ASIAN SEMINAR ON RURAL DEVELOPMENT
The Indian Experience

CMA Monograph 120

ASIAN SEMINAR ON RURAL DEVELOPMENT
The Indian Experience

edited by

M.L. DANTWALA
RANJIT GUPTA
KEITH C. D'SOUZA

OXFORD & IBH PUBLISHING CO. PVT. LTD.
New Delhi **Bombay** **Calcutta**

ISBN 81-204-0150-6

Published by Mohan Primlani for Oxford & IBH Publishing Co. Pvt. Ltd.
66 Janpath, New Delhi 110 001 and printed at
Sunil Printers, Ring Road, Naraina, New Delhi 110 028

Contents

Part III: Choice of Implementing Agencies

Part IV: Reconciling Growth and Social Justice

Part V: Other Asian Experiences

Preface

The Indian Society of Agricultural Economics and the Centre for Management in Agriculture at the Indian Institute of Management, Ahmedabad (IIMA), organised a four-day seminar in December 1984 in collaboration with the International Development Research Centre "to evaluate the rural development experience generally in Asian countries and in India in particular". About 40 eminent social scientists, planners and development administrators from seven Asian countries, including India, participated in the seminar and discussed in depth the issues and themes which were identified earlier. This volume presents the papers and proceedings of the seminar.

The seminar was an outcome of nearly two years of intensive work involving identification of key issues, classification of the issues in terms of broad themes or topics for preparation of papers and case studies by individuals well-conversant with the problems, and consultation and exchange of ideas to facilitate the organisation of the seminar and make it a worthwhile exercise. As a first step in this direction, a preliminary note outlining the purpose of the seminar was prepared and sent to a large number of individuals well acquainted with the subject with a view to eliciting their suggestions and participation.

Outlining the purpose of the seminar the note emphasised:

> This kind of exercise has no doubt been made before and often. The main reason which has spurred us to do this exercise once again is a near unanimity among those who have studied the subject on the finding that, despite the many experiments, there is practically no abatement in rural poverty and unemployment. If so, it would be cyni-

> cal to argue that the issue of rural development has been discussed exhaustively and nothing worthwhile will be gained by discussing it further. Such an attitude would be tantamount to taking to academic *sanyas*—renunciation.
>
> But this imposes a heavy responsibility on the seminar participants to ensure that at least an attempt is made to evoke some fresh thought. This does not imply that all past details have been irrelevant and the seminar will, therefore, strain its ingenuity to be original. Undoubtedly, much that has been said on the subject must be still relevant, and if so it must be stressed again. In fact, besides exploring new approaches, the seminar must critically scrutinise the analyses and solutions suggested in existing literature on the subject and either repeat or refute them.

The comments and suggestions the note evoked helped in identifying the key issues and classifying them into the following five themes:

1) *Evaluation of rural development strategies*: Basic strategy of rural development adopted in India since Independence. Evolution of thinking and approaches. Critical evaluation of successive strategies. Findings and suggestions.

2) *Consistency between macro and micro planning*: Policies, strategies, programmes. Instances of inconsistencies. Ways of reconciling macro and micro policies: centre-state, state-district, district-block-village.

3) *Rationale and limitation of decentralised planning*: Modalities of two-way planning. Necessity of central intervention with the objective of reducing regional inequalities in natural endowments, entrepreneurship, checks on local power groups—class, caste, religious—for protection of minorities. Is planning from below feasible?

4) *The choice of implementing agencies*: Bureaucracy, professional groups, voluntary agencies—with government patronage or people's support—community action, organising the disadvantaged. How to achieve a combination of professional competence, administrative support and local initiative and participation in rural development.

5) *Reconciling growth with social justice*: Different approaches, group conflicts, proletariatisation of the rural population. Pres-

sure groups—political, social, economic. Building countervailing forces—structural and institutional changes: priorities, sequence.

Eleven papers and case studies on these themes analysing the Indian experience were specifically prepared for the seminar and discussed at length on the first three days after they were presented by the respective authors. The experiences of other Asian countries participating in the seminar—Bangladesh, China, Japan, Nepal, Philippines, and Thailand—were presented, orally or in writing, by the participants from these countries.

This volume reconstructs the seminar by putting together the papers presented and the discussions which took place. The volume consists of five parts, one for each of the themes of the seminar. Part I presents two papers on the theme, "Evaluation of Rural Development Strategies": one by Prof. V.R. Gaikwad, the other by Dr. Dipankar Gupta.

Gaikwad's paper traces the rural development strategies followed in India since the turn of the century and evaluates them in terms of their contribution to economic and technological progress, and the building of a just social order. Gupta's paper on the other hand evaluates one of the on-going government programmes—the Integrated Tribal Development Programme—in Birbhum district of West Bengal. The focus of the paper is on identifying and analysing the strengths and weaknesses of the programme.

Part II includes two papers: *Consistency between Macro and Micro Planning* by Dr. D.T. Lakdawala, and *Rationale and Limitation of Decentralised Planning* by Prof. M.L. Dantwala. Together, the two papers provide insights into the relationship between macro and micro planning in India, the Indian experience of centre-state relations vis-a-vis development planning, the implications of this experience, and the rationale and limitations of decentralised planning in realising the goals of poverty alleviation, regional equality, and people's participation.

Part III examines issues pertaining to the problems of implementation of rural development programmes.

Mr. Nirmal Mukarji looks at the problems of implementation from a macro perspective and makes a strong plea for the creation of district government envisaging significant structural changes in the administrative set-up. The case studies by Dr. Kamla Chowdhry, Prof. Nirmala Murthy, Prof. Ranjit Gupta, and Dr. Biplab Dasgupta evaluate the progress and performance of eight non-governmental agencies involved in rural development activities in different parts of India and analyse their strengths and limitations, approaches to development, management and organisation, problems and potentialities.

The two papers included in Part IV, one by Dr. C.T. Kurien and the other by Prof. M.L. Dantwala, examine the dilemma of reconciling the imperatives of economic growth with the values of social justice. While Kurien argues that the crucial issues to be addressed are not only those related to the adoption of a development strategy but also those related to the changes required in the basic structure of the economy, Dantwala questions the idea that poverty cannot be alleviated unless preceded by structural change. He argues that structural change can be brought about by modifying the "consequences" of the structure—a prospect that is much easier to achieve given the formidable problems that direct changes in structure would entail.

Part V provides a brief overview of the experiences of other Asian countries in the field of rural development.

Development of Small Towns in the Delta of Yangtze River by Prof. Yuan Bao-min provides one example of Chinese efforts at socio-economic transformation of rural small towns. Dr. Antonio Ledesma's paper, *Rural Development Strategies in the Philippines: Some Perspectives*, recounts the experiences of the Philippines against the background of turbulent social and political changes. The brief accounts of the experiences of Bangladesh, Japan, Nepal, and Thailand, recorded in this part, are based on oral presentations by the participants from these countries.

The *proceedings* which precede each of Parts I through IV contain summary previews of the papers presented and reports of the discussions which followed the presentations.

* * *

Towards the close of the seminar an attempt was made to recapitulate the core problems in rural development discussed in the various sessions. There was general agreement that while considerable efforts have been made to promote rural development in the country, a number of issues relating to strategy, planning and implementation remain unresolved.

The seminar recognised that well intentioned macro strategies for eradicating poverty and socio-economic inequalities are inadequate unless they are accompanied by micro-level strategies specific to the varied needs and conditions of the local areas where the crux of implementation lies. Decentralised planning cannot be effective unless the roles of local bodies are recognised by the national and state governments, clearly demarcated, well coordinated and backed by adequate resources. In India, these aspects have often been neglected. Another area of concern which emerged from the seminar was the lack of people's involvement in planning and implementation. Popular participation is not only a laudable objective by itself but is also a necessary precondition of meeting the objectives of macro-level planning. Planning has neglected to take into account the inherent social and economic inequalities which facilitate the usurpation of power over local bodies by vested interests and sidetrack the interests of the rural poor.

One of the measures suggested for making decentralised planning more effective is the creation of a planning authority at the local level to replace the existing hierarchical system. A more radical measure suggested is the democratisation of development administration through the setting up of a third tier of representative government at the district level. But this raised the question: how to ensure that such a district government would be truly representative of the people? Would not the same inequalities which today facilitate vested interests to control local bodies favour their chances of winning "representation" in an election? The experience with the working of the panchayati raj institutions in the country suggests that these institutions, which were supposed to be vehicles of grassroots participation, are too often dominated by local vested interest groups.

Another reason for the lack of people's participation seems to be the lack of motivation on the part of the people themselves. But even this lack of motivation can be attributed to past failures to involve the people in the development process.

If people find that they can obtain some benefits—meagre though these may be—without participating in planning and implementation, they are unlikely to feel motivated to participate at all. Development administration needs to find ways and means to convince the people that they have much to gain by their involvement.

The seminar also found evidence to support the belief that a greater role for voluntary agencies would facilitate more effective implementation of anti-poverty programmes. Voluntary agencies, it was felt, are better at mobilising and sustaining the involvement of people in development activities than governmental agencies which tend to suffer from bureaucratic inflexibility. However, given the scale on which development work needs to be done, voluntary efforts by themselves cannot serve as a substitute for governmental efforts.

Discussion on the theme of reconciling growth with justice highlighted the areas of agreement as well as disagreement. There was general agreement with the idea that growth and justice cannot go together unless structural change to even out socio-economic disparities is brought about. But there were strong differences of opinion on the nature of structural change required. Some participants were of the opinion that since social, economic and political power in the rural areas is associated with the pattern of land distribution and ownership, growth and justice can only be reconciled when land is redistributed more equitably. Others felt that land redistribution is no longer a viable solution. Since land as a resource has now been tapped almost to the point of exhaustion, they felt, attempts to redistribute the scarce available land would only lead to conflict between various interest groups without furthering egalitarianism. The experiences of some Asian countries such as the Philippines were cited as examples of the limited effectiveness of land reform measures. Whereas land reforms in the Philippines were relevant and necessary about 20 years ago, they are not so today when the density of population is so high that there is not enough land to go round. Besides, even when land reforms were carried out in the past, it was found that the reforms simply replaced one exploited class by another because those who had benefited from the reforms moved into the urban areas leaving the cultivation to be done by the remaining landless peasants.

Instead of depending on land reforms as a means of structural change, some participants felt, it is necessary to develop and implement appropriate policies to distribute other resources which have not yet been tapped or only partially tapped like underground water, forests, and other common property resources. It would be easier and more useful to ensure their equitable distribution since vested interests in these resources have not yet been firmly established. As a first step, measures have to be taken to prevent the privatisation of common property resources both in the rural and urban areas.

Japan's experience illustrates that growth with a measure of equity can be brought about by alternative means such as improvements in the absorbtive capacity of the non-agricultural sector to accommodate landless people by a redistribution of the non-land factors of production, or by the setting up of institutional mechanisms like farmers' cooperatives to safeguard common ownership and control of scarce resources. A judicious mix of labour intensive and capital intensive technologies, as in Japan, could increase employment and improve the quality of production.

Structural change, as the experiences of some of the Asian countries show, can be a politically and socially volatile issue. The success stories of rural development in these countries suggest, as one of the participants mentioned, that some kind of a strongarm government or political force may be necessary to push through structural reforms, as happened in Taiwan and Japan under the occupation forces after World War II. "But a strongarm government," he cautioned, "is like a two-edged sword that can cut to heal or to wound. Martial law in the Philippines was initially a powerful instrument of socio-economic reform, but it subsequently lapsed into becoming an agent of repression and injustice."

Thus, it is not political force *per se* but the character of political force that is important for change toward greater equity and growth. In the long run, it may be slower but more effective for pressure in favour of reform to come from grassroots movements. The precondition for this is the mobilisation of the silent majority in society.

The seminar deliberated on many more issues and raised a number of questions. To name a few: How can the poor be organised more effectively to assert their rights? How do developing countries create institutions that can harness the enormous, but often dormant, power of the people for change? How do we institute reforms in the existing social, economic and political structures which continue to thwart growth with social justice? Such questions often do not have immediate answers. But, as the seminar emphasised, the search for the answers must continue.

M.L. Dantwala
Ranjit Gupta
Keith C. D'Souza

Acknowledgements

This volume is the product of the participation of many people. We are grateful to all of them. In particular, we wish to record our deep appreciation and thanks to:

Dr. David J. King, Mr. Vijay G. Pande, and Dr. Abe Weisblat of the International Development Research Centre, and Mr. J.N. Barmeda of the Indian Society of Agricultural Economics for their valuable support.

Dr. N.R. Sheth, Director, Prof. A.H. Kalro, Dean, and the Chairman and faculty of the Centre for Management in Agriculture, Indian Institute of Management, Ahmedabad for their encouragement and help to organise and host the seminar.

The contributors of papers and case studies and all those who participated in the seminar, especially those who came from abroad, for their stimulating participation and contributions.

The rapporteurs at the seminar—Mr. Rakesh Basant, Mr. Indranil Chakrabarti, Dr. Gunvant M. Desai, Mr. Saurabh Kumar, Dr. Nirmala Murthy, Dr. Girja Sharan and Dr. Pravin Visaria—who helped us piece together the many diverse points raised in the discussions.

The numerous support staff at the IIMA, in particular Mr. T. Kameshwaran, Programmes Officer of the Centre for Management in Agriculture, who provided the material comfort in which to deliberate upon sometimes uncomfortable issues.

Ms. Rohini Patel of IIMA's Publications Division who patiently and cheerfully provided editorial assistance from the stage of preparing the papers for the seminar up to the publication of this volume, and Ms. Svati Desai who assisted in editing the papers for the seminar, Ms. K. Barathi who provided willing and meticulous secretarial assistance, and Mr. B.N. Nayak who ably substituted for her in her absence.

Contributors

DR. KAMLA CHOWDHRY

Chairman, National Wastelands Development Board, New Delhi. Formerly Executive Director, Society for the Promotion of Wastelands Development, New Delhi; Hon. Director, Institute of Rural Management, Anand; Programme Adviser, Ford Foundation, New Delhi; Professor at the Indian Institute of Management, Ahmedabad.

PROF. M.L. DANTWALA

Emeritus Professor of Economics, Bombay University. Eminent teacher and author. Chairman and member of several commissions. Founder President of the Indian Society of Agricultural Economics, Bombay.

DR. BIPLAB DASGUPTA

Professor of Economics, Calcutta University. Formerly Executive Vice-Chairman, West Bengal Comprehensive Area Development Corporation, Calcutta.

MR. KEITH C. D'SOUZA

Doctoral student in the Organisational Behaviour Area at the Indian Institute of Management, Ahmedabad. Prior to joining the Institute worked in the field of human resources development in BEML, Bangalore. Currently, completing his doctoral dissertation on the organisational design of non-governmental development agencies in India.

DR. V.R. GAIKWAD

Professor at the Centre for Management in Agriculture, Indian

Institute of Management, Ahmedabad. Done extensive research in the field of development administration and rural development.

Dr. Dipankar Gupta

Associate Professor, Centre for the Study of Social System, Jawaharlal Nehru University, New Delhi.

Prof. Ranjit Gupta

Professor at the Centre for Management in Agriculture, Indian Institute of Management, Ahmedabad. Previously, Chairman, Centre for Management in Agriculture, IIMA; SBI Chair Professor of Rural Development, IIMA. Done extensive work in the field of rural development.

Dr. C.T. Kurien

Director, Madras Institute of Development Studies, Madras. Done extensive research on problems of rural development.

Dr. D.T. Lakdawala

Hon. Director, Centre for Monitoring Indian Economy, Bombay. Eminent professor and scholar. Former Vice-Chairman, Planning Commission. Former Director, Sardar Patel Institute of Economic and Social Research, Ahmedabad.

Prof. Nirmal Mukarji

Research Professor at the Centre for Policy Research, New Delhi.

Dr. Nirmala Murthy

Professor at the Indian Institute of Management, Ahmedabad. Specialisation: Systems Analysis and Simulation, Evaluation and Control of Non-profit Organisations.

Seminar Participants

1. MRS. TAHRUNNESA ABDULLAH
   4-B Amynabad Cooperative Housing Society,
   Siddheswari, Dacca-17, Bangladesh

2. PROF. YUAN BAO-MIN
   Professor of Agricultural Economics and Farm Business Management, Nanjing Agricultural University,
   C/o President, Chinese Association of Agricultural Sciences Societies, Beijing, China

3. DR. J.N. BARMEDA
   Hon. Secretary, Indian Society of Agricultural Economics,
   46-48 Esplanade Mansions, Mahatma Gandhi Road,
   Bombay 400 023

4. MS. NAFISA BAROT
   Mahiti Project, 83/387 Saraswatinagar,
   Near Azad Society, Ahmedabad 380 015

5. DR. KAMLA CHOWDHRY
   Chairman, National Wastelands Development Board,
   Government of India, Ministry of Environment & Forests,
   Lok Nayak Bhavan, New Delhi 110 003

6. PROF. M.L. DANTWALA
   Founder President, Indian Society of Agricultural Economics,
   46-48 Esplanade Mansions, Mahatma Gandhi Road,
   Bombay 400 023

7. DR. GUNVANT M. DESAI
   Indian Institute of Management,
   Vastrapur, Ahmedabad 380 015

8. MS. ANILA R. DHOLAKIA
Self-Employed Women's Association,
Opp. Victoria Garden, Ahmedabad 380 001

9. DR. V.R. GAIKWAD
Indian Institute of Management,
Vastrapur, Ahmedabad 380 015

10. DR. DIPANKAR GUPTA
Jawaharlal Nehru University,
68 New Campus, New Mehrauli Road,
New Delhi 110 067

11. PROF. RANJIT GUPTA
Indian Institute of Management,
Vastrapur, Ahmedabad 380 015

12. MR. SANJOY DAS GUPTA
Project Director, IRDP,
Karwar 581 301, Karnataka

13. SHRI R.N. HALDIPUR
Director, Institute of Rural Management, Anand,
Anand 388 001

14. DR. S. HIRASHIMA
Director, International Exchanges Department,
Institute of Developing Economies,
42 Ichigaya Hommura-Cho, Shinjuku-ku, Tokyo 162, Japan

15. MR. AZIZ-UL HAQ
30-A University Staff Quarters,
Fuller Road, Dhaka, Bangladesh

16. MR. DEEP JOSHI
Programme Officer, The Ford Foundation,
55 Lodi Estate, New Delhi 110 003

17. MR. B.B. KHADKA
Member Agriculture, National Planning Commission,
His Majesty's Government of Nepal, Ramshah Path, Kathmandu, Nepal

18. Dr. David J. King
Rural Development Specialist, Social Sciences Division,
International Development Research Centre, Tanglin,
P.O. Box 101, Singapore 9124

19. Dr. C.T. Kurien
Director, Madras Institute of Development Studies,
79 Second Main Road, Gandhi Nagar, Madras 600 020

20. Dr. D.T. Lakdawala
Hon. Director, Centre for Monitoring Indian Economy,
110-120 Kaliandas Udyog Bhavan, Near Century Bazar,
Worli, Bombay 400 025

21. Dr. Antonio J. Ledesma SJ
Faculty of Agriculture,
Xavier University, Cagayan de Oro City, Philippines 8401

22. Mr. Vijay Mahajan
Executive Director, PRADAN,
250-A DDA MIG Flats, Rajouri Garden,
New Delhi 110 027

23. Dr. Suzzane Mowat
Programme Officer, Social Sciences Division,
International Development Research Centre, South Asia
Regional Office,
11 Jor Bagh, New Delhi 110 003

24. Prof. Nirmal Mukarji
Research Professor, Centre for Policy Research,
Dharma Marg, Chanakyapuri, New Delhi 110 021

25. Dr. Nirmala Murthy
Indian Institute of Management,
Vastrapur, Ahmedabad 380 015

26. Mr. Vijay G. Pande
Regional Director, South Asia Regional Office,
International Development Research Centre,
11 Jor Bagh, New Delhi 110 003

27. Dr. C.H. Hanumantha Rao
Member, Planning Commission,
Government of India, Yojana Bhavan, New Delhi 110 001

28. Dr. V.M. Rao
Senior Fellow, Institute for Social and Economic Change, Nagrabhavi, Bangalore 560 072

29. Dr. Girja Sharan
Indian Institute of Management,
Vastrapur, Ahmedabad 380 015

30. Dr. Ammar Siamwalla
Senior Research Fellow, Thailand Development Research Institute, Rajapark Building, 163 Asoke Road,
Bangkok 10110, Thailand

31. Mr. M.P. Vasimalai
State Project Coordinator, Tamil Nadu, Association for Sarva Seva Farms,
9 Power House Road, Madurai 625 001

32. Dr. Pravin Visaria
Director, Gujarat Institute of Area Planning,
New Brahmakshatriya Society,
Pritamrai Marg, Ahmedabad 380 006

33. Dr. Abe M. Weisblat
Visiting Professor, The State University of New Jersey, RUTGERS Cook College, Department of Agricultural Economics & Marketing,
P.O. Box 231, New Brunswick, New Jersey 08903

34. Dr. Ram P. Yadav
Deputy Director, International Centre for Mountain Development,
P.O. Box 3226, Kathmandu, Nepal

PART I

Rural Development Strategies

Proceedings

Rural development has had a fairly long history in India going back to several decades before Independence, although it was perhaps only after Independence that fresh, concerted efforts were made. The first session of the seminar took stock of the past experience in the hope that the lessons of history would provide cues by which the future of rural development can be determined.

V.R. Gaikwad's paper, "Rural Development Strategies: Evaluation of Some Early Experiments in India", evaluates rural development strategies from a historical perspective, tracing the path that they have followed over the last 82 years or so, and the major projects which embodied the strategies.

Rural development strategies are weighed against two criteria: The extent to which they have contributed to the achievement of democratic India's objective of building a technologically progressive economy, and the extent to which they have helped move the country toward an ideal social order based on justice and equal opportunity for all.

Early well-known experiments such as the Sriniketan, Martandam, Gurgaon, and Etawah, according to Gaikwad, contributed little to enhancing technological development, justice and equity. Often they were only of cosmetic value in that they were concerned mainly with those aspects of poverty and inequity which hurt the eye most; they usually remained confined to the experimental areas failing to bring about a diffusion effect on surrounding villages; and success, whenever it was achieved, was marginal. The reason for this is ascribed to inherent defects in the programmes such as their excessive concern with spiritual and philosophical ideas which appealed to emotions rather than with substantial socio-economic changes, lack of scientific temper, focus on the individual instead of community, and passive acceptance of the prevailing socio-economic and political structures. A majority of these programmes were initiated and carried out either by well-intentioned foreigners who saw in underdeveloped India opportunities to perform their good deeds in life or by prominent Indians who were strongly influenced by foreign ideas.

The Community Development Programme (CDP) introduced shortly after Independence at the instance of Chester Bowles and with the support of US aid was not much different in its strategy. The basic elements of the CDP design continued to be similar to those in earlier designs: focus on the individual cultivator, restructuring and reorganisation of district administration, provision of facilities to individual cultivators, and provision of welfare facilities at the block level. The design neglected the development of small and medium agro-industries and cottage industries which would have helped reduce the pressure on land and develop new entrepreneurial skills and crafts. The CDP, apparently, was a mere palliative, meant to satisfy the needs of the masses just enough so that India would not turn to communism and to provide political stability together with a semblance of development.

Gandhiji's efforts in the area of rural development represented a different approach, inextricably linked with his strategy of achieving political freedom for India. His actions had a unique blending of two components: a simple outward looking act which had great mass appeal, one which would kindle a sense of power in the masses, and an inward principle to provide spiritual sanctity to the effort.

Two other approaches of a different nature were the one used by the framers of the Nilokheri township project and the other used by Gadgil and Kurien in building agro-processing industries. The focus of the former was on vocational training and cooperative action for industry and trade, the primary purpose of which was the establishment of a new township to rehabilitate persons displaced from Pakistan after the partition. The latter experiments were intended to bring about rural transformation by involving people in agro-industrial enterprises through the establishment of cooperative institutions. This approach facilitated the effective and efficient integration of various aspects of rural development.

The design that emerged from the agro-industrial township approach was characterised by the use of policy instruments to facilitate agro-industrial growth, the facilitating role of administration, the integration of welfare and economic development through farmers' cooperatives, and the participation of every member of the organisation in its management. This design, according to Gaikwad, has the potential for building a socially relevant, technologically progressive economy.

In the second presentation of the session, the focus and scenario shift from 'early experiments' to one of the on-going programmes: the Integrated Tribal Development Programme (ITDP) in Birbhum district of West Bengal. On the basis of his study Dipankar Gupta argues that ITDP follows a target group approach and works toward the elimination of exploitation and poverty. It attempts to bring development to the tribals and at the same time to take steps to protect their cultural identity and heritage from the onslaught of 'modernisation'. It includes measures for economic protection and uplift, promoting popular participation of tribals in decision making, providing and improving social welfare facilities, and facilitating the learning of new occupational skills and techniques.

Because the Santhals who inhabit Birbhum are predominantly peasant-farmers, the ITDP's major thrust is toward improving agricultural practices through irrigation improvements and assistance in the form of agricultural implements, seeds, and mini-kits. Economic protection is afforded by guarding tribal lands from encroachment by non-tribals and giving the tribals special privileges for securing the produce from forests and grasslands. The large-size multipurpose societies (LAMPS) were introduced to generate and promote tribal employment schemes. Social service measures were taken, such as the setting up of hospitals and schools and improving hygiene and drinking water facilities.

The ITDP in Birbhum has done much by way of transforming the lives of the Santhals, but it suffers from a number of drawbacks. The main problems are the incongruities in the administrative structure of the ITDP, the lack of control over resources, the absence of initiative from the beneficiaries, the inability or failure to follow up on programmes, and the failure to institute a proper system of monitoring the various schemes.

The most serious drawback of the ITDP has been its inability to project a multi-sectoral integrated thrust. This is mainly because of the uncertainty regarding the availability of funds which compels ITDP to tailor its plans to fit available resources instead of the other way round, end the lack of coordination among the different sectors which work jointly with the ITDP office. The hope that ITDP would end exploitation and poverty was belied, although it had begun well by trying to restore the confidence of the tribals through education and popular participation. Attempts to elicit the participation of the tribals by involving the panchayats did not succeed because, although the panchayats are important institutions in West Bengal, the tribals have very little representation in them. The author concludes that the ITDP has been an operation which has succeeded only in keeping the tribals alive, but has failed to achieve any economic breakthroughs or make any worthwhile social changes in favour of the tribal community.

The main issue which dominated the discussion following the presentations by Gaikwad and Dipankar Gupta was the role of people's participation in rural development. Many participants shared the conviction that the involvement of the common people in the process of planning and implementation is a prerequisite to successful rural development. Many of our failures in the field of rural development, R.N. Haldipur contended, can be traced to the absence of people's participation. Policy makers and implementers often only pay lip-service to the idea of people's participation and appear to work on the assumption that 'all wisdom comes from outside'. Such an attitude has nursed a dependency syndrome among the people. Rural development programmes are unlikely to succeed until the instruments of development are vested in the hands of the people and professionals working for rural development recognise their roles to be those of 'employees of the people' rather than those of masters.

Institutional weaknesses were seen to be one of the major factors impeding effective people's participation. In India, village panchayats are relied upon as a means of enlisting popular participation, but the constitution of the panchayats often does not help serve this purpose because the really poor and underprivileged who are supposed to be the target beneficiaries of development programmes rarely find adequate representation in the panchayat institutions. Aziz-ul Haq cited the similar experience of Bangladesh with regard to Tribal Area Development Programme. The panchayats which were expected to play a facilitating role in the programme, in fact, had very few tribals among their members.

Another problem, according to Vijay Mahajan, is that governmental patronage to development efforts have almost always proved counter-productive for rural development programmes. The link between development agencies and the government often led to such agencies becoming 'sub-contractors' to the government, and the infusion of bureaucratic culture into rural development agencies alienated them from the people they were supposed to serve.

Both Haq and Kamla Chowdhry took up the issue of involvement of foreigners in development programmes. Although the initiation of programmes by foreigners unfamiliar with the Indian context may have diluted the effectiveness of the programmes, they felt that foreigners cannot be blamed for the failure of development programmes. After all, the failures in the case of indigenous development efforts have been monumental. Most westerners who were involved in early programmes were well-intentioned people and many of them, like C.F. Andrews, were more Indian than many westernised Indians.

Responding to some of the issues raised by the participants, Gaikwad said that in most rural development programmes the attitude of the administration towards beneficiaries was one of: "I manage, you participate". There was little in the planning and implementation of the programmes that made participation worthwhile. Despite liberalism and other positive influences, early rural development programmes lacked scientific temper. Little attempt had been made to utilise scientific and technological innovations to improve the conditions of the poor.

Dipankar Gupta felt that the absence of people's participation in ITDP was primarily due to the fact that instead of resources being tailored to development, the plans were being tailored to resources. Resources flowed to ITDP in a haphazard manner, and it was left to the officials to decide how and where they should be allocated. At this level, there was no participation from people because they were not consulted. There was scope for participation in the LAMPS programme because it did not affect matters which were of critical importance to powerful vested interests. If programmes like the LAMPS could be multiplied, greater involvement and participation of tribals outside the panchayat would be possible.

Summing up the proceedings of the session, the Chairman, M.L. Dantwala, noted that the session had raised basic questions about people's participation, self-reliance, professionalism, and bureaucracy. How these aspects could be brought together into a viable working arrangement and how coordination between the various organisations involved in development could be brought about were questions that needed to be taken up in the seminar.

Rural Development Strategies: Evaluation of Some Early Experiments in India

V.R. Gaikwad

EVOLUTION OF RD STRATEGY

Since Independence in 1947, India has applied various strategies for planned economic development. Rural development during the First Five Year Plan was one such strategy and it has to be understood in the context of overall planned efforts.

From the beginning, a two-fold objective has guided India's planned development: to build up by democratic means a rapidly expanding and technologically progressive economy, and to establish a social order based on justice and offering equal opportunities to every citizen.[1] These objectives are sought to be achieved on the basis of systematic and vigorous economic planning. Planning was intended, in the words of the Government Resolution of March 1950, "to promote a rapid rise in the standard of living of the people by efficient exploitation of the natural resources of the country, increasing production, and offering opportunities to all for employment in the service of the country."[2] In December 1954, Parliament adopted the resolution with the following clauses:

1) The objective of economic policy should be a socialistic pattern of society; and

2) Towards this end the tempo of economic activities in general and industrial development in particular should be stepped up to the maximum extent.[3]

Thus, from the beginning due emphasis was, and still is, given to develop a strong industrial base. There has to be, therefore, emphasis on development of basic industries, power generation, mining, and organised industries, and on infrastructure required for industrial development such as communication, transport, human resources in science, technology and management, and financial institutions [1]. Self-sufficiency in food and other necessities of life, to the extent possible without affecting industrial development, is another area. Social and economic development of large masses of people living in villages and in deep poverty would require huge investments, and these could be done only at a cost of industrial development. Yet, in the hands of these people was the fate of democratic political system and political stability; and India needed continuous political stability to achieve a rapidly expanding and technologically progressive economy. At this phase of development India opted for a strategy of 'low cost', 'special programmes'. The strategy was to keep hopes and aspirations of the rural people as well as their faith in democratic institutions and the government alive, and progressively satisfy these with increasing gains from industrialisation that would provide a continuously expanding economic and technological base for more effective programmes for economic development and welfare of the rural masses.

Thus, during the last 35 years, the introduction of various programmes and activities that could be listed under 'rural development' has essentially been a dimension of political strategy to ensure political stability, integrated with the strategy for long-term economic and social goals. It was, in essence, a strategy to gain time in the absence of any viable alternative.

There were three other situational factors that guided and supported such a strategy.

1) India had to depend mostly on its own resources for economic development. Indian independence came just after the Second World War. Europe had been bled white by the war and the entire energy of the U.S.A. and the European nations was concentrated on reconstruction of the European economy. The U.S.A. had the additional responsibility of strengthening Japan, Korea and Taiwan as a defence against expansion of communism. She could therefore spare little funds, even if she

so desired, for India's development. Yet, there was the bitter lesson from China. India has to be encouraged on the path of democracy, and for this it needed political stability. It was in the interest of the Western countries to help India gain time as that would also give them some breathing time before they could regain their traditional economic strength and later on exercise influence on the world affairs. Thus, the West too, was in search of a "low cost" strategy to keep India away from communism, and this primarily determined its support to India in the form of the Community Development Programme (CDP).

2) There was already a legacy of colonial administration which could not be wiped out or even modified in a short span of time. Britain's interest in the economic development of its colony were directly or indirectly linked with its own economic and political interests. Economic development of the rural masses was never its primary concern. For that matter, historically Britain has no worthwhile experience of 'rural development' in its own country which could be of use to India [2].[4] Its administrative system was designed for keeping the unorganised rural masses under control through regulatory mechanisms. After the Russian Revolution of 1914 and under rising political opinion in the country, some welfare and relief activities were introduced. But, these were isolated and meagre. Even if England wanted to take up such activities on a large scale, it could not have done much. After the First World War, Europe was in shambles. Great Britain and North America had to pump in huge resources in Europe, especially in Germany to rapidly repair the ruins of the war [3].[5] These had to come from the colonies. Hence, the administrative system had no experience of or orientation in welfare and economic development activities. There was little about rural development that the planners could have borrowed from a colonial government, except the administrative structure and its regulatory and maintenance orientation and marginal experience of welfare and relief activities supported by periodic grants. This readily available administrative system could be effectively put to use for implementing the 'low cost' rural development programmes. As we shall see later, the nature of development programmes was such that these could be easily managed by this system without requiring any drastic changes in its

century-old organisational structure, rules and procedures of district administration.

3) Over the century a school of thought emerged on the Indian scene which was concerned with safeguarding India against the onslaught of Western materialism. Tagore and Gandhi were the great exponents of this school. They were also influenced by Western humanism, democratic political system, and social philosophies. Their idea of a new Indian society was basically rural, self-governing, decentralised and cooperative. They emphasised the importance of spiritual values in building modern India. Self-mastery, self-help, virtue of simplicity, and dignity of labour, were some of the essential aspects of their approach. Over the years, many experiments for rural reconstruction and rural transformation were conducted by them and others following this approach. A large number of urban intellectuals, social workers and social reformists were attracted to this approach. There was pressure on the planners to adopt this approach for rural development. As discussed later, the results of various early experiments were not very encouraging, in terms of improving the economic condition of rural people. Yet, the approach has three strengths: a great mass appeal due to its religio-philosophical base, social welfare orientation, and possibility of large area coverage at a low cost. As such, it was readily adopted by the planners in their "low cost" strategy for rural development.

Effectiveness of Present Strategy

The strategy for rural development was formulated in the form of a Community Development Programme (CDP) while finalising the country's First Five Year Plan. It was designed and partially funded by the United States. From the beginning, rural development was linked with growth of agriculture and allied sectors, infrastructure development in rural areas and social welfare activities. Some of the important programmes for rural/agricultural development initially launched were: CDP, Intensive Agricultural District Programme (IADP), and High Yielding Varieties Programme (HYV). These were followed by the creation of Small Farmers' Development Agencies (SFDA) and Marginal Farmers' and Agricultural Labourers' Development Agencies (MFAL) to provide assistance to poorer sections of rural population. A special programme known as Drought Prone Areas Programme (DPAP) was introduced in 1970-71 in chronically drought-affected areas. More recently, the Integrated Rural Development Programme (IRDP), based on methodology and administrative practices evolved during the implementation of SFDA, DPAP, Command Area Development Programme (CADP), etc., was initiated. Throughout this period, various social welfare programmes pertaining to health, nutrition, sanitation, family planning and education, were initiated.

All these programmes have led to manifold increase in agricultural production, and, to some extent, to the self-sufficiency in food. However, social and economic development of an increasingly large mass of people living in rural areas below the poverty line is still to be achieved.

From the overall national perspective the rural development strategy followed during the past 35 years has achieved its twofold objective: (1) keep the hopes and aspirations of rural people alive and thus provide political stability which helps the country move on the democratic path, and (2) provide time and resources to build a strong industrial base.

Over the years, India has achieved considerable progress in terms of:

1) a reasonably sound agricultural base,
2) sufficiently strong industrial and technological base,
3) human resources in science, technology, and
4) physical and institutional infrastructure.

These are the first generation tasks which provide a foundation for rapid economic growth in future. Based on the above, the country has to plan the second generation activities that would take the fruits of science, technology and industrial development to the rural masses and contribute to their economic and all-round development. This would require appropriate changes in the existing strategy for rural development.

In national planning, long-term development strategies are evolved keeping in mind the economic, technological, social and political realities at a given stage of development. The planned efforts by their very nature change the realities over a period of time. It follows that to suit the new set of realities, new, long-term strategies have to be evolved. In this sense, no strategy is ever-lasting and sacrosanct; once it achieves most of its objectives, a strategy loses its force, its importance; hence it must give place to a new strategy. In the context of a country's achievements on the industrial and agricultural front, one can say that India has reached a stage of development where it has to think of a new strategy for rural development for continuing political stability and economic development. A critical appraisal of various experiments which determined the design of present strategy would help in understanding the in-built limitations of present strategy for the tasks of future, and in identifying appropriate modifications.

Framework for Evaluation

Over the span of about sixty years the notable rural development experiments and programmes conducted in India are:

EARLY EXPERIMENTS (1920-46)

—Sriniketan Experiments of Rabindranath Tagore
—Martandam Project of Spencer Hatch of YMCA
—Gurgaon Experiment of F.L. Brayne
—Baroda Rural Reconstruction Movement of V.T. Krishnamachari
—Mahatma Gandhi's various experiments
—Firka Development Scheme of Madras Government

1940s THROUGH 1960s

—Etawah Pilot Project of Albert Mayer
—Nilokheri Nucleus Township Project of S.K. Dey
—Fifteen Pilot Extension Projects of Ford Foundation
—Community Development Programme designed by Chester Bowles and funded by the U.S.A.
—Cooperative Farming

1960s THROUGH 1970s

—Intensive Agricultural District Programme of Ford Foundation
—Farmers' Service Cooperative Societies
—Special Programmes like SFDA, DPAD, etc.

These experiments and programmes were conducted at different points of time, in different regions, and under different politico-economic conditions. The experiments and programmes varied in terms of area and population coverage and financial and other resources. The background of experiments also varied considerably. Each designed the experiment according to his perception of problems and needs of rural people. All these variations make comparative evaluation of these experiments and programmes rather difficult. To be just to the experimenters it would be most appropriate if each experiment is evaluated independently in terms of approach, performance, and effectiveness against the stated objectives. At the same time, a comparative evaluation is also essential for understanding the undercurrent of thinking that has influenced the policies and strategies after Independence.

Comparative evaluation, however, requires some common denominator in terms of some conceptual framework against which the objectives, activities and performance of each experiment/programme/project could be evaluated. To be of practical use in formulating new strategies for rural development, such a framework has to take into account persistent realities in rural areas, that is, those present in the past, continued even after planned efforts of 35 years, and likely to continue in future if the present strategy for rural development remains unmodified.

The persistent realities are:

1) Dependence on primary production (subsistence agriculture, food gathering economy such as subsistence traditional fishery, collection of forest produce, traditional animal husbandry, etc.) by a large percentage of population; such production by *direct application/use* of human and animal power in raw form.

2) Extremely low purchasing power of those involved in primary production and food and natural product gathering activities due to very low net income earned from such activities. This low income is sufficient to replace the human and animal energy expended in the production/gathering activities.

3) Lack of application of science and technology even to primary production process [4] resulting in low productivity and consequently low net income.

4) Complete lack of scientific understanding about natural resources, especially the flora and fauna of the region, and their potential for commercial and industrial exploitation for econo-

mic development, among the local people as well as local administrators [5].[6]

5) Little or no value addition to primary produce through processing by the producer-farmers, gatherers or collectors of food and natural products.

6) Little or no share of the local people, especially producers in management and ownership of the commercial and industrial enterprises exploiting the local natural resources (e.g. agricultural raw materials and byproducts; inferior minerals like limestone, marble, sand and sandstone; even forest—even though the forest tribes lived in forests for generations and by natural right the forest belonged to them). Only gain to the local people is in the form of some marginal income from the sale of agricultural raw materials and from wages.

7) Due to reason (6), almost all the profits/surplus generated (value added) by the commercial and industrial activities based on local resources taken out of the locality; no capital formation in the locality and consequently, no further industrial development and/or social welfare activities in the locality; no employment generation; no human resource development; no transfer of modern science and technology to the rural people for optimum exploitation of potential natural resources, and their own produce.

8) As a corollary of the above, the absence of strong economic organisations of local people which otherwise could be evolved around commercial/industrial enterprises based on local resources for collective benefit of local community.

9) As a further corollary of the above, stagnant social environment where energies of the members of traditionally dominant families/groups/castes/class in rural areas could not be deliberately and fruitfully diverted from traditional ways of satisfying their urge and desire for power and maintaining higher socio-economic status. In the absence of any alternative channel, their major preoccupation would be dominating the weak by using the one and only instrument of power in rural areas, namely, the ownership of land.

10) Century-old, routine, administrative tasks, activities given to local administration with the primary purpose of maintaining *status-quo* (especially economic stagnation). These tasks provide little or no opportunities for innovativeness, creativity,

or for playing leadership role to the educated, often well-trained, local officials.

These are some of the persistent realities of rural India [6]. It is these which forced the society to remain rural in the 20th century. One may even say that the term "rural" connotes the presence of such realities. The basic purpose of experiments/programmes for rural 'transformation', 'reconstruction' and 'modernisation' would then be to overcome these realities.

Against this framework, rural development experiments/programmes/projects listed earlier are evaluated in this paper. To what extent were these realities considered while designing the experiments/programmes/projects? If these realities were considered, what activities were undertaken to overcome these realities? What were the limiting factors? To what extent were the experiments/programmes successful in overcoming these realities? This is the line of thinking followed in this paper.

EARLY EXPERIMENTS (1920-1946)

Any critical appraisal of rural development efforts in India requires reference to early experiments. The names are well known, though few scholars have first-hand knowledge of all these experiments. Three were initiated around 1921: the Sriniketan experiment of Rabindranath Tagore, the Martandam project of Spencer Hatch of the YMCA, and Brayne's Gurgaon experiment. Krishnamachari's Baroda Rural Reconstruction Movement was started in early 1930s. Mahatma Gandhi initiated various experiments, especially Champaran (1917) and Sevagram (1936). The Firka Development Scheme in Madras State was initiated in 1946; and, Albert Mayer's Etawah Pilot Project in 1947-48. The Community Development Programme (CDP) was initiated in 1952 to which I will draw attention later on.

Data on early experiments (1920-1946), unfortunately, are scanty. Very few systematic, objective appraisals of these experiments were conducted during the early implementation stages. There were articles and books written by the social workers associated with these experiments. However, generally the tendency was to emphasise the philosophy, ideals, approach and process, and give some illustrations of startling or unusual events. Little or no information was provided on financial aspects of these experiments: sources of funds, investments, break-up of costs, financial returns, increase in net income of farmers and others, direct and invisible costs of social welfare activities; extent to which economic activities were self-generating, etc. As such, we really know very little about these experiments.

Studies conducted afterwards were, by and large, descriptive. Some were recollections of the social workers involved in the experiments. These primarily described the personalities of key persons (who initiated the experiment and/or were involved in the experiment), their philosophy and perception of rural problems and needs, approach, method and process, major activities, a few illustrations of rural peoples' response to the experiment, and cursorily, the results obtained. A good deal of emphasis was on the philosophical aspects of the experiment. Often the writers were awed by the philosophy and vision of the initiator of the experiment, and that affected their objectivity. Overemphasis on the spiritual and philosophical aspects of these experiments often put such a gloss on the subject of rural development (especially the economic aspects) that it has falsified the perspective. Since some of the key persons, like Tagore and Gandhi commanded great respect, everything directly or indirectly connected with them was considered sacrosanct. So much so, that even the practical aspects of the experiments were not critically examined by these writers.

All these experiments were conducted during the colonial rule. During the last couple of centuries, Indian thinking and actions were at their lowest ebb. On economic and commercial as well as scientific and technological fronts it was both narrow and shallow. There were many social reformers and educationists [7], but on economic matters there were no giants. The thinking and actions were by and large devoid of scientific temper. The role of scientific curiosity and new technologies (and consequent industrialisation) in economic development and social change, as experienced in Europe and America, did not seem to excite the minds of the social thinkers then. Besides this limitation, British rule naturally did not encourage or tolerate any ideas or experiments that hurt its basic interest in keeping the unorganised rural population subjugated and exploiting the natural and human resources of the colony for its own benefit. The aforementioned experiments, therefore, had these two aspects against them to begin with.

Some of the experiments were inspired by a mixture of humanism as developed in the West and the spiritualism of ancient India. The first was primarily due to the exposure of the initiators of early experiments to the already industrialised societies of Europe and America. The exposure, however. was one-sided. They were impressed by the democratic political system, and social philosophies. On the other hand, their exposure to scientific and technological aspects of Western culture was cursory or nil. They neither imbibed, nor made attempts to inculcate the scientific temper of the western culture among the rural masses through their experiments in rural India.

Compared to the free, dynamic, industrialised countries of the West, the scenario in India then was of political subjugation, dismal poverty, complete absence of science and technology and aggressive commercial and industrial entrepreneurship. The end result was, on the one hand, little economic development and material prosperity, and on the other hand, a sense of inferiority complex and fear of loss of identity. Perhaps, partly as a reaction to this, and partly as a long-term solution to India's plight, the spiritual aspects of life and social reforms became the guiding principles for rural reconstruction experiments.

This humanistic, spiritual, egalitarian mixture did not endanger British interest. Experiments or movements carrying any germs of technological revolution from the industrialised West to rural areas would have hurt the interest of rulers in the long run. Early experiments did not carry any such germs. Further, experiments or movements carrying the germs of socio-economic transformation from the Russian Revolution of 1918 would have been equally dangerous to the British rule [8]. The pragmatic and far-sighted British knew too well the likely effects of any approach of trying to organise rural masses around economic, production-oriented enterprises such as collective or cooperative farming. Though all the experiments mentioned above were conducted *after* the Russian Revolution, none borrowed any ideas from it.

Since these experiments did not hurt the economic or political interest of the West in general and of Britain in particular, these were tolerated, sometimes even encouraged.

This gave direction to rural development efforts in India, which, as we will see later, continued even after independence [9].

These experiments were not initiated or managed by Indians alone. A number of well-meaning, socially-oriented Westerners initiated and/or contributed substantially in the management of these experiments. For example, C.F. Andrews was involved in Tagore's Surul experiment; Leonard Elmhirst, a young Englishman played a key role in the Sriniketan experiment; Miss Gretchen Green, an American lady looked after the clinic in Sriniketan, Dorothy Payne Whitney Straight financed the enterprise at Surul from the outset and continued to do so until 1947. Dr. Spencer Hatch, an American, managed the Martandam Project of the YMCA for 18 years; the Gurgaon scheme was initiated by F.L. Brayne, an Englishman who was posted as deputy commissioner; the Pilot project Etawah was initiated and managed by Albert Mayer, an American. Even after Independence the Westerners were in the forefront in moulding the rural development strategy and programmes in India. The Fifteen Pilot Extension Projects were initiated and funded by the Ford Foundation, and the Community Development Programme, contrary to popular belief, was designed by Mr. Chester Bowles, the then American ambassador, and funded by the U.S. Government. These foreigners have had their own perception of rural India and what India ought to be and motivations to work in India. They brought with them many skills, especially organisational skills, and often provided funds to support the programmes they recommended.

It could be said without much hesitation that the influence of foreigners on the design of rural development (approach, methods, organisation and activities) has been substantial in the past as well as after Independence. As we shall see later in this paper, different approaches suggested by some Indians were either absorbed rather superficially in the foreigners' design, or ignored due to scarcity of funds (foreign funds were never available to support the Indians' ideas), or due to political exigencies.

All such environmental factors have to be taken into account while evaluating the early experiments.

It is difficult to give detailed descriptions of all these experiments in this paper. Salient features of these experiments and certain important aspects and analyses are presented here.

SRINIKETAN EXPERIMENT

Tagore's Ideas

This experiment was one of the many efforts to translate in practice ideas of Rabindranath Tagore who appeared on the Indian scene as a great poet-educator just at the beginning of this century. Born in 1861 in a rich *zamindar* family of West Bengal, from an early age, Tagore, a person of great sensitivity and poetic disposition, was influenced by the reformist movement. Two forces influenced him greatly. From his father and other religious and social reformers of his time he had imbibed an understanding and love for India's cultural and spiritual heritage. On the other hand, through contacts with the western world, he realised the stark materialistic orientation of the West born out of industrial revolution. Being a poet, he was also acutely sensitive to a variety of impulses flowing around him—the beauty of nature, the poverty and helplessness of *ryots*, the sterile 'babu' mentality, contempt of 'John Bull' towards everything Indian, the Hindu nationalism and anti-Westernism of the revivalists, the dehumanising effects of uncontrolled urbanisation and industrialisation, and so on.

In 1890, he was sent to take charge of the *zamindari* of his father in East Bengal. From his early writings, we get the glimpses of how his sensitive, philosophical mind perceived the rural scene, not in isolation but in a variety of perspectives.[7] He was touched by sufferings of his *ryot* and became aware of their immediate problems of cultivation, of credit and marketing, and their utter slavish mentality and child-like dependence on the *zamindar* and District Collector for each and every little thing.

Tagore's concern, however, was not merely the immediate sufferings of the masses as has often been emphasised in the literature on rural development. He was a poet, humanist and visionary. His perspective was very different. From the immediate sufferings of human beings he moved towards the much larger issues faced by human society, and like many sages in the past, towards the perception of ultimate realities, similar to the teachings from the *Upanishads* [10].[8] He was an educationist. His concern was 'blending of life's diverse work with the joy of living'. He believed in international cooperation, and tried to bring into harmony the ideals of the East and the West. But, as Jawaharlal Nehru observed, "his feet have always been planted firmly on India's soil and his mind has been saturated with the wisdom of the *Upanishads*."[9] As Mukerji observed, he neither subscribed to fighting Hindu Nationalism, nor the anti-Westernisation of the revivalists, nor the westernisation supported by a few 'England-returned' Indians. He was not a reformer in the usual sense. "He was more interested in society than in the urban roots, and more in the invigoration of the rural roots than the grafting of the foreign notion of nationalism on the branches or the trunk. His new society was basically rural, self-governing, decentralised, and cooperative." Mukerji found certain areas of similarity between the thinking of Tagore and Gandhi.

> Both (he and Gandhi) knew that India lives in the villages, both wanted villages to be the growth-cones of India, both believed in decentralised economy, and both wanted self-mastery, 'self kingdom' (Swaraj) before exchange took place. Negatively, too they were similar—they both failed to point out the way of absorbing the new social forces which the west had released through science and its application to large-scale production. Tagore saw them as power uncontrolled by social sense and morality, while Gandhiji saw them evil, even when he considered some machines as necessary.[10]

This opposition to science, technology and industrialisation, and emphasis on the spiritual aspects of life found predominance in Tagore's experiments in education, as well as in many other earlier experiments.

In the early period, Tagore made some efforts to see whether the Bengal villager could learn to stand upright upon his own feet with self-help. His efforts at Surul failed. In fact, they gave negative rather than positive results.[11]

Santiniketan

In 1901, at the age of 40, Tagore started a school named

Brahmacharyasram later changed to Brahma Vidyalay.[12] Sometime around 1913 when he got the Nobel Prize, the name was changed to Santiniketan School. The use of the term 'Brahmacharyasram' and 'Brahma Vidyalay', clearly indicates the influence of vedic spiritual teachings on Tagore. It is believed that he started this school "to solve the problems of his own children's education the charge of which he could not as a conscientious father entrust to any institution then known to him."[13]

In translating his ideas into practice, Tagore faced many challenges. The first principal of the Ashram made it a training ground of a rigid religious cult. He left after a year due to differences between him and Tagore. Another principal gave excessive stress to bookish studies. In 1905-1907 came the challenge of the Swadeshi movement of which Tagore was one of the leaders, but he did not like the frenzy of the movement and withdrew to his Ashram. Then in 1914-1915 came the influence of Gandhi who spent a month at Santiniketan. He brought with him the ideas of 'self-support', self-help, and social service. While Tagore appreciated Gandhi's ideas, he was worried that Gandhiji's practical programme might degenerate in unwary or untrained hands into mere utilitarian labour, unabashed vocationalism. According to Sarkar, Tagore "firmly and wisely tackled this by subordinating all experience and activity to the atmosphere which he himself created of 'joyous adventure'."[14]

For creating a 'complete man' with a 'fully developed personality' Tagore's emphasis was on creativity in various fields of art and craft, music, literature, even work, with tools and machines (for handicraft and cottage industries). The type of personality he liked and conjured up was an "honest dissenter, emotionally rich, rational and tough enough to die for a cause—a man essentially the affirmative-creative type." But as Mukerji puts it, "unfortunately, however, the type that was immediately produced by his influence was the literary-romantic one believing more in the spontaneity of talent than in discipline, a soft and tender type, in fact, effeminate."[15]

Sriniketan

This rather detailed presentation of Tagore's Brahma Vidyalay or Santiniketan School provides a useful background for study of the Sriniketan experiment, initiated in 1922, essentially as an extension of Santiniketan. The Santiniketan experiment had little to do with 'rural development' *per se* for the first 20 years. In 1913, Tagore received the Nobel Prize. In 1921, the Vishva Bharati University was inaugurated. Tagore wanted to develop a centre to extend his ideas on education in a rural setting. Between 1920 and 1921 a second attempt for some constructive work at Surul, under the inspiration of C.F. Andrews was made once again but it failed miserably. In fact, it gave negative results. Tagore was in search of some person to build his centre at Sriniketan. By that time he was already 60 years old.

In 1921, for building his centre, Tagore recruited a young Englishman, Leonard Elmhirst, on the recommendation of his two American friends. He was an M.A. in history and had completed courses in Agricultural Economics from Cornell. About him Tagore mentioned, "Help came to us from an English friend who took the leading part in creating and guiding the rural organisation work connected with the Vishva Bharati. He believes, as I do, in an education which takes account of the organic wholeness of human individuality that needs for its health a general stimulation of all its faculties, bodily and mental."[16]

According to Sarkar, "Mr. Elmhirst represented 'progressivism' in education, which was then spreading fast over the U.S.A. and the U.K. as a new movement of considerable force, to a point of extreme experimentalism, an exaggerated insistence on the 'freedom' principle and on non-academic activities and occupations which perhaps were not entirely in keeping with Tagore's ideas. But it was only a question of greater or less emphasis on certain aspects of the experiment."

Elmhirst had full freedom to conduct the experiment. It was he who named his work 'Village Construction Work' which was later acknowledged by Tagore.

Elmhirst arrived at Santiniketan on 28 November, 1921.[17] In January 1922, Tagore asked him to go to Surul (where Sriniketan was to be established) which was a mile from Santiniketan. Here, Tagore had some twenty *bighas* of land purchased some 20 years back. On the land was the empty house of the former superintending engineer and the derelict sheds to which the parts of the East India Railway engines were sent in 1870s to be assembled. Elmhirst and his team reached Surul on 5th February 1922 by a Ford lorry. The next day, the first problem was of emptying the latrine buckets. Elmhirst himself emptied the buckets. Some others followed. It was a part of training.

Contact with villagers was established through first-aid help when there was a riot in a village. Then villagers invited Elmhirst to visit the village to treat a sick woman. He treated her in somewhat amateur fashion and luckily the woman recovered. Afterwards, Elmhirst asked permission of the village elders to teach drill and games to young boys. First the request was refused, but one day there was a fire in the village. Two days later Elmhirst visited the village and trained the boys as a fire brigade. There was a mock trial and villagers were impressed. Thus, the confidence of the villagers was won. Monkeys used to destroy crops. Villagers requested Elmhirst to shoot the monkeys and when asked by him, they even agreed to pay for the cartridges.

All this took six months. The team told Tagore that the chief obstacles to the villagers pulling themselves up out of their depression were monkeys, malaria and mutual mistrust.

> The monkeys eat the fruit and vegetables, dig up potatoes and destroy sugarcane and other crops. Only the rice is left and that is polished, so there is no vitamin in the village diet, almost no protein, and so no resistence to malaria at harvest time. The result is poverty, indebtedness and then fear of constant oppression by one group of another until cooperation for any constructive or common end has become almost impossible.[18]

On such a simplistic analysis the foundation of future activities of the Centre were developed. Elmhirst found his knowledge of 'agricultural science' from Cornell of little use. However, the Centre introduced a number of schemes. Earlier they did introduce new breeds of poultry and cows, new vegetables and some new implements and manures. These only gave marginal results. Still they persisted in their efforts.

They were in search of some activity which would provide

"the readiest path to the hearts, affection and so to the confidence of the village." Obviously, it was medicine and medical treatment, as found long back by the missionaries all over the world. With the help of an American lady, Miss Gretchen Green, who had some knowledge of nursing and first aid, a clinic was opened. Next came the cooperative village health societies which were formed by adopting the method and approach of the Anti-Malarial Cooperative Society of Bengal. Those villages which were too poor (especially of *Muchies*, Baynes, and Santhal tribals) to pay even the meagre membership fees, were allowed to join the scheme and pay their contributions in labour on the Society's farm.

The other activity was Baden-Powell's Scouting system adapted for village use. Sriniketan staff were sent for training as scoutmasters. Troops of village boys called *brati balaks* were formed. Other students also became scoutmasters. Later, girls were also included as *balikas*. These scouts learnt to grow vegetables, put out fire, give first aid, act dramas, sing songs, play games and administer quinine.

As the team discovered that traditional craftsmen were near starvation, so slowly training workshops for the *muchies*, the lac workers, the weavers, the carpenters, were set up, and later they started production. The famous artist Nandalal Bose and his young artists from Kalabhavan helped the team in the early stages. Two Japanese carpenters also joined the team. A number of staff members of the Centre were sent to different parts of India and abroad to acquire new designs and skills. As regards marketing of products, Elmhirst's candid observations are worth quoting: "The difficult problem of orderly marketing was left out, as it so often is, till much too late. How little we know about it! We thought that goods well made should sell themselves, and did not realize how important it was to study consumer needs and preferences, and then to perfect every step and link in the chain of production from source of raw material to the finished article."[19]

After two years in 1923, Tagore pulled Elmhirst away to give the Indian staff a chance to find its own feet. He took Elmhirst with him to Kathiawar and later to China, Japan, Argentina and Itlay.

During 1924, Tagore founded another school named Siksha-

Satra at Santiniketan which was later shifted to Sriniketan. It was a 'Home School for Orphans' started with six students between the ages of 7 and 10. According to Sarkar, Tagore founded this school "with a few boys who either were orphans or whose parents were too destitute to be able to send them to any school whatever."[20] According to Elmhirst it was a boarding school where village children came by the week. The boys arrived on Monday morning, each with his little sack of rice, enough for five days, and went home on Saturday.[21]

Elmhirst was associated with this school from its inception and prepared the plan of work for it. Majumdar, who was in charge of the school from 1924 to 1926, called it an experiment in village education, but for Tagore and Elmhirst, Satra was a continuation of the Santiniketan experiment to apply the universal principles of education. The arrangement was very flexible. "Nothing was decided regarding the total number of students to be admitted, the age of admission or the duration of the boys' education at Satra."[22]

At school, these little boys carried out a variety of duties: cooked their own food, kept the dormitory and compound clean, washed utensils, clothes, did the shopping. Some time in morning was set aside for weaving and an hour or perhaps two in the afternoon for studies. Everyday they had to work in their gardens and look after poultry and dairy. As regards curriculum, there was no fixed curriculum nor was there any guarantee of a minimum standard of attainment within a definite period. Boys' academic work primarily consisted of reading, writing and simple arithmetic.[23]

Elmhirst worked at Sriniketan for about four years (1921-25). In 1925, at his request, Tagore agreed to release him so that he could marry Dorothy Payne Whitney Straight, who had financed the enterprise at Surul from the outset and who continued to do so until 1947.

Initially, the Sriniketan experiment covered a limited area of three neighbouring villages. After Elmhirst's departure, while the basic approach and activities continued over the years, the experiment was thinly spread over to about 85 villages by 1953. More activities were established or strengthened at the Centre itself, and over the years Sriniketan became a centre of many institutions for research, extension and education. It maintained a demonstration farm, a dairy and poultry unit, an outdoor clinic, a department of cottage industries (Silpa Sadana), and a village school (Siksha-Satra). These agencies were to treat the villages as their laboratory to identify problems and test their ideas. The villagers were expected to approach these agencies through the village workers to obtain solution of their more pressing problems. The social worker lived in the village working with the people and neither 'for them' nor 'on behalf of them' in isolation.[24]

Dasgupta reported[25] that at Sriniketan Centre, agriculture, dairy and poultry were the foremost activities. Schemes of land development and tree plantation were given due importance. Experiments on paddy, sugar cane and cotton were undertaken. Improved seed, vegetable seedlings, fruit grafts and saplings were distributed. New breeds of cattle were introduced. Through Silpa Sadana local artisans were trained in cottage industry. Other activities were village scout movement, village development council, health cooperatives, circulating library, village fairs, Siksha-Satra and Siksha-Charcha (for school teachers).

All this expansion of activities and area coverage seems contrary to Tagore's ideas. On December 27, 1939, two years before his death in 1941, he wrote to Elmhirst:

> My path, as you know, lies in the domain of quiet, integral action and thought, my units must be few and small, and I can but face human problems in relation to some basic village or cultural area. So in the midst of world-wide anguish, and with the problems of over three hundred millions staring us in the face, I stick to my work in Santiniketan and Sriniketan hoping that our efforts will touch the heart of our village neighbours and help them in re-asserting themselves in a new social order. If we can give a start to a few villages they would perhaps be an inspiration to some others—and my life work will have been done.[26]

After the initiation of Community Development Programme in 1951, Sriniketan completely lost its identity as a number of government sponsored institutions were established at Sriniketan. In 1951, the Institute of Rural Reconstruction, Sriniketan, was redesignated as the Department of Rural Reconstruction when Vishva-Bharati (Santiniketan) was made a Central University.

Other government sponsored institutions established at Sriniketan were: Social Education Organizers' Training Centre (1953), Agro-Economic Research Centre (1954), Headquarters of Bholpur Development Block (1955), Home Economics Training Centre (1955), Institute of Rural Higher Education (1956) (afterwards in its place came College of Agriculture and Department of Social Work). After CDP lost its momentum SEOTC was converted to Family and Child Welfare Training Centre. Silpa Sadana started running job-oriented courses sponsored by the Khadi Committee, the Government of West Bengal and nationalised banks.

Results

What are the results during the 62 years of 'experiment'? To what extent was the vision of Tagore fulfilled? One can say, what Tagore was striving for was perhaps too Utopian, or could not be achieved in a short span of time and under the pressure of on-going socio-economic and political processes (since India was no isolated island). Still, in the experiment there was investment of 62 years of time, unknown quantity of money (which must be fairly large), and the personal efforts of deeply committed Indian and foreign social workers. To what extent these contributed to the removal of poverty, to improving the economic and social condition of *ryot* and artisans and landless at least in the original three villages and other intensively covered villages?

Unfortunately, literature on Sriniketan is rather silent on these questions. Statistical information on many aspects of the experiment is missing. What is, once again, available is generalised statements.

In his article published in 1963, Elmhirst gave the following generalised impressions about the results.

> Notable results were achieved in a small area and in a few villages. Economic returns were such that the rising standard of living in the area was very noticeable. New confidence arose among the villagers, They felt able to tackle new things, to defeat pessimism and to achieve results together. But time and again problems were such that, without much more university research on the one hand,

> whether scientific, economic or sociological, and without more intimate contact between us and government officials, and between officials and villagers at village level, on the other, there could be no progress over the wider areas around us. We knew we were not equipped either with means or men to tackle them ourselves. When and if we attempted half measures both we and the village would get discouraged.[27]

As we have seen above, since 1953 university research, and initimate contacts between the centre and the government agencies through CD block and other institutions were established. Yet the results were not much different. Elmhirst earlier pointed out the weakness in the field of marketing of goods. That also continued. Other reasons according to him were: lack of professional guidance as needed by the people; market rate of salary were demanded by trained men and women and when cheap compromises were attempted these did not work; the idea of local government sharing responsibility for rural development and welfare was new during that period and not generally accepted by the secretariat; the administrative machinery tended to work on a mechanical routine, on a day-to-day basis, with much form filling: collection of revenue and administration of justice occupied too great a proportion of administrators' energy.

Thus Elmhirst put the blame on trained persons who asked for the market rate of salary, and government machinery. That there might be some weaknesses in the approach itself, the methods and the activities, did not cross his mind.

Based on a comparative survey conducted in 1959 (37 years after the inception of the experiment), Sugata Dasgupta looked into both material and non-material achievements. According to him:

> Even a casual review of the impact of the work of the Institute of Rural Reconstruction will reveal that the activities of Sriniketan have not borne uniform results in all the 85 villages which lay within its area of operation. The face of some villages has hardly changed. Some of them appear like most other villages anywhere else.
>
> The causes of these failures of the programmes of

> Sriniketan were many, the most important of which were lack of resources and dearth of trained personnel.

His other observations are:

> From study of various reports and records of work, it was evident that the total programme of rural reconstruction based on principles recommended by the poet, had never had a systematic trial over a sufficiently long period of time to bear finite results. It is, therefore, a matter of no surprise that the programme had not been able to produce the desired results and introduce far reaching changes in all the 85 villages.[28]

Yet, Sugata Dasgupta provides some stray incidents of great success: Between 1939 (base line) and 1953, in the village Laldaha, thirteen miles away from Sriniketan, there was a thousand per cent rise in the per capita income of the people, employment available for each individual, no infant mortality in six years, consumption pattern substantially augmented, and literacy shot up hundred per cent. In Ballarpur village of fifty families, women's literacy rate was 96 per cent, the grain bank of the village stored paddy worth Rs. 2,000 in value which represented the total savings of the community. In Benuria village a Health Society was in existence for 30 years. In some other villages where people were poor, the village as a whole was allowed to become a member of the Health Society and it was entitled to pay contributions in labour on the Society's farm.

These findings could also be interpreted differently. Sriniketan was initiated in 1922, the base line year was 1939, i.e., 17 years after initiation, and survey was in 1953. Thousand-fold increase in per capita income could be deceptive unless one knows the distribution. Also, during the first seventeen years of experiment, it must have been very low in spite of the experiment. Two thousand rupees total saving of 50 families means an average saving of Rs. 40 after 31 years of efforts. If the villagers could not afford to pay even five rupees as membership fees of the Health Society after 31 years of efforts then it speaks rather poorly of the experiment. Instead of sharing the burden of the poor, asking him to pay by working on the society's farm is not much different from the practice followed by feudal landlords, unless the wages were paid at the market rate.

Even though Sriniketan introduced several schemes, in all about 47, yet, as reported by Dasgupta, instances were not lacking when villagers of particular areas had continued to remain stagnant and were unable to secure any impressive results in spite of the best efforts of Sriniketan.

Siksa-Satra was introduced in 1924. From the beginning there was confusion about its organisation, method and activities. Over the years the confusion was compounded. Sarkar observed, "The Siksa-Satra School attracted the attention and praise of a number of distinguished educationists from India and abroad. There is evidence of a strong body of opinion that the Satra experiment was far too important to have been allowed to languish and ultimately cease."[29]

It is rather a harsh, though sad, reality that by and large, the Sriniketan experiment failed on many fronts. This, in spite of more than 31 years of efforts (up to 1953) by many highly educated and committed social workers. There were always a few examples of success in isolated areas and fields of activities. This is a normal phenomenon. In conditions of extreme poverty, even a little relief would be appreciated, and the results seen against the benchmark of extreme poverty look surprisingly impressive. But such results were, in fact, marginal and temporary. The introduction of numerous schemes did not solve the problems of acute poverty. Each scheme mostly provided some temporary, marginal help to a few in isolated pockets. It was the nature of technology and the economy that determined the end result. Extreme poverty and subsistence living conditions defied all attempts to bring social change. Occupational pattern remained the same; agriculturists remained agriculturists, artisans remained artisans and *muchies* remained *muchies*, and the economy also remained stagnant.

The initial results in a locality, though marginal, were satisfying and encouraging to the social worker. But after a couple of years, when no further gains could be made, the normal tendency was to cover or shift to other villages and perform the same or similar activities, which once again would give some marginal gains. This is how the experiment, initiated in three villages, spread to 85 villages. The other normal tendency was to start simultaneously highly structured training institutions which ultimately became the most important activity. These institutions did not cater to the needs of the people of the first three villages or of the 85 villages, but of the state and even the country. Thus, Tagore's idea of conducting his experiments in education in a few and small units ultimately ended up in a stereotype centre for a variety of training, the type of which are numerous in the country.

Many reasons were provided for failure of the experiment. Trained, professional, competent, persons were blamed for demanding market rate of salary. It should be realised that not all persons were imbibed with the social work zeal, nor were all financially as well-off as the social workers who initiated the experiment. Blaming the administrative machinery afterwards does not make sense. It should have been thought of as a given constraint even before launching the experiment.

But there were many other reasons which were generally overlooked. The experiment, in practice, was reduced to keeping a section of people permanently rural which means bound to agriculture—that too subsistence agriculture—and at a low level of economy. In the entire scheme there were no efforts to develop some central dynamic enterprises to work as a driving force for economic progress. This was because of the value system, as well as the background of the social workers involved in the experiment. They could not think of any new enterprise which would provide such driving force; add value to farmers' produce; exploit potential of other unused natural resources; bring capital to rural areas; generate more employment opportunities; demand and develop new skills and thus develop human resources; make it worth for the people to shed their stagnant way of life, thinking and behaviour; provide opportunities for leadership of a new type and entrepreneurship: integrate other economic and social activities around it; and so on. They were no entrepreneurs; they were social workers who could at best contribute a little bit to literacy and some health facilities and a few new designs to artisans; and for economic problems simplistic isolated solutions like the use of improved seeds, poultry birds, and milch cattles. All these could at best provide marginal, temporary relief to a few.

Tagore was extremely sensitive to the possibility of India's cultural and spiritual heritage being adversely affected by the forces released by the West through its science and technologies. But trying to safeguard Indian heritage by keeping a poor section of population permanently 'rural' was rather an extreme step. It was not realised that perhaps the Indian culture and value system could be sufficiently strong, deep-rooted and resilent to absorb new forces generated by science and technology [11]. The cumulative effect of all this was that very little efforts were made to introduce new technologies and industries already in operation in Western countries and even in parts of India. It was not appreciated that technology could, in addition to adding value to raw materials, also reduce the drudgery of work, take over the hard and dirty aspects of work which otherwise have to be done by some human beings.

Many casually reported little events in this experiment indicate how the typical value systems of the social workers influenced the actions. The following observations may look a bit harsh and even unjust. However, these could be justified on the ground that similar approaches and activities were followed in many other "past experiments", and are followed even now, and that while evolving new strategies for rural development these could provide a different perspective.

Elmhirst used a Ford lorry to go to Surul which was only a mile west of Santiniketan. He used a modern technology himself because it provided convenience and comfort and because he could afford it. At other place, there is reference to a gun for shooting monkeys that damaged the crops. Thus, he had another modern technology. He did not help the villagers to get a gun and kill the monkeys themselves, or train the boys to catch them and if possible sell them somewhere. Either the philosophy of 'self-help' was forgotten, or he had no expertise in catching the monkeys, or he knew that poor could not afford to purchase a gun even for their survival, or he did not want a modern technology like a gun to corrupt their life. He mentions about himself and others carrying the buckets of night-soil. The technology of siphon water closet and the sanitary fixtures trap were already widely used in England and other Western countries in the latter part of the 19th century.[30] But such available technologies were ignored. Elmhirst's limited purpose was to inculcate among his fellow workers and others the respect for even the dirtiest, meanest, toughest kind of manual work. His purpose was not to remove the very need for doing such work, a thing the technology would have achieved. Perhaps he and many others after him, did not realise how intervention of such a technology, to take care of the dirtiest, meanest aspect of the work in a village setting, would have contributed to far-reaching social change. Even if he wanted to introduce such technology, there was still the question of assured water supply, and of investment for all these, which poor villagers could not afford. So the easier option was to inculcate the virtue of doing the meanest manual work.

Both Elmhirst and Sugata Dasgupta referred to scarcity of resources—both money and professionally competent personnel. But this was because the work was expanded from the original three villages to 85 villages over the years without taking into account financial and other realities. Secondly, even if funds were available, under the principle of 'self-help' these could not be spent directly on the poor villagers. It seems funds were available, otherwise how could Tagore have sent the members of his staff to different parts of India and even abroad to acquire new skills and designs? And to be more critical, how could Elmhirst and Tagore travel in 1923 to Kathiawar and later to China, Japan, Argentina and Italy? It seems that the shortage of funds was primarily in relation to work at the village level and payments to teachers and professionals. The principle of 'self-help' then became a convenient, handy excuse to shirk one's responsibility of finding much needed finances for investment and social welfare activities in the village.

In short, the experiment was weak on many fronts: its purpose, the value system it was trying to inculcate, the approach, the personnel, the programmes, the activities, financial planning, implementation, timely evaluation, and so on. It is no surprise it failed to excite the minds of villagers, for the experiment had nothing new to offer. The failure of Sriniketan was, in fact, a victory of the villagers who by their native intelligence, instinct, and cunning (which helped them to survive in an extremely hostile environment) knew from the beginning that even the most profound philosophy and aesthetics could at best provide some solace to the soul, but not food for the belly and cloth for the body and would never take them out of the subsistence living. By their response to Sriniketan experiment they clearly pointed out that that was not what they wanted, and that the Sriniketan experiment could not be a model for 'rural reconstruction'.

OTHER EARLY EXPERIMENTS

We have covered the Sriniketan experiment rather exhaustively because it was one of the earliest ones, most reputed and often quoted, and many other experiments followed similar approach, programmes and activities, and with similar results. These other experiments are described in brief.

MARTANDAM PROJECT

Just when the Sriniketan experiment was being initiated in eastern India by Elmhirst, an Englishman, another project of rural development was taking shape at Martandam near Trivandrum in South India under the leadership of Dr. Spencer Hatch, an American.[31] He too arrived in India in 1921 but for permanent service with the Young Men's Christian Association (YMCA) [12].[32] His experience and qualifications were: like Elmhirst, education at Cornell University, College of Agriculture, but majoring in sociology; youth spent on a stoney farm in Northern New York where "real effort, ingenuity and science had been necessary to earn our livelihood," and three years' experience in relief and education services with expeditionary forces on the northwest frontiers of India, in Wazaristan and in Mesopotamia. These were essentially dry, arid or semi-arid, and/or hilly areas mostly inhabited by nomadic tribes. In contrast, Travancore—Cochin had tropical climate, seashore, settled agriculture, and a high density of population. However, Dr. Hatch reported that his three years' experience in the northwest frontiers and other places provided him "with some of the fundamental knowledge needed".

Even before the arrival of Dr. Hatch, the YMCA had developed in Travancore and Cochin about a hundred village associations of rural people mostly managed by honorary officers who worked in their spare time without pay. These village

YMCAs needed guidance, training, and a more rounded, balanced, programme of work.

The then Indian General Secretary of the National Council of the YMCAs, India, Burma and Ceylon, Mr. K.T. Paul, had an idea of establishing a demonstration centre in the midst of a rural area from which people of the villages around could learn. Paul and Hatch selected Martandam for such a centre which was amidst a well-populated area, easily accessible, on a good road to facilitate marketing of goods, and reached by bus. Martandam was a market place for the forty surrounding villages within a radius of three miles. It was selected because, "People were very poor, the land pretty well worn out. A really hungry man is of all men most interested in something to eat; it seems we could expect active response to a programme which could promise better living." Another reason for selecting the place was that for seven years, S. Manuel, the then YMCA Secretary, had been helping the people successfully to establish cooperative credit societies. The spirit of honorary service was strong. There was also a government high school.

According to Hatch, their new movement was called 'Rural Reconstruction', a name coined and proposed by K.T. Paul (it may be recalled that at that time Elmhirst also called the Sriniketan experiment 'rural reconstruction').

The centre initially concentrated the main programme within a radius of three miles covering 40 villages and a population of about 41,600. A survey of the three mile radius region was undertaken. It revealed that there were 36 elementary schools with 5,282 pupils and 186 teachers. The Martandam High School had 560 pupils. Still, only one person out of seven could read. There were few cottage industries, the quality of products was poor, and wages pitifully poor. Cows gave little milk, working cattle were underfed, poor, and weak. Native poultry birds laid a few very small eggs. Agriculture stood in great need. Annual rainfall from two monsoons was forty inches but all within short periods. Water was a problem. More crops, tools, seeds and methods were needed. Debt was prevalent. Interest rates soared as high as 300 per cent. Health needed attention. Expectancy of life was only 27 years and infant mortality was high.

The main programmes undertaken by the demonstration centre were:

1) To improve literacy; organise night schools with the help of enthusiastic colleagues from existing schools.

2) On the weekly market day, set up a portable tent with teaching equipment, and exhibit better poultry and livestock.

3) Guide village associations into wider activities; help the villagers develop the activities they had already organised and in which they were interested enough to work. This was basically an extension service. To help some enthusiastic villages beyond the three miles radius, the earlier plan was modified to 'reach out along lines of interest'.

The 'Pillars of Policy' of the centre were:

1) Building on what the village and the people have.

2) Make certain the programme is the people's own.

3) Help the people to help themselves upwards on all sides of life.

4) Include all people. (A variety of communal organisations were in evidence. Even existing cooperatives were formed on communal basis.)

5) Reach the poorest. (For example, poor were given loans for purpose which could produce profit. "We charged such persons on the book for white leghorn eggs and took our pay later in chickens, or charged for a beehive and took our pay in honey.")

6) Maintain a comprehensive programme: Besides teaching better culture of the land, the centre taught many cottage industries. Pure bred cocks of white leghorn were circulated from village to village to breed their flocks. For better marketing, the centre established the system of testing eggs for freshness and grading for size for the first time in India. The Martandam Cooperative Egg Marketing Society, the first such in India, was formed. Bee-keeping was introduced and soon Bee-keepers' Cooperative was formed for sale of their products. Other cottage industries and activities demonstrated and taught at the centre were: improved pineapples, garden products, milk from improved Surati goats, improved cows sired by Schindi breeding bulls, mats and baskets, refined Palmyra sugar, and handwoven cloth products. "By improving the quality of the arti-

cles and introducing better marketing practices, all products brought better prices."

7) Refuse to be rolling stones or emergency kits: They decided to concentrate on only one centre instead of going about starting new centres all over the place. All the early staff remained with the centre for long periods.

8) The spiritual base: Spiritualism was considered the foundation of the programme. "The deep spirituality of the Indian people demanded this." At the centre there were morning and evening periods of united worship.

9) Keep simplicity the keynote: "Unless the whole rural reconstruction movement remained simple, it would cost too much and perforce would stop short of benefits to millions of rural people. . . . Classroom benches could just as well be cheap floor mats, made by the local people. . . . Staff travelled on bicycles, buses, and on foot. . . . Gandhi's teaching and example helped us in our campaign to glorify the necessary principle of simplicity."

10) Honorary, unpaid service: "By 1940, we had in our extension service in Travancore and Cochin states, 1300 devoted, unpaid workers, every one of whom gave a substantial part of his or her time. . . . It helped make an efficient and highly productive extension service." (This, incidentally, means availability of on an average one unpaid worker for every forty persons or eight households in the three-mile zone of the Centre's activity.)

11) Cooperation and Coordination: Government also cooperated and helped the Centre in many ways such as free lumber for making beehives cheaply, breeding bulls, pure breed poultry from government farms, occasional grants to encourage cottage industries, lectures by government officials about health, sanitation, agriculture, livestock, economics, physics, cooperation etc. Other cooperating agencies were the London Mission and the Mission Hospital at Nellore.

12) Educational emphasis in training of workers: Short summer schools for workers were organised. The first was held in 1926.

In the mid-thirties, the Centre shifted from its old rented site to a nearby two-acre plot purchased for this purpose. There they put up a small headquarters building, a weaving shed, a permanent exhibition hall, a library, a simple model living room. A good well was also dug.

Benefits

Dr. Hatch and his wife stayed with Martandam for 18 years. About the benefits he reports, "We have no evaluation as such for the accomplishments and extent of influence of the Martandam work." However, after one year some efforts were made to measure the progress on bee-keeping. Dr. Manuel carried a simple questionnaire with him on his extension trips. But he informed Dr. Hatch that if he really counted the beehives; the amount of honey sold, given away, or eaten, he would have no time at all for his regular work. So the survey work was left uncompleted. But this experience encouraged the workers greatly. "They kept a rough appraisal of their successes and reverses, analysed them at staff conference and learned a great deal even from this inadequate method." Record-keeping was often neglected. "Our progress may have been slow but it was progress and it accumulated as it developed."

The centre received many invitations to assist elsewhere. For example, Gaekwar of Baroda invited Hatch to start a rural centre at Kosamba in Gujarat. Manuel worked there until Martandam could train a secretary and his wife to head the Baroda work. Assistance was provided to the Governments of Pudikkottai and Cochin State, and government centre in Mysore and Hyderabad, both established by the YMCA secretary Stephen. The centre also trained social workers/YMCA workers from other countries such as Egypt, Burma, and Ceylon, who started similar centres in those countries.

Lessons

Like the Sriniketen experiment, this project also dealt in easily identifiable, stereotype activities, e.g. bee-keeping, improved poultry and cows, some handicrafts and literacy. These could at best provide some marginal gains to some families. The programme and activities were, however, somewhat better organised than Sriniketan, due to the organisational strength of YMCA. The organisers were also more pragmatic in so far as they primarily concentrated on income generating activities to attract poor people to the centre. The emphasis on marketing of output, especially the formation of cooperative Egg Marketing Society and Bee-keepers' Cooperative, supported the production activity. In the marketing efforts the YMCA was in a better position due to its organisational capabilities, and linkage and association with various institutions and organisations. The overall approach and method of the Project, however, were such that dependence of village people on the centre continued indefinitely. Started with a limited objective of improving the life of people in a three-mile radius, over the years the centre developed into a training institute trying to provide expert advise and trained workers for the vast population of India, Burma, and Ceylon.

GURGAON SCHEME

The Gurgaon scheme in northern India was contemporary of Sriniketan and Martandam.[33] Towards the end of 1920, Mr. F.L. Brayne, an Englishman, was posted as Deputy Commissioner of Gurgaon district. About his educational background, information is not readily available. According to Verma, Brayne "took more than usual interest in the welfare of rural people and made extensive tours in the villages to study the conditions of the people." For revenue purposes the district was classified as 'insecure' as it was liable to periodic conditions of scarcity. Rainfall was uncertain or scanty, and means of irrigation were meagre. "The people were extremely poor, dirty, and unhealthy, with no conscious desire for anything better, because they had no idea that anything better was possible."

In his visits, Brayne was invariably accompanied by Mrs. Brayne. He became popular as he mixed with people freely. In his daily routine, Brayne used to do most of his work with his own hands. "He would even remove night-soil to set an example, and in this way he preached to the people the dignity of labour."

After about seven years of study and experiment Brayne evolved a scheme called 'The Gurgaon Scheme'. According to Mr. Brayne, "Our object in Gurgaon has been to jerk the villager out of his old groove, convince him that improvement is possible, and kill his fatalism by demonstrating that both climate, disease and pests can be successfully fought. He must be laughed out of his economic and unhealthy customs, and taught better ways of living and farming. Further, the secrets of our success were to deal with the whole of village life, to take the whole District as the field of operations and to deluge the areas with every form of propaganda and publicity that we could devise or adopt or afford. Uplift is a mass movement, a combined assault, and no area, no part of life, and no method of attack can be neglected."[34]

The activities introduced by Brayne were as follows:

1) In 1925, a School of Rural Economy for training of village guides. The first year batch consisted of 42 school teachers and four *patwari* candidates. In the second year, 80 agriculturists were enrolled. The trainees received scholarship of Rs. 10 to Rs. 15 per month. The school managed a farm of 51 acres on long lease for practical training. The curriculum of studies included scouting, cooperation, agriculture, first aid, infant welfare, public health, domestic and village hygiene and sanitation, stock breeding and elementary veterinary training.

2) Village guide for each *zail* to develop cooperatives take up public health work, cleaning of villages by digging of manure pits, putting in windows, ventilators in the houses, and demonstrate and sell improved ploughs, other implements, improved seed, persian wheel, etc.

3) In 1926, a Domestic School of Economy under Miss E.M. Wilson, an English woman, to train a group of women in Women and Child Welfare work. The school taught reading and writing up to primary standard, and some instructions in sewing, knitting, cutting, and making clothes, embroidery work, toy making, cooking, hygiene, sanitation, first aid and child welfare, etc.

4) Health Association which ran five health centres in the district. The nurses at the centres also acted as health visitors. Local women received training in midwifery. It organised baby shows and arranged health and sanitation weeks and exhibitions.

5) A Women's Institute at Gurgaon to manage the ladies' garden in Gurgaon and to organise games, lectures, first aid classes, etc.

Both Mr. and Mrs. Brayne carried on intensive propaganda on rural sanitation. He gave elaborate instructions for using manure pits as latrines. According to Brayne, "The Gurgaon village houses are the direct successors of the caves of prehistoric man." He suggested windows in these houses. Preventive treatment against small-pox, plague, cholera, malaria was encouraged. Since some people were superstitious, Brayne managed to get the head Imam of Jama Masjid from Delhi to announce by *fatva* that vaccination was not against Islam. On the agriculture front, improved seeds. improved Gurgaon ploughs, manure pits, killing of rats and monkeys, harmful insects, etc., were encouraged. People were advised to keep good cattle and selected cows for breeding, and to maintain milk registers. Hissar stud bulls were distributed to various villages on subsidised basis (25 per cent villages, 75 per cent District Board). The Persian wheel was introduced.

On the education front four new high schools and 152 night schools for adult literacy were opened. Scouting and coeducation were introduced. Under his guidance credit cooperatives made progress. Propaganda for social reforms was carried out (prohibition of child marriages, co-education, abolition of *purdah*, etc.).

According to Brayne:

> There is nothing new in the details of the Gurgaon Scheme. The only new thing is the coordination of efforts or rather the popularisation and application, by a specially trained staff of propagandists, of the many benefits which the various departments of Government have in store for the villager.

In view of the 'pioneering' work done by Brayne, the Punjab Government appointed him as Commissioner of Rural Reconstruction in 1933.

As regards the 'results', Verma laments,

> It marked a definite departure in the technique of village improvement and attracted India-wide attention. It looked grand—but alas, it was not to last or take roots.[35]

Brayne's candid observations are worth quoting:

> Good work, excellent work is going on all over the Punjab. *You can travel all day and find nothing that offends either eye*

or nose. Village after village and *zail* after *zail* have been turned into models of the new life. Marvellous changes have been made and there is a feeling of life and movement in the air. Have we found the incentive then? Will this work last and spread? Alas, no! This work is not being done by villagers determined to live a better life but by villagers determined to please their District Officers. A good enough motive in its way but not the motive we are looking for. There is no permanence about this kind of work. What if the District Officer's attention is diverted elsewhere, or he wants something different done, or in a different series of villages?

Comments

Elmhirst, Hatch and Brayne were contemporaries. Brayne's approach and activities were similar to those of the other two. All were concerned about those things in rural India which 'offended the eye and nose', of urbanites, more so of foreigners. That these were like poisonous mushrooms on the squalid bed of poverty, a product of subsistence economy, was overlooked. What Brayne achieved was rather superficial and that too temporary, since the motive force was a district officer. He was worried that without the constant attention of district officer whatever results were obtained would be lost. But, in case of Martandam, Hatch stayed for eighteen years and in Sriniketan there was a continuous stream of social workers working for the project. Yet, the results were not much different. Brayne's major contribution was to draw attention to the problem of coordination in the given structure of district administration, which incidentally continues even today. But the nature of activities undertaken by him were such that each could be implemented by the relevant department more or less independently. There was no *central* activity requiring coordination of various activities and tasks. Like Elmhirst and Hatch, his primary unit of operation was 'individual' and marginally village. Hence, effective coordination would mean coordination of activities at the individual family level, and village level, and thus depended on the decision of individual and the community. The results indicate that the poor villagers did not find the project activities sufficiently attractive to continue on their own, especially considering their economics. In the project there was no coordination of agriculture production oriented activities with output marketing. And output marketing was the primary concern of farmers, so also of village craftsmen, as ultimately his entire economy depended on the amount his produce/product fetched. There the exploitation and market forces continued to operate. Dr. Hatch, at least, made some contribution in this field through marketing cooperatives for eggs and honey. But he, too, ignored the marketing of the main agricultural outputs. Elmhirst too ignored this. He encouraged the production of new and better designed products by artisans, and realised, rather late, the importance of marketing.

BARODA EXPERIMENT

Baroda was a princely state in western India.[36] Under the enlightened rule of Maharaja Sir Sayajirao Gaekwar, this state made considerable progress starting from the late 19th century in the field of education, agriculture and welfare as compared to many other princely states and British India.

During the late 19th century, when Sayajirao was a minor, his minister Raja Sir T. Madhavrao created certain essential preconditions for further reforms and development. The first school in the State was started as early as 1870. While the Raja appreciated the need for education of masses, he emphasised the importance of higher education. At one time he observed:

> Education of masses is certainly important. But my profound conviction is that higher education though necessarily for a smaller number is still more important in present conditions and circumstances in India. I am fully convinced that one native to whom higher education has been imparted at an expense of Rs. 1000 contributes definitely more to the general progress of the community than 333 natives only slightly or superficially educated at a charge of Rs. 3 per head.[37]

Kavoori observes that to the Raja, a highly educated man was a 'hydraulic bellows', and that he believed in the leadership of truely 'educated'. Such orientation distinguished the Raja from many others of his time. During his firm and enlightened rule he restored political stability and social stability. Security of life and property was guaranteed. A number of basic amenities and other development services were provided by him. Public works of various kinds, provision of medical services, irrigation, roads and transport provided basic amenities to rural people and also opportunities for self-propelling development. During his time, Baroda State had the highest percentage of area covered by rail and road and the largest number of schools. As Desai and Chowdhary observed, all these were the essential conditions for further development.[38]

Sayajirao gave special emphasis to rural welfare in the total administrative set up, and a number of supportive legislations. Under him the central focus of the entire administrative machinery in Baroda was rural development.

The programme introduced by Raja Madhavrao and Maharaja Sayajirao were as follows:

1) Education

In 1893, compulsory elementary education for boys and girls in one district on an experimental basis; by 1923 this was extended to the entire state. Responsibility for this was given to village *Patel.* Except for certain categories of persons, those parents who did not cooperate were fined. This coersive measure was supplemented with education of people for the need of education; special attention was given to schools for tribals and Vagharis, girls' education, vocational classes with agricultural and technical bias. As early as 1886, 2,000 girls were in primary schools; there were night schools as early as 1890 and *zanana* schools for older women. Library movement was started in 1893.

In 1888, a committee under Professor T.K. Gajjar recommended a central institute of technical education, later known as *Kalabhavan*, which is today a part of Baroda University. "Its objectives were to improve the local industries and to induce the poorly-paid government employees to become well-paid artisans".

In 1887, for the first time in India agriculture biased schools were opened in Baroda State. By 1926, things rapidly changed and by 1936, a full-fledged agricultural college was established. The agricultural education was much diversified and in addition to long-term one or two year courses, there were short-term courses on such subjects as fruit preservation, virginia tobacco, oil engines, and tractors, etc.

2) **Cooperatives**

In the late 19th century, the cooperative movement was introduced, about 16 years before it was officially launched in the country. Over the years a number of legislative measures were introduced to strengthen the cooperative movement. By 1940, the movement became "comprehensive as an economic measure and an instrument for providing social infrastructure". The concept of a multipurpose society was practised. The societies organised even night schools and cottage industries. Between the twenties and thirties an apex cooperative institute took shape and it trained departmental personnel.

3) **Village Panchayat**

In as early as 1904 the village panchayat was an integral part of the democratic administration. In a village panchayat 50 per cent members were elected and 50 per cent nominated. Next to the panchayats were taluka councils, district councils and State Assembly. At each level 50 per cent of the representatives were indirectly chosen for the next higher tier by the tier immediately below it.

4) **Village Economy**

There was emphasis on agricultural development. Under this irrigation facilities were developed such as medium and minor irrigation projects, power-driven tube wells, pumping schemes from rivers and canals, etc. Other programmes were: soil conservation and contour bunding; production and distribution of improved seeds: education in agriculture and supplementary occupations. A Central Cottage Industries Institute (Kalabhavan) gave training in weaving, calico printing, block engraving, metal work, etc. Training classes were held in villages for various cottage industries.

In all these efforts various renowned persons like R.C. Dutt and V.T. Krishnamachari played an important role. Under V.T. Krishnamachari, who joined the Baroda State in the thirties, agriculture became the heart of rural development. Notable work was done in this, especially the introduction of rural reconstruction centres (RCC) with the help of Dr. Spencer Hatch of the YMCA.

The first RCC was established at Kosamba in 1932 following the model of Martandam Centre. Dr. Hatch spent two months initially and kept visiting as adviser for the project. Many persons for this centre were trained at Martandam Centre.

As per Government order, the Centre was expected to do the following:

1) "Aim at effecting an improvement in all aspects of rural life—changing in fact the outlook of the agriculturists, the problem being 'the development of the desire for a higher standard of living'."

2) Undertake intensive work in a group of villages where the superintendent and his trained co-workers could establish personal contact with practically all agriculturists.

3) Develop village leadership of the best type.

4) Undertake programmes for economic development such as: subsidiary occupations (kitchen gardening, weaving, poultry-farming, bee-keeping etc.), "Marketing of products must be arranged for. This test is most important;" every village was expected to carry out farm improvements in cotton and other crops recommended by the Agricultural Department; every village was expected to have at least one cooperative society, and village panchayat discharging such functions as providing water supplies, improving sanitation, building village roads, etc.

5) Educational and moral programmes: adult education, development of community sense, propaganda against evils like early marriages and unreasonable customs, use of village libraries, scout movement, etc.

The Baroda Administration Report of 1933-1934 also laid down, "The Centre can regard its work as completed only when a large proportion of the agriculturists in the village have adopted some subsidiary occupation or other and when all the other activities mentioned above have made satisfactory progress and not till then."[39]

The activities of Kosamba Centre initially covered 10 villages and over the years expanded its activities to cover 35 villages. Two new centres were also established in two other areas. In areas not covered by these Centres intensive efforts were made on the same principles by district technical officers working together. In every district there were: (i) intensive zones; and (ii) areas outside intensive zones. Intensive zones covered 20 to 25 villages and graduate assistants concentrated on agricultural production and strengthening of cooperatives. As trained workers became available the number of such zones was steadily increased. By 1942-43, there were 24 intensive units serving 487 villages.

The Baroda Government passed many important social and economic legislations such as Hindu Remarriage Act, Divorce and Inter-caste Marriage Act, Rent and Land Regulation Act, Debt Regulation Act (1935), Debt Reconciliation Act (1938), Consolidation of Holding Act, and so on.

With the help of the ICAR, a Village Rehabilitation Scheme was undertaken to study the influence on economic, social and other aspects of village life under various land-tenures such as lease tenancy, personal proprietorship, cooperative farming and collective farming. The scheme worked for a number of years. In 1951, ICAR reviewed the scheme and recommended its continuation in a suitably amended form. However, as reported by V.T. Krishnamachari, "No definite results of value emerged as to the respective merits of the different systems of land-holding."[40]

Results and Comments

The Baroda Experiment was not an experiment in the sense that Sriniketan and Martandam were. It was not limited to a few villages and a few activities. Its social programme covered the entire state, and the economic development programmes intensively covered hundreds of villages spread over all the districts of the state. It covered human development, organisational infrastructure and legislative support. For nearly 50 years, the entire state administrative machinery was involved in welfare administration and rural development in an integrated fashion supported by various legislations. The overall results of these massive efforts could not be easily measured, though some information about people's reactions to various programmes as well broad conclusions drawn by various administrators and scholars are available.

The major contribution of the Baroda State's efforts was in

the field of mass education. By 1942, it outpaced all British provinces and other princely states except Travancore and Cochin, with 229 literates for every 1000 population. The strong state support also helped in the wider spread of the cooperative movement. The emphasis on agricultural production through demonstration, extension and training did help in creating a general awareness among farmers about new varieties and practices. However, there is little evidence that fifty years of efforts in strengthening the cooperative movement and agricultural development made the economy of villages of Baroda State substantially better than that of other provinces.

The village panchayats did not work as expected in spite of all legislations. Around 1925, after about twenty years of efforts, the then *diwan*, Manubhai Mehta reported "creeping aversion on the part of people to shoulder responsibilities, and unpreparedness for taxation for promoting the new schemes, however, sound." He further noted: "Advantages of village conciliators and communal mediators were not easily understood and the progress in the art of self-government was poor in the basic stages." However, he did not recommend abrogation of the panchayat and self-rule.[41] In 1928, a special committee recommended that financial resources of self-governing bodies be increased.

In the Baroda Experiment, as in other experiments and programmes, then, and even now, the stark reality of the financial capacity of local bodies, to continue welfare schemes and civil amenities provided by the state or any other agency, has not been seriously taken into account. The economic condition of the people was such that they could not afford to support such activities. Mobilisation of funds through any form of taxation (cash or kind) could be only at the cost of satisfaction of more pressing needs. Either the economy of a large number of people must develop substantially so that they could support welfare schemes and other amenities, or funds must continue to flow from outside to support these activities. The tendency was to avoid this responsibility by propounding the concepts of 'self-help', 'local self-government', and allow the scheme to run somehow or die. (It is worth noting here that situation is not much different in present days, and even in developed countries.) About the U.K., Baviskar observed, "Those who remained in the countryside, despite the forces favouring rationalisation of the rural economy, were either cushioned by welfare state apparatus, or were able to more easily earn a material improvement in their standard of living."[42]

After the establishment of the rural reconstruction centres and intensive efforts. it was reported that "On the whole there were appreciable increases in production in spite of the widespread depressions in agriculture from 1931 and the effects of the war." The Administrative Report for 1944-45 mentioned, "While production figures are fairly impressive, there is a steady change in the outlook of the villagers which is a matter of real satisfaction."[43] Neither V.T. Krishnamachari, nor the Administrative Report refers to an increase in the net income of the farmers due to 'appreciable' increase in production, or the extent to which the depression affected the villagers.

The scheme of consolidation of holdings, through cooperative societies, did not find favour with the villagers. Even on act was passed in this connection, "But the movement did not take root." The 1942-43 Report mentioned, "There were 41 societies, of which 22 were cancelled during the year, and 12 are under liquidation. Most of the remaining societies are stagnant, and no appreciable work is being done by them."[44] This, in spite of about 50 years of state support to development of cooperative movement. It was not realised that mere consolidation of holdings through cooperative farming or collective farming could not increase agricultural production and net income of member farmers. Cooperative or collective was only a form of organisation to bring individual farmers in an organised fold, so that other welfare and development activities could be provided, and control could be exercised more effectively and efficiently. In the absence of other investments and facilities, there was nothing attractive for the farmers in the cooperative action.

The Rural Reconstruction Centre started in 1932 was abruptly closed down in 1946. Whether it achieved its stated objectives or not is not known.

Kavoori summarises the impression still carried by old village people and officers who were earlier involved in the experiment: "The government machinery was superior; work discipline of officers was high; officers were knowledgeable; primary education was considered with general pride as a very progressive measure; social legislation stands very high in the minds of people; clear and unequivocal preferences for cooperative societies: the number of people interested in development was smaller but they were more genuinely interested."[45]

It is worth noting that in this summary of impressions, there is no reference to agricultural production or economic benefits. Perhaps, not much was achieved in this field which could have left some lasting impressions in the minds of the village people and officers.

Kavoori observes, "Maharaja produced a unique instance of democratic revolution from the top. But the revolution has to come from below. Therefore the correct policy well-formulated and well-begun and with the might of the State behind them did not succeed as much as was expected."

The experiment did not succeed, but perhaps not for the reason given by Kavoori.[46] The approach itself carried the germ of failure. Considering rural reconstruction mainly in terms of literacy, welfare, civil amenities, cottage industries, agriculture, and credit cooperatives has not been very effective in transforming the society. There was no force in these activities, individually or collectively which could move the society on the path of economic progress.

In his article, V.T. Krishnamachari observed, "Two preliminary points should be made. Firstly, the programme of rural reconstruction was to be part of a wider programme for bringing about a rapid increase in the standard of living. Industrialisation—establishment of large-scale, small-scale and cottage industries—formed an important part of this programme; also rapid expansion of the educational system. Secondly, the Baroda Government, recognising that increased agricultural production lay at the root of all development, progressively expanded programmes necessary for this purpose."[47]

Yet, in spite of such awareness in the entire Baroda Experiment, the link between rural reconstruction and industrialisation was completely missing. Perhaps, the failure of the Baroda Experiment and all other such experiments could be explained by this missing link.

GANDHI'S EXPERIMENT

There is no comparison of Gandhi's 'experiments' with other

experiments, considering the motivation, objectives, scope and activities. He spoke and wrote on numerous occasions on numerous aspects of Indian life, and there is always a danger of misquoting him, and/or misleading the reader by partially quoting him. Though his basic philosophy towards life remained constant, his views on many issues changed over the years.

To understand his 'construction' programmes two things have to be kept in mind: First, he was primarily a political strategist having the primary objective of leading India towards freedom from the British rule through mass movements. As such, each of his actions has to be interpreted with this perspective and in the light of socio-political and economic conditions prevailing during a particular period. Second, as a corollary of above, his every action or view on a subject has a singular blending of two components: a very simple looking outward act having tremendous appeal to masses, and which would help in awakening the sense of their own power; and the inward principle which would provide a spiritual sanctity to the whole effort. The ultimate purpose of the whole was to overcome Britain's power in India.

Born in 1869, Gandhi went to England at an early age to finish his education and obtain a full training as a barrister-at-law. After a successful law practice in Natal, South Africa, he devoted his time to oppose the oppressive racist regime. For this, two new principles evolved and followed in practice by him were: fight a moral, non-violent war of passive resistance against the oppressor, and develop inner strength through self-discipline, self-control and purification.

In 1915, at the age of 46, Gandhi returned to India, and straightaway plunged into the freedom movement. First three years he spent moving in villages, gauging the feeling, understanding the real implications of poverty, experimenting with his ideas developed during the South African movement. In 1917, he started his experiment in Champaran. The emphasis was on educating children in various arts and science subjects as well as crafts. Adults were taught hygiene, making village roads, sinking wells, etc. The team workers swept the roads, cleaned the wells, etc., and persuaded the villagers to take up such work themselves. *It was more a training to his team workers, and a creation of awareness for need of mass movement among the villagers, than a mere effort to improve literacy or sanitation and economic condition.* At Champaran, for the first time he actually offered passive resistance (*satyagraha*) in order to remedy the evils that were connected with the indigo plantations.

During 1917-18, he was also busy organising *satyagraha* at Khaira district in Gujarat for suspension of land revenue collection till the ensuing year as the year was an exceptionally bad one for the villagers.

In 1919, under Martial Law, the British betrayed their war mentality. General Dyer massacred large number of innocent men, women and children in Jallianwala Bagh, Amritsar. But in 1920, the House of Lords refused to pass a resolution condemning General Dyer, and the Hunter Commission Report wavered in its own condemnation of official action.

1920 was a landmark in the life of Gandhi. All these years, his passive resistance—the moral struggle—gave him positive results and gained a slight advance both in social and political freedom for people of India. All these years he expressed loyalty to the British Constitution as he had faith that it was founded upon justice. But after the Jallianwala Bagh massacre he completely lost faith in British Government in India. His indignation against the British rule came up forcefully as reflected in the terms he used in his writings of those days: Satanic Government treachery of Mr. Lloyd George, exploiters of India's resources, wickedness, a system that is vile beyond description, and so on.

It is from this background his strategy of 'non-violent Non-Cooperation' emerged. The programmes under this strategy were Village *Swaraj* (self-government or self-rule) and *Swadeshi* (indigenous) movement. Under these two programmes, he introduced apparently extremely simple activities such as *Charkha* (spinning wheel) and *Khadi* (handmade cloth), in opposition to the use of foreign (British) made cloth, revival of village handicrafts and household industries, village sanitation, hygiene, Wardha scheme of education for harmonious development of the whole personality built around manual skills, and so on. Removal of untouchability and social disabilities became part of his strategy to strengthen unity among people and mass movement. *In his strategy, efforts to achieve Indian political freedom and work on the constructive programmes were inseparably linked.*

After intensive political work between 1920 and 1924, Gandhi withdrew from political activity from time to time to devote his time to 'constructive programme', which, as mentioned above, included such things as communal unity, abolition of untouchability, fostering of hand spinning and other handicrafts, 'cow protection', advancement of women, prohibition of alcohol and drugs, and so on. In 1936, he settled in Sevagram, a village near Wardha. He served the villagers by undertaking various activities like road sweeping, revival of handicrafts, introducing improved agricultural practices and new varieties of crops. Since he mixed with untouchables and was using excreta as manure, people from surrounding villages did not cooperate in his experiments.[48]

He advocated a 'self-sufficient village economy' and 'self-reliant village community', and emphasised utilisation of local resources for development.

In 1942, when he was already 73 years old, he said,

> My idea of village Swaraj is that it is a complete republic, independent of neighbours for its own vital wants, and yet interdependent for many others in which dependence is a necessity. Thus, every village's first concern will be to grow its own food crops and cotton for its cloth. It should have a reserve for its cattle, recreation, and playground for adults and children. Then if there is more land available, it will grow *useful* money crops, thus excluding *ganja*, tobacco, opium and the like. The village will maintain a village theatre, school and public hall. It will have its own waterworks ensuring clean water supply. . . . As far as possible every activity will be conducted on the cooperative basis . . . . The government of the village will be conducted by the Panchayat . . . . Here there is perfect democracy based upon individual freedom.[49]

In his nationwide campaign for village reconstruction, Gandhi emphasised revival of *Khadi* and village industries linked with *Khadi* production. For his rural reconstruction programme he created or was associated with several organisations such as the All-India Spinners' Association (1925); the All-India Village Industries Association (1934); the Adamjat Seva Sangh; the Harijan Sevak Sangh; the *Go* (cow) Seva Sangh (1941); the

Hindustani Talimi Sangh; the Kasturba Trust (for village women and children services organisations); and the Gandhi Seva Sangh (1920-40).

There were real differences of opinion between Gandhi and Tagore. Tagore did not support Non-Cooperation Movement. He could not understand why Gandhi's entire stress was on the manufacture of *Khadi*, as though other things were not important. In reply to Tagore's criticism on the boycott of foreign cloth and Gandhi's call of the spinning wheel, Gandhi wrote,

> The Bard of Santiniketan has contributed to the *Modern Review* a brilliant essay on the present movement. It is a series of word-pictures such as he alone can paint. . . .
>
> The Poet tells us summarily to reject anything and everything that does not appeal to our reason or heart. . . . A reformer who is enraged because his message is not accepted must retire to the forest to learn how to watch, wait and pray. . . .
>
> With all this we must heartily agree, and the Poet deserves the thanks of his countrymen . . . .
>
> It is good, therefore, that the Poet has invited all who are slavishly mimicking the call of the spinning-wheel boldly to declare their revolt. . . . I regard the Poet as a Sentinel warning us against the approach of enemies called Bigotry, Lethargy, Intolerance, Ignorance, and other members of that brood.
>
> But, . . . let me assure him that if happily the country has come to believe in the spinning-wheel as the giver of plenty, it has done so after laborious thinking. I am not sure that even now educated India has assimilated the truth underlying the spinning-wheel. He must not mistake the surface dirt for the substance underneath. Let him go deeper and see for himself whether it has been accepted for blind faith or for reasoned necessity.[50]

In his other letters also Gandhi sharply replied to Tagore's criticism of Non-Cooperation Movement. Gandhi also thoroughly studied Brayne's Gurgoan Scheme and critically reviewed his book, *The Remaking of Village India* which was second edition of his *Village Uplift in India.* His criticisms of Brayne were: He made use of his official position to put as much pressure as he could upon his subordinates and the people. But he could not carry conviction by force. Brayne was impatient and wanted to cover long distance in one stride, and he failed. When an official becomes a reformer people do things more to please the official than to please themselves. Brayne relied more upon money for the success of his experiment than upon his faith in himself and the people. So in spite of his having had Rs. 50,000 a year, he complains that many things await development only for want of money. There is much exaggeration in his description of the defects in the villages. Indian villagers' method of farming are certainly not bad. His observation about 'absurd expenditure' by villagers is only his imagination. Vast majority of the masses have no money to spend on any ceremony. Millions of village women have no jewellery except some hideous stones or wooden pieces. 'Absurd expenditure' is confined to the fewest people. People have rejected modern implements because most of these are useless. More than once Brayne betrayed ignorance of the chronic economic distress of the seething millions of India. It is prefectly useless to suggest remedies which are beyond the present means of the people. What the people may be capable of doing when the reformer's dream is realised is irrelevant to a consideration of what they ought to do whilst the reform is making its way among them.

Gandhi, however, also praised Brayne for a number of programmes such as women's programmes, taking care of dogs in the villages, village education, using school teacher as genuine village leader, etc.[51]

It is commonly thought that Gandhi was against industrialisation, wanted to abolish machinery and return to a pre-industrial life. As I mentioned earlier, what Gandhi said after 1920 and during his Non-Cooperation Movement about *Swadeshi* Movement has to be seen in the context of that time. *His emphasis on Khadi was an outward component of his political strategy.* As a man of extremely critical mind and trained in law, he presented unrefutable arguments against the use of foreign goods and propagation of *Khadi*. One has to go through his arguments carefully to understand the real implications of his strategy. He mixed religion, culture, economics—everything possible in support of *Swadeshi* to ultimately hit Britain where it would hurt the most: its economy. Some of his choicest arguments presented in Andrews' book are:

—What the British Empire means to India is exploitation of India's resources for the benefit of Great Britain (p. 239).

—During the first quarter of the 19th century Indian villages were better off with millions of village people having work all the year round, but now whole of the agricultural population remains without work for at least half of the year (pp. 150-151).

—People say why only *Khadi*, why not try dairying? Well, India is not Denmark, which easily possesses 40 per cent of the butter trade of England. In 1900, Denmark received 8 million pounds sterling from England for butter, and 3 million for bacon (p. 152).

—After 70 years of cotton industry, and having some 50 crores of capital, the cotton magnates only claim to have given their daily bread to 1½ million souls (p. 153).

—*Khadi* does not require any capital or costly implements, does not require any higher degree of skill and intelligence, raw material can be cheaply and locally obtained, little physical exertion is involved; has been done traditionally so no ground has to be prepared (pp. 154-155).

—A stiff protection duty upon foreign goods is needed: Natal, a British Colony protected its sugar by taxing the sugar that came from another British Colony, Mauritius. England has sinned against India by forcing Free Trade upon her. It may have been food for England but it has been poison for this country (p. 125).

—If not a single article of commerce had been brought from outside India she would be to-day a land flowing with milk and honey (p. 124).

—I think of economic *Swadeshi* not as a boycott movement undertaken by way of revenge, but as a religious principle to be followed by all. I am no economist, but I have read some treatises which show that England could easily become a self-contained country, growing all the produce she needs (p. 124).

—Is it not madness to send cotton outside India, and have it manufactured into cloth there and shipped to us? (pp. 242-243).

—India cannot live for Lancashire, or any other country, before she is able to live for herself; and she can live for herself only if she produces everything for her own requirements within her border (p. 124).

—The Lancashire cloth, as English historians have shown, was forced upon India, and her own world-famed manufactures were deliberately and systematically ruined (p. 242).

Gandhi's arguments were based on two factors:

i) enforced idleness for nearly six months in the year of an overwhelming majority of India's population owing to lack of suitable occupation supplementary to agriculture and the chronic starvation of the masses that results therefrom;

ii) *Khadi* "alone offers an immediate, practicable, and permanent solution of the problem"; "it does not compete with or replace any existing type of industry". He observed that

> There would be no place for the spinning-wheel in the national life of India, comparatively small as the remuneration that can be derived from it is, if these two factors were not there."[52]

There is a general impression that Gandhi was against all machines. On this he said:

> How can I be, when I know that even the body is a most delicate piece of machinery? The spinning-wheel itself is a machine. What I object to is the craze for machinery, not machinery as such. The craze is for what they call labour saving machinery. Men go on 'saving labour' till thousands are without work and thrown on the open streets to die of starvation. I want to save time and labour, not for a fraction of mankind, but for all. I want the concentration of wealth, not in the hands of a few, but in the hands of all. To-day machinery merely helps a few to ride on the backs of millions, the impetus behind it all is not the philanthropy to save labour but greed. It is against this constitution of things that I am fighting with all my might. . . . Scientific truths and discoveries should first of all cease to be the mere instruments of greed. Then labourers will not be overworked, and machinery, instead of becoming a hindrance, will be a help. I am aiming, not at the eradication of all machinery, but its limitation.[53]

EXPERIMENTS AROUND INDEPENDENCE

Compared to Gandhi's construction programme, the other experiments were mere pygmy, and their failures made them still more insignificant. Not only that, it looks as if Sriniketan, Martandam and Gurgoan experiments were encouraged on the Indian scene around 1921, just when Gandhi launched his vast Non-Cooperation Movement, to oppose, or at least minimise Gandhi's influence. In this sense, these experiments could also be considered treacherous to India's freedom struggle. Available evidence does not indicate their support to Gandhi's Movement. On the contrary Tagore, The Bard of Santiniketan or the Poet of Asia, who was fast becoming the Poet of the World as Gandhi referred to him, vehemently opposed the Movement for one reason or another. And for this he was squarely criticised by Gandhi and many others, in spite of his Nobel Prize.

Yet, over the years, the failures of these experiments and the indifference or opposition of their mentors to Gandhi's Movement for freedom was forgotton, and many, in their ignorance of the past, considered these as the model for India's rural development. Around 1947, the year of India's Independence, the language of these experiments was revived—the philosophy, approach programmes and activities. This time, it was the influence and money of the United States that played an important role as could be seen from the Mayer's Etawah Project, Ford Foundation's Fifteen Pilot Extension Projects and US Ambassador Chester Bowles' Community Development Programme.

THE PILOT PROJECT ETA WAH

Like in many other states planned development of rural areas was first introduced in Uttar Pradesh in 1937. A Rural Development Board was set up. Chiefs of all development departments, non-official constructive workers and M.L.A.s were its members. There was some success due to the unprecedented zeal of the non-officials. But within two years the Board got officialised, after the first non-official Chairman of the Board resigned. In 1939, with the beginning of the Second World War, the main functions of the Board were procurement of rice and recruitment of farmers for military purposes. It soon acquired great notoriety in rural areas and became entirely unpopular. The Congress Government which resigned in 1939 came back to office in 1946, and again took up the task of revitalising life in the villages which was at its lowest ebb. It was at this stage an American architect Albert Mayer, who was a soldier in India during the war, came on the scene.

After convincing the then Prime Minister Nehru and Chief Minister of U.P., G.B. Pant, he started a three-month tour, visiting the rural areas in Uttar Pradesh and some other states. It was during this tour that the ideas of a model village came to him. During 1947-48, he formed a team of four specialists—a town and village planner, an agricultural extension specialist, an agricultural engineer and a rural industries specialist. On September 15, 1948, Mayer and his team submitted their Pilot Intensive Project for Etawah district in Uttar Pradesh. The project was started in October 1948 in Mahewa village. The objectives of the Etawah Pilot Project were:

1) To know the degree of productive and social improvement, as well as of the initiative, self-confidence and cooperation that can be achieved in the villages of the district;

2) To find out how quickly these results could be attained;

3) To know whether the results remain permanent part of people's mental, spiritual and technical equipment and outlook after the special pressure is withdrawn; and

4) To assess how far the results were reproduceable in other places.[54]

During the preparation of the project proposal, Mayer studied various early and on-going efforts such as rural reconstruction efforts in U.P. during 1937-39, Brayne's Gurgoan experiment, Gandhi's construction programme, missionary activities in India, etc. He was aware of the weaknesses in these efforts and developed the project proposal keeping weaknesses in mind.

Mayer evolved the philosophy, "We must work with the people, not tell them; we must demonstrate by doing with our own hands in their own villages and fields."[55]

In contrast to earlier experiments, there was a systematically developed organisational structure in this pilot project. At the state level, the development commissioner with his secretarial staff was involved in coordination work. He was assisted by a planning officer and four American experts. At the district level, the rural analyst, executive engineer and district development officer, with officers of agriculture, cooperative and livestock departments formed a team. During the initial stages of the programme, the assistant development commissioner provided administrative facilities. The district magistrate (collector) initially did not play any part in the project.[56] At Mahewa, the team at the project level comprised four deputy development officers (one each for agriculture, village participation, engineering and training), one senior economic intelligence inspector and a number of assistant development officers, namely workshop supervisor, overseer, sanitary inspector and field teacher. At the village level, there was a 'multi-purpose' village level worker (VLW) with four or five villages under him.

As Planning and Development Advisor, Mayer made several visits to India between 1946 and 1957. At some stage the project also employed Horace Homes, an agricultural specialist from Tannessee, to assist in the training works. The entire project was sponsored and funded by the Government of U.P. The Ford Foundation, which took keen interest in CDP in India, was not involved during the pilot project stage.[57]

"The programme of work under the project was by and large similar to earlier projects: introduction of improved variety of seeds, chemical fertilisers (new activity), green manuring, compost-making, improved implements, irrigation, plant protection measures, horticultural development, soil conservation, improved cultural practices; animal husbandry through upgrading of cattle, disease control; provision of cooperative societies for credit, production, marketing and supply; better sanitation and health services, maternity and child welfare services; improvement of roads, water supply, drainage and other public utility works; improvement of housing, broad based social education programme by means of adult literacy classes, study tours, farmers' fairs, village leaders' training camps, mass contact programme."

The total expenditure in the Pilot Project for the first four years (1948-49–1951-52) was Rs. 1.54 million. Of the total expenditure, about 28 per cent was spent on supervision and administration, 53.3 per cent on capital expenditure, engineering project and equipments, temporary accommodation, office equipment and spare equipments, 1.3 per cent on grants-in-aid, roads, and agricultural demonstration, and the remaining 17.4 per cent on participation, soil conservation, cooperation, tube-wells, land reclamation and village planning.

Thus, the project distributed very little money as grants-in-aid and subsidy. It also did not distribute material of any kind free of cost to the people. The emphasis was on self-help. Advise alone was provided free. Materials such as fertilisers and seeds were provided on deferred payment basis or on loan.

Initially, the work was started in 64 villages. After about a year the number of villages covered by the project went up to 97. In October 1951, another group of 125 villages was taken up. In 1956, a third group of 112 villages was added. The project ultimately merged with the National Extension Service block.

The most convincing achievement of the project was in agriculture. It was claimed that production went up considerably due to the use of improved seeds, fertilisers, green manure and water. The pilot project was not able to solve the problem of unemployment and underemployment of the population. The project did not solve the problem of balance in human and resources ratio.[58] Success gained at Etawah could not be maintained and the work became sluggish after Mayer's departure in 1957.

Comments

The Etawah Project design and results indicate that Mayer did not pay much attention to the results of earlier experiments, and repeated more or less the same approach, programmes and activities. There was no linkage of industry with agriculture, even though the project was launched in the middle of the 20th century. After initial 'spectacular' results, ultimately the project failed to deliver the goods. Yet in 1951, when the pilot project was only about three years old and without any 'spectacular results', Chester Bowles, after a quick visit to the project, was 'impressed' by the results and designed his rural reconstruction programme, later known as Community Development Programme, on the model of the Etawah project. Incidentally, as we will see later, the CDP also failed miserably within five years of its launching in 1952 and had to be continuously revitalised by other means.

NILOKHERI EXPERIMENT

The Nilokheri experiment was different from earlier experiments. Its primary purpose was to develop a new township to rehabilitate displaced persons from West Pakistan. The new township Nilokheri was built in 1947-48 on a swampy, barren land by the refugees with self and government help under the leadership of S.K. Dey, an engineer by training. Dey was building this new refugee township at the same time (1947-48) Mayer was experimenting with his rural reconstruction project in a few villages in Etawah.

Dey's experiment started in a refugee camp at Kurukshetra, near Delhi. His approach was a practical one. "The people should be given work so that they could earn. That would, among other things, restore among the refugees the self-confidence they lost during the turmoil. Once work for their livelihood was arranged, other things would follow as a natural consequence. With the money earned they could have homes for the family, adequate clothing, and schooling for the children; medical aid and other amenities would also follow. But the starting point was that their right to live and to work for a living had to be recognized."[59]

Dey made a survey of the immediate needs and requirements of the camp population. He found that there were some artisans like weavers, tailors, carpenters, blacksmiths, etc. among the refugees, who could be trained to produce useful materials and provide services needed by the camp population. A vocational training-cum-production centre was accordingly started in 1948. There were 750 trainees, 250 trained workers, besides 50 instructors, supervisors and others administering its activities. Thus, about a thousand persons were kept productively busy.

Prime Minister Nehru who visited the place in April 1948, was greatly impressed with the activities. He declared that he would like to see thousands of townships in India "humming with the music of muscles".

Encouraged by the results of his experiment, Dey launched a new scheme, a more elaborate one, known as Mazdoor Manzil, resulting in the construction of a new township, Nilokheri. The basic concept here was to stop the one way traffic of labour, material, skill, and culure from villages to town. The emphasis was on a decentralised administration and decentralised economy that would eventually lead to an agro-industrial economy as the future economic pattern of the country.[60]

Mazdoor Manzil scheme envisaged a nucleus township housing a population of about five thousand. The township was linked with the surrounding villages. The idea was that the township with the surrounding villages would not only be an economic unit but a unit of administration as well.

Within the township, facilities such as hospitals, schools, institutions for technical and vocational training, veterinary aid, and agricultural extension services were planned to be set-up. Recreational activities were provided in the form of libraries, reading rooms, cinema, drama, music and other cultural activities.[61]

As regards the surrounding villages, it was thought that in each village the school would grow as the community centre. "Agriculture, animal husbandry and the local crafts would all be taught in the village school. Both the children and the adults in the village would benefit from such a school. Under the existing circumstances a wholesale remodelling of the villages was not possible, nor necessary either. They were to be reconditioned and made better for living purposes. But the townships were to be built anew."[62]

For this new experiment a plot of part marshy and part jungle land near Delhi was allotted by the government. On this land a new township named Nilokheri sprang up. The polytechnic formed the core of the township. The trainees came from prospective permanent residents of Nilokheri, from Kurukshetra and other refugee camps, and from surrounding villages. Buildings, water, electricity, and services were provided by the government to all those willing to work for a living and organising themselves into groups for industrial production. As far as possible, responsibility for production, supplies and sale was entrusted to cooperatives. Slowly, cooperatives of spinners, weavers, tailors, shoe-makers and other craftsmen came up.

Nilokheri was not without its problems. "The cooperatives

had their teething troubles. Though joining hands for a common purpose, the cooperators unfortunately could not imbibe the spirit of a joint family. There was also the difficulty that Nilokheri, being a small township, failed to offer a wide enough base for different types of cooperatives. A contradiction was growing from the beginning. This contradiction was in all spheres—technical, managerial and ideological."[63]

Some industries were organised by the government, some were in private hands and some were run by cooperatives. Industries which required special skills for management and which had a vital impact on the economy of the colony were under government management. Small industries were handed over to enterprising and skilled technicians. Farmland in the colony was entrusted to individual farmers at the rate of six acres per head. They also received bullocks, implements and a small amount of capital. Activities in which there was no wide gulf between the skill and the emolument of the supervisors, and the manager and common run of workers were retained under cooperative management.[64]

The *panchayat* (local government) was revitalised to look after political and social aspects of community life in the colony. It was given the responsibility for law and order, sanitation, and community welfare including assistance to the weaker sections of the community. It operated through sub-committees.

Prime Minister Nehru on his second visit to Nilokheri observed: "I want ten thousand Nilokheris spread over the whole of India."[65] On his third visit, he observed: "I have seen one Nilokheri from its birth to its present development. I am deeply struck by the effort made by the people to revive themselves and build their future. I want 9999 Nilokheris to implement the message of Nilokheri."[66]

Nilokheri township was subsequently handed over to the Government of Punjab. After the bifurcation of Punjab, Nilokheri went to Haryana State. Its economy was geared to private and state enterprises, and the cooperatives receded into the background to some extent.[67]

Nehru was very impressed by Nilokheri Experiment, and on his request government appointed a committee, with P.A. Narielwala of the Tata Industries as Chairman and S.K. Dey and Konisberger as members, to study the Nilokheri project and examine the possibilities of its duplication. *This committee strongly recommended the adoption of agro-industrial economy for the development of rural areas.* Little is known about government's reaction to this committee's report. Perhaps, top administrators who had no experience of industries and had experience only in colonial administration under which they were providing some stereotyped welfare and simple agricultural development services, felt uncomfortable with this report and 'killed' it. Or, perhaps, this model somehow did not fit into the overall strategies then formulated by the national leaders for Indian's economic development. Dey observed, "The Committee visualised an agro-industrial town to support, and being supported by the hinderland of villages, each complementing the other. But the time was still not ripe for this. Therefore, the report just added to the weight of the archieves."[68]

It is during this period that American influence started operating in India. Ideas generated by the Indians themselves were set aside, and instead a low cost, non-industry oriented rural development programme, suggested and funded by Americans, was adopted.

THE FORD FOUNDATION AND 15-PILOT PROJECT PROGRAMME

In mid-1951, a high power team of American Ford Foundation (FF) visited India to explore the possibility of the Foundation collaborating with some development programme. The team consisted of Paul Hoffman, the then President of FF, John Cowles, Trustee of the Foundation, Chester Davis, Vice-President and John Howard of the staff. Hoffman had been a high executive in the Studebaker Motor Corporation in America and was the Administrator of the Marshall Plan in Europe before he took up the office of the President of the Ford Foundation.

One day in mid-1951, Dey received a trunk call from Prime Minister's office to urgently come to Delhi to meet the Team. Dey recalls, "To my utter surprise I found this ace Administrator and Industrialist talking to me all the time about the supreme importance of rural development as the foundation for the further growth of this country in science, technology and freedom."[69]

Dey, however, did not explain what prompted him to forget his 'agro-industrial township programme,' and join the Americans in their rural reconstruction programme.

The dialogue between Dey and Hoffman resulted in the formation and initiation of a set of 15 Pilot Projects each covering about 100 villages. This decision was taken in August 1951 and the programme received the approval of the government in December 1951. The programme was organised under the leadership of Centre and state ministers of food and agriculture and financed by a Ford Foundation grant of $1.2 million. Douglas Ensminger, who took over the charge as Ford Foundation Representative in India in November 1951, was associated with the CDP till his retirement in 1970.

According to Dey, "The Programme primarily envisaged agriculture, rural sanitation and allied activities based on self-help by the people. Government was to provide a nucleus staff for the purpose and some very limited funds as nuclei for promoting the programmes. A village level worker was envisaged for every 5 villages who would receive special orientation in Agricultural Extension spread over a period of 3 months. The same could be offered for the other staff at the headquarters of each of the project. Five agriculture colleges in India were adopted for the development of an Extension Wing to carry out this special orientation programme."[70]

The Pilot Project was in operation from April through September 1952. Up to early 1954, the projects maintained their 'pilot' character. According to Ensminger, "with the launching of the community projects in October (1952) and with the national spotlight focused on this new and intensive effort, the experimental projects began to lose their pilot emphasis. By 1954, they were no longer thought of as pilot areas and were therefore integrated into the National Extension Service (NES) arm of the community development programme, with Foundation funds no longer required."[71] Thus, the life span of original fifteen pilot projects was brief—about 2½ years.

CHESTER BOWLES AND 55 CD PROJECTS

Even before the actual planning and implementation of these pilot projects one more source began to exert its influence at the highest level. Chester Bowles came to India in 1951 as the Ambassador of the United States. "He had in his pocket a provision of 50 million dollars on behalf of the U.S. Government to assist finance India's development."[72] At the instance of Nehru, Dey met Chester Bowles in December, 1951. Chester Bowles and Mrs. Bowles spent a day and night at Nilokheri at the instance of the Prime Minister "to examine the feasibility of multiplying the Nilokheri Growth Centre scheme throughout the country."[73]

According to Dey, at the instance of Bowles, he made a visit to Etawah project which was then about four years old. "An examination of the Project at Etawah revealed to me that Etawah was moving more or less in line with the Ford Foundation Project of Rural Extension in Agriculture and related subjects, and constituted in a way the rural counterpart of the 'Mazdoor Manzil' composite scheme which formed the basis of the urban counterpart we were working out at Nilokheri."[74]

"A scheme therefore evolved for working out a composite rural-cum-urban programme involving the building up of both a Growth Centre nucleus as well as the development of the rural hinterland based on the experiences already gathered at Nilokheri and Etawah as well as in the 15 Ford Foundation Pilot Projects. The new programme envisaged. . . coverage of all fields of development in the village—agriculture, animal husbandry, fishery, poultry, irrigation, soil conservation, communications, public health, education, social education, rural industrialisation, women's and children's programmes, indeed every element that entered into the life of the villager."[75]

The new scheme was known as the community development programme. A formal scheme was drafted and an agreement with the United States was signed on May 31, 1952. This agreement is known as Operational Agreement No. 8. The initial programme was to have 55 projects of 3 blocks each, each block covering about 100 villages. The 55 community projects were formally launched on October 2, 1952, on the birth-day of Mahatma Gandhi.

Operational Agreement No. 8

According to the Agreement, "The central object of Community Development Project is to secure the fullest development of the material and human resources of the area. The attainment of this object in rural areas demands urgent measures for a rapid increase in food and agricultural production. Work will also be undertaken for the promotion of education, for improvement in the health of the people, and for the introduction of new skills and occupations so that the programme as a whole can lift the rural community to higher levels of economic organization and arouse enthusiasm for new knowledge and improved ways of life."[76]

It further stated: "The proposed projects will be of the rural development type including irrigation, fertiliser application, agricultural extension, health measures, and education. Six of the 55 projects, however, will be of the composite type including, in addition to the foregoing, activities in small and medium scale industries, township planning and development, etc."[77]

The Agreement provided a detailed list of activities to be undertaken. It covered: (a) agricultural and related matters (eighteen areas of activities); (b) communication (three areas of activities); (c) education (three areas of activities); (d) health (six areas of activities); (e) training (five areas of activities); (f) social welfare (five areas of activities); (g) supplementary employment (four areas of activities); and (h) housing (two areas of activities).

The Operational Agreement also stated that only six out of 55 agreed projects would be eligible for expenditures from dollar and rupee budgets for supplementary employment, namely "encouragement of medium and small scale industries to employ surplus hands for local needs or for export outside project areas". It was stated that "such areas will be provided with some equipment (both for training and for use) for small industries and possibly small thermal power stations."[78]

Since the community development programme covered the activities of almost all the development and welfare departments of the state and central governments, a Central Committee was formed with the Prime Minister as the Chairman and the members of the Planning Commission and the Minister of Food and Agriculture as members. Various ministries were directed to collaborate with the programme through community project administration, headed by an Administrator. Dey was appointed as Administrator.

Comments

Chester Bowles is very candid in his explanations why he supported and pushed the CDP based on the Etawah model, even though the pilot project was not fully tested. In his book[79] he does not even refer to a visit to Nilokheri mentioned by S.K. Dey, nor his reaction to the Nilokheri experiment. He has completely ignored Nilokheri experiment and the recommendations of the Narielwala Committee for building new agro-industrial townships as a strategy for rural development.

Bowles' all pervading concern was to keep communism out of India and his mind was already made up as to what India should do to keep communism out. He refers to the work of James Y.C. Yen in pre-communist China which influenced his thinking about India. Dr. Yen was a graduate of Yale University and returned to China after the First World War "fired with determination to help set his people free from the bonds of ignorance, poverty and disease."[80] Yen introduced a team approach involving three workers—one each for agricultural development, literacy and public health—who went to villages as a team to develop abroad, coordinated development programme. At a later stage he realised that local governments should be controlled by villagers themselves and as such introduced the fourth functionary whose job was to encourage democratic self-government. Yen, who was Minister of Education in Chiang Kai-Shek's Nationalist Government, asked the Generalissimo for resources so that his village development efforts could spread into all of rural China. However, the Generalissimo, though impressed by Yen's approach, gave first priority to victory over the communist forces. According to Bowles, "Yen is said to have replied, 'But you cannot defeat communism on the battlefield, until you have first conquered it in villages and rice fields; it is the poverty and helplessness of the peasants which is giving Mao his chance'."[81]

Bowles remarks: "when I know that I was going to India, all that I had learned from Dr. Yen came to my mind. In theory at least his techniques seemed superior to the more diffused development programmes which were being started in most of the underdeveloped countries through the United Nations Specialized Agencies and America's Point Four."[82] Bowles was convinced that Yen's integrated plan would have good impact. "When Steb, Cynthia, Sally, Sam and I visited the Etawah development project in Uttar Pradesh two or three weeks after our arrival in India I became convinced that this was right. . . . I saw in action the very principles of multipurpose development which Dr. Yen had developed in China."[83]

After returning from Etawah, Bowles prepared a memorandum and armed with $54 million sanctioned by the U.S. Congress under the technical assistance programme met Nehru in November 1951. He reports:

> I opened the conversation by suggesting to Mr. Nehru that one of the most crucial questions was whether Asian democracy could compete with Asian communism unless it, too, organized its village efforts on a massive scale, substituting persuasion and cooperation for violence and concentration camps. . . . I told him that I had been authorized by my government to offer India $54 million in economic assistance to assist some such village campaign and on other programmes.[84]

Nehru accepted his offer and the CDP on the Etawah pattern was introduced in India.

Chester Bowles' premise was that communism gained strength in China because Yen's approach was not supported by the generalissimo. He thought that a similar situation would develop in India if development programmes were not undertaken urgently on the lines suggested by Yen. To him, the CDP was a defence mechanism against his perceived threat of communism to India. It could be said that Bowles' influence at a crucial and psychologically important moment pushed India to opt for the Etawah model.

The *Operational Agreement No. 8: Community Development Programme*, is an important document in many respects. The Agreement specifically listed a large number of activities. The activities covered provision of inputs, facilities and technical knowledge required for agricultural production to individual cultivators, and provision of communication, education and health facilities at the rural settlement level. For implementation and administrative coordination of activities it envisaged restructuring and reorganisation of traditional district administration by establishing a new administrative unit known as development block covering about 100 rural settlements.

The four basic elements of the CDP design were:

1) Focus on individual cultivator,

2) Restructuring and reorganisation of district administration, especially by establishing new administrative units on area (block) basis,

3) Provision of facilities (including extension of knowledge) for agricultural production to individual cultivator through cooperatives and block agency, and

4) Provision of welfare facilities by the block agency at the block level and partly at rural settlement level.[85]

Thus, the focus of this design, as in case of all early experiments, was on *individual* cultivator. There was no emphasis on collective, community action for community welfare and on building community assets for common economic development. The design envisaged development of the rural people through concentration of efforts on individuals (primarily cultivators) and marginal reorganisation of government machinery at district level and below (as evolved during the colonial period), but not through development of new organisations of the rural people for collective economic and other benefits. In this design there was no scope for development of small and medium agro-industries and cottage industries which could help in reducing pressure on land, add value to farmers' produce and develop entrepreneurship and new skills. The design also did not provide any help to rural artisans and craftsmen who were constantly adding to the number of the landless.

Thus, this design was not much different from 30-year-old Brayne' Gurgaon experiment, and in terms of activities, from all earlier experiments. This design also failed miserably to improve the economic condition of rural people or to create a dynamic force for rural development. *It, however, did serve its main purpose, namely, provide political stability in a democratic framework.* Contrary to popular belief, its contribution to agricultural production was, at best, marginal. The real breakthrough in agricultural production came after high-yielding varieties responsive to higher doses of fertilisers and controlled irrigation were introduced.

Even after its failure within the first five years, this design was kept alive by various means. Community development itself has remained an enigmatic concept even after 30 years of operation and countless books and articles. Most of the early literature on CDP reflect the typical emotional appeal, excitement and euphoria generated by CDP. Most of the writers had a tendency to eulogise the programme, extol its virtues, glorify small achievements, overlook its genesis and inherent weaknesses, and blame the bureaucracy for its failures. The publicity the programme received through speeches of national leaders, seminars, conferences, workshops, symposia, training programmes, and especially, writings of foreign scholars, swept the academic world as well. Many academicians joined the bandwagon and vied with each other in praising the programme. Among the ambitious administrators (both national and international), foreign promoters who formulated and financed the scheme, and the enterprising researchers looking for trips abroad and grants to support further stereotyped researches, there was little inclination for a critical examination of the basic assumptions.

For the next 30 years, this design determined, and still determines, the strategy and instruments for economic development and welfare of the rural people. It also determined the direction in which internal resources and external aids were to flow. This design was constantly nurtured and financially helped to survive by introducing, one after another, various schemes and programmes such as Intensive Agricultural District Programme (IADP) designed and funded by Ford Foundation in 1960, the programme failed miserably); the Drought Prone Area Programme (DPAD); the Command Area Development Programme (CADP); Intensive Cattle Development Programme (ICDP); Small Farmers' Development Agency (SFDA); etc. all following the CDP design, but excluding the welfare component. Earlier, the failure of CDP was attributed to lack of people's participation. To overcome this 'weakness' panchayati raj was introduced, which, however, did not in any way improve the programme. Various other schemes on nutrition, women and child welfare also followed the same design with unimpressive results. In all such agricultural and welfare development programmes, there was some tinkering with the district administrative machinery such as appointment of project officers, subject matter specialists, more extension officers, field workers, etc. There were neither changes in the structure and management of co-operative institutions, nor any efforts for organising farmers for utilisation of their and community's resources for common benefits. The new cooperative structure like Farmer's Service Cooperative Societies (FSCS) where emphasis was on marketing of farmers' produce and agro-industries failed miserably due to excessive control as well as hostility of CDP oriented "development administrators.[86]

INDIGENEOUS FARM-INDUSTRY LINKAGE EFFORTS

While the low cost, relatively simple to administer, community development programme approach for rural development was adopted on the national scale, in some parts of the country farmers, on their own, made efforts to improve their economic condition by establishing agro-industrial cooperatives. These efforts also received support from the government. In these efforts one can see an alternate/supplementary approach to rural development somewhat on the lines suggested by Narielwala Committee. Unfortunately, these have not found place in the CDP influenced, stereotyped, massive literature on rural development in India. Few have studied these efforts systematically, and as such literature on these efforts is rather scanty. Some literature which can provide insight into some of these efforts is available only in local languages.[87] What is presented here is based on a few available studies, government statistics, and data collected during personal visits to a number of agro-industrial cooperative organisations.

The process of rural transformation with local participation around an agro-industrial enterprise was initiated some 35 years back with the establishment of Pravaranagar Cooperative Sugar Factory in Ahmednagar district in Maharashtra by Shri Vikhe Patil and Professor D.R. Gadgil. During the same period a modern cooperative dairy industry (AMUL) was established by Shri Tribhuvandas Patel and Dr. V. Kurien at Anand in Gujarat State. This commodity output based (such as sugar and milk), capital intensive industrial cooperative approach for rural transformation was not followed in any of the earlier and even contemporary rural development efforts. These were initiated when Albert Mayer, Chester Bowles, and Ford Foundation experts (who can be considered as 'representatives' of *industrialised* West) were designing the non-industrial models such as Etawah project and CDP. The sugar and milk industrial cooperatives were developed by local initiative. While milk cooperatives received some support from Cooperative League of the USA, UN agencies and other aid agencies, the sugar cooperatives developed mostly by local support—members' contribution and government funds.

Following the success of Pravaranagar factory, about 209 co-operative sugar factories (as on 30th June 1984) have been established in India. These produce nearly 50 per cent of total sugar production in the country. About 1.5 million sugar cane farmers own and participate directly or through their representatives in the management of these agro-industrial activities.[88] Detailed statistics up to 1980 for 184 cooperative sugar factories indicate that about one thousand million rupees of share capital was raised by about 1.2 million growers from about 82,000 villages. This share capital was about 40 per cent of the total paid-up capital of these societies.[89] Many societies have even paid back the entire state contribution to share capital as loans. Most of them have been paying, year after year, a higher sugar cane price than that paid by the private sugar factories as well as the floor price fixed by the government. Thus, these farmers' enterprises contribute to the income of more than 1.5 million farmer members, most of them being small and marginal farmers.

Such an agro-industrial cooperative enterprise provides an *anchor*[90] around which various productivity enhancement and other economic development and welfare activities are integrated. Most of the sugar cooperatives assist farmer-members by providing extension services, good variety of seeds, and development of irrigation facilities. These also assist in supply of inputs and credits in collaboration with village level primary cooperative societies, and arrange harvesting and transport of sugar cane.

Many have utilised part of surplus for expansion/diversification, and part for social welfare activities such as schools, colleges, hospitals, consumer stores, medical stores, recreation, etc., as well as for the development of off-farm activities such as cooperative poultry and dairy.

Each such enterprise located in rural area has developed a small township of its own. These are labour intensive enterprises. For example, an average size of sugar factory with 2,500 MT/day capacity and command area of about 10-15 thousand hectares spread over 30-40 villages employs about 700-800 persons on permanent basis (office and supervisory staff and skilled and unskilled workers). In addition, it provides employment to about 2,500 persons (for harvesting/transporting of cane) for about 150-180 (harvesting/crushing period) per year. Besides, it generates secondary employment in the business, transport and service sectors in the region.

The value of the annual output of sugar alone of a single factory of 2,500 MT/day capacity is about Rs. 200 million. This is many times the budget of the average district local government body like zilla panchayat. The industrial activity of these societies is not limited to production of sugar. Many have established plants for processing by-products/waste matter such as alcohol and other derivatives from molasses, liquor for alcohol, paper from bagasse. These by-products/waste matter processing add further value to the agricultural produce of the farmer, and consequently: (a) add to their net income, (b) support further expansion of industrial and other economic activities, (c) generate further employment, and (d) contribute to more sophisticated welfare activities.

One of the most important contributions of these agro-industrial cooperatives is human resource development. In backward, often barren or newly developed rural areas, these enterprises have exposed illiterate, poor rural people to modern science and technology, management systems and industrial culture. Various categories of farmer-members and others participate in this dynamic economic activity generated in a compact area of 30-40 villages. On account of employment opportunities new skills are taught and learnt.

These agro-industrial organisations are the outcome of rural entrepreneurship. The entrepreneurial achievements of local persons, the political processes generated in a compact area of 30-40 villages, and the managerial activities pertaining to running of a modern industrial plant, all created an educational environment for the local, backward, illiterate rural community. In the process, the base for entrepreneurship and creative leadership was expanded, and over the years, second-generation entrepreneurs, leaders and managers emerged from the rural community.

From the visits to sugar cooperatives in Maharashtra State (such as Pravaranagar, Sangli, Warnanagar, Krishna, Panchganga, etc.) and Gujarat (e.g. Bardoli) one gets the feel of this process of rural transformation. One gets similar feeling during visits to the command areas of dairy cooperatives (such as AMUL Mehsana).

It is worth mentioning here that the contribution of socially oriented cooperative entrepreneurs, such as, Vikhe Patil, V. Kurien and many others was nationally recognised when the Government of India awarded *Padmashri* to Vikhe Patil and Kurien, and *Padma Bhusan* to Vasantdada Patil. Incidentally, few following the traditional rural development approach of the CDP type received such recognition in the country. It is reported that as early as 1955, Pandit Nehru observed, "Of all the many types of assistance India is receiving from many friendly countries and bilateral aid agencies this type of help that has enabled the building of this type of farmers cooperative institution is the one India will most value."[91] In 1964, Lal Bahadur Shastri observed, "If we can transplant the Spirit of Anand in many other places, it will also result in rapidly transforming the socio-economic conditions of the rural areas and in our achieving the objective of a socialistic pattern of society."[92] Similarly, in 1982 Indira Gandhi observed, "This is one of our success stories of which we are all proud. May the spirit of AMUL spread far and wide in our country to help, instruct and inspire our farmers."[93]

In 1965, the Ministry of Agriculture, GOI, constituted the National Dairy Development Board (NDDB) "to replicate the Anand pattern dairy cooperatives in other parts of India in an effort to improve rural incomes by giving the farmers a price for milk based on price in the metropolitan cities. The NDDB is today working in 136 milkshed-districts in 19 states and 3 Union Territories in India." About 34,523 Anand Pattern village milk cooperatives have been formed so far covering about 3.6 million producer-members. The NDDB provides turnkey as well as consultancy services to set up dairy and cattle feed plants and other projects owned and operated by farmers through professionals employed by them. The sale of milk through urban dairies in the organised sector based on cooperative procurement exceeds 183 crore litres per annum, valued at some Rs. 700 crores. The dairy cooperatives in addition to procuring their members' milk, also provided inputs such as artificial insemination and veterinary services, balanced cattle-feed, concentrates, and minikits for fodder development to lakhs of producer-members to improve their milch animal productivity. In addition to such activities which directly help the producer-members, the NDDB takes up major projects to support the cooperative dairy industry. Some of these are Indian Dairy Machinery Company, Paper Laminating Plant, Pilot Project on an Alternate Structure for Vegetable and Fruit Marketing, Bhavnagar Vegetable Products Unit, and Oilseeds and Vegetable Oil Projects. Interest of dairy industry is closely linked with cattlefeed industry, a major component of which is de-oiled cake. As such, NDDB is assisting in development of Anand Pattern oilseeds growers' cooperatives in various parts of India.[94]

Various case studies and project research on Anand Pattern of dairy cooperatives indicate the dynamic nature of such farmers' enterprises.[95] As Kurien observed, this approach provides a way of "putting the instruments of rural development into the hands of the producers."[96] This farm-industry linkage approach has been successfully tested during the last 35 years. Even after 35 years, farmers' organisations like AMUL, Pravaranagar and many other sugar cooperatives are full of energy, working efficiently and expanding and diversifying their activities. These gave a sense of permanancy, continuity and concrete achievement. In contrast, nothing much was left in the field by early traditional rural development experiments such as Tagore-Elmhirst's Sriniketan, Brayne's Gurgaon, Mayer's Etawah, and Bowles' CDP.

The milk and sugar cooperatives are not without their critics. Sugar cooperatives have often been criticised for the misuse of funds by corrupt leaders, dominant-caste politics, inefficient operations due to interference of leaders into legitimate work of managers, and so on. About two years back Claude Alvares' feature article, 'The White Lie' in the *Illustrated Weekly* (October 30—November 5, 1983) describing the White Revolution 'as a blatant lie', challenged the very philosophy on which Operation Flood was based. Alvares' article, Kurien's reply[97] and newspaper debate on the issue[98] are worth studying to understand how different segments of population look at farmers' cooperative efforts as well as government's efforts to improve their lot.

The sugar and milk cooperatives provide a model, a new approach to technology oriented rural development. These emphasise the importance of an *Anchor* activity in development of integrated rural development organisation. The lesson is: wherever possible, depending upon the available local agricultural and other natural resources, bio-mass handling/processing industry/activity should be the central or anchor activity of organisations for integrated rural development. Around this anchor could be developed backward linkages (credit, inputs, extension, support services and procurement, etc.), forward linkages (marketing of produce and finished products and by-products), infrastructure (roads, electricity, irrigation etc.), social welfare facilities (housing, health, education, recreation), and supplementary economic activities. The command area of each such organisation would depend upon the capacity and nature of the central, anchor activity. The organisational structure of such integrated rural development cooperative enterprises would vary according to the nature of commodity and economic activities, and cannot be uniform, stereotyped as under CDP or existing IRD programme.[99] Potential for developing such anchor activity is very high in case of many commodities such as sugar cane, paddy, maize, cassava, oilseeds, coconut, cotton, jute, various plantation crops, medicinal plants/roots/herbs, fruits and vegetables, as well as domesticated and wild animals, and marine products.[100]

SUMMING UP

Early experiments were, at best, poor examples of rural reconstruction, considering their tall philosophical ideas, narrow and shallow base of thinking on material aspects of life, and poor and transient impact on the economy of rural people. These kept the society 'rural'. In these experiments there was not much that would build 'a technologically progressive economy' which rural India needed badly. This happened in spite of the close involvement of the people from the West. One would like to consider persons like Andrews, Elmhirst, Miss Green, Dorothy Straight, Dr. Hatch, Brayne, Mayer, etc., as 'representatives' of technologically and industrially advanced western societies. Yet, they introduced very little of 'industry' and technology of the West in their experiments. To be kind to them, one would say, perhaps, they were the misfits in their own societies, unable to stand the pressure of industrial culture then sweeping their societies, and found a safety valve in the experiments supporting agrarian economy and society with a little touch of welfare services. In contrast, Bowles was most candid about his country's objectives. His CDP was designed with the sole objective of 'managing the rural poor' in such a way that they would not become communist. This strategy of 'managing the poor' came most handy to Indian planners, who used it most efficiently (at low cost) and effectively (India remained a democracy) to keep the poor's hopes and aspirations alive and thus buy time to build strong industrial infrastructure. It is to the credit of Indian politicians and planners that they simultaneously encouraged agro-industrial cooperatives which seems to have taken a strong root during the last 35 years and are helping in the transition of an agrarian economy and society into an industrial economy and society.

NOTES

1. As could be seen from Plan Outlays (Appendix I), there was increasing outlay in power, industry, and mining sectors. Except in the First Plan, around 24 per cent of the total outlay was allocated for agriculture and allied sectors including Cooperation and Community Development, Irrigation, and Village and Small Scale Industry. About 15-16 per cent was allocated to social services. Thus, 50-60 per cent of the Plan Outlay was for building an industrial base.
2. In the U.K., historically, the need for special efforts for development of rural areas was not felt due to the continuous migration of rural people to industrial centres in the U.K. and to British overseas colonies and New World countries (North and South America, Australia, and New Zealand). The heavy migration led to the depopulation of rural areas and reduced pressure on land. Even now, as reported by Baviskar and others, "The U.K. government has no formal Rural Policy just as it has no Urban Policy. Its organisation reflects a strong bias in favour of the functional, rather than territorial principle." As ragards on-going rural development activi-

ties they observed a lack of clarity about objectives of rural development, only lip-service being paid to the notion of integrated rural development, and local authorities being weak, especially when it came to playing development role. Historically, in many parts of the U.K., local authorities have never been endowed with a central development function and have primarily fulfilled regulatory and maintenance functions. Local governments and local authorities were firmly under the thumb of the central government and did not generally enjoy active popular grassroots support. They may do only what central government allows them to do, or requires them to do; they have very little discretion to concert development on their own terms, according to their needs. The weakness of local authorities as development media has been used to justify special, central-state sponsored development agencies on regional scale. These have been more technocratic than democratic. Many of them were mere grant-giving bodies, and so on.

3. After the 1914 War, while about £ 1,000 million of German assets were appropriated by the victorious powers, more than £ 1,500 million went a few years later to Germany given principally by the United States of America and Great Britain. Most of this had to be written off later.

4. It may be noted here that even a hundred years back, many technologies which could contribute to agricultural development, and improvement in quality of living by removing drudgery or dirty part of work were already developed and in use in industrialised countries of the West. Windmills for irrigation, electricity generation sets and electrically operated pumpsets, steam engines etc., were already in use in those countries. By the turn of the present century, new technologies for better sanitation (septic tanks and flush-latrines) were introduced. Some of these technologies were also in use in India.

5. It is worth mentioning here that in Western Societies even in the 18th and 19th centuries, science and technology orientation was of a high order, and this orientation played an important role in transformation of these societies. Even in India since the second half of the 19th century, scientific information about the numerous economic products from raw materials produced in rural areas was available. Curiosity about and interest in the use of such information among the early experimenters is a subject worth exploring.

6. There are other well-known realities such as skewed distribution of land ownership, illiteracy, unemployment and under-employment, poor health, casteism, over population, etc. Some of these are symptoms of deep-rooted maladies Land redistribution, already in process, by itself cannot change the subsistence nature of agriculture. It provides temporary relief to some. It cannot improve the lot of the landless, nor the life of tribals and shepherds and fishermen and artisans. Some of these, like casteism, which is bad in itself, cannot be made responsible for persistent poverty.

7. Mid-decades of the 19th century are generally known as the age of Indian Renaissance. Some of the great social and religious reformers and educationists of that period were Raja Ram Mohan Roy, Isvar Chandra Vidyasagar, Maharsi Debendranath Tagore, Keshab Chandra Sen and Ramakrishna Paramahansa. There were many literary stalwarts like Isvar Gupta, Michael Madhusudan Dutta, Bankim Chatterjee, who spread the fire of patriotism and nationalism. There were also a few industrial entrepreneurs in the field of textile and jute industry, and a few isolated cases of scientists and engineers. But compared to social reformers and educationists their number and influence were negligible.
8. It is worth noting that the three well-known early experiments, Sriniketan, Martandum and Gurgaon, were more or less simultaneously initiated during 1920-21, i.e., two to three years after the Russian Revolution. All received support from the British, and praise in the West. A number of administrative/political reforms such as local government were also introduced during that period. It is for the students of history to find out whether simultaneous initiation of these experiments and other reforms was a mere coincidence or a strategy of the British to give direction to political movement in India.
9. The Community Development Programme was introduced in many developing countries, so also the RD and IRD programmes afterwards. Once again it is for the student of history to find out whether it was a coincidence or a part of a strategy of the West to guide the development processes in a particular direction in these countries.
10. The influence of Vedic literature on Tagore was well-known. For comments on this see Reference 8.
11. India has been exposed to science, technology and value systems of the West for more than 150 years. However, there is not yet any convincing and confirmed evidence that due to this exposure, there has been systematic, deep erosions in the Indian culture and value systems, or that basic teachings from *Upanishads* are altogether forgotten. On the contrary, it seems that with more and more exposure, there is an increasing awareness about traditional culture, philosophy and value system, and desire to maintain them, and these continue to mould the life of people.
12. "The aim of the YMCA is to develop high standards of Christian character through group activity and citizenship training. It is a lay movement, nonsectarian and nonpolitical. Christian but without doctrinal views."

References

[1]Government of India, Planning Commission, *Third Five Year Plan*, p. 4.

[2]Government of India, Planning Commission, *Fourth Five Year Plan: 1969-74*, p. 2.

[3]*Ibid.*, p. 2.

[4]Baviskar, B.S., A.U. Patel and J.B Wight 1983. *Development Institutions and Approaches in the Three Rural Areas of the United Kingdom* (The report of the 1982 Arkleton Trust Study Tour of Mid-Wales, the Western Isles and the Grampion Region of Scotland) The Arkleton Trust, Scotland, U.K., pp. 31, 34-35, 60-61, 72-73, 79-84.

[5]Churchill, Winston S. 1950. *The Second World War*, Vol. 1: The Gathering Storm, Cassell and Co., London, pp. 8-9.

[6]George, Watt, *A Dictionary of Economic Products of India*, (Six Volumes prepared during 1882-1896, Publication starting from 1889), Second Reprint 1972, Periodical Experts, 42D, Vivek Vihar Shahdara, Delhi.

[7]Tagore, Rabindranath. 1921, Indian Edition 1960. *Glimpses of Bengal*: Selected from the Letters of Rabindranath Tagore-1885 to 1895, MacMillan and Co., pp. 19, 28-29, 34-36; 96-99, 102-108, and 142-144.

[8]Nehru, Jawaharlal. 1946. *The Discovery of India*, The Signet Press, Calcutta, pp. 57, 61, 294.

[9]*Ibid*, p. 294.

[10]Mukerji, D.P. 1956. *Diversities*: *Essays in Economics, Sociology and Other Social Problems*, People's Publishing House, pp. 34-35.

[11]Elmhirst, Leonard. 1963, 1973. "Rabindranath Tagore and Sriniketan", in GOI, *Evolution of Community Development Programme in India*, p. 1.

[12]Sarkar, S.C. 1961. *Tagore's Educational Philosophy and Experiment*, Vishva-Bharati, Santiniketan, p. 176.

[13]*Ibid.*, p.133.

[14]*Ibid.*, pp. 148-153.

[15]Mukerji, *op. cit.*, p. 36.

[16]As reported by Sarkar, "A Note on Siksha-Satra: The Influence of Elmhirst" in his book, *Tagore's Educational Philosophy and Experiment*, *op. cit.*, p. 183.

[17]This description of Sriniketan Experiment is based on Leonard Elmhirst's paper *op. cit.*, pp. 1-14.

[18]Elmhirst, *op. cit.*, p. 7.

[19]*Ibid.*, p. 9.

[20]Sarkar, *op. cit.*, p. 180.

[21]Elmhirst, *op. cit.*, p. 10.

[22]Sarkar, *op. cit.*, p. 186.

[23]*Ibid.*, p 186-191.

[24]Dasgupta, Sugata 1976. "Tagore's Experiment in Rural Reconstruction: A Poet and a Plan" *In History of Rural Development in Modern India*. Mittal and Khan (ed.), Vol. IV, Gandhian Institute of Studies, Varanasi, 1976, p. 215.

[25]*Ibid.*, p. 6.

[26]Elmhirst, *op. cit.*, pp. 11-12.
[27]*Ibid.*, p. 13.
[28]Dasgupta, *op. cit.*, p. 224.
[29]Sarkar, *op. cit.*, p. 198.
[30]*Encyclopaedia Britannica*, 1970 Edition, Vol. 18, p. 63.
[31]The description here is based on Spencer Hatch's article "Early Times at Martandam Project," in GOI, *Evolution of Community Development Programme in India*, (1st edition 1963), revised edition 1973, pp. 15-26.
[32]*Encyclopaedia Britannica*, Vol. 23, p. 910.
[33]Based on the article of S.R. Verma. 1973. "The Gurgaon Experiment", in GOI, *Evolution of Community Development Programme in India*, pp. 27-35.
[34]As quoted by Verma, *op. cit.*, p. 27.
[35]*Ibid.*, p. 34.
[36]Based on the following articles: J.C. Kavoori. 1976. "Baroda Experiment," *In History of Rural Development in Modern India*, Mittal and Khan (eds.) Vol. IV, Gandhian Institute of Studies, Varanasi, pp. 190-202; I.P. Desai and Banwarilal Chawdhary, 1977. *History of Rural Development in India*, Vol. II, Impex India, Delhi, pp. 7-13; V.T. Krishnamachari, 1973. "Community Development in Baroda State", in GOI, *Evolution of Community Development Programme in India*, pp. 36-44.
[37]Kavoori, *op. cit.*, p. 192.
[38]Desai, *op. cit.*, pp. 7-8.
[39]Krishnamachari, *op. cit.*, pp. 39-40.
[40]*Ibid.*, pp. 43-44.
[41]As quoted by Kavoori, *op. cit.*, p. 197.
[42]Baviskar, Patel and Wight, *op. cit.*, p. 80.
[43]Krishnamachari, *op. cit.*, p. 41.
[44]*Ibid.*, p. 43.
[45]Kavoori, *op. cit.*, p. 202.
[46]*Ibid.*, p. 202.
[47]Krishnamachari, *op. cit.*, p. 37.
[48]*Harijan*, 19th June 1937.
[49]Gandhi, M.K., *Rebuilding Our Villages* (edited by Bharatan Kumarappa), Navajivan Publishing House, Ahmedabad, 1956, pp. 5-6.
[50]As quoted by, C.F. Andrews, *Mahatma Gandhi's Ideas Including Selections From His Writings*, George Allen & Unwin Ltd., London (First Published 1929) Third Impression 1949, pp. 259-260.
[51]Gandhi, *Rebuilding Our Villages*, *ibid.*, pp. 102-110.
[52]Andrews, *op. cit.*, p. 149.
[53]Andrews, *op. cit.*, pp. 335-336.
[54]Mayer, A. and Associates, *Pilot Project India*, Berkeley: University of California Press, 1958, pp. 40-41.
[55]———, *Interim Report on Pilot Development Project, Etawah and Gorakhpur*, Berkeley: University of California Press, 1951, p. 23.

[56]Kavoori, J.C. and B.N. Singh, *History of Rural Development in Modern India*, Vol. I, New Delhi: Impex India, 1967, pp. 125-128.

[57] *Ibid.*, p. 112.

[58]*Ibid.*, p. 408.

[59]Government of India, Ministry of Agriculture, "The Nilokheri Experiment" in *Evolution of Community Development Programme in India*, 1973, p. 82.

[60]*Ibid.*, p. 84.

[61]*Ibid.*, p. 85.

[62]*Ibid.*, p. 85.

[63]*Ibid.*, p. 87.

[64]*Ibid.*, pp. 87-88.

[65]*Ibid.*, p. 87.

[66]*Ibid.*, p. 89.

[67]*Ibid.*, p. 89.

[68]Dey, S.K., *Power to the People? (A Chronicle of India 1947-67)*, Orient Longmans, Bombay, 1969, p. 11.

[69]———, "Introduction", in Ensminger, Douglas, *Rural India in Transition*, All India Panchayat Parishad, 1972, p. 2.

[70]*Ibid.*, pp. 2-3,

[71]Ensminger, D., *Evolution of Community Development Programme in India*, New Delhi: Ministry of Community Development, 1973, p. 96.

[72]Ensminger, D., *Rural India in Transition*, New Delhi: All India Panchayat Parishad, 1972, p. 3.

[73]*Ibid.*, p. 3.

[74]*Ibid.*, pp. 3-4.

[75]*Ibid.*, p. 4.

[76]*Ibid.*, p. 105.

[77]*Ibid.*, p. 105.

[78]*Ibid.*, p. 107.

[79]Bowles, Chester, *Ambassador's Report*, Collins, London, 1954, pp. 132-148.

[80]*Ibid.*, p. 132.

[81]*Ibid.*, p. 133.

[82]*Ibid.*, p. 133.

[83]*Ibid.*, pp. 133-34.

[84]*Ibid.*, p. 135.

[85]For a sub-system analysis of this design *see* Gaikwad, V.R. and Parmar, D.S., *Rural Development Administration under Democratic Decentralisation*, Wiley Eastern Ltd., New Delhi, 1980, pp. 55-57.

[86]*See* Gaikwad, V.R., *Serving Small Farmers, A Study of Farmers' Service Cooperative Society*, Bidadi, CMA, IIMA, 1982.

[87]For example, the biography in Marathi language of Tatya Saheb Kore, who established the Warnanagar Co-operative Sugar Factory in Kolhapur district: *see* Tatya Saheb Kore, *Me: EK Karyakarta*, Gajanan Press, Miraj, 1974; For a Case Study (in English) based on

this biography, *see* V.R. Gaikwad, "Saranga Cooperative Sugar Factory", Case Unit, IIMA, 1982.

[88]National Bank of Agriculture and Rural Development, *Important Items of Data: Credit and Non-Credit Co-operative Societies: 1983-84*, NABARD, Bombay, 1985, p. 74.

[89]National Bank of Agriculture and Rural Development, *Statistical Statements Relating to the Co-operative Movement in India 1979-80, Part-II, Non-Credit Societies*, NABARD, Bombay, 1983, p. 17.

[90]For elaboration of the 'anchor' concept *see* author's paper "Organisational Designs for Technology Oriented Integrated Rural Development", Working Paper No. 565, June 1985, Indian Institute of Management, Ahmedabad.

[91]As reported in V. Kurien, *A Black Lie*, NDDB, Anand, 1984, p. 11.

[92]*Ibid.*, p. 2.

[93]*Ibid.*, p. 4.

[94]For details of NDDB operations *see* NDDB, *Annual Report*: 1984-85.

[95]For example, C.G. Ranade, D.P. Mathur, B. Rangarajan and V.K. Gupta, *Performance of Integrated Milk Co-operatives* (A Study of Selected Co-operative Dairies in Gujarat and Maharashtra), Centre for Management in Agriculture Monograph Series No. 111, IIM, Ahmedabad, 1984; Case studies by D.K. Desai, V.K. Gupta and D.P. Mathur, "Dudhsagar Dairy"; C.G. Ranade, "Dhudhsagar Dairy Revisited", 1982, Case Unit, IIM, Ahmedabad.

[96]V. Kurien, "Putting the instrument of rural development into the hands of the producers", Ramon Magsaysay Award Foundation Workshop, Los Banos, Feb. 7-9, 1977. (Copies available with NDDB, Anand): V. Kurien, "Public Service by Private Persons", Leslie Sawhny Programme of Training for Democracy, No. 22.

[97]V. Kurien, *A Black Lie*, NDDB, Anand, 1984.

[98]For example, *see Business India*, February 13-26, 1984, pp. 35-53.

[99]V.R. Gaikwad, "Some Considerations for Appropriate Organizational Designs for Integrated Cooperatives", Paper prepared for Policy Level Workshop on Appropriate Management Systems for Agricultural Cooperatives (AMSAC), jointly sponsored by FAO of UN, NCDC and IIMA, at IIMA August 28-30, 1985.

[100]See V.R. Gaikwad, "Application of Science and Technology for Integrated Agriculture and Rural Development", Case Unit, Indian Institute of Management, Ahmedabad, 1985.

APPENDIX 1

Percentage Distribution of Plan Outlays by Heads of Development: Centre, States and Union Territories

Head of Development	I Plan (1951-56) Actuals	II Plan (1956-61) Actuals	III Plan (1961-66) Actuals	Annual Plans (1966-69) Actuals	IV Plan (1969-74) Actuals	V Plan (1974-79) Actuals	1979/80 Actuals	VI Plan (1980-85) Outlays
1 Agriculture & Allied Sectors	14.8	11.8	12.7	16.7	14.7	12.3	16.4	13.6
2 Irrigation & Flood Control	22.1	9.2	7.8	7.1	8.6	9.8	10.6	9.7
3 Power	7.6	9.7	14.6	18.3	18.6	18.8	18.4	19.8
4 Village & Small Industries	2.1	4.0	2 8	1.9	1.5	1.5	2.1	1.8
5 Industry & Minerals	2.8	20.1	20.1	22.8	18.2	22.8	19.6	20.9
6 Transport & Communications	26.4	27.0	24.6	18.5	19.5	17.4	16.8	15.9
7 Social Services & Miscellaneous	24.2	18.2	17.4	14.7	18.9	17.4	16.1	18.3
7.1 Education			6.9	4.6	4.9	4.4	2.2	2.6
7.2 Scientific Research			0.8	0.7	0.8		0.7	0.9
7.3 Health			2.6	2.1	2.1	1.9	1.8	1.9

7.4 Family Planning			0.3	1.1	1.8	1.3	1.0	1.0
7.5 Other Programmes			6.8	6.2	9.3	9.8	10.4	11.9
Total	100	100	100	100	100	100	100	100
Total Absolute Amount, Rs. Crores	1,960	4,672	8,577	6,625	15,779	39,426	12,177	97,500
Average Per Year, Rs. Crores	392	934	1,715	2,208	3,156	7,885	12,177	19,500

Source: For I & II Plan—*Basic Statistics Relating to the Indian Economy*, Commerce Research Bureau, Bombay, 1973.
For the rest—*Economy Survey, 1981/82*, Government of India, 1982.

[illegible]		[illegible]	[illegible]	[illegible]	[illegible]	[illegible]	[illegible]	[illegible]	[illegible]	[illegible]
[illegible]		[illegible]	[illegible]	[illegible]	[illegible]	[illegible]	[illegible]	[illegible]	[illegible]	[illegible]
Total	100	100	100	[illegible]	[illegible]	[illegible]	[illegible]	[illegible]	[illegible]	[illegible]
Total Absolute Amount, Rs. Crores	[illegible]	[illegible]	[illegible]	[illegible]	[illegible]	[illegible]	[illegible]	[illegible]	[illegible]	[illegible]
Average Per [illegible] Rs. Crores	[illegible]	[illegible]	[illegible]	[illegible]	[illegible]	[illegible]	[illegible]	[illegible]	[illegible]	[illegible]

Source: [illegible] Statistics Relating to the Indian Economy, [illegible] Research Bureau, [illegible]
For [illegible] Series, 1951-52, Government of India, [illegible]

Integrated Tribal Development Programme: An Evaluation of ITDP in Birbhum District, West Bengal

Dipankar Gupta

The paper, initiated by a field study, enquires into the Integrated Tribal Development Programme (ITDP) in practice in Birbhum district of West Bengal. There were three reasons why Birbhum was chosen. Firstly, West Bengal was ruled by the Left-Front Government. It was, therefore, assumed that there would be a greater inclination on the part of the government and the people to make the programme successful. Secondly, Santal, which is supposed to be the most advanced tribe, inhabits Birbhum to the near exclusion of all other tribes. The ITDP in Birbhum can, therefore, be expected to be at its best. Finally, since this region is contiguous to the Santal Paragana and very nearly so to the Chota Nagpur belt which is the heartland of the tribals, one could also estimate links of the tribes in Birbhum with the contiguous areas of Bihar.

Extensive visits to as many areas as possible were conducted since the express purpose of the study was to evaluate the ITDP. Four blocks were visited: Bolpur and Illambazar in Eastern Birbhum, and Rampurhat and Rajnagar in Western Birbhum. In addition, some time was spent with the ITDP officials in Suri, which is the headquarters of Birbhum district.

Origin and Scope

The ITDP was formally launched in 1974 with the Fifth Five Year Plan (1974-79). But its seeds were sown several years ago. The Renuka Ray Report of 1959 pointedly referred to the need for an integrated approach to tribal development.[1] This was followed by the setting up of the Scheduled Areas and Scheduled Tribes Commission in 1960 under the chairmanship of U.N. Dhebar. The Dhebar Commission looked into a large number of factors, met numerous delegations, and interviewed several people in the course of its existence.[2] It stressed an integrated approach for it believed that "the problem of economic development for the bulk of the tribals cannot be solved unless the resources of land, forests, cattle wealth, cottage and village industries are all mobilised in an integrated way."[3] But apart from mentioning desirable objectives in a somewhat general way, nothing was clearly spelt out. The S.C. Dube Committee (1972), which was set up to advise on tribal development in the Fifth Plan, was asked to formulate a more concrete strategy. By this time, the belief was that time-bound integrated area development programmes could no longer be postponed because it was absolutely urgent, as the Planning Commission document of the Fifth Plan put it, to improve the quality of life of the tribals.[4] The ITDP was thus concretised with the Fifth Five Year Plan, and it was enjoined that the sub-plans be drawn up by the states which would detail the ITDP at the state level.

The programme was called an integrated programme for two reasons: (1) in terms of its external and ostensible performance schedule, management, and allocation of resources; and (2) in terms of its orientation towards the concept of planning itself. On the first count, the ITDP was considered integrated because various sectoral resources were to be integrated under its aegis so that a balanced thrust could be provided in the developmental process. It was believed that the lack of coordination between the different sectors such as industry, agriculture, power and energy, health, and education were functioning in a disjointed manner; there was no general conception of what was really required for the tribals in each region. Nor was care taken to ascertain whether the benefits were reaching the tribals.[5]

The second, a less ostensible reason for calling the ITDP an integrated programme arises out of a concern with the first. If one is to know what the tribals need—the 'felt need'—then it is necessary to plan from the grassroots level. But stating this by itself was not enough as the tribals and the poor in general were as yet unable to participate wholly and effectively in rural decision-making bodies. Hence the notion of generating popular participation arises. The importance of popular participation should be stressed because it does form an important component of the planning methodology envisaged under the tribal sub-plan from the Fifth Plan onwards. It should perhaps also be mentioned here that the role of cooperation was also underlined in the Fifth Plan, especially with regard to tribals. The large sized multi-purpose cooperative societies (LAMPS) were to play an important role in coordinating institutional finance, credit, and marketing facilities for tribals.

All those blocks or tehsils where more than 50 per cent of the population comprised tribals were to be included in the tribal sub-plan for the implementation of ITDPs.[6] This, however, excluded tribal-majority States like Nagaland, Meghalaya, Arunachal Pradesh, Mizoram, and the Union Territories like Dadra and Nagar Haveli and Lakshadweep since the development plans for them would be only for the tribal population living there. It was hoped that with the introduction of ITDP more resources would flow into tribal areas for tribal development.

The tribal sub-plan was to be financed by resources gathered from state plan resources, investment by central ministries, the Ministry of Home Affairs under the rubric of "special central assistance", and financial institutions.[7] Financial resources were to be made available on the basis of the total population of the sub-plan area, the geographical area, the comparative level of development, and the state of social services.

The ITDP had a wide scope; it had to work towards eliminating exploitation, promoting productivity, and providing educational facilities.

In the Fifth Plan period the ITDP was initially conceived of and implemented as an area development programme. But it was later realised by the government that under this dispensation it was not easy to identify concrete benefits to the tribals, and it was quite likely that the non-tribals gained more out of the ITDP. In the Sixth Plan, therefore, the tribal sub-plan, which guides and positions the ITDP, took a special note of this and converted the ITDP into a target group approach where individual families were to benefit concretely from the programmes. These families would be selected on the basis of their absolute economic status, the poorest being given the first preference.

The family-based or the household-based approach would not only prevent resources meant for the development of the tribals from being siphoned-off by the relatively well-endowed, but it would also demand a greater allocation of divisible funds than of indivisible ones. The emphasis so far was on indivisible funds. Greater emphasis was thus placed on beneficiary oriented schemes rather than on capital intensive sectoral programmes in the Sixth Plan which would restore the balance. The role of education and popular participation which was stated somewhat *sotto voce* earlier was clearly emphasised in the Sixth Plan.

Planning Methodology and Process

Since the ITDP aspires to meet the specific needs of the tribals on the basis of a comprehensive development of the tribal family, planning has to be initiated from the lowest unit. Each constituent block of an ITDP should come out with its formulation for a five year period. From the lowest level onwards, the formulators are enjoined to take into account the natural resources of the ITDP area and the genius and the avocations of its inhabitants in formulating their proposals. It is necessary to take cognizance of this if the tribals are to consolidate and sustain the development programmes set up with the help of the ITDP. It also underscores the importance the planners attach to popular participation as a key to the success of the ITDP. The planners should also recommend an appropriate administrative structure for recruitment in the region. This is more applicable to the higher levels—levels which sanction posts and provide employment in the administrative structure.[8]

The Block Plans which are thus formulated are then coordinated at the ITDP level. These ITDP plans are then aggregated, coordinated, and meshed at the state level into a Tribal Sub-

Plan of the State where resources are matched with the need-based proposals which have come from the lower levels. The state authorities then communicate to the project authorities a detailed outlay for the entire five year period as well as for each individual year.

It was not the intention of the government to have heavily staffed ITDP offices. The ITDP was, after all, going to be the agency through which the various sectors were to be integrated. The ITDP in each district is headed by a Class I Project Officer who would coordinate activities with the District Level Technical Officers who are, in turn, under the supervision of the District Collector who is the Chairman of the ITDP level projects. The Project Officer would be vested with some power and authority over the sub-formations of the District Level Technical Officers. The Project Officer is also a member of the District Welfare Board. Different states have worked out different structures by which "the physical and administrative gulf" can be bridged.[9] The involvement of popular representatives like the members of legislative assembly, members of parliament, and panchayat samiti chairmen are also formalised at the District Welfare Committee level, or at the ITDP Committee level, or both.

The problem, however arises in the selection of personnel; they must have empathy and work with dedication in the ITDP. The Maheshwari Prasad Committee (1979) recommended that adequate monetary and non-monetary incentives should be given to those who are posted in tribal areas. The Seventh Finance Commission also made an award in favour of various states to enable them to remunerate suitably those who work in tribal areas. For monitoring the ITDP at the grassroots level, a team comprising the village level workers and foresters, among others, was to be set up. But it has already been acknowledged by the Government of India that such monitoring teams have not yet come about.[10]

This brief sketch of the ITDP ought to be sufficient to provide a general understanding of the ITDP as well as a suitable backdrop against which the ITDP approach can be compared with other approaches to development. It would also help to comment on issues like popular participation or the desirability of *structural change* versus *target-oriented developmental pro-*

grammes. It should also supply some basis to discuss the issue of integrating the tribals in the mainstream.

Integration versus Seclusion

Anthropologists like Verrier Elwin and anthropologist-administrators like W.G. Archer had tried to demonstrate the dangers the tribals are exposed to as a result of the spread of communication, commerce, and modern economic structures to areas which were traditionally tribal strongholds. But the Government of India is not convinced that the tribals should be kept outside the pale of developmental activities of a modernising nation-state, though spreading development efforts and communication networks sometimes provides more opportunities to exploiters from outside the tribal areas.[11] The efforts to spread and develop communication networks in tribal regions should not be held back, but measures, including legal measures, should be instituted to protect the tribals from exploitation of the worst kind—from usurpers of tribal lands, traders, merchants, and contractors.[12] To those familiar with the literature on the subject, it is quite clear that all these 'professions' can be combined into one. They also know how poverty and simplicity have deprived the tribals from economic pursuits they know best. The Sixth Five Year Plan, therefore, stresses that even the transfer of techniques initiated by the ITDPs should be such that it does not destroy the tribal economic base, but strengthens it along the lines the tribals are particularly adept at, such as agriculture, horticulture, and animal husbandry.[13]

Though there is an element of brinkmanship in what the Government of India proposes to do in exposing the tribals and yet protecting them, the alternative approach of secluding them altogether is perhaps a trifle romantic and unreal. After all, tribal regions are now accessible, and if the technology exists, and if the pickings from tribal areas can be lucrative, it is unreal to assume that by governmental fiat the logic of technical-cum-economic structure can be kept under the wraps in tribal regions. Even if the government ordains that tribal areas be secluded, it is not necessary that they may in fact remain so. There are problems in the seclusion approach at the practical level too. To make sure that the tribals are not exploited, or even to ensure that there are no encroachers on tribal lands, it is necessary to have some sort of governmental supervision, control and communication. This makes it almost impossible to make tribal areas "out of bounds".

Further, the government cannot ignore the vital resources which are found in most tribal areas. Forest and mineral resources abound in most tribal regions, and since these are scarce resources the government ought to utilise them. This leads to "exploitation" by government too, if we consider the amount of tribal lands appropriated by the government for industrial purposes. Further, for the development, running and maintenance of these enterprises, communication and traffic with the non-tribal population cannot be avoided.

If one were to operate within the established parameters then brinkmanship alone can attenuate the exploitation of tribals and help them to salvage some of what they have already lost due to extortionate manipulations of contractors, usurers, and others. Finally, it is impossible to segregate an area and keep it in historical limbo, especially when the contiguous landmass is in the grips of the historical process. This is the assumption with which the ITDP functions.

Features of the Integrated Approach to Development

There are three known approaches to development which are conceived and mooted by governments. In the first approach, technical and managerial innovations are introduced to that stratum which is considered to be the most receptive. Thereafter, the government adopts a kind of night-watchman attitude. This approach should be called *diffusionist approach* in contrast to *trickling down* or *coffee percolator approach*. Diffusion implies regeneration even at the highly receptive levels, and the effects of diffusion are not restricted to the contents of the original input. Rather, it is hoped that the effects will become increasingly diverse.

The second approach may be called the *grants-in-aid approach*. Aid is given to those who seem to need it the most, sometimes accompanied with the hope that this push will set off the deprived sections onto a path of independent and sustained development. But very often even the probability that this will take place in the short run is not entertained, and the aid is given only to allow the needy to tide things over, as a short-term measure. No permanent resource base is sought to be created under programmes of this sort.

The third approach is the *integrated approach*. This approach views the community, or the target group holistically, and various material and non-material factors responsible for poverty and backwardness are taken into account so that developmental thrusts can be integrated and they may become less traumatic, more permanent in terms of their effects, and less likely to become uneven and perverted over time.[14]

The integrated approach has two important features. The first is that it is not concerned only with those factors which are ostensibly economic. It is the integration of economic with non-economic factors that is sought to be consolidated.[15] The second feature is that it encourages popular participation. The beneficiaries of the programme are not merely passive recipients; they become actively engaged in the programme, tackling the governmental machinery and dealing with the official personnel when needed.

Popular Participation

Without being explicit, the proponents of the integrated approach are actually commenting on the power structure and on the sociology of power when they insist on popular participation in developmental programmes. They are alert to the fact that the poor and deprived sections in most societies have no effective means of asserting their rights or of even communicating their problems. The information and communication channels that exist are not accessible to them. On matters unambiguously political, the poor lack confidence to assert themselves because of the elite-officialdom tie-up and have, as a result, become cynical, or at best, indifferent towards developmental programmes. Therefore, unless confidence is rekindled all developmental efforts would prove fruitless. But first, cynicism and indifference have to be removed. This cannot be done by exhibiting goodwill alone towards the poor; one has to place one's ear to the ground. One has to learn from them of their travails, hopes and disappointments, as well as of their thoughts on what they consider necessary and appropriate in their environs.

To look at it from another angle, where the hiatus between the elites and the poor is vast then a programme, however well-intentioned, runs the risk of not meeting the 'felt needs' of the people. This will prevent not only popular participation but also popular cooperation. The group one wants to reach out is unmoved and, quite naturally, popular participation is not forthcoming. The tendency has been to explain this indifference by blaming the 'victim'. He is deemed to be the prey of superstition, ignorance, and tradition; a bearer of the 'culture of poverty'.

But such explanations are wearing thin, at least among those who advocate the integrated approach. Ignorance, superstition, culture, etc., are good explanatory devices only because nobody bothers to put his ear to the ground and tap the well of popular initiative.[16]

Recognising this should not result in confusing populism with actively aiding the cause of popular participation. The distinction between the felt need and the real need is still real for the integrated approach to planning and development. Because development initiators are able to view the social scope on a larger and supra-local scale, there arises a two-way learning process: the people are educated by the agent, and the agent is educated by the people.

An issue on which a lively debate is going on is the issue of commitment versus inducement to sustain the bond between initiators or officials of the development project and the people. While nothing could be better than finding self-motivated people to work as development agents, it is true that not many committed people are forthcoming. Therefore, the alternative seems to be to induce people to work in these projects and offer them attractive terms.[17] This, however, does not guarantee that the better people will take up such offers. It is quite likely that the mediocre and the uncommitted will continue to staff these positions but only at a greater cost. This issue still bedevils the integrated approach to development and is especially evident in schemes which demand round-the-year attendance at the project site.

The ITDP as an Integrated Approach

ITDPs are found all over India, and the most urgent tasks

and targets of an ITDP differ from state to state as indeed from block to block and division to division. But even so, certain uniform features underpin the ITDPs regardless of where they are situated.

It is a known fact that the tribals are a particularly disadvantaged community because their original way of life was quickly disintegrated in not-too-distant past. In large parts of India, tribals have been absorbed in and dominated by the economy of non-tribal India. Many anthropologists have recorded that the majority of tribals are now peasants.[20] As a matter of fact, at present there are no tribal economies which are anywhere near viable. This is further compounded by the fact that the tribals have not yet lost their cultural heritage. If in the past their symbolic, ritual and religious behaviour was integrated with their mode of livelihood, the very fact that the latter has undergone a remarkable transformation would put the former under tension. So the integrated approach to tribal development has to take this into account as well.

Secondly, there were, till the first British inroads were made into the tribal region, different forms of tribal economy and land usage from which the tribals found near-total sustenance (though they were never prosperous). Some elements of that labour process were kept alive, even though the total economy as such was disrupted. The tribals were particularly adept at living off forest flora and fauna. No special efforts were made to take care of the fauna, but measures were taken from time to time to allow a certain leeway to the tribals in terms of forest produce such as fruits, leaves, seeds, and grass. Today this finds expression in measures to protect tribal lands and prevent it from going into the hands of non-tribals. Over time, in spite of governmental regulations, much of tribal land has been taken over by non-tribals, and very little remains of what used to be their traditional *khuntkhatti* land (lineage-held land), and what remains is sought to be made inalienable. In addition, even plots of land held by tribals individually cannot be sold to non-tribals without being cleared by the government. This measure was instituted so that the tribals are not cheated by non-tribals and parted from their land.

Thus, there is justification for a separate development programme for tribals which should not be subsumed under a general programme for the poor. Even so, the ITDP shares many features which are commonly associated with other rural development programmes for the poor. The ITDPs can be grouped under the following rubrics: programmes designed for economic protection; programmes designed for economic uplift; programmes designed to involve tribals in the decision-making process and to promote popular participation; and programmes to further social service facilities to tribals in order to render both humanitarian service to them which was hitherto unavailable and to enable them to overcome the handicaps they face in terms of skills required to promote themselves economically in the contemporary world.

Programme for Economic Protection

Any non-tribal (or encroacher) on tribal lands has ceased to be recognised since 1977.[21] Those who have been on tribal lands prior to 1977 are screened and in no case are *pattas* given to them which exceed one acre. The government provides free permits to tribals to collect (free of charge) brush wood, leaves, flowers, and seeds of *mahua*, *peasal*, etc. Suitable price support is provided by the government for minor forest produce. The government also restores all those tribal lands which have been illegally acquired. Simultaneously, attempts are made to protect the tribals from contractors, traders, and money lenders.

Programme for Economic Promotion

These programmes have a lot in common with the kind of programmes that have been planned for the rural poor; the special feature in tribal areas are the LAMPS, set up to initiate tribal employment schemes and to increase the number of mandays for which tribals may be gainfully employed. The LAMPS are also supposed to aid the tribals in securing loans and credit in order to promote agriculture, sericulture, animal husbandry, poultry, piggery, etc. The LAMPS are meant to provide such facilities for the tribals that the possibility of extortion by contractors and users is decreased. They also provide easy access to the various state institutions which can give the much-needed succour for economic development.

Tribals are also to be encouraged in all downstream activities for processing forest produce. In addition, in those tribal areas which are rich with mineral deposits the scope for tribal employment is sought to be increased. But by far the greatest portion of resources and energy is directed towards improving agricultural prospects of the tribals. Attention is paid to irrigation, soil conservation, bunding and flood control measures. The tribals are also provided with improved seeds and fertilisers.

Since the tribals are keen on animal husbandry, they are encouraged to keep goats, cows, sheep, and poultry, and all necessary services for their procurement and up-keep are provided.

Decision Making and Participation

The government tries to promote tribal development by actively seeking their participation. To this end, the ITDP officials have been instructed to learn the tribal language of the group they are involved with. At the ITDP level and the block level, the traditional tribal panchayats are also represented. Statutory panchayats are being associated with the ITDP to make the latter a people's movement.[22]

Social Service Measures

Hospitals and schools are provided to the tribals. It is imperative that hygienic conditions be improved in tribal areas and safe drinking water be provided. But if the communication system is to remain as poor as it is today, then there is the possibility that opportunities available outside the local area for the tribals to improve their condition will not be utilised. Tribals are also encouraged to take courses in sericulture, pisciculture, etc., from institutes specially set up.[23]

* * *

Though the ITDP has been in existence officially since 1974, it took an organised shape in Birbhum district only after 1980 when the ITDP office was set up in Suri. The tribal sub-plan for West Bengal includes 12 project districts consisting of 33

ITDP areas.[24] Each ITDP area is further sub-divided into *mouzas*. *Mouzas* are traditional revenue collection units and comprise, at times, several villages. Each district has one ITDP Project Officer, and under him in a direct chain of command is the Sub-Assistant Engineer, followed by inspectors, social workers, upper and lower division clerks, a peon, and a driver. In addition, there are ITDP personnel in each field office. A field office is staffed by one inspector and three social workers. The ITDP Project Officer, in turn, works under the supervision and control of the District Magistrate. There is also an ITDP committee where the District Magistrate is the chairman. The function of this committee is to formulate programmes and guide projects. The ITDP Project Officer also liaises on behalf of the ITDP with other agencies such as the District Welfare Committee of which he is an ex-officio member. He is a member of the governing body of District Rural Development Society (DRDS) too.[25]

An important feature of the ITDP in West Bengal is the attention given to the recording of sharecropper's rights. Even in the sub-plan for West Bengal a good deal of emphasis is given to land reforms and to the registration of sharecroppers under the Operation *Barga* scheme (*barga* is a sharecropper). Operation *Barga* not only guarantees security of tenure but also a larger share to the sharecropper in the crops grown. As a large number of sharecroppers are tribals, the ITDP is supposed to see to it that the tribals get what they are legally entitled to. But to ensure that an impoverished community gets what it is legally entitled to get requires more than making statutory provisions. As in the case of vested l nds released on account of land reforms, it is contended that on this issue too West Bengal has a more successful story to tell.[26] The ITDP officials are directed to be vigilant in this matter and to make sure that the tribals get the vested lands that have been released.

It is, however, not clear how the ITDP should involve itself in the land reform or in the Operation *Barga* programme. The ITDP officials, after all, have no authority over the agriculture or home departments, nor is the Project Officer given such powers. Nor do the ITDP officials have a say in the disbursement of crop loans or *barga* loans. Similarly, the ITDP officials cannot ensure that workers get paid their minimum wages whether they work for agriculture, industry, or construction. Only in those fields where the ITDP officials have complete control and supervision can they be held responsible. In this sense the section devoted to land reforms in the Tribal Sub-Plan of West Bengal for 1980-85 is a redundant accretion.

Birbhum District

In terms of its soil condition Birbhum district can be classified into two regions. The eastern region has alluvial tracts of land which are good for paddy crops. In this region *babla* (*acacia-arabica*), jack-fruit, and mango trees grow in abundance. The western region has infertile laterite soil. The area under forests in this region is somewhat greater. A large number of trees like *sal*, *piar*, *mahua*, *kend*, *palas*, and *neem* grow in this region.

The district is at the western extreme of West Bengal, and it borders the Santal Paragana in Bihar. Blocks in Birbhum district which are close to the hilly slopes of the Santal Paragana along the West Bengal-Bihar border are different in many ways from the areas around Bolpur or Labpur. The soil conditions are quite different in these two regions. In addition, there are obvious variations in the land-ownership pattern among the tribals. In the western region the infrastructure is somewhat poorer, and this feature is aggravated by the remoteness of the region in terms of communication, commercial and marketing facilities. The headquarters of Birbhum is Suri.

The tribe with which the study is concerned is the Santal tribe which inhabits Birbhum to the near exclusion of other tribes. The Santals are the most developed tribe because they had taken to peasant farming much earlier and more thoroughly than had other tribes of the region. They are not autochthonous to the district but are migrants from the Santal Paragana. They are not particularly devoted to artisanry or craftsmanship for their livelihood and are, with rare exceptions, dependent on agriculture. There are no big landowners who are Santals in Birbhum, but all other agrarian classes have Santals in sizeable numbers (Appendix I). Quite expectedly, the Santals work primarily as agricultural labourers, even though some of them own small parcels of land which are nowhere near sufficient.

The Santal people's culture and way of life have been detailed by scholars and administrators (for instance, W.G. Archer[27]).

EVALUATION OF ITDP IN BIRBHUM

Appendix II gives preliminary information of the ITDP blocks in Birbhum district.

Irrigation and Agriculture Programme

The ITDP spends the largest portion of its funds for the purposes of economic promotion. In the sector economic, expenditure on agriculture and irrigation has been the highest. According to the sub-plan of West Bengal tribal earners are encouraged to engage in agriculture, forest and livestock in the ratio of 10 : 2 : 1.[28] Appendix III gives an idea of the manner in which the ITDP has spent money in different programmes in different parts of Birbhum district.

An amount of approximately Rs. 25 lakhs has been spent on irrigation facilities in the entire district of Birbhum. A further amount of Rs. 12,29,000 has been spent on other agricultural facilities, such as seeds, fertilisers, and agricultural implements. In terms of irrigation facilities there is a clear bias in favour of blocks in the western region of Birbhum such as Mohammad Bazaar, Rampurhat, and Rajnagar. But this can be justified since these areas are neither recipients of earlier irrigational facilities, nor is the sub-soil water easy to tap there, nor even are there many tanks and ponds—natural or man-made. There is also another important consideration: the soil is rocky and infertile in this region and thus requires more water.

Except for two major river lift irrigation schemes launched by the ITDP, it is the deep-dug wells that have received most attention. The wells have also been constructed in the western region. Since the soil in Rampurhat, Rajnagar, and Mohammad Bazaar blocks is very hard, the construction of deep-dug wells has to be done under professional supervision with funds from the government. From 1981 onwards greater emphasis has been laid on the construction and re-examination of tanks. It is argued by the ITDP officials that the excavation of tanks has the advantage of not being greatly dependent on professional expertise and other agencies. The panchayat takes a major share of the initiative in organising the excavation or re-excavation of tanks.

The terms and conditions under which these tanks are made available are not always uniform. In Andahara-Digidhanga (Bolpur block), while the water was to be shared by all those who had land around the tank, the returns from pisciculture (which is also encouraged in every tank where the ITDP has had a hand in construction) were distributed in the following way: 50 per cent was for meeting the cost of production, 25 per cent was paid as rent to the owner of the land on which the tank was built, and the remaining 25 per cent was used for developmental works in the village. In Salbadra (Rampurhat block) the land on which the tanks were built was owned by four tribals who were related. While there was an agreement to give water equally to all those who had lands contiguous to the tank, the returns from the sale of fish from the tank went entirely to the four owners. Pisciculture in this tank was, however, neither initiated nor aided by either the ITDP or by LAMPS of that region. In another tank in Salbadra, because LAMPS had invested in pisciculture the owner would get 50 per cent of the proceeds from the sale of fish from the tank and the rest would go to LAMPS. Pisciculture is not of any significant consequence in any of the three tanks, but the variations in the terms and conditions of tank construction is an indication of how such things are often arrived at the local level after negotiations and consultations between the owner of the land on which the tank is built, the panchayat and the ITDP officials.

The land on which the re-excavation of the tank in Andahara-Digidhanga took place was owned by a non-tribal. The land surrounding the tank was also owned by non-tribals, and it is these non-tribals who benefited the most from the tank. The total area irrigated by this tank was 13 acres, but of this only three acres belonged to tribal households, and the remaining ten acres belonged to non-tribals. Further, when irrigation takes place with the aid of such tanks, generally the water requirement of those with lands nearest to the tank is met first, and then water flows down to the next plot of land. Therefore, the more distanced the land from the site of the tank, the less water it is likely to get. Thus, in this case by the time water reached the tribal-held land of three acres, it was reduced to a trickle. The rule all over Birbhum is that at least three feet of water must be left in the tanks for the fish to survive. When this tank was renovated by the ITDP, a committee of five was formed, and all five members of this committee were tribals. This is perhaps an indication of the impotency of tribals in committees where they are only formal members.

In Salbadra, the other case cited, the situation was somewhat different because the land on which the tank was built was owned by tribals, as also were the contiguous plots of land. But of the 20-25 bighas that can be cultivated by this tank, one Enos Murmu owned at least 12 bighas. The ITDP was originally planning to construct a tank on land owned by a non-tribal, but then ceased work when they came to know that Murmu was willing to give his land for excavation of a tank. A case almost completely similar in details with the Salbadra tank case is that of the tank at Kanhaipur in Rajnagar block. But in that case the land belonging to the owner of the tank was not more than five bighas, and the tank irrigated about 20 bighas in all. Kanhaipur was an all-tribal village made up of 55 households. In Dholtikuri (Bolpur block) some 15 tribals had bought some fallow land for constructing a tank. The Kankalitala panchayat claims to have forwarded this demand to the ITDP for funds, but it is nowhere on the ITDP records.

Most of the dug wells constructed by the ITDP with great cost have yet to be used for irrigation purposes. There were about nine deep-dug wells in Aligarh *mouza* in Rajnagar block, especially around the villages of Baganpara and Khoiraghar. In this area there are about 165 tribal households, but not one of them is a beneficiary. This is because none of them had the apparatus required to draw water from the deep-dug wells in order to irrigate fields. There was sufficient water in these wells, but it was lying unused. It is very difficult to apportion blame officially to the ITDP officials because while funds were made available for the construction of the wells, no money was sanctioned for the installation of the lifting apparatus. A matter as blatant as this should have been noticed and rectified either by the ITDP officials, by the irrigation department or by the local panchayat. It seems that the ITDP officials had not visited these villages with the express purpose of inspecting these dug wells after they were constructed.

It may be mentioned that unlike tanks, the deep-dug wells are not the property of any one household but belong to the village. In this case the wells are not built on the agricultural fields but some distance away. In addition to the lifting apparatus *nullahs* have to be constructed for carrying water to the fields. This has not been done in any of the 12 deep-dug well-sites. Nor had any thought been given as to who would draw water from which well, and so forth. But in Asadullapur (Bolpur) money was sanctioned and 'spent' on a deep-dug well, and it had not been constructed. The local panchayat members were unaware of it as also were the block development officials of Bolpur.

Although concentrating on the construction of irrigational facilities in the western block of Birbhum seems justified, the near-neglect in providing irrigational infrastructure in the eastern blocks (for instance, in Bolpur), is difficult to justify. Bomerpukur in Boiradihi *mouza* of Bolpur has about twenty tribal households, and there is no irrigational facility at all for tribal lands. Again in Benodepur in Ruppur panchayat of Bolpur block, there is a complete lack of irrigational facilities for the tribals. In Patharghata there was one tribal with one bigha of irrigated land, but he had received the land from the pool of vested land. In the above-mentioned villages the land-areas owned by non-tribals were situated near the river with proper provisions for drawing water. This perhaps creates the impression that there is no great urgency to provide irrigational facilities to ITDP villages in Bolpur block.

Appendix III (b) details the assistance given to individual tribal households in the form of implements for agricultural purposes, seeds, and mini-kits. According to the calculations based on the ITDP records in Suri, about 7,000 tribal households benefited from these schemes. But the ITDP figures have not been organised under appropriate headings. Secondly, the panchayat decides who is needy and distributes funds accordingly. In the nine *mouzas* in Ruppur and Kankali panchayats in Bolpur block not a single person was found who had received agricultural implements either from the ITDP or from the panchayats. It is possible that there were people who had received help, but they could not be traced. But if such implements had been given through the popular panchayats someone would have remembered.

The situation is however different in the western region. In Bhokikhol, Aligar, and Kanaipur in Rajnagar block, 11 tribals had received *donis*—a *doni* is an elongated metal tray which helps in drawing water from shallow waters. There were no hand-sprayers or dusters which were procured at cost; they were supposed to have been distributed among the tribals. In any case *donis* are of little use for the quality of land the tribals cultivate and the crops that they grow, which are mainly coarse cereals and some maize.

The agricultural mini-kit story is somewhat different. One mini-kit is about six kg in weight, sufficient for about half a bigha of land. The mini-kits have been distributed to tribal households even in Bolpur block, but they always arrive too late to be of use, and hence go waste. In the western region LAMPS distributed the mini-kits on time as a rule; the records of Aligar and Salbadra LAMPS were particularly good in this matter. In other words, whenever distribution is done at the village level through panchayats the efficiency is much lower than when it is done through the LAMPS. It appears that official as well as non-official agencies fail to reach out to people, but when people are expected to come forward to claim benefits, they do come forward.

LAMPS in Birbhum

The LAMPS set up in the ITDP areas have the objective of economic and social development of the tribals, and they function in close coordination with the ITDP in those areas. As a matter of fact, the special attention devoted to LAMPS in the ITDP blocks and the variety of functions they are enjoined to carry out are the outcome of the formulation of the ITDP itself. The LAMPS amalgamate various functions so that the tribal people do not have to go to various institutions for assistance.[29]

Till 1981 the Cooperative Inspector acted as the officer-in-charge of the LAMPS in each block. After 1981, an official was posted in charge of LAMPS with the designation of Executive Officer. The LAMPS perform a variety of functions: their primary job is to arrange credit, both long-term and short-term; supervise the disbursement of subsidies; purchase minor forest produce from the tribals; sell cloth and essential commodities to the tribals at a fair price; etc. In addition, the LAMPS also hand out mini-kits and agricultural implements. Some LAMPS are getting into the construction of gobar gas plants as well.

The facilities offered by the LAMPS are availed of by those who live nearby. For instance, in a village such as Barkananda in Rajnagar, the tribals in recent times did not benefit from the LAMPS in Aligar, which is about 25 km away, although they knew about its existence. Three LAMPS were visited for the purpose of the study: at Aligar in Rajnagar Block, at Sewrakuri in Mohammad Bazaar, and at Salbadra in Rampurhat. An overwhelming number of LAMPS members were tribals: in Aligar, about 1,364 were tribals out of the total of 1,446; in Sewarkuri, 900 out of 1,658; and in Salbadra, 1,400 out of 1,750. The nine-member managing committee of the LAMPS was entirely made up of tribals. Only the executive officer in all cases was a non-tribal, and he was the secretary of the managing committee.

These LAMPS functioned successfully as an outlet for the distribution of rationed commodities, though performing this function is not as easy as it is in the cities because the LAMPS have no vehicles. The transport problem is often further compounded by bad roads. For instance, the road between Mallarpur and Salbadra is such that the owners of automated vehicles are reluctant to rent out their vehicles for reaching supplies to Salbadra. Nor are the villagers in Salbadra willing to lend their bullock carts for this purpose.

The LAMPS are important as institutions through which loans and subsidies are given out. But the LAMPS alone do not disburse these funds. It is possible for those who qualify under various schemes to get their money through the various agencies like the Drought-Prone Area Programme, DRDA, Primary Agricultural Credit Societies, and nationalised banks which have been specially entrusted with the task of providing credit.

The LAMPS are meant to provide various types of loans for animal husbandry and small irrigational works. They provide consumption loan to their Scheduled-Tribe members, interest subsidy to convert all loans given through LAMPS into the differential rate of interest loans, loans to tribal defaulters, and aid and subsidy under the Special Component

Plan for *bargas*. (The *kishani* system, where the tiller only provided his labour, is now subsumed under the *bargadar* scheme.) This Special Component Plan also includes the *pattadars*, i.e. those who have received vested land.

The Special Component Plan and the ITDP both finance the supply of *donis* through LAMPS at 75 per cent subsidy. A *doni* costs about Rs. 250.

Even the payment made under the National Rural Employment Programme (NREP) is made through LAMPS. The Aligar LAMPS have made payments in cash and kind under this scheme. This, however, depends on where a particular NREP is launched.

In addition to this, the Tribal Development Corporation provides consumption loans of up to Rs. 100 to poor landless tribals. There is also the Agricultural Cooperative Bank which gives crop loans on the basis of amount of land owned, and the Primary Agricultural Cooperative Society (PACS) which in Bolpur operates through the United Bank of India. A tribal can become a member of this society by purchasing a share worth Rs. 10 while paying only Re. 1. This enables him to get a loan of Rs. 100. The PACS is directed to lend more to the weaker sections.[31]

Wewrakuri LAMPS reported that in 1983-84 the return on loans taken by tribals was about 80 per cent in contrast to the previous year when it was only 15 per cent. The meagre return was due to the very poor harvest. In times of drought and floods the LAMPS propose to the Reserve Bank of India via the State Corporation Bank to convert all short-term loans into mid-term loans.

The discussion so far covers well the area of LAMPS operation in this field, though it is not exhaustive.

The Aligar LAMPS encourages the tribals to collect *sal* seeds and *kendu* leaves. It lacks transportation facilities like others and cannot market *sal* leaves to places where they are in demand. The officials in Aligar suggested that the transit charge in respect of *kendu* leaves should be dropped by the forest department, but this has not been agreed to. The charge works against the interests of the tribals in the region because the *kendu* leaves grown in the region are of poorer quality than those grown in Orissa and in Palamau. The minor forest produce is sold in Rajnagar P.S., except for a small part which is sold at Khoirashole P.S. In Laujore there is also a warehouse for *kendu* leaves leased by the ITDP to the LAMPS.

Pump sets are in great demand by the members of the LAMPS. Two of the four pump sets given to Aligar LAMPS were damaged due to overuse and were not repaired. In the Salbadra LAMPS, 46 members had requisitioned and used pumps for drawing water from July 1983 to January 1984. Of these, 18 were Santals.

The Aligar LAMPS has set up a bakery which is much talked about in the official circles, but has in fact not created much impact among the tribals. The bakery has been set up in Rajnagar with Rs. 86,845 sanctioned by the government. It employs 25 people, 11 of them are Santals, though the operational supervision is in the hands of a non-tribal. It was primarily seen as a scheme to engender profits to finance LAMPS operations in other sectors. The tribals neither buy the products of this bakery, nor do they sell them. At one point it was envisaged that the tribals would be given the charge of selling the products, but it was soon realised that the tribals would be cheated by customers.

The LAMPS also takes part in *tasar* cultivation and in imparting training to tribals to take up this activity. At one point the Sewrakuri LAMPS in Mahammad Bazaar was thinking of protecting the workers in the Pachim Hatgachi quarry.[32] But it pulled out of this venture because only about 20 per cent of the workers in the quarry were tribals.

Through a number of activities mentioned so far, the LAMPS seeks to perform economic functions which are both promotive and protective. The major problem in the functioning of the LAMPS, according to the officials, is the lack of transport facilities.

The LAMPS officials function with a good deal of efficiency and commitment. It is true that neither the LAMPS nor the various financial institutions have been able to get rid of the usurer, although they seem to have made a noticeable impact. Subsidy (a mere Rs. 100) given out to the poor marginal and landless tribals is hardly sufficient, and not everybody gets even that. The LAMPS has made no impact in strengthening cottage industries which fit the genius of the people either.

Activities like rope making, bidi making, and oil crushing have gone almost completely neglected, though the LAMPS were supposed to play a role in encouraging them.[33] This could again be justified on the ground that agricultural operations are primary and hence, attention should be paid to them first. Even so, one cannot deny the fact that as a majority of the tribals are poor farmers and landless labourers who generally get only three months of regular agricultural work a year, these other industries would, if promoted, aid them substantially in the years to come.[34] Only about Rs. 90,000 have been spent on cottage industries by the ITDP so far. The neglect of these areas and the explanation for this neglect can be traced to over-reliance on the existing forms of economic activity. Branching out to newer forms of activities should be thought about.

Other Programmes

A total of approximately Rs. 6,75,000 was spent on animal husbandry, fishing, and poultry keeping. The ITDP officials select livestock and poultry and get them certified by the veterinarian as healthy before purchasing them. Then they are handed over to panchayats for distribution; the ITDP is not involved here.

In two villages in Bolpur and in four villages in Rampurhat, several tribals had received goats, pigs, or cows from the ITDP. It was difficult to ascertain how many of the listed beneficiaries actually received what was supposedly given to them since the records were not clear.

The more important question was to what extent these hand-outs actually helped them. In Benodepur in Bolpur block the tribals were not able to maintain livestock because there was no veterinary surgeon to look after them. The veterinary surgeon, it was alleged, never came. His compounder and assistant sometimes did, and they charged Rs. 5 for each case. (They would come down to Rs. 2 on occasions!) A member of the Kankali panchayat in Bolpur said that the tribals looked upon the charge levied by the veterinary surgeon's assistants as a 'fine' for accepting animals and livestock from the government. In Patharghata, the mortality rate of livestock given by the ITDP was 100 per cent. The situation was not very different in Rampurhat block. The animal insurance scheme also ran into difficulties. The legal requirement is that the carcass of the animal must be brought to the veterinary surgeon of the block who would certify it as dead before the owner can claim insurance money for it. But neither could the tribals afford to take the carcass to the veterinary surgeon at the block headquarters, nor would the surgeon come round. The body has to be disposed of, and the officials accuse the tribals of having feasted on it. This state of affairs explains the findings of the Agricultural Finance Corporation of Bombay which states that in Birbhum only 5 per cent of cases were brought by tribals to the veterinary hospital, even though they made up 50 per cent of the population.[35] Although the study attributes such low percentage to a low level of literacy among the tribals, poor service facilities appear to be the cause.

A large amount of money has been spent on forestry in Birbhum (Appendix III d). Although the amount spent, Rs. 24 lakh, is disproportionate in view of the strategy of the West Bengal Tribal Sub-Plans to encourage tribals to engage in agriculture, forestry, and livestock in the ratio of 10 : 2 : 1, one may commend the ITDP for spending such a large amount on forestry. These forests have been recently planted, and the benefits are yet to accrue.

Land Reforms and Operation *Barga*

The major thrust of the ITDP should be on scheduled caste *bargadars* and assignees of vested land according to the *Tribal Sub-Plan for West Bengal for 1980-85*. A prompt recording of *bargadars* and identification of lands beyond the ceiling are also recommended.[36] This might lead one to believe that the ITDP is involved in the Operation *Barga* in its own areas, but that is not the case. The ITDP does not have either the structure or the authority to intervene in the Operation *Barga*. Neither can it aid in the identification of land beyond the ceiling, nor is it expected to do any of these. These functions have already been entrusted to other authorities.

The system of crop sharing was not uniform even among different villages. In most places if the *barga* has registered himself, then the crop share is in the ratio of 50 : 50. If the sharecroppers are well organised, then they give only 25 per cent to the landowner and keep 75 per cent of the crops for themselves. This is incidentally the ratio which has been legally ordained in Operation *Barga*.

The most tangible benefit that has accrued to the tribals in the first flush of the Operation *Barga* is that they now have security of tenure, larger share of the crops, and are able to claim *barga* loans. The question of *bargadars* is relevant both in the eastern and the western regions of the district, but in the border villages like Bhokhikol in Rajnagar block, or Sulunga and Salbadra, it is not important since only a handful of tribals are landless in these places.

As regards the distribution of vested land, almost every village visited had four to seven people who had received land. But the vested land called *danga* land is uniformly of poor quality. There was only one case where the assignee had received half a bigha of fertile land (this was in Bonerpukur in Bolpur). The distribution of vested land never exceeded one bigha per assignee.

The discussion so far shows that in spite of statements made in the sub-plan, the ITDP has in fact nothing to do with land reforms. But this does not mean that there is no scope for the ITDP to play a positive role in it. If the ITDP could help in the registration of *bargas* and aid in the identification of land beyond ceiling, then it could get involved at the grassroots level in an integrated manner and nurture popular initiative.

Finally, it may be noted that the issue of alienation of tribal-lands does not arise in this region as it does in Orissa, Bihar, and Madhya Pradesh because Birbhum's tribal population is composed entirely of migrants, though they are not recent migrants. The kind of initiative and programmes that are required in other states for the protection of tribal lands and forests are, therefore, not necessary here. (Appendix IV provides information on restored tribal-lands.)

The issue of forestry and forest produce does not play a significant role in this area because there are no tribals forests as there are in other states, but the forest department occasionally initiates an afforestation programme for tribals' benefit. In such cases the tribals plant saplings as was done in Alokshonday in Rajnagar.

Popular Participation

Both the *Tribal Sub-Plan of West Bengal* and the *Report of the Working Group on Tribal Development During the Sixth Plan* state that without popular participation, the plans would never be implemented, and the ITDP would not be a fully integrated approach. Although planning in the ITDP was supposed to be from the block level, the eventual sanctioning of funds was decided at the state level. The statutory panchayats are only very tenuously associated with the ITDP; the ITDP distributes its livestock or implements through the panchayats. The ITDP has no structural arrangement to interact with the beneficiaries directly. Even the *upa panchayats* were not sure if they knew what ITDP stood for.

The structure of the ITDP makes no provision for popular participation. The traditional tribal leaders are in no way involved in this project. The single line administration system of the ITDP gives no scope at any level to popular participation in decision making. It remains then, even in areas where its presence can be felt, a project which doles out benefits to tribals. The monitoring system too is severely deficient. The ITDP officials are unable to get any feedback from the people. The Block Development Officer (BDO), on whom the ITDP in the district has to depend, is not in any way responsible to the Project Officer of the ITDP. The BDO is in the administrative wing, and his confidential report is written by the panchayat samiti chairman. The ITDP has no mechanism by which it can project a high profile in the blocks and villages under its jurisdiction.

Popular participation has surely not worked out the way it was envisaged in the declaration in the ITDP's official plan documents and proposals. There appears to be a hiatus between what the documents proclaim and what the officials in the Planning Commission or the ITDP believe. Time and again, officials deny that there is room for popular participation in the ITDP, but documents speak otherwise. The importance of this shortcoming cannot be overstated, but what is perhaps most deleterious to the ITDP is the near-universal ignorance of its presence at the popular level. The very knowledge that there exists a certain programme for the tribals would itself generate a great deal of confidence among them. After all, does not the

ITDP aim at removing age-old barriers, barriers which are erected because of the leviathan structure of administration and against which tribals feel a sense of helplessness? Must it be repeated again and again that a great gulf separates the poor, especially the tribal poor, from the administrative structure in this country? And, has not the recognition of the need for a new approach to tribal development given birth to the ITDP?

Social Services

Education has been recognised as a key to the success of the ITDP. Accordingly, schools have been established in Sainthia, Lotabani (Suri II), Kusunidihi (Sainthia), and in Sisal Farm (Rajnagar). They admit about 20 tribal children (each) who live more than 8 km away and whose parents earn less than Rs. 3,000 a year. In Sainthia there is also the Narainpur Boarding School for tribal children run by the missionaries. There are other such schools in Birgram and Bandgora (Bolpur) and Timbuni (Rampurhat), but only four of them have been set up by the ITDP.

Only Rs. 1,22,450 were spent in opening the Primary Ashram Schools for tribals from 1974 to 1983 by the ITDP (Appendix III c). The government spends Rs. 100 per student for boarding, lodging, and other school-related needs. There is no record of any other expenditure on schools. The ITDP report prepared in 1976 asks for 42 additional primary schools; it may be added as a matter of cynical detail![37]

But it is not enough to set up schools; it has to be ensured that tribal children go to school. In Bolpur villages (Bonerpukur, Patharghata, and Amdahare) there are schools nearby and yet a large number of tribal children do not go to school. In Bonerpukur only seven out of 45 tribal children go to school though in Patharghata nearly every tribal child goes to school.

Surprisingly, however, in the more backward western regions the idea of going to school is taken more seriously. In Bhokhikor, for instance, about half the tribal children go to school. From Salbadra, tribal children even go to school in Mallarpur, which is about 8 km away. These children have gone as far as Birgram and Bandigora in Bolpur and stayed in hostels for their education.

In Bhokhikol there was a tribal who was educated at

Viswabharati but has never returned to his village. In Salbadra, there were four tribals who had passed school but were idle.[1]

Facilities for drinking water existed in every place visited (except Bonebukur), though this may not apply to the entire area.

The ITDP in Birbhum has spent over Rs. 14 lakh on the construction of roads linking tribal villages to the outside world. The road constructed between Aligar to Kurulmetia in 1982-83 was at a cost of over Rs. 4 lakh, and the ITDP officials and the villagers in Kurulmetia consider this a great success. It is over 8 km long and is not metalled yet. It is a *moram* road, built by crushed stone-chips, pressed down and packed with earth. Salbadra was connected to Mallarpur by road; the work was initiated by the ITDP though two km of it had not yet been sanctioned. Not receiving sanction was an oft-repeated complaint of the ITDP officials. The construction of this road, when completed (if the road department makes the money available), would connect Salbadra with the outside world through Mallarpur. Incidentally, the panchayat members of Kankali in Bolpur also wanted some roads to be constructed for tribal development but had shown no inclination towards other programmes where only tribals would benefit. A vented causeway was built in Adityapur which also linked a large number of villages in that area.

But what have these constructions to do with the integrated approach as envisaged by the planners? Road construction could have taken place before the adoption of the ITDP. If it is claimed that the new approach brought about a jump in financial resources made available to the ITDP then it is only a quantitative jump and not a qualitative one.[2]

It may be mentioned that the increase in ITDP funds is because area development resources have now been linked to the ITDP in a large number of cases.

* * *

The lack of awareness of the ITDP has already been remarked upon. This may be considered a failure primarily of the ITDP structure which has not made any actual provision for popular participation Where there is a possibility of tangible benefits accruing to tribals as a consequence of participation, such as in the case of LAMPS, a perceptible degree of awareness among the tribals ("something was going on") was found. As a matter of fact, only in panchayats where the LAMPS are situated there was some awareness of the ITDP. In Tantipura panchayat, not far from Rajnagar LAMPS, there was no awareness at all of the ITDP. Indeed, the ITDP had even set up a well for drinking water in 1980 in one of its villages, but this was seen as any other governmental activity—and quite correctly! The construction of a lonely well or a rig bore tap in a random village does not mean that a new approach to integration is at work.

If one were to view the ITDP from the perspective of what it has accomplished given its structure, then one might say that in Birbhum the ITDP is ticking efficiently, and it is trying very hard to succeed. On the other hand, if one were to look at the incongruities in its administrative structure, its lack of control over resources and hence its inability to plan in an integrated way, the complete absence of popular initiative, its inability to do a follow-up of its programmes, its non-involvement with popular bodies, and the complete failure of its monitoring system, then one may conclude that the ITDP has fallen far short of its aims. A balanced evaluation would have both these perspectives in mind.

It was hoped initially that the ITDP would end exploitation and eliminate poverty, but it was a completely unrealistic expectation. Later, the Planning Commission reformulated the position and the ITDP is now supposed to mitigate exploitation and alleviate poverty. The ITDP began on the right note, emphasising the need to restore confidence through education and popular participation among the tribals, but it has been unable to achieve its goal.

Two things come to mind in this connection. One, Operation *Barga* and the land reforms movement in Bengal; and two, the LAMPS. Although there are shortfalls in Operation *Barga*, for two years after it was launched, it mobilised a number of poor peasants and attained dimensions of a movement. Today, Operation *Barga* has run its course and has nothing more to offer, nor have any other measures been taken to take over from where it left off. In several villages, especially in Bolpur block, several tribal sharecroppers did not register as *bargadars* because they had come to an understanding with the landowners. In some cases landowners had taken the matter to court. But there is a clear advantage which the poor secured as a result of Operation *Barga.* They could no longer be pushed around and made to perform corvee-like services with the same confidence as before by the landowners in the rural areas.[3] The ITDP could have capitalised on this achievement and could have built structures in its overall administrative framework to tap this vital energy. This could have made Operation *Barga* a greater success in tribal areas, and it might also have released more vested land for tribal use.

The LAMPS, small and inadequate as they are, were the only places which were humming with activities associated with agencies involved in tribal welfare and development. This is because of the greater scope given to popular participation of the tribals in the LAMPS. Many more LAMPS should be built, perhaps one in each tribal *mouza*, and they should be linked with other ITDPs. It would be perhaps better if the LAMPS could become an agency of the ITDP. In other words, replication of what is happening in Aligar, Sewrakuri, and Salbadra LAMPS appears to be one way of involving the tribals, creating confidence in them, and cementing their solidarity. Through the LAMPS the ITDP could start industries at local level which can be easily run by tribals and which would augment their earnings.

The panchayats are very important institutions in West Bengal, perhaps more so than anywhere else in this country. But the tribals are not always adequately represented in them. Hence, the ITDP cannot equate involving the panchayats at formal level with liaising with popular tribal bodies.

The ITDP in Birbhum is manned by conscientious officers led by the Project Officer. But given the structure of the ITDP, if the officials change for some reason, then the whole programme can be seriously affected (as it is, the ITDP office in Suri has many vacant posts, and of the four field offices sanctioned the one for Rajnagar has not yet been set up). But the most serious drawback of the structure of ITDP is in the nature of the finances that flow to it, and in the way the ITDP has to match its programmes according to the funds received each year from different sources. Rather than the ITDP getting money and resources to match its plans, the plans have to be tailored according to the amount ITDP receives from different agencies. It is, therefore, unable to give the project an integrated thrust of the multi-sectoral kind, except that from time to time it works in different sectors.

Planning ministry officials and those who have been involved with the making of the ITDP have stated that initially the programme was meant to be quite different. The ITDP was to be an agency through which different sectors would work jointly, and the ITDP office would have a major say in the use of funds in its project regions. This is also how the Sub-Plan and the Planning Commission documents read. But because each sector is reluctant to give up its powers—and probably also because re-organisation required for this purpose would be quite extensive—a simpler structure was evolved which does not allow the working of an integrated approach.

Heavy expenditure is undertaken in building roads, weirs, etc. It is not that they are unnecessary, and many tribals at Kurulmetia and Salbadra were quite satisfied with the construction of roads. But the question is, to what extent can such development work be said to have been inspired by a new approach to tribal development.

The ITDP programme was reoriented in the Sixth Plan and it is no longer an area development programme but a beneficiary oriented programme. Frankly, a distinction of this kind is not always easy to draw, but it has been drawn quite sharply by the planners. This distinction is not reflected in the pattern of expenditure undertaken in Bolpur by the ITDP in the Fifth and Sixth Plan periods. It seems that items of indivisible expenditure such as on weirs, bakeries, and roads have been undertaken, paradoxically, in the latter phase (Appendix IIIc.) Obviously, such policy decisions at the top cannot be translated at the action level. In a way perhaps it is just as well or people in Kurulmetia and Sulunga would have been without roads as also those between Adityapur and Zahanabad. But surely such constructions need not have been financed from the scarce ITDP funds. If they have to be, then the ITDP should perhaps take over charge of the entire tribal block, subsuming both area development and the comprehensive family development schemes. Eventually the question remains: who decides that the ITDP should go in for this or that expenditure? The broad plans are too broad and serve the ITDP like the directive principles serve the functionaries of the states. When a certain amount of money is turned over to the ITDP from time to time from different agencies in a highly unpredictable manner, the ITDP officials or the ITDP committee decides where to invest it.

In the ultimate analysis, the ITDP in Birbhum is, at best, an operation to keep the tribals alive—a staving-off operation: it has dug wells, distributed mini-kits, allotted livestock, but it has neither been able to raise tribal elan and confidence, nor improve their lot in economic terms. The resources available with the ITDP, of course, do not allow for an immediate economic breakthrough, nor has the ITDP ever claimed, even in its most sanguine documents, that it would change the social structure radically. But even within the system, even allowing for the fact that the ITDP is primarily interested in pushing tribal development in an integrated, multi-sectoral way, the ITDP fails because the very structure of its administration is not conducive to it. When this is seen in conjunction with the total lack of popular participation—and indeed the fact that there is no opening for it—one wonders if the ITDP as an integrated approach was ever really intended to be practised.

Notes

1. The father of one of them, who was disillusioned, said, "When my boy was away in boarding, he did not want to come here even on holidays because he got tomatoes to eat at school. Now that he is here and without a job he is not much help. When he goes to work in the field the stones and shells hurt his feet. He is unhappy and grumbles every day."
2. If one were to take the instance of the causeway in Adityapur, then one would probably agree with Professor B.K. Roy Burman who said, "After the formulation of ITDP if one were to construct a five-star hotel in an ITDP area it would be shown as an investment for tribal benefit. The increase in developmental finance after ITDP is basically a question of accounting jugglery." It is not as if the causeway in Adityapur is as irrelevant as a five-star hotel, but not all programmes launched by ITDP exemplify a new or integrated approach.

3. This is not true of all places. For example in Benodepur there are no unpaid labourers, but there are in Bonerpukur—both the villages have a common panchayat.

REFERENCES

[1]*Report of the Working Group on Tribal Development During Sixth Plan (1980-85)*, Government of India, Ministry of Home Affairs, October 1980, p. 10.

[2]*Sub-Plan for the Tribal Areas of West Bengal*, Government of West Bengal, Scheduled Caste and Scheduled Tribe Welfare Department, 1975, p. 31.

[3]*Report of the Working Group, op. cit.*, pp. 10-11.

[4]*Ibid.*

[5]*Ibid.*

[6]*Sixth Five Year Plan, 1980-85*, Government of India, Planning Commission, p. 420.

[7]*Report of the Working Group, op. cit.*, p. 3.

[8]Bhupinder Singh, *Tribal Development in Retrospect and Prospect*, Ministry of Home Affairs, Government of India, May 1983, p. 26.

[9]*Report of the Working Group, op. cit.*, pp. 33, 34.

[10]*Ibid.*, pp. 7, 40.

[11]*Tribal Development in Retrospect, op. cit.*, p. 13.

[12]*Report of the Working Group, op. cit.*, p. 15.

[13]*Sixth Five Year Plan, op. cit.*, p. 420.

[14]Haque, Wahidul, Mehta, Niranjan, Rehman, Anisur and Wignarya Poona 1977. "Towards a Theory of Rural Development", *Development Dialogue*, Vol. 2.

[15]*Ibid.*

[16]*Report of the Working Group, op. cit.*, pp. 37-39; and *Tribal Sub-Plan of West Bengal, op. cit.*, p. 34.

[17]*Report of the Working Group, op. cit.*, p. 36; *Tribal Development in Retrospect, op. cit.*, p. 34.

[18]*Report of the Working Group, op. cit.*, p. 17.

[19]*Ibid.*, p. 2.

[20]Bose, N.K. *Culture and Society in India*, Bombay: Asia Publishing House, pp. 179-180.

[21]*Tribal Sub-Plan for West Bengal, op. cit.*, p. 13.

[22]*Ibid.*, p. 34.

[23]*Report of the Working Group, op. cit.*, pp. 99-109.

[24]*Tribal Sub-Plan of West Bengal, op. cit.*, pp. 1-2.

[25]*Tribal Development in Retrospect, op. cit.* pp. 67-91.

[26]*Tribal Sub-Plan of West Bengal, op. cit.*, p. 20.

[27]Archer, W.G., and McAlpin, M.C., Report on the Condition of the Santhals in the Districts of Birbhum, Bankura, Midnapore and North Balasore, Calcutta: Bengal Secretariat Press, 1909.

[28]*Ibid.*, p. 35.

[29]*Integrated Tribal Development Project in Birbhum District, West Bengal*, Bombay: Agricultural Finance Corporation, 1976, p. 88.

[30]*Tribal Sub-Plan of West Bengal, op. cit.*, p. 28.

[31]*Ibid.*, p. 93.

[32]*Integrated Tribal Development Project in Birbhum District, op. cit.*, p. 106.

[33]*Tribal Sub-Plan of West Bengal, op. cit.*, p. 28.

[34]*Integrated Tribal Development Project, op. cit.*, p. 83.

[35]*Ibid.*, p. 253.

[36]*Tribal Sub-Plan of West Bengal, op. cit.*, p. 19.

Appendix I

Percentage of Tribal and Non-tribal Labour Force by Occupational Categories

Occupational category	Tribal	Non-tribal
Owner cultivator	8.2	13.0
Sharecropper	12.5	10.7
Owner cultivator-cum-sharecropper	10.5	9.6
Owner cultivator-cum-agricultural labourer	4.2	3.3
Agricultural labourer	23.5	20.1
Sharecropper-cum-labourer	17.4	12.4
Owner-cultivator-cum-sharecropper-cum-labourer	5.7	4.4
Dairy	0.5	0.9
Agriculture-cum-dairy+poultry+piggery	1.9	2.4
Agriculture+dairy+poultry+goat-keeping	1.6	2.8
Cottage industry	1.7	3.0
Agriculture+cottage industry	1.8	2.5
Forestry	1.2	1.6
Business	1.1	1.9
Labour (other type)	5.9	5.4
Others	1.2	3.0

Source: *Integrated Tribal Development Project: Report on Birbhum District, West Bengal* (Agricultural Finance Corporation Limited, Bombay, 1976).

Appendix II

ITDP Blocks in Birbhum District, West Bengal (1980)

ITDP project no.	Name of the block	*Mouzas*	Total population (1970)	Tribal population (1970)	Col 5 as % of col 4	Total projected population (1980)	Projected tribal population (1980)
10	Rajnagar	27	7,974	4,201	52.68	9,808	5,083
11	Sainthia, Suri, Illambazaar	66	22,262	12,882	57.86	27,382	15,587
12	Bolpur, Labpur	51	21,726	11,516	53.00	26,723	13,394
13	Mohammad Bazaar, Rampurhat	65	32,161	18,115	56.32	39,558	21,919

Source: *Tribal Sub-Plan of West Bengal for 1980-85 and 1981-82, Government of West Bengal* (S.C. and S.T. Welfare Department), November 1980, pp. 8-9.

Appendix III

ITDP Expenditure in Birbhum

(a) *Irrigation*

Year	Amount spent (Rs.)	Purpose	Location and number
1975-76	1,50,000	16 dug-wells, (one dug-well irrigates 8 to 10 bighas)	9: Rampurhat—1, 3: Suri 2: Illambazaar
1976-77	1,15,470	10 dug-wells	7: Rajnagar, 3: Rampurhat—1
1977-78	20,000	2 dug-wells	1: Rajnagar, 1: Suri
	3,00,000	3 River-lift irrigation (each irrigates up to 250 bighas)	3: Rampurhat—1
1978-79	14,500	1 dug-well	Mohammad Bazaar
1979-80	20,000	2 dug-wells	1: Mohammad Bazaar, 1: Sainthia
1980-81	3,00,000	For dug-wells initially, but because of drought, the amount was transferred to principal Agricultural Officer, Birbhum district	
1981-82	3,02,152 79,847	River-lift irrigation 12 tanks are re-excavation of tanks	3: Rampurhat—1 different panchayats. Not ascertained but informed that one was in Bolpur
1982-83	1,50,000	Tanks	
1983-84	11,00,000 approx	To construct 9 tanks deep tubewells and to construct weir scheme	Not ascertained Illambazaar Rampurhat—1

Appendix III (*Contd.*)

(*b*) *Agricultural Implements, Seeds, etc.*

Year	Amount spent (Rs.)	Purpose	Location and number
1975-76	—		
1976-77	—		
1977-78	—		
1978-79	—		
1979-80	25,000 5,15,000	Purchase of seeds, manure, implements hand sprayer, hand-duster, wheat mini-kit, basic slag (manure)	Equally distributed to 9 panchayats samitis. 1: Rajnagar, 2: Sainthia, 3: Mohammad Bazaar, 4: Suri—1, 5: Suri—2, 6: Bolpur, 7: Labpur, 8: Rampurhat—1, 9: Illambazaar
1980-81	34,000 4,20,000	Seeds and implements hand sprayer, hand-duster, *doni* wheat mini-kit, mustard mini-kit, mung mini-kit, basic slag, foot sprayer	—do— (at the rate of Rs. 100 per head) —do—
1981-82	2,35,000	Pumpsets, *doni* and other agricultural implements	6 pumpsets for 3 LAMPS
1982-83	—		
1983-84	Amount to be spent not clear*		Not mentioned

*But of the 1,100,000 mentioned under irrigation money will also be used on the following items: 10,000 coconut seedlings, 431 *donis*, 800 packets or agricultural mini-kits, 6 pumpsets.

APPENDIX III (*Contd.*)

(*c*) *Social Services*

Year	Amount spent (Rs.)	Purpose	Location and number
1975-76	—		
1976-77	81,460	19 tubewells	9 blocks
	45,000	8 masonry wells	Rajnagar and Rampurhat—1
1977-78	9,000	Housing	Suri—11, Rajnagar
	1,84,665	21 masonry-wells	all 9 panchayat samitis
1978-79	95,400	Clinic van for veterinary aid	Salbadra
	21,000	Houses	
	1,00,000	Road	Kuruthnetia
	72,450	Primary ashram schools (through school boards)	One each in Suri—I, Sainthia and Rajnagar
1979-80	50,000	Primary ashram school	Sainthia
			All 9 panchayat samitis
	44,996	17 masonry-wells	
	12,000	Housing (1,500 per house)	Mohammad Bazaar
1980-81	6,25,704	Vented causeways	Connecting Adityapur (Bolpur) villages
1981-82	39,000	Water supply, 6 masonry wells	
	4,01,388	Roads	Mallarpur to Salbadra (Rampurhat—1)
	76,000	Village industries	
1982-83	4,01,764	Roads	Kurulmetia (Rajnagar)
	40,000	4 masonary-wells	
1983-84	1,32,550	Bakery	Tatarpur
	66,000	Expansion of Rajnagar LAMPS	Rampurhat—1 LAMPS
			Rajnagar
	1,450	Bamboo works aid	Bolpur
	40,000	4 masonry wells	Not ascertained

APPENDIX III (*Contd.*)

(*d*) *Forestry*

Year	Amount spent (Rs.)	Purpose	Location and number
1975-76	25,000		
1976-77	1,99,500	Mandays created—33,273	
1977-78	—		
1978-79	2,71,000	Mandays created—33,982	
1979-80	2,45,000	Mandays created—25,585—31,000	
	2,94,000		
1980-81	—		
1981-82	4,25,000	—41600	
1982-83	6,16,225		
1983-84	4,09,000	Mandays created—43,610	

APPENDIX III (*Contd.*)

(*e*) *Animal Husbandry, Fishery, Dairy, Poultry etc.*

Year	Amount spent (Rs.)	Purpose	Location and number
1957-76	47,750	Goats demonstration centre	Suri—1
1976-77	43,181	Goat-keeping 25 units (5 she-goats+1 he-goat=1 unit) sheep—25 units, dairy —10 units (2 cows+2 calves=1 unit)	Mohammad Bazaar and Rampurhat—1, through LAMPS 20 beneficiaries, distributed through panchayat
1977-78	4,400	2 units of goats (20 goats+20 kids=1 unit)	20 beneficiaries, distributed through panchayat
1978-79	2,200	Goat-keeping	Not ascertained
	70,235	Animal husbandry	Not ascertained
1979-80	4,400	Goats, 2 units (20+2 making one unit)	Not ascertained
	84,565	Sheep—9 units, dairy —6 units, Goats—23 units, pigs—5 units	Not ascertained
	4,400	Livestock	Not ascertained
	71,500	Cows—6 units, goats —20 units, Sheep—10 units, poultry—60 units (10 chicks per unit), pigs—10 units (6 pigs per unit)	Not ascertained
1980-81	—		
1981-82	—		
1982-83	—		
1983-84	3,00,000	Dairy—54 units, goats—95 units (5 she-goats+1 he-goat=1 unit) Sheep—95 units (5 she-sheep+1 he-sheep=1 unit) duck-keeping—95 units (10 chicks=1 unit) poultry—96 units (10 chicks=1 unit	Not ascertained
	44,C00	Fisheries	

Appendix IV

Tribal Lands Alienated and Restored in West Bengal

Year	Land alienated (in acres)	Land restored (in acres)
1960-61	933.66	4.32
1966-67	1138.75	15.15
1968-69	1115.04	10.55
1973-74	1249.75	6.06
1976-77	49.85	368.08
1978-79	69.54	181.64

Source: *Tribal Sub-plan of West Bengal for 1980-85 and 1981-82*, Government of West Bengal, S.C. and S.T. Welfare Department, November 1980.

PART II

Multi-Level Planning

Proceedings

Presenting his paper, "Consistency between Macro and Micro Planning", D.T. Lakdawala deals with five themes: the relationship between macro and micro planning in India in the context of plan objectives, the Indian experience of centre-state relations in the sphere of development planning, the implications of this experience for local level planning, and the limitations of decentralised planning in achieving the twin goals of poverty eradication and regional equality.

The various plans formulated through multi-level planning in India have all shared the common goal of poverty eradication with emphasis on removal of unemployment and underemployment, elevation of the standard of living of the poor, and the provision by the State of the basic needs of the poor. The structural transformation required to meet these objectives requires strategies that have to be carried out at the macro-level. At the same time, if anti-poverty programmes are to be effective, they have to be specific to areas and communities that require state action. This can be achieved only when micro-level planning constitutes an instrument of macro-level planning. Macro and micro planning have to complement each other; they are neither contradictory to nor independent of one another.

The Indian five-year plans have been attempting to integrate these two aspects of planning. The federal nature of the Indian Constitution necessitates planning by the centre as well as by the states. While such a set-up has the potential for generating conflict between parties, and in fact has done so, centre-state conflicts in planning have been avoided because of the clear demarcation of the powers and functions of the parties involved, the sharing of a common ideology, and the presence of integrative bodies such as the National Development Council and the Planning Commission.

The picture of planning at the local level, however, has not been as rosy. The powers and functions of local bodies are not recognised by the Constitution, and local bodies are therefore left to the mercies of state legislations. Even in states which have experimented with it, decentralised planning is marginal. Planning for the districts is mainly done at the level of state departments which often have no regard for the special circumstances of the individual districts. The non-representation of districts in the formulation of district plans has forestalled state-local conflicts but the basic objectives of planning are not realised. If district planning is to be successful, a number of changes have to be instituted by way of demarcation of functions and finances between the state and the districts, provision of greater discretionary powers to local bodies, setting up of a single body to control and coordinate plan activities at the district level, better utilisation of local resources and manpower for satisfying local needs, building up of districtwise data banks on demographic and other data relevant to planning, and setting up of competent planning teams that can look into local level matters and link them with national and international objectives.

Although decentralised planning may be the key to success in vital national endeavours, there are some dangers which it has to guard against. In a heterogeneous society like India, a holistic perspective may be lost in decentralised planning and it may reinforce the prevailing inequalities both within and between districts. On the whole, decentralised planning is a slow process requiring considerable patience and political commitment which are not easily forthcoming. In addition, attempts at decentralised planning may be thwarted by the powerful tendencies towards centralisation which mark the Indian political arena.

The second presentation by M.L. Dantwala, "Rationale and Limitation of Decentralised Planning", also touched on similar issues. While arguing forcefully in favour of decentralised planning, he cautioned against some problems which planning from below, entails. Planning from below assumes that the planning process should begin at the village level, but all the problems of the village or area do not necessarily originate in the area and their causes may lie outside the purview of local authorities. A more important consideration is that people's involvement in planning assumes the existence of a harmonious society—an assumption that cannot be applied to India. In an unequal society like ours where the planner is confronted with the conflicting interests and aspirations of the powerful and the powerless, he inevitably succumbs to pressures from the former and is likely to cater to the interests of the powerful to the detriment of the weaker sections. Given the problems of planning from below, planning has to be a two-way process and it has to involve different levels: centre, states, districts, blocks and villages. This will of course give rise to disputes about the sharing of authority or financial resources, but this is a part of the democratic process.

According to Dantwala, decentralised planning in India has not succeeded in contributing to greater social justice. This can be attributed partly, but not entirely, to the failure to bring about social reconstruction or structural change involving property relations and to opposition from vested interests. The blame for very many of the failures of decentralised planning has to be laid squarely on inefficiency, bad planning, and poor implementation. The major lacuna in decentralisation experiments has been the failure to constitute a planning authority at the local level and a reliance on an outdated hierarchical administrative system which controls planning right from the state to the local levels. Decentralisation can play a more effective role in poverty eradication if a planning authority as the district level is set up with adequate sanctions and resources.

The applicability of foreign know-how to promote development under Indian conditions, the role of foreign agencies, and issues relating to decentralised planning and people's participation in development planning, dominated the discussion following the presentations by Lakdawala and Dantwala.

Girja Sharan observed that professionals in the field of development tend to depend on ideas and plans formulated abroad, even though many of them are trained in the West where self-reliance is a part of education and training. Instead of accepting ideas from abroad non-critically, it is necessary to develop indigenous capabilities that are congruent with our own environment and needs. The absence of appropriate expertise has hindered the success of rural development programmes in many developing countries. V.M. Rao illustrated this point by citing the experience of Sri Lanka in setting up IRDP. Despite the availability of funds, the district level planning system could not be implemented because line departments did not possess adequately qualified personnel to prepare schemes.

Not everyone, however, shared the view that the aims of rural development will be achieved through the development of appropriate expertise and a judicious mix of the two-way planning process. Kamla Chowdhry felt that even more important than these was the need for village communities to assume an activist role that will liberate people from their condition of dependence. The Jawaja experiment initiated by Ravi J. Matthai and some of his faculty colleagues at the Indian Institute of Management, Ahmedabad, was a good example of how people can be induced to assume such an activist role.

Some participants raised questions about the role of foreign agencies in rural development programmes. Pravin Visaria felt that the United Nations and other foreign agencies often have little that is new or relevant to offer by way of programmes. Their programmes, however, are accepted only because foreign exchange becomes easier to obtain when the programmes are linked with World Bank loans and credit facilities. Once funding is assured, it becomes unimportant whether the programmes are effectively implemented or not, except when the funding agencies themselves insist on reviews and appraisals. Programmes which are proclaimed to be successes, according to Dipankar Gupta, are usually those which receive strong political support because they maintain the existing social order and do little to change prevailing socio-political and economic structures.

Some participants felt that the real test of the success of the development programmes of international agencies lay in whether the programmes brought about changes in asset distribution in favour of the poor. Thus judged, they said, many programmes would fail to make the grade.

The *raison d'etre* for decentralised planning also figured in the discussion. Haldipur contended that development would take place only when the poor pose a threat to established interests. Such a threat would not be forthcoming as long as planning is done only at the central level. The instruments of development have to be put in the hands of the people to close the gap between planning and implementation. Besides, if a development plan has to be realistic, it must take into account cultural and social factors. Such factors vary from place to place and can be given due importance only when district level planning is carried out.

But the experiences of several Asian countries have shown that decentralisation is difficult to implement. The problem lies not only in the absence of political commitment, but also in that, as Haq pointed out in the case of Bangladesh, talents at the local level are often very scarce. Another difficulty is the lack of will on the part of local level functionaries who often become disillusioned because of bureaucratic and other obstacles.

C.T. Kurien drew attention to the problem of coordination in decentralised planning. Currently, much of what passes for coordination is done at the national level. This practice is inconsistent with the promotion of decentralisation. Despite verbal commitments to the ideal of decentralisation, national plans, including the Seventh Plan, have neglected or ignored local plans and have often been finalised even before local plans are ready. If the need for plan formulation at the local level is recognised, then a state level plan cannot be formulated without taking into account local plans. The national plans in turn must await finalisation of state level plans. In the absence of mechanisms for linking higher level plans with local plans, coordination poses formidable problems.

Kurien also referred to the role of the market as coordinator of various plans. The market coordinating mechanism has to be examined in terms of its compatibility with social objectives. This is especially pertinent at the local level if plans are taken seriously because at the local level it is very difficult to distinguish between public and private sector activities. Unless the role of the market is clearly defined, the market may turn out to be a counter-coordinator of planned social objectives.

The role of rural development programmes in combating poverty in the country was questioned by Dipankar Gupta who felt that the issue of poverty was too complex to be adequately dealt with by development programmes. The removal of poverty implies structural changes which are not within the scope of development programmes. However, what could perhaps be dealt with is the problem of acute poverty because this is mainly an organisational problem. Kamla Chowdhry emphasised that poverty in rural areas is linked with the exploitation of women. In the rural areas, women have to manage many of the subsistence resources such as fuel and fodder and, therefore, women have to be involved in any real efforts at eradicating poverty. If this is to be done, the problem of vested interests in terms of gender will have to be sorted out first.

Ranjit Gupta took up the issue of talent decentralisation posed by Dantwala. While Dantwala appeared to confine himself to decentralisation of talent only within the government or the bureaucracy, he emphasised that it was necessary and feasible to look into talent decentralisation in other channels. One such channel is the voluntary agency. In the last ten years, a large number of young, talented persons have taken up work in the field of rural development. Often they find it difficult to get the kind of opportunities they seek to work independently. Therefore, they join a voluntary agency which is dependent on external funding agencies and take up activities which are approved by the funding agencies. As a result, many such people do not find adequate scope for self-expression and creativity. The Jawaja experiment was an instance where young, independent volunteers were encouraged and supported to work on their own. But even these volunteers, when they branched out on their own, often had to fall back on some funding agency. Is it not possible, he asked, to create some autonomous corpus of funds so that interested, dedicated volunteers could be enabled to contribute to development work without being tied down to some organisation, and at the same time without having to fear shortage of resources?

Towards the end of the session Lakdawala and Dantwala responded to some of the major issues raised by the participants in reaction to their presentations.

The reason why international schemes almost always find ready acceptance in our country, Lakdawala explained can be seen in the system of plan assistance to states. The states are always short of resources, and they find special advantage in obtaining funds from the World Bank or other UN agencies because 70 per cent of such assistance is directly passed on to them. On the other hand, the assistance they get from the centre is only a part of the general assistance that the centre provides to the states.

Lakdawala conceded the point made by Nirmala Murthy that not many people in policy-making bodies take the planning exercise seriously. But once the planning has been done, the allocations of resources are taken seriously because they have serious consequences for certain groups and classes and because funds, once allocated, cannot be changed easily. While there do exist instances of misuse of funds, they are stray examples and difficult to eradicate. If we wish to retain faith in the system of decentralised local planning, then these minor aberrations have to be tolerated.

Whether the strategy of planning should be geared towards the removal of poverty or the removal of acute poverty depends on the time frame that planners have in mind. When we are talking of poverty in the Indian context we are concerned about families that cannot afford even the minimum calorie intake necessary for subsistence. It is the abolition of this extreme poverty which is envisaged in the plans for the next 10 or 15 years. If we do not do this, then the whole planning process will lose its meaning.

On the question of coordination between the central and state level plans, Lakdawala said it was difficult to decide which must come first. Plans at all levels have to be looked at with reference to each other; no central plan can be finalised without taking into consideration the state and local plans which have to have an all-India perspective.

Lakdawala agreed that the market as a coordinator of planning is being ignored. But ours is a mixed economy, and often plan efforts are intended to direct and regulate market forces. Measures such as land ceiling, organising land credit, and replacing moneylenders by cooperative credit facilities, are means of changing the market structure. To the extent these measures fail, the plans have to be readjusted. Often the failures lie in the implementation of policies rather than in the plan policies themselves.

Dantwala, in his reply, emphasised his commitment to the philosophy of decentralisation. He highlighted the constraints under which decentralised planning has to function. These constraints should caution rather than deter policy makers in decentralising planning. He suggested that schemes for the generaiton of employment should take into account the pattern of demand that is likely to be generated by the application of advanced technology to agriculture and rural industry requiring a variety of new skills, instead of thinking primarily in terms of providing unskilled work on a mass scale through government sponsored schemes of public works. The rural labour force should not be perpetually condemned to unskilled work. He felt that in the next decade the nature of demand for rural labour will undergo a qualitative change.

When talking of the need for education, Dantwala said, what he had in mind was not the creation of literacy but the creation of awareness or conscientisation. Such awareness will inevitably give rise to class conflict. To this extent, rural development is a "bitter pill", but conflict is the price that we will have to pay for development. It is for this reason that one entertains scepticism about UN aided projects which normally avoid conflict. If we want reduction of poverty and redistribution of assets as the objectives of rural development, we must reconcile ourselves to the fact that rural development is and will remain a painful process.

Dantwala also agreed with Abe Weisblat's suggestion that instead of harping on the subject of redistribution of existing wealth, which is a complicated issue, the strategy of planning should be the generation of resources which are predominantly for the weaker sections. We should order our investments in such a way that a major portion of additional resources which may become available is channelled toward building up the assets and skills of the poorer sections of the population.

Consistency between Macro and Micro Planning

D.T. Lakdawala

Introduction

This paper is divided into five sections. The first section discusses the relationship between macro (central) and micro (state and local) planning in India in the context of plan objectives. It concludes that there is no dichotomy between the two and that the latter can usefully be regarded as an instrument to further the objectives of the former. In the second section, an attempt is made to analyse the experiments that India has made in the field of centre-state planning. Because of the federal nature of our constitution, Indian planning has to be both central planning and state planning in one. The Indian Five Year Plans are attempts at integration of both. We have acquired rich experience in the problems of centre-state planning, the likely conflict in its course, and the various devices to promote their reconciliation and harmonisation. The third and fourth sections try to extend the lessons learnt from centre-state planning relationships to local planning. Even in the states, which have experimented long with it, decentralised planning is marginal. Planning for the districts is mainly done at the level of state departments. District-level schemes pay no regard to the special circumstances and requirements of the

Grateful thanks to Dr. Babubhai Patel, Gandhian Labour Institute, Shri Sudarshan Iyangar, Gujarat Institute of Area Planning and Shri D.H. Chauhan, Centre for Monitoring Indian Economy for help in the preparation of this paper.

individual districts, and there is a general reluctance of district officials to go outside them, as fresh technical sanction has to be obtained. The district sectoral allocations are made by the state departments, which also can make changes in the plans approved by the District Planning Board. Since the districts have hardly any effective voice in the formulation of district plans, there is no state-local conflict, but also the basic objectives of planning are not realised. The various changes that need to be made for successful district planning are listed. In the atmosphere prevalent in the country, it is likely that we may look to decentralised planning as the missing key to success in all our vital national endeavours. Section five draws attention to its limitations in achieving poverty eradication and regional equalities and the threats that may arise from local power structure.

I

The problem of consistency between macro and micro planning can be examined meaningfully in the context of what is sought to be achieved through multi-level planning. Based on the pressing needs of the times, past experience of the experiments in planning and the insight of the planners, the objectives of different plans show wide variations, but the common aim of poverty elimination runs through all of them. The Draft 1978-83 Plan aptly puts the principal objectives as "(i) the removal of unemployment and significant under-employment; (ii) an appreciable rise in the standard of living of the poorest sections of the population; (iii) provision by the State of some of the basic needs of the people in these income groups."[1] While the Approach to the Seventh Plan specifies the continuing guiding principles as "growth, equity and social justice, self-reliance, improved efficiency and productivity", it stresses the need for "a sharper focus on employment and poverty alleviation."[2] In fact, rapid rate of economic growth, greater self-help, reduction in grave personal and regional inequalities and modernisation, which are often mentioned as other objectives, are at the present stage of Indian economic development only worthwhile as a means to poverty reduction. In the Indian context absolute poverty cannot be tackled only through redistribution of income, assets or credit; relief measures can only be resorted to during emergencies or for very small selected groups. The poor have not only to be employed, but employed more productively so that they will have enough purchasing power to buy the elementary needs of life which the state cannot freely provide. Table 1 gives the additional sectorwise employment that the Sixth Plan was estimated to create. The state will ensure the provision to all its citizens throughout the country a minimum of services like education, public health, drinking water and roads.

Table 1: Estimated Sectoral Employment Creation in the Sixth Plan: 1980-85

(Million standard person year)

	Employment		Additional employment
	1979-80 (1)	1984-85 (2)	(2—1)
Agriculture	72.184	85.237	13.053
Forestry	6.207	7.794	1.587
Fishing	1.940	2.220	0.280
Mining and quarrying	0.724	0.894	0.170
Manufacturing	22.012	27.759	5.747
Construction	9.286	11.321	2.035
Electricity, gas and water supply	0.723	0.927	0.204
Railways	1.662	1.704	0.042
Other transport	7.109	8.677	1.568
Communication	0.800	0.917	0.117
Trade, storage and warehouses	13.278	16.640	3.362
Banking and insurance	1.038	1.225	0.187
Real estate and ownership dwellings	0.028	0.032	0.004
Public administration, defence and other services	14.119	16.042	1.923
Special programmes for employment generation, including National Rural Employment Programme		4.000	4.000
Total:	151.110	185.389	34.279

Source: Planning Commission, *Sixth Five Year Plan: 1980-85*, New Delhi, March 1981, p. 54.

The structural transformation needed for this purpose demands a great deal of institution-building, strategies, policies and programmes which can only be carried out at the national level. Rapid increase in savings and capital formation through monetary and fiscal measures, nationalisation of banking and insurance, control over imports and exports, control of capital issues and industrial licensing to conserve scarce capital and other resources, price control and allocation of vital scarce materials, distribution of food and other important consumption goods in shortage (both involving regulation of inter-state trade and commerce), protection of small and cottage industries, starting and running of large state enterprises in risky industries, and institutional changes in the organised sector can only be brought about at the top level. Planning necessitates the extension of state regulation and activities and, therefore, increased possibilities of inter-state conflicts and need for inter-state coordination, and these have to be resolved and brought about at the higher level. Horizontal transfer of resources, an important means to regional equalities, can only be undertaken through action at the higher layer.

While the realisation of plan objectives demands macro-level planning as an essential prerequisite, by itself it is woefully inadequate. Planned economic development demands state assistance, help and intelligent cooperation in the administration of central rules and regulations. Some idea of the overlap can be obtained from the distribution of public sector plan outlays between the Union government and the states (Table 2). The list of subjects in the Indian Constitution on which the state legislature has the exclusive power to make laws is fairly impressive. Agriculture, irrigation, industries (with certain exceptions), labour, trade and commerce (except inter-state), production, supply and distribution of goods, regulation of mines and mineral development (with certain exceptions), education and public health are all mentioned in List II of the Seventh Schedule. Much of the success in planning depends on policies and programmes in these spheres. The Central government can directly lay down production policies and targets in most of the public sector, and directly and indirectly influence production in the other organised sectors. Through the supplies of the inputs supplied by the public sector and their demand

Table 2: Sixth Five Year Plan Public Sector (Centre and States) Outlays

(Rs. Crores)

	Centre	States	Union Territories	Total
1	2	3	4	5
1. *Agriculture*	2,450.13	3,199.02	125.92	5,695.07
Agricultural research and education	340.00	197.67	(a)	537.67
Crop husbandry	293.00	906.50	34.48	1,233.98
Soil and water conservation	90.00	323.16	20.41	433.57
Animal husbandry and dairying	398.00	430.56	22.82	851.38
Fisheries	174.00	185.13	12.29	371.42
Forestry	105.00	559.54	28.10	692.64
Land reforms	30.10	272.62	1.91	304.63
Management of natural disasters	15.00	—	—	15.00
Agricultural marketing	46.65	48.55	0.91	96.11
Food storage and warehousing	294.00	38.61	5.00	337.61
Investment in agricultural financial institutions	664.38	156.68	—	821.06
2. *Rural Development*	2,314.87	3,020.03	28.83	5,363.73
Integrated rural development and related programmes	997.55	1,508.09 (for both items)	1.00	3,486.64
National rural employment programme	980.00			
Community development and panchayat institutions	7.17	335.29	9.74	352.20
Cooperation	330.15	566.00	18.09	914.24
Special employment programmes	—	610.65	—	610.65

Table 2 (*Contd.*)

1	2	3	4	5
3. *Special Area Programmes*	—	1,480.00	—	1,480.00
Hill areas	—	560.00	—	560.00
Tribal areas	—	470.00	—	470.00
Northeastern council	—	340.00	—	340.00
Development of backward areas	—	110.00	—	110.00
4. *Irrigation and Flood Control*	635.00	11,395.48	129.55	12,160.03
Major and medium	90.00	8,301.46	56.90	8,448.36
Minor	70.00	1,710.70	29.60	1,810.30
Command area development	300.00	555.92	0.35	856.27
Flood control including anti-sea erosion	175.00	827.40	42.70	1,045.10
5. *Energy*	11,995.00	14,293.56	246.88	26,535.44
Power	4,725.00	14,293.56	246.88	19,265.44
New and renewable sources of energy	100.00	—	—	100.00
Petroleum	4,300.00	—	—	4,300.00
Coal	2,870.00	—	—	2,870.00
6. *Industry and Minerals*	12,771.47	2,185.86	60.24	15,017.57
Village and small scale	923.40	815.11	41.94	1,780.45
Large and medium	11,848.07	1,370.75	18.30	13,237.12
7. *Transport*	8,418.64	3,707.34	285.99	12,411.97
Railways	5,100.00	—	—	5,100.00
Roads	830.00	2,398.87	210.09	3,438.96
Road transport	70.00	1,111.40	14.15	1,195.55
Ports	575.00			
Light houses	12.00	63,85	43.75	1,414.60
Shipping	720.00			

1	2	3	4	5
Inland water transport	45.00	24.36	2.30	71.66
Civil aviation	850.00	6.30	2.80	859.10
Meteorology	43.00	—	—	43.00
Tourism	72.00	102.56	12.90	187.46
Farakka barrage	50.00	—	—	50.00
INSAT—space segment	51.64	—	—	51.64
8. *Communication and Information and Broadcasting*	3,101.98	28.61	3.67	3,134.26
Communication	2,810.00	0.15	0.12	2,810.27
INSAT—space segment	51.65	—	—	51.65
Broadcasting and television	210.33	—	—	210.33
Information and publicity	30.00	28.46	3.55	62.01
9. *Science and Technology*	848.15	17.05	—	865.20
Atomic energy	248.98	—	—	248.98
Space	245.80	—	—	245.80
Scientific research	304.87	17.05	—	321.92
Ecology and environment	40.00	—	—	40.00
National test houses	8.50	—	—	8.50
10. *Social Services* Education	4,453.42	8,830.88	750.96	14,035.26
a) General education	515.75	1,493.09	153.39	2,162.23
b) Art and culture	51.00	31.85	1.05	83.90
c) Technical education	168.00	99.13	10.48	277.61
Health including medical	601.00	1,091.19	128.86	1,821.05
Family planning	1,010.00	—	—	1,010.00
Housing	300.00	1,065.95	124.92	1,490.87
Urban development	110.00	780.77	106.76	997.53
Water supply and sanitation	614.22	3,123.65	184.15	3,922.02

Table 2 (*Contd.*)

1	2	3	4	5
Welfare of scheduled castes, scheduled tribes and other backward classes	240.00	709.00	11.30	960.30
Special central additive for scheduled caste component plant	600.00	—	—	600.00
Social welfare	150.00	109.78	12.19	271.97
Nutrition	14.95	214.55	8.64	238.14
Labour and labour welfare	78.50	111.92	9.22	199.64
11. *Others*	261.34	532.17	17.96	801.47
Statistics	68.87	24.56	2.01	95.44
Rehabilitation of displaced persons	154.12	—	—	154.12
Planning machinery	20.07	—	—	20.07
Stationery and printing	12.00	26.06	1.49	39.55
Public works	—	190.30	4.87	195.17
Training for development	2.28	—	—	2.28
Other unclassified services	4.00	281.25	9.59	294.84
Total (1 to 11)	47,250.00	48,600.00	1,650.00	97,500.00

Source: Planning Commission, *Sixth Five Year Plan*: *1980-85*, New Delhi, March 1981, pp. 57-58.

for inputs from outside, it can have an impact on production in the unorganised sector also. But the most important infrastructure, irrigation and power are mostly in the state sector, and the state administration which can be used to bring relevant information and knowledge and influence and guide the public, has to reach much lower down.

Experience has revealed a major defect of macro-level planning. Because of the heavy costs of obtaining detailed information, it pays little regard to the spatial aspect, and as a result the specific inter-departmental localitywise linkages tend to be ignored. All-India norms and an all-India pattern of staffing are laid down which do not suit the vast diversities in the country. As a result, we often have instances of wells being subsidised in tracts where there is no adequate discharge of underground water, electric pumps being encouraged in places where there are no certain prospects of electric power supply, and land under irrigation being worked uniformly at so many acres per well irrespective of its contour or the nature of its soil. In his address to the Regional Workshop on District Planning at Gandhinagar, Shri Sanat Mehta, Minister for Planning, Government of Gujarat, referred to a UNICEF scheme for nutrition programme for children, in which vegetables were to be grown in an area which had no water for irrigation.[3] The costs of a countrywide or statewide programme are sometimes similarly estimated on a uniform basis and need substantial revisions before implementation. This may explain much of the gap between physical and financial planning, which can be filled by micro-level planning. Macro-level planning has to be content as far as the unorganised sector is concerned with building up facilities for credit, marketing, input supplies, etc. A large number of technically feasible and economically sound and productive schemes are promised credit and other facilities, and listed for adoption. But skill-training, extension works, and all further planning can only proceed on more specific decisions regarding which industries or trades are suitable for an area of resident families. The anti-poverty programmes have to be area and community specific in order that their benefits may be widespread. Otherwise, the tendency would be to select the easily accessible areas and groups. The numerical targets may, thus, be attained but the basic purpose of the programme is partially defeated. The studies conducted by the National Committee on the Development of Backward Areas revealed that even in sheep and goat acquisition programme, which unlike dairying does not require good transport connections, remote areas were neglected,[4] though sheep units need adequate grazing land which is often not found near well-linked roadside villages. Abuses, leakages and other transaction costs abound in the operation of bank credit schemes. It has been estimated that of the subsidies given to the poor in loan-cum-subsidy schemes, 50-75 per cent are spent in getting them. To incur these preliminary expenses, high interest personal loans have to be resorted to. A review of the Food for Work Programme in Tamil Nadu revealed that the amount of employment for the rural poor that it generated was rather small in relation to the estimated need because of very small food quantities being released for the creation of suitable assets, irregularity in supply, poor quality and bad timing. "The programme was not successful in the achievement of any of its objectives."[5] The coordination between beneficiary-oriented schemes with area development measures at the local level was found to be very ineffective.[6] These defects could be more easily detected and corrected if there were efficient local authorities in charge of micro-level planning and monitoring.

Evaluation studies have revealed that just as production facilities are not fully availed of, social service facilities are also poorly utilised. Minimum needs provision is being made on a large scale in the states, but many powerful socio-economic obstacles, their extent and prevalence varying with local milieu, prevent their utilisation.[7] A primary school may be provided practically in every village; to ensure regular teaching facilities, more than one teacher may be appointed, but a number of children of school-going age may not join it. What is more common, having entered it they may not attend regularly and there may be drop-outs. Only one-third of the school-joining children, on an average, go to Standard V. The percentage varies mainly with the economic conditions of families but also with sex, community and culture. Detailed on-the-spot investigation of the working of adult classes has revealed that the experience is much worse there. Even when pure drinking water is available within one kilometre of the residence, some people continue to use the old impure source because of ignorance or inertia. Often the pumps are out of repair. Health facilities available at a primary health centre are availed of only within a short distance. In an article in the *Gujarat Economy: Problems and Prospects*, (Ahmedabad, 1983) Dr. S.M. Shah reports the disappointing results of an ICDS survey carried out at Chotta

Udaipur.[8] When it comes to the extremely delicate subject of family planning, the responses vary more widely. Micro-level planning can aim at basing its strategy and programmes on a careful marshalling of all available evidence, a study of the constraints limiting progress in desired directions, and the steps needed to remove these constraints.

Slowly but surely, the need for micro-planning as an instrument of macro-planning has been recognised. The Planning Commission Working Group on District Planning noted that only two of the states had some hesitation in 1982 on their preparedness for decentralised planning and later on even they revised their stand.[9] It is no longer true that there is a dichotomy between micro-planning which stands for social justice and macro-planning which emphasises growth.[10] As the National Committee on Backward Areas clarified, the former is not only selective development aiming at certain target groups but comprehensive area development with special concern for the weaker sectors. Programmes like water control, land shaping conservation of land, pest control, social services, have to be carried out on an area basis.[11] These, however, will be worked discriminatingly in favour of the poor and tied up with their needs so that they can take full advantage of them. All efforts including special programmes will be made to remove their disabilities.

II

Because of the imperatives of the Indian Constitution, state planning had to be an inherent part of national planning. There is, therefore, a long experience of how central-state planning can work in unison, the problems that arise, the mechanisms that can be evolved to tackle them and how far they can work. In the history of well-established federations, centre-state conflicts are not unknown. The most acute arise from the widely divergent interests of different states and the failure to evolve a consensus of codes, rules and regulations by which all will abide irrespective of the temporary inconveniences they may be put to or the sacrifices they may be called upon to make. The American Civil War is an extreme instance of the dangers to be guarded against. The Indian planners believe in a mixed economy, in the large-scale coexistence of the private and public sectors in a judicious mixture of the market mechanism with controls. The philosophy of abiding by market discipline, which makes some of the inter-state conflicts of interests more easily manageable, does not command allegiance. High protective tariffs, quantitative import controls, export duties and controls to regulate domestic supplies and prices, export subsidies, inter-state movement controls to ensure equitable distribution, production control regulatory taxes to encourage production of certain commodities and adoption of certain techniques, etc., raise sharp questions of the application of equity in matters which would almost automatically be resolved in free market economies. Each of the above steps may harm one state more than another. For instance, in times of food scarcity, movement control to ensure procurement by the Food Corporation of India is resented by the food-surplus states, but for the deficit states it is a welcome step as it augments their scarce food stocks. Free inter-state movement of commodities like groundnut oil is disliked in a groundnut oil-surplus state but appreciated by regions which do not cultivate groundnut on a wide scale. States interested in powerlooms or textile mills do not approve of various measures to protect the handloom industry. The adoption of industrial licensing has raised controversies regarding industrial location policy. Compared to the possible areas of centre-state conflict, the actual differences in the field of planning have been hitherto limited and mainly financial. The acute centre-state relations controversies have not been in the economic field as much as they have been in the political field regarding the discretionary powers of the Governor, the use of the Central Reserve Police Force, the control of All India Radio and Doordarshan. The differences seem to have mainly originated not in inter-state conflicts but in centre-state conflicts.

The relative success in avoiding sharp centre-state conflicts in planning can be attributed to the clear demarcation of powers and functions between the two, the sharing of a common ideology of planning by both, the existence of an all-India administrative service cadre liable to be transferred between the centre and the parent state, and the mechanisms that have been built to clear misunderstanding and suspicions. The powers of both the Union and the state governments are clearly defined. There is a Union list of 97 items, a state list of 66 items and a third concurrent list of 47 items where both can make laws, but in case of any inconsistency the Central legislation will prevail. The lists are fairly comprehensive, but to remove any ambiguity, Article 248 lays down that Parliament will have the power to legislate regarding residuary items. The list of items on which the state has the power to make laws is, as we have already seen, formidable, but there are provisions and wide exceptions which have been liberally used. Not only industries declared by law to be necessary for purpose of defence or for the prosecution of war, but also industries the control of which is declared by Parliament to be expedient in public interest are in the Union list. A similar provision is repeated for regulation of mines and mineral development. Commercial and industrial policy, production, supply and distribution of foodstuffs, price control, trade unions, industrial and labour disputes, employment and unemployment and above all economic and social planning are placed in the concurrent list. With such a comprehensively defined division of powers providing for a large degree of flexibility fully availed of by Parliament and the Central executive, the need for changes would be small. Normally amendments would be difficult as they would require to be passed in each house by a majority of total membership of that house and by not less than two-thirds of the members of that house present and voting, and also require to be ratified by the legislatures of more than one-half of the states. Article 249, however, empowers Parliament to make laws with respect to any matter in the state list, if the Council of States by a two-thirds majority of the members present and voting declares by a resolution that it is necessary or expedient in public interest to make laws in that matter. This extraordinary bias in favour of the flexibility of Union powers can be ascribed to three main factors: the crucible of partition and the aftermath which the country passed through, the experience of wartime controls and the needs of planning as visualised at that time.

A clear demarcation of powers between the Union government and the states could only settle questions of jurisdiction in legislative matters. By itself it cannot assure that a well-conceived plan of Indian economic development is formulated and smoothy implemented. This was achieved through the evolution of four major devices: the National Development Council, the Planning Commission, plan assistance, and several autonomous economic institutions like the Reserve Bank of India aimed at settling controversies regarding detailed application of economic policies in a non-political atmosphere. The one major untried mechanism is the inter-state council provided in Article 263 of the Constitution. The National Development Council (NDC) presided over by the Prime Minister of India has among its members the Deputy Chairman of the Planning Commission, the Minister for Planning, Members of the Planning Commission and Chief Ministers of States. Important Central Ministers, whose presence and advice would be useful in discussions, and State Planning Ministers are invited to the meeting. It provides the highest forum for discussions of and decisions on problems of planning. The Draft Five Year Plan is placed before it for detailed discussion. If it is approved, it becomes a nationally accepted plan. Generally speaking, discussion of an Approach Paper placed before the NDC precedes the formulation of the plan which takes account of the discussions, and there is, therefore, no difficulty in the general acceptance of the Plan. The individual States' Five-Year Plans are formulated by the Planning Departments of the States and finalised in one or more rounds of discussion with the Planning Commission. Generally, the discussions are conducted in an understanding atmosphere and there is satisfaction of a job well done at the end. The plan as it emerges is a public sector plan with targets for the private sector hoped to be achieved through input facilities, incentives, technical aid, extension and demonstration, and monetary, fiscal and detailed control policies. It has been the aim of the Union and state governments to set up in these matters corporations and semi-autonomous organisations which will operate freely within the guidelines and subject to directives which may be given in writing by the ministry.

It is recognised that a state is a better judge of its economic potential and of the needs of its people, but it has freedom to operate only within the constraints of national resources. It has also to pay due regard to the basic national objectives and needs. These have been agreed to at the NDC meeting and are well understood. The Planning Commission as a body of technical experts can take an expert view of the Centre's plan needs. There is no parallel body at the state level, and sometimes political considerations or views of the more powerful departments get the upper hand, but with its prestige and competence, the Planning Commission is able to convince the state about the need for correction. The more difficult task for the Planning Commission is to convince a state that its allocation between the needs of Central versus state planning is well-founded. This task has hitherto not been difficult because the states have recognised in the Planning Commission a friend whom they can trust to deal fairly by them. More recently, however, some states have demanded that the Planning Commission should be made responsible to the NDC.

It is well recognised that the states have to frame their plans within their plan resources. The Constitution clearly demarcates between the Union and state sources of revenue and while everybody is agreed that the latter are ill-matched with their functions and needs, there are few worthwhile suggestions for transfer of tax powers from the Centre to the states. It fact, the increasing economic integration of the country makes that highly unprofitable, so that there are quite a few suggestions like centralisation of agricultural income tax and measures like levying of additional excise duties in lieu of sales tax in the other direction. There has, therefore, to be a systematically vertical transfer of tax revenues from the Union government to the states. The Finance Commissions appointed every five years or less examine the needs of the Centre and the states and decide on the quantum of transfer mainly through sharing of income tax and central excises and Article 275 grants to weaker states. Successive Finance Commissions have made efforts to ensure that: (a) large sums representing roughly the same proportions of Central tax revenue are transferred to the states, (b) more of these accrue through tax-sharing rather than grants, and (c) the transfers are made more progressive. However, since the grants are given mainly for meeting non-plan needs, the grant recipients will have little surplus from the prevalent tax levels and service charges left for the plan. On the other hand, the states which have a surplus on non-plan revenue account even before tax devolution will have large surpluses on non-plan revenue account because of the Finance Commission's policy of relying on tax-sharing rather than grants. It is gratifying to note that even non-plan capital gap of the states is referred to the Finance Commissions from the Sixth Plan onwards and their recommendations for writing off of a part of debt and rescheduling of debt are more or less faithfully implemented.[12]

Once the Finance Commission has completed its work the Planning Commission takes over and, on the basis of its calculations of revenue surpluses on non-plan account (modified in the light of its needs and new development), and its own estimates of possible new resource mobilisation through additional taxation and new capital receipts (including foreign borrowings) arrive, at the funds that can be made available for planning. In formulating its resource-based Plan, the Planning Commission attempts at distributing this between the Centre and the states on the basis of optimum national welfare, and thus arrives at the size of their plans. The difference between the Central plan size and the resources it can spare for planning gives the measure of plan assistance to the states. This should ideally be distributed among the States on the basis of the gap between their assessed plan needs and their assessed resources. This was attempted till the Third Plan but several difficulties were experienced. The idea of encouraging states to formulate plans on the basis of their needs without any resource constraint could not be continued for long. It led to exaggerated expectations of Central plan assistance, and the Planning Commission had to ruthlessly cut down the size of the plan to an extent where the original exercise proved counterproductive. Self-reliance was soon discounted and a detailed schematic pattern of assistance was evolved which put the states in a strait-jacket[13] and culminated in the weaker states getting more of their plan assistance through loans and less through grants. The Planning Commission was under great pressure to evolve a system of assistance which was less discretionary, and it gave more freedom to the states to formulate their plans in their own way. After detailed discussion, the Gadgil formula of plan assistance was adopted. While the special category states were given liberal plan assistance on the basis of the desired plan size for them, and some money was set apart for hill areas, tribal areas and NEDC, the other states were given share of plan assistance based on the weightage of population (60 per cent), deviation of state's per capita income from the average all-India income (10 per cent), per capita tax burden as percentage of state income (10 per cent), continuing plan expenditure on irrigation and power (10 per cent), and special problems (10 per cent). This formula has worked well and has been revised only in two major aspects. When it was decided at the NDC meeting in 1979 to reduce the plan expenditure on central and centrally-sponsored schemes and pass on the savings to the states in the form of general plan assistance, it was agreed that this should be distributed according to the IATP (Income Adjusted Total Population, i.e. reverse of per capita income × population). In order to provide a special incentive to the states to prepare schemes for international aid, 70 per cent of the external finance of projects sanctioned for them is being given to them as additional central assistance. For the Sixth Plan, 20 per cent instead of 10 per cent of plan assistance was set apart for the poorer states, and the sum set apart for continuing works was withdrawn as it could lead to greater time lags in implementation of major power and irrigation schemes. A convention has also grown that aid for special problems will only be given to poorer states.

While the formula of plan assistance continues to be subject to vigorous criticism, mainly on the grounds of not being progressive enough to take care of the inability of poor states to raise adequate plan resources on their own (Table 3) and not taking adequate care of the spatial aspects of planning, its acceptance at the National Development Council meeting makes negotiations between the Planning Commission and the individual states much easier. Every major state knows that its plan size will be limited by the resources it can harness and central plan assistance, and the latter is hardly negotiable. It has, therefore, to plan within these financial contours. Plan assistance is subject to the approval of the plan by the Planning Commission which has to ensure that the guidelines are observed, that national plan targets will be fulfilled, that proper provision is made for core plan items, and that the state makes adequate efforts to mobilise resources for its plan. While the assistance is only tied for a few important plan items, a shortfall in the approved plan may invite the penalty of a proportionate cut in plan assistance. State plan schemes in irrigation, power and agriculture costing more than Rs. 5 crores need the technical approval of the Central

Table 3: Plan Assistance and Plan Outlays*

	Average: 1981-84		Col. 1 as % of col. 2	Per capita transfer under Seventh Finance Commission (Rs.)	Average per capita: 1981-84		
	Plan assistance (Rs. crores)	Plan outlay (Rs. crores)			Plan assis-tance (Rs.)	Plan out-lay (Rs.)	Per capita income in 1981-82 (Rs.)
*Major states**							
Punjab	66	389	17	250	39	232	3,164
Haryana	52	334	16	239	40	259	2,581
Maharashtra	200	1,326	15	273	32	224	2,496
Gujarat	121	765	16	283	35	224	2,192
West Bengal	171	503	34	293	31	92	1,595
Karnataka	113	517	22	271	30	139	1,541
Andhra Pradesh	193	602	31	285	36	116	1,536
Kerala	100	300	33	302	39	118	1,447
Rajasthan	140	361	39	263	41	105	1,441
Assam	236	242	98	261	119	122	1,380
Tamil Nadu	141	727	19	311	29	150	1,373
Uttar Pradesh	427	1,179	36	299	39	106	1,313

Orissa	147	307	48	373	56	116	1,308
Madhya Pradesh	215	756	28	306	41	145	1,241
Bihar	279	582	48	317	40	83	995
Other states							
Himachal Pradesh	89	129	69	756	207	300	1,773
Jammu & Kashmir	205	179	115	628	342	298	1,630
Meghalaya	50	49	102	1,032	385	377	1,236
Manipur	58	47	123	1,386	414	336	1,045
Tripura	51	54	94	952	243	257	—
Nagaland	57	44	130	3,007	713	550	—
Sikkim	26	26	100	1,228	867	867	—
All States	3,138	9,436	33	309	46	140	1,758**

*Ranked by last column
**All-India

Water Commission, the Electricity Authority and the Indian Council of Agricultural Research respectively, and those between Rs. 1 and 5 crores are scrutinised by them on a *pro forma* basis.

The Planning Commission has one more form of assistance which involves more detailed supervision, and has, therefore, been subject to greater criticism. There are subjects lying entirely within the state sphere where national interests demand that a certain course of action should be uniformly followed throughout the country. States or their people left to themselves because of their particular situation or limited vision may not attach the same priority to this, but some financial inducements may do the trick. Conditional grants are a recognised method of achieving this objective. In India family planning, prevention of spread of infectious diseases, inter-state transmission of power lines, encouragement of cultivation of scarce food items like pulses and oilseeds, special areas of anti-poverty programme like DPAP, IRDP, CADA, ITDP, SFDA, MFAL, NREP, etc. have been recognised as being in this category. The two questions that have arisen and not been satisfactorily solved are: the types of conditions and the degree of supervision involved, and the coverage of conditional assistance. The general complaint has been that while the essential conditions should pertain to successful performance, unnecessary detailed conditions like staff pattern, pay scales, etc. are imposed. A National Development Council meeting in 1969 resolved that central and centrally sponsored schemes should be limited to one-sixth to one-seventh of plan assistance for the states. When it was found that the 1978-83 Draft Plan provided for a much larger share of centrally-sponsored schemes, it became subject to severe criticism at the NDC meeting, and it was decided to severely curtail the number of centrally-sponsored schemes. The 1980-85 plan once again witnessed a big increase in the importance of these schemes which now account for more than 40 per cent of the plan assistance to states. It seems that the debate was mainly utilised by the states to get more general plan assistance, and once this was settled, they did not seriously mind an increase in the scope of centrally-sponsored schemes.[14]

Besides the setting up of specific institutions where Union-state differences on planning could be resolved and a common policy evolved, there are some general climatic factors which largely explain the smooth working of centre-state planning. The chief objectives of plans have commanded a large degree of consensus. This has been helped by the predominant position of one party in the centre and the states, but even the opposition parties have not had widely different objectives for the nation. Many of the policy differences between the Centre and the states are recognised as inter-state differences, for their reconciliation of which the Centre obtains the cooperation and active help of most of the states. While the other states recognise this reality, they realise the wisdom of abiding by this arrangement in their own long-term interests.

III

The question of planning at the local level is entirely different. In the first place, the entity of local bodies is not recognised in the Indian Constitution and so their powers and functions receive no mention. Local government is included in the state list of legislations and it is for the states to pass legislation defining their scope and authority. An article of the Directive Principles of State Policy lays down that the state shall take such steps to organise village panchayats and endow them with such power and authority as may enable them to function as units of self-government. Not being enforceable in a court, this provision has no teeth and has not been enforced. Thanks to the recommendations of the Balvantrai Mehta Study Team and the Asoka Mehta Committee, local bodies have been established almost everywhere but their functions and powers vary widely from state to state. The functions and moreso the finances are limited. The inadequate tax sources remain unexplored so that whenever efforts are made to get planning works done through them, they have to be liberally financed from above. Local bodies are the creature of state legislation and can be superseded at its discretion. While decentralised planning has been talked of for a long time and the first guidelines for the formulation of district planning were laid down in as early as 1969, the activity has remained a "non-starter".[15] The topic can, therefore, be discussed only with meagre experience and hypothetically.

As in the case of states, the first prerequisite for the working of decentralised planning would be a clear demarcation of functions at the local, let us say, district level. In planning terminology, a district can only plan and operate district-level schemes defined as those which have no inter-district implications. This definition is helpful but a rigorous application of it is not possible. Many of the engineering departments have functional jurisdiction spilling beyond a district and their exclusion from district planning would leave little for it to do.[16] Some overlapping and revisions are, therefore, to be expected. In Maharashtra up to 1976-77 major irrigation and package schemes of incentives for industries were classed as district level schemes. Subjectwise, agriculture, forestry, horticulture, fishery minor irrigation, district roads, primary and secondary education, adult education, primary health and drinking water would be proper spheres of district planning, but in most cases the state would also be spending on them. For instance, in Gujarat State for 1980-83, 80 per cent of the plan expenditure on agriculture and allied activities, 75 per cent of that on road development, 60 per cent of that on village and small industries, 40 per cent of social service expenditure and 36 per cent of irrigation expense were incurred through districts (Table 4).[17] This gives a broad idea of the departmental interdependencies between the state government and the districts.

The next need is the demarcation of finances. According to the detailed division of work, the state government (planning department) works out the optimum distribution of plan expenditure between the state and the districts as a whole. The percentage of plan expenditure thus worked out would vary from state to state depending on the importance attached by the planners to district level versus state level schemes. In states like Punjab and Haryana, where power and major and medium irrigation would claim a very large share of plan funds, less would be left for district level schemes. An exercise in Uttar Pradesh arrived at 70 per cent of the state plan allocation as being necessitated by state level schemes, leaving 30 per cen for district planning. Gujarat and Maharashtra, with greate per capita plan expenditure and a tradition of local self-government, spare more of their plan funds—35 to 40 per cent for this purpose. Even there, however, no effort is made to sound local

Table 4: Average Percentage Share of Outlays for District Level Schemes out of Total Outlays Provided in State Annual Plan for Different Sectors during 1980-81 to 1982-83

Sector/Sub-sector of development	Average percentage of outlay for district level schemes to total outlay for sector/ sub-sector
1	2
1. *Agriculture and Allied Services*	80.1
Agricultural research and education	—
Crop husbandry	44.4
Land reforms	97.2
Minor irrigation	98.3
Soil and water conservation	76.9
Command area development	67.1
Animal husbandry	53.1
Dairy development	55.7
Fisheries	85.5
Forests	86.3
Investment in agricultural finance institutions	—
Marketing, storage and warehousing	63.9
Community development and panchayats	88.5
Development of backward areas	100.0
Special programme for rural development:	
National rural employment programme	99.0
Integrated rural development programme	97.6
Drought prone area programme (with D.D.P.)	102.7
Antyodaya	100.0
Strengthening and supporting special programme organisation	100.0
Local development works programme	100.0
Abhinav gram nirman karyakram	100.0
Off-season unemployment relief works	100.0
Block level planning	92.4

Table 4 (*Contd.*)

1	2
2. *Cooperation*	44.7
3. *Water Development (Irrigation)*	35.7
4. *Power Development*	7.3
5. *Industries and Minerals*	34.7
Village and small-scale industries	59.7
Large and medium industries	1.8
Mining	—
6. *Transport and Communication*	55.0
Ports, lighthouses and shipping	—
Roads and bridges	75.5
Road transport	—
Tourism	—
7. *Social and Community Services*	40.2
General education	53.4
Technical education	—
Science and technology	—
Medical, public health and sanitation	28.2
Social inputs	100.0
Sewerage and water supply	37.4
Housing	30.8
Urban development	9.4
Capital project	—
Information and publicity	95.1
Labour and labour welfare	90.0
Welfare of backward classes	54.1
Social welfare	1.4
Nutrition	104.7
8. *Economic Services*	32.2
Secretariat Economic Services (Planning Machinery)	—
Economic Advice & Statistics	20.0
Training of development personnel	—
Administrative machinery for TASP	104.8
Civil supplies corporation and consumer movement	—
Total (1 to 8)	37.0
9. *De-centralised District Planning*	98.3
Grand Total	40.0

Source: *Report of the Working Group on District Level Planning*, Vol. II, pp. 33-35.

opinion on the entire district level expenditure. A part of the sum allocated for district planning is kept at the state level. In the 1983-84 Maharashtra budget, of the total plan expenditure of Rs. 1,500 crores, Rs. 646 crores were allocated for district planning; of this Rs. 191 crores (nearly 30 per cent) were earmarked for the state pool of district level schemes. In Gujarat, in order to provide latitude to the departmental heads, the ceilings indicated to the District Planning Boards are lower than those likely to be provided in the State Annual Plan. In 1983-84, these were Rs. 240 crores and Rs. 316 crores respectively—a difference of 24 per cent.[18] It may be noted that 30 per cent of the excess sum spent on a district from the state pool of district level schemes in Maharashtra is adjusted next year against its regular allocations. The total district plan outlay is distributed among the districts largely on the basis of population and various indicators of economic backwardness. Since unlike the States none of the districts is in a position to spend much from its own resources,[19] this ensures that plan expenditure will be progressive among the districts and will in due course ensure that insofar as difference in public expenditure is the cause of economic backwardness, it will be removed. Hitherto public expenditure has operated in the reverse gear, less per capita being spent in backward areas.

The unsatisfactory part of district planning is that even when it is most developed, as in Gujarat and Maharashtra, it is more of planning for the districts by the departments at the state level than by or of the districts. In the first instance, the sectoral allocations for the districts were made by the department at the state level, and inter-sectoral changes were difficult at the district level. This made it impossible for district planning to take adequate care of inter-sectoral linkages and activity sequencing. The "district level schemes" were a misnomer, because they were prepared at the state level without taking into account the specific needs and circumstances of the districts. As they were technically approved, choice from among them (522 in Gujarat in 1981) was appealing and convenient. Even a slight departure would necessitate a fresh technical appraisal and imply the risk of inviting a large number of objections[20] and consequent botheration and delay. The district officials were, therefore, loath to think of new schemes, and regarded themselves as free only to choose a package from among the sanctioned schemes and decide their location. District planning, thus, became a programming exercise.

The entire process of district planning is not done at the state level. A large District Planning Board (or District Planning Development Council in Maharashtra) with the Minister as the Chairman, the Collector and President of the District Panchayat as Vice-Chairman (in Maharashtra, Collector as Secretary), and several elected representatives of the people discuss, approve and review the plan, and a smaller executive planning committee meets every month for more detailed discussions. But these get poor technical assistance. To help the Collector and the Member Secretary of the Planning Development Council in Maharashtra, there is the official apparatus of a District Planning Officer helped by two research assistants, and two clerks to piece together the planning schemes of various departments at the district level. Gujarat had a somewhat bigger and better staff. The District Planning Board was till recently provided in addition to a District Planning Officer with a research officer, two research assistants, three statistical Assistants and a deputy mamlatdar. It is unlikely that they could do anything more than an arithmetical exercise. The plan, as it emerged, was more likely the result of pressure and negotiations rather than a reasoned view of the means needed for achieving the plan goals and an analysis of the inter-departmental linkages. The monitoring was ritualistic. It was provided that before making changes in the district plan at the state level, these would be discussed with the district authorities. On the ground that the timetable of finalisation of the state plan with the Planning Commission does not leave enough time for such discussion with the district plan authorities, no such discussion has been carried on till 1983-84 both in Gujarat and Maharashtra. To ensure agreed consensus, in Gujarat, the Minister who presides over the District Planning Board has the final say.[21] Shri Sundararajan and Dr. K.V. Sundram sum up the role of the District Planning Board in Gujarat as being at best "marginal", there being no vigorous consultation or relay of information between district level officials and State controlling officials, and all traffic being one-way.[22]

Some encouraging signs in decentralisation experiments in

Gujarat and Maharashtra may be noted. The former has made a far-reaching experiment on a limited scale in decentralisation by laying down that 15 per cent of the district plan expenditure will be at the entire discretion of the district authorities and 5 per cent will be by way of incentives to be released, on the condition that half or quarter of this, depending on whether the district (now the taluka) is advanced or backward, is raised by the district. At least 67 per cent and hopefully 75 per cent of the discretionary amount will be distributed among the talukas on the basis of a formula and will be spent in consultation with the taluka representatives. The remaining amount can be spent on schemes having an impact on more than one taluka or other important district schemes. It is interesting to note that the districts have enthusiastically responded to the incentive scheme and raised most of the money needed to earn incentive money. The pattern of discretionary spending has been different from that of the other district plan expenditure (Table 5).[23] Almost

Table 5: Average Sectoral Distribution of the Outlay for Normal District Level Schemes and Percentage Distribution of Allocation made by 18 District Planning Boards Out of Decentralised District Planning Funds Given to Them : 1980-81 and 1981-82

Sector/Sub-sector	Average distribution of outlay for normal district level schemes during 1980-82	Distribution of allocation made by 18 districts in 1980-82 from discretionary and incentive outlay
1	2	3
1. *Agriculture and Allied Services*	34.5	20.3
Agricultural research and education	—	—
Crop husbandry	4.0	2.2
Land reforms	0.9	—
Minor irrigation	7.4	9.2
Soil and water conservation	1.6	0.1

Table 5 (*Contd.*)

1	2	3
Command area development	0.5	—
Animal husbandry	0.7	2.4
Dairy development	0.1	0.1
Fisheries	1.5	0.3
Forests	6.5	0.2
Investment in agricultural financial institutions	—	—
Marketing, storage and warehousing	0.1	0.1
Community development and panchayats	0.7	4.7
Development of backward areas	0.3	—
Special programme for rural development		
National rural employment programme	0.7	—
Integrated rural development programme	2.7	—
Drought prone area programme (with D.D.P.)	1.8	—
Antyodaya	0.3	—
Strengthening and supporting special programme organisation	0.1	—
Local development works programme	1.0	1.0
Abhinav gram nirman karyakram	1.8	—
Off-season unemployment relief works	0.4	—
Block level planning	1.2	—
2. *Cooperation*	1.5	0.6
3. *Water Development* (*Irrigation*)	22.8	—
4. *Power Development*	5.2	7.7
5. *Industries and Minerals*	5.2	1.0
Village and small-scale industries	5.1	1.0
Large and medium industries	0.1	—
Mining	—	—
6. *Transport and Communication*	13.7	30.1
Ports lighthouses and shipping	—	—
Roads and bridges	13.7	30.1
Road transport	—	—
Tourism	—	—

7. *Social and Community Services*	17.2	37.6
General education	2.3	14.4
Technical education	—	—
Science and technology	—	—
Medical, public health and sanitation	1.3	7.2
Social inputs	0.2	—
Sewerage and water supply	3.5	10.7
Housing	2.6	1.3
Urban development	0.2	1.5
Capital project	—	—
Information and publicity	0.1	—
Labour and labour welfare	1.8	0.1
Welfare of backward classes	4.4	0.8
Social welfare	—	1.2
Nutrition	0.8	0.4
8. *Economic Services*	0.1	2.7
Secretariat economic services (Planning machinery)	—	—
Economic advice and statistics	—	—
Training of development personnel	—	—
Administrative machinery for TASP	0.1	—
Civil supplies corporation and consumer movement	—	—
Others	—	2.7
Grand Total	100.0	100.0

Note: Percentages for Minimum Needs Programme and other than Minimum Needs Programme have been merged in respect of these sub-sectors of development.

Source: *Report of the Working Group on District Level Planning*, Vol. II, pp. 40-42.

two-thirds of it has been spent on "minimum needs". The missing links have also been provided. It cannot be said whether the different pattern of discretionary spendings arises from a feeling that the other equally pressing or more pressing needs have already been provided, or there are different priorities which would influence other spendings if they were left with the district authorities, but it does provide a release mechanism from the uniformity of a state authority finally deciding district priorities.[24]

In Maharashtra, after the district annual plan is approved, the District Planning Development Council can ask for reallocation and reappropriate from one department to another. State approval is easily given (90 per cent of cases). The departments concerned have to carry out the necessary revision in their budgets. This curtails their powers of reappropriation within the departmental budget. For the districts, however, it is a freedom from severe restraints of departmentwise allocations. The District Planning Development Councils will be asked to carry out exercises allocating districtwise plan expenditure among District Level Schemes, Reserved Allocation for Block Level Schemes, and Block Level Schemes in the proportion of 25 : 10 : 65, the last being distributed among blocks on the basis of population and area.[25] The block-funds will be non-transferable. Block level planning will, thus, be introduced in Maharashtra on a full scale.

IV

Serious problems of inconsistency between planning at the state and local levels have hardly arisen because there has been no district planning. District planning has been by the state government. Consistency has to be judged with respect to a purpose, and if the purpose is not achieved, mere mechanical consistency has no virtue. Consistency has, therefore, to be examined from first principles. Even like state planning, local planning has to accept certain basic limitations. It must work within central guidelines and those of the State Planning Department as well as other technical departments. The district plans must be approved by the state government before they become operative. But that is no reason why changes should be made in the district plans as approved by the District Planning Board without discusssing them with the Board. Multi-level planning implies a process of reiteration, of repeated discussions and dialogues,[26] and the fact that the time table of discussions with the Planning Commission leaves no time for this procedure is no adequate ground for suspending this essential element of decentralised planning. It gives both sides an opportunity to understand and appreciate each other's viewpoint, may enable reconciliation of differences on the spot, and lead to agreements regarding further data gathering and studies for future resolution of conflicting viewpoints. The need for getting local plans approved by the state and the almost 100 per cent financing by the state give it a powerful handle for making its judgement prevail in the final instance, but it must be sparingly and skillfully utilised as the last resort. Schemes on the basis of conditional grants to achieve specific aims, which it is feared the local bodies would not be equally enthusiastic about or to which they would not attach the same priority, cannot be ruled out, but they do raise serious doubts about the extent of local autonomy. The latter demands that in the functions attached to them, the level at which these should be performed within the constraint of financial resources should be decided by the local bodies themselves. While national and state planning demand that the autonomy principle should be modified through the guidelines and the general approval of the plan by the higher level authority—a sort of "cooperative federalism", the further modification by way of special programmes to be implemented through specially set agencies should be confined to the minimum. The conditions should only be those essential for the attainment of the goals. Planning within the limited spheres of local bodies should be with a single authority. Bodies like the District Manpower and Employment Generation Council should not be independent, but a part of the planning machinery. If the major function of a planning body is to closely examine inter-departmental relationships and linkages, all plan activities should be within its jurisdiction. It should be its duty to chalk out a plan strategy, to determine the tasks to be done within a given time frame, and to allot the jobs among various departments and agencies. It may derive its funds from more than one agency, and the funding agencies will define the tasks they want performed. But all the planning activities must be vested into an overall district planning framework. This alone can avoid the tendency to fragmented decision-making which can obstruct the planning progress. The administering departments and agencies will have the freedom to formulate individual plan schemes in technical and financial detail and to frame their own rules and the procedures to perform best the assigned tasks, but the annual plan review will examine their success and in case of marked shortfalls ask for remedial measures. It will also provide for ex post facto coordination of plan activities where called for.

Observance of the logic of decentralised planning only ensures that if the initial conditions and set up are favourable the aims will be achieved. The goal of decentralised planning may be defined as the full utilisation of local resources, including local manpower, for satisfying local needs. A district profile will, therefore, have to be prepared based on needs and potentialities. The Indian masses need, in general, food, clothing and shelter, but the specific consumption needs will differ according to climate, income, habits etc. To the extent their satisfaction is not to be dependent on imports from other localities, they will have to adjust to the types of crops that can be locally grown and the raw materials available. Local tastes and choices are important in planning for appropriate employment but it may be found that there is scanty demand for local easily available labour or local skills. However, there may be good opportunities coming up in other spheres.[27] Most of the local areas have a potential for growth if certain measures are taken. These have to be identified. For instance, somewhere within the district a major/medium irrigation or power scheme or a large industry may be coming up and will create new employment demand. Export-based growth may offer rich promises. In these cases, there is need for arranging a marriage between the two. Even in the very difficult case of drought-prone districts, the National Committee on Development of Backward Areas notes the availability of a large number of technological innovations with research stations for increasing their productivity. Only the appropriate technology for each specific watershed has to be transferred to the inhabitants of the locality.[28] An appropriate pattern of settlements and development foci must be devised so that growth impulses are quickly transmitted and get reinforced.

Purposive action is data based, and in the three decades of planning, notable efforts have been made to collect useful data. The decennial Population Census, the quinquennial Livestock and Agricultural Machinery Census, the Annual Survey of

Large-scale Industries, and the Economic Census more recently carried out are based on universal or wide coverage, and, therefore, can yield reliable and useful district-level data if quick tabulation can be arranged. There are ambitious national and state level Sample Surveys which are so devised as to yield reliable regionwise results but the district estimates derived from them are not trustworthy. It should be earnestly examined if it is worthwhile redesigning some of them so as to yield districtwise information. The available district data are widely scattered; they should be available at one place. Some of the information needed like employment, unemployment, contemplated new employment, or self-employment activities, and the preparedness to undergo training and acquire skills with reference to local possibilities have to be gathered from all village families—a sort of labour survey. It is surprising that in spite of the great importance of agriculture and allied activities, not much effort has been devoted to gathering data on vegetables, fruits, dairy, fishery, etc. Agencies to encourage cottage and rural industries have worked for quite some time and they must have valuable data on raw materials, marketing and employment of the industries they cover, but these have not been collected on a district basis. Data on district income and its sectoral breakdown and regional inflows and outflows of goods and services must be built up.

In the course of their limited experiments with decentralised planning, some of the States have taken some strides and even adopted novel devices. In its initial efforts, Maharashtra covered fairly ambitious technical resource survey of districts in major fields of primary production, collected districtwise development data and prepared an indicative framework of the proposed perspective for district development. Andhra Pradesh experimented with aerial photos and remote-sensing techniques and Gujarat has collected detailed information regarding village amenities which it has computerised.

The guidelines for district plans prepared in 1969 emphasised the need for drawing upon all available sources of information besides statistical and administrative data. If persons administering schemes set their minds to examining the success of the schemes, the constraints they operate under, and ways and means to overcome them, they could contribute a great deal to plan formulation. Apart from public sector production which does not occupy an important role in district planning, the components of the Indian Plan are the economic and social infrastructure and facilities which will provide productive opportunities for private investment and make possible increased production in the private sector. The final success of planning depends, therefore, on the responses of farmers and entrepreneurs. Their experience and knowledge may greatly help in incorporating a proper set of plan inputs. The interests of the unorganised poor who normally go unrepresented, will have to be specially taken care of.

The composition of the planning team is another matter which needs to be looked into. The team must have enough competence, expertise and perspective to take a view of the district economy, the way it should be directed and regulated in the course of 15-20 years to realise its potential, and the definite steps that should be taken in various fields over time. It must be well acquainted with national and international developments and be permeated with national ambitions. It must keep itself abreast of the developments in the state economy, and be in touch with the plans of other districts, especially the neighbouring districts in the state, as a developing district economy tends to be increasingly export-based. It was sad to note that at some of the district offices there was no copy of the national plan[29] and there was substantial ignorance of the programmes of rural development under the plan in various sectors. Regarding the more vexing economic, sociological or managerial problems, it should have the foresight to draw upon expertise from outside. It should sternly resist pressure from vested interests in the government and outside, and command enough public confidence and faith in impartiality to be allowed to do so. It should have sympathy with the problems of the poor but not be led into basically relief programmes. To arouse public enthusiasm, elicit public cooperation, and bring about needed institutional changes, it should draw upon the experience and help of voluntary organisations to the utmost.

Keeping these varied requirements in mind, the Working Group on Block Level Planning laid down that the district planning team which was to prepare block plans, should consist of a core group of seven, comprising: (1) chief planner,

(2) economist/statistician, (3) cartographer/geographer, (4) agronomist, (5) engineer, (6) industry officer, and (7) credit planning officer. In addition, specialists may be engaged according to the needs of the area of the programme.[30] The manual on IRDP prepared by the Rural Development Ministry in 1980 had, perhaps on grounds of economy, provided only for a three-member planning team—an economist/statistician, a credit planning officer and a small/cottage industry officer. The state governments had further economised in the matter, as seen earlier. More recently in December 1982, however, the Planning Commission agreed to give 50 per cent assistance to the states accepting decentralised planning and approved a staff of one chief planning officer, one economist, five other specialists from a suggested list of six and two research assistants. Advantage should be taken of this offer to build up a planning cadre for which qualified officers from other departments could be seconded and trained. Provision should be made for lateral entry of outsiders.

If decentralised planning is to succeed, the vertical line of command which makes for a complete departmental hold over district staff should be loosened. This can be done by putting all developmental staff under a single head. On grounds of prestige and convenience, the collector could be the head but the collector will be too heavily preoccupied with non-developmental work to spare adequate time for developmental administration. If the idea is to make the Zilla Parishads (DPRIs) entirely responsible for district planning in conformity with democratic principles,[31] the executive offcer of the Zilla Parishad should be built up for this role.

While the public sector outlay and credit disbursals are based on different principles, the latter being given only for bankable schemes and more dependent on the attitudes of the applicants, success in planning requires that the two work in unison. This is most easily seen in the loan-cum-subsidy schemes for poverty removal. The local planning authorities and the financial institutions, banks and cooperative societies should be in close touch with the requirements of each other and their ability and preparedness to meet them. The district credit plans of the financial institutions must be based on an intimate knowledge of the economic infrastructure existing and planned in the district. For achievement of final production goals, the district plan is dependent on a certain credit quantum for its bankable project. There have been three rounds of district credit plans, but they have so far not been integrated with district plans. While the bank's annual action plan is announced in advance, the district plan comes late. The bank's annual plan ends by December and the district plan for the financial year is only available by September. This makes the job of coordination difficult. The banks have no idea of the credit requirements of the district plan.[32] The bridge between the two needs to be built at the earliest.

V

In the last thirty years, we have learnt to critically assess our planning effort and realise its major deficiencies. While the pre-Independence stagnant economy has begun to move and we have established many sophisticated capital goods and basic industries, our rate of growth does not compare well with that of other fast-developing economies, and we have not been able to make a worthwhile impact on the all pervading disturbing facets of the Indian economy—poverty and unemployment. Various measures have been tried from time to time to improve the situation but to no effect. There may, therefore, be a natural tendency to rely disproportionately on untried remedies of which decentralisation is one.[33] It may, therefore, be worthwhile to note the limitations of decentralisation, of what it cannot do.

An examination of the working of the Indian economy during the last few years reveals a major weak spot in the industrial field. Organised industrial growth has considerably slackened after the Third Plan. There has been intense effort to identify the causes of this low growth. Slowing down of public investment, lack of adequate infrastructural facilities like coal, power and transport, rigid price control, antiquated methods of production which would make the industry non-competitive in international goods, and in certain phases undue import liberalisation coupled with world recession and sudden large credit restriction have been located as important causes of the slowdown. There is little that decentralisation can do in these spheres. All the major issues are within the power of the Central government and one, electricity, with the state government. Another major field of low performance, exports, is also largely a matter of Central government policy. As a matter of fact, progress in the unorganised sector, which predominantly belongs to micro-planning, is dependent on the central and state policies of differential taxation, wages, reservation, marketing and credit infrastructure. If macro-planning is deficient, micro-planning however carefully devised, cannot deliver the goods.

One of the major motives in decentralised planning has been the objective of removing inter-district inequalities. Among the two objectives in introducing district planning in Maharashtra, one was to attain parity in the matter of socio-economic infrastructure facilities over a period of 15 to 20 years so that inter-district disparities in levels of development are ironed out. The Dandekar Committee[34] went into this question in great detail. For operational reasons it defined economic backwardness in each important indicator separately as being behind the districts' average without combining the indicators in an index, avoiding the problem of weighting. It obtained the districtwise expenditure on 29 of them and worked out the cost of making up the physical deficiencies of the backward districts. It found that considerable backwardness still remained in spite of progressive district-level expenditure, and if the districtwise pattern of expenditure remained the same, it would in several cases take the backward districts a long time to make up the lag. In the meantime, the average itself would rise, and with it the lag. The per capita aggregate book value expenditure on the building up of infrastructure over a period did not really measure the quantitative extent of these as the spending pattern over time differed. More recent progressive expenditure could not atone for the past neglect of backward areas. If this was to be quickly remedied, a different approach was necessary. In all fields where districtwise expenditure could be determined, and this was to be an expanding area, for all districts above the average (developed districts) plan expenditure on the indicator should be stopped except an allowance to keep up with population growth in all districts and to continue on-going schemes in non backlog districts. The whole should not exceed 15 per cent of the sectoral plan expenditure. The entire remaining balance of 85 per cent of the funds should be earmarked and spent on the district backward on that indicator in proportion to their lag behind the average. The radical reorganisation that would be needed to put through this programme can be gauged from the fact that for 1983-84, it would have meant that only one-third of the usual collection of district level schemes would be distributed among the districts according to the formula, the rest would go to the State Pool for the Removal of Specific Backlog. If more data of districtwise details could be obtained, more money would go to the pool. Even now, in almost half the items the estimated Seventh Plan allocations would not be enough to remove the existing backwardness (Table 6).[35] It

Table 6: Cost of Backlogs in Maharashtra Districts Compared to Anticipated Outlays in the Seventh Plan

(Rs. Crores)

Sector/Sub-sector/ Scheme/Programme	Aggregate backlog	Estimated cost of backlog in Seventh Five Year Plan	Seventh Five Year Plan estimated outlays	Number of years to remove the backlog
	(1)	(2)	(3)	(4)
Main roads	279.79	419.69	393.78	6.3
Other roads	320.50	480.75	211.66	13.4
Irrigation	1,385.92	2,078.88	3,355.86	3.7
Rural electrification	54.90	82.35	482.02	1.0
Energisation of pumpsets	185.75	278.63	464.40	3.5
Primary education	38.56	57.84	47.48	7.2
Secondary education	31.10	46.65	164.94	1.7
Pre-university and University education	20.38	30.56	41.38	4.3
Adult education	1.51	2.27	11.04	1.2
Industrial training institutes	39.32	58.97	38.01	9.1
Technical high school/ centres	10.25	15.38	9.11	9.9

Technical training in higher secondary schools	0.34	0.51	12.29	0.2
Vocational courses	0.20	0.29	16.37	0.1
Polytechnics	33.30	49.95	19.49	15.1
Primary health sub-centres	4.08	6.12	10.29	3.5
Primary health centres	—	—	57.72	—
Rural cottage hospitals	34.22	51.50	27.75	10.9
Hospital beds	182.91	274.37	20.42	79.0
Water supply by dug/bore wells	11.33	16.99	296.91	0.3
Piped water supply to problem villages	80.17	120.25	394.11	1.8
Piped water supply to others villages	—	—	—	—
Urban water supply	286.75	430.12	240.82	10.5
CADA works	82.29	123.44	25.00	29.0
Land development in non-CADA areas	0.90	1.35	25.52	0.3
Contour bunding	43.80	65.69	11.36	34.0
Terracing	23.63	35.44	14.03	14.9
Nala bunding	24.32	36.47	28.51	7.5
Land development-cum-horticultural development	2.84	4.26	5.14	4.9
Veterinary institutes	7.75	11.63	26.38	2.6

Note: Col. (4) $= \frac{\text{Col. (2)}}{\text{Col. (3)} - 15\%} \times 5$ as 15 per cent of the district plan outlays may be set apart to take care of the growth in population and for continuing schemes.

Source: Planning Department, Government of Maharashtra, *Report of the Fact Finding Committee on Regional Imbalances*, pp. 385-386.

would further imply a very serious curtailment of the DPDC's power of sectoral allocation.

(Rs. lakhs)

	1983-84 Plan	Schemes examined by committee	1983-84 Plan modified
State Level Schemes	85,334.78	25,381.38	59,953.40
District Level Schemes in the State Pool	19,075.00	6,373.50	12,701.50
Other District Level Schemes	45,590.22	28,931.69	16,658.53
State Pool for Removal of Specific Backlogs	—	—	60,686.57

If this principle is extended further to all facilities, it would mean that no district will be permitted to improve per capita facilities given to its people unless it becomes backward. This demands a great degree of sympathy and understanding on the part of developed districts. We are afraid that states may not be prepared to enforce such strict discipline and sacrifice.[36]

Even if equal public infrastructure facilities were built up in all districts, other causes of district inequalities would remain. Access to bank credit and institutional finance, easy availability of skilled labour, natural endowment, access to prosperous or fast growing areas, quality of management and entrepreneurship and more mundane things like capacity of people to work hard and to cooperate with one another, are important factors which go to determine the income of a district. The Dandekar Committee was content with the goal of equal public facilities (State and district) to all districts, but one of its members, Dr. V.B. Borkar[37] went much further. He demanded the extension of this principle to the commercial sector, and called for compensatory public action to make up for natural deficiencies. He was right in a sense, for even with equal public infrastructure, district inequalities could persist and even thrive, though it would be a different, more tolerable and perhaps more easily remediable type of inequality.

One of the major tasks of micro-level planning is to serve as a communicator of central and state facilities to the district people, and put them in a position through direct contact and otherwise to avail themselves of these. Different areas will be able to do that in different measures and the local potential itself will differ from place to place. As a consequence of micro-planning, while every district can be reasonably expected to be better off, it is not unlikely that district inequalities increase initially. It may defeat the purpose of self-reliance and encouragement of initiative if every time it happens there is an effort to redistribute resources.

Decentralised planning works best in a homogenous society where there are no large differences, because common decisions are easy to take and their implications easy to realise. Common courses of action help people more or less equally. In an unequal society, even a programme like road-building is more beneficial to those with marketable surplus for sale outside the locality. Public works which have a large appeal outside their immediate employment effects soon get exhausted. Much of land consolidation, conservation, and productivity improvement work remains outside the orbit because of its effects on private rights. The corrective measures have to be taken at the central or state level, but vested interests at the local level can thwart the administration of beneficial measures taken from the top.[38] Decentralised planning may strengthen the existing power structure and make life more difficult for the poor. The vested interests also exist at the central and state levels but with more enlightened elements to contend with, they have to operate within certain restraints. This is seen from the fact that the aggrieved interests appeal frequently against local authority to higher authority with some success. At the local level, opposition to vested interests cannot remain anonymous; it has to come out in the open, can be easily identified and may invite wrath and violence. On the other hand, however, while many progressive measures are enacted at the central and state level, they cannot be implemented without active local support and because of the lack of it most of them remain on paper. Micro-level planning at the local level will ensure that local opinion becomes organised on these vital issues. This organisation will also help in the productive employment of the population. Different localities will show different degrees of organisation and strength but if there are a few successful cases, their examples will prove infectious.

Decentralised planning is likely to be a painfully slow process. The fact that we have talked of it for the last few years without giving it a genuine trial even in one State, and that we are not prepared to entrust it to the popularly elected representative of the districts is a grim indicator of the obstacles ahead. In the political field, there has been a powerful tendency towards centralisation. Administratively, the vertical hierarchy has a strong hold; the limited decentralisation that has taken place below the state level is more by way of information-feeding, restricted delegation of authority, and implementation of decisions already taken, rather than genuine decision making. Micro-planning can only flourish in a culture of decentralisation and independent cogent thinking which are yet to evolve. To achieve its purpose, it must be accompanied by a change in the value system.

There may be a legitimate doubt about the district being the lowest proper unit for micro-planning.[39] The discussion has been conducted in terms of the district because of three major advantages. Data are easily available at the district level, and it is more often a question of classification and tabulation of existing data rather than collecting fresh data; at the district level almost every major department has a responsible officer, who can act independently if given a chance; and by long tradition the Collector has a natural leadership position in the district, which can hopefully be transferred to the Executive Officer of the Zilla Parishad. But the district has various units of hetrogeneous development and there is nothing to ensure that the benefits of what happens at one place in the district will automatically pass to others. There is a natural tendency for greater representation of the more developed talukas at the district level and their being more vocal. This is the major reason why in both Gujarat and Maharashtra, some formula for distribution of the district expenditure among blocks is laid down. It may be necessary to extend the job of the DPO and his staff to the talukas also, so that money is spent to the best long-term advantage. Even the block may, however, be too big an area, and the Asoka Mehta Committee suggested a Mandal as being more appropriate. Dr. V.M. Rao, who has examined at length the question of disparities among neighbouring villages in Tumkur district suggests a small cluster of villages which should be so planned and linked with each other that people think as one.[40] The process of group identity consists of much more than physical interconnections and takes considerable time for completion, but it may be worthwhile building up so that the growth impulse is immediately transmitted. The prerequisites for micro-planning at this level, the data, the planning, personnel, etc., render this course impracticable.

References

[1]Draft Five Year Plan 1978-83, 1.25, p. 3, Planning Commission, Government of India, 1978.

[2]The Approach to the Seventh Five Year Plan 1985-90, para 2, page 1, Planning Commission, Government of India, 1984.

[3]Report of the Working Group on District Planning, Planning Commission, Government of India, 1984, Vol. II, p. 276.

[4]NCDBA Report on General Issues Relating to Backward Areas Development, Planning Commission, Government of India, 3.22, p. 24.

[5]*Ibid.*, 3.65-3.75, pp. 30-32.

[6]*Ibid.*, 3.78, p. 32.

[7]For a detailed account see: D.T. Lakdawala—Planning for Basic Needs, Centre for Monitoring Indian Economy, 1981, pp. 11-13.

[8]Evaluation of the ICDS Services Project in Chhota Udaipur (Gujarat), A Case Study, pp. 627-640, in Gujarat Economy: Problems and Prospects, SPIESR, Ahmedabad, 1983. Section VI of the volume on Education and Health gives several instances of inadequate utilisation of social services in Gujarat.

[9]Report of the Working Group on District Planning, Planning Commission, Government of India, 1984, Vol. I, 2.2, p. 31.

[10]For example, see Thimmaiah's remarks "All growth oriented activities appear to be confined to macro and meso-level planning process and anti-rural poverty is pushed down to micro-level planning process." Block Level Planning, Evaluation of Karnataka's Plans, *Financial Express*, March 27, 1982.

[11]Report, NCDBA, 8.4 & 8.5, p. 85.

[12]D.T. Lakdawala, "Eighth Finance Commission's Recommendations", *Economic and Political Weekly*, September 1, 1984, pp. 1529-1534.

[13]"The system of Central assistance introduced considerable confusion, delay and uncertainty in the process of planning. The initiative of the States was crippled". The Planning Process in India: An Appraisal and Framework, Report of the Study Team, Administrative Reforms Commission, 1967, p. 14.

[14]For fuller details of plan assistance and its problems, see my article on "Plan Finances in a Federal Economy" in Singh and others (ed.) 'Economic Policy and Planning in India', Sterling Publishers Private Ltd., 1984, pp. 363-376.

[15]Report of the Working Group on District Planning, Vol. I, 4.51, p. 62.

[16]*Ibid.*, Vol. II, Proceedings of the Regional Workshop at Srinagar, para 32, p. 341.

[17]For detailed distribution of itemwise expenditure, see *Ibid.* Vol. II, Status Paper on Decentralised District Planning in Gujarat, pp. 33-35.

[18]*Ibid.*, Vol. II, p. 20.

[19]It is estimated that in Maharashtra in 1981-82, as against Rs. 463 crores expenditure on district planning, only Rs. 23 crores were spent through Zilla Parishads and Panchayat Samitis. Only 5 per cent of the expenditure was from own sources. Report of the Fact Finding Committee (Dandekar Committee) on Regional Imbalance in Maharashtra, Planning Department, Government of Maharashtra, Bombay, 1984, p. 93.

[20]Dr. R.H. Dholakia and Shri Sudarshan Iyengar note that more than 100 objections were raised by the Irrigation Department to a minor irrigation tank project in the Panchmahals. District Project Planning Cell—Panchmahals—An Experience in Action Research 1978-81, (cyclo) SPIESR, 1981, p. 9.

[21]Proceedings of the Workshop on District Planning at Gandhinagar, Report, Vol. II, para 23, p. 280. The reasoning for this procedure makes queer reading. "This enabled them to overcome the difficulties that generally arise when opposition parties were in majority in a particular local body, leading to conflicts."

[22]*Ibid.*, Vol. II, para 7, page 100 of "District planning in its true sense is still in its infancy, even in Gujarat". Sanat Mehta, Inaugural Address, National Workshop on Perspective Planning at the District Level, Department of Rural Studies, South Gujarat University, p. 5.

[23]*Ibid.*, Vol. II, pp. 40-42.

[24]Two likely unfavourable results of discretionary spendings may be noted. In an interesting unpublished paper, Shri Sudarshan Iyengar has made an attempt to classify by size groups the villages for which the discretionary schemes were proposed for 1981-82 in the Panchmahals District Planning Board. He found the bigger the

village size, the more likely it was to attract a proposal. The economies of scale operated (Rural Upliftment—Politicians, Verdict) The Multi-level Division of the Planning Commission regarded the discretionary and incentive components as being not integrated in the state plan, making district planning in Gujarat a "limited as well as isolated exercise" (Report, Vol. II, p. 201.)

[25]*Ibid.*, Vol. I, 8.4, p. 124.

[26]"A multi-level plan has to adopt a multi-stage planning procedure." KN Kabra: Planning Procedure in a District, IIPA, New Delhi, 1977, p. 17.

[27]"Programmes which were acceptable to the people were limited by numbers whereas other programmes which did not have ready acceptance had large opportunities". Report NCDBA, 8.12, p. 87.

[28]*Ibid.*, 5.77, p. 56.

[29]Report of the Study Group on District Planning, Vol. I, 3.20, p. 42.

[30]Report of the Working Group on Block Level Planning, Planning Commission, 1978, 10.11.

[31]Cf. "There is no getting away from the reality that the political authority has to have a decisive voice on all major issues pertaining to planning". Dantwala Committee Report.

[32]"The district functionaries are not able to indicate even broadly how much of their programme would be credit-based. Credit plans drawn by the banks remain unrealistic, since they are not related to district plans." H.B. Shivamaggi (Executive Director, Reserve Bank of India), Report of the Working Group on District Planning, Vol. II, p. 254.

[33]See M.L. Dantwala: Two-way Planning Process, Scope and Limitations, Indian Journal of Agricultural Economics, June 1983, p. 154.

[34]Report of the Fact Finding Committee on Regional Imbalance in Maharashtra, Planning Department, Government of Maharashtra, Bombay, 1984.

[35]*Ibid.*, Table 17.2, pp. 385-86.

[36]It is interesting to note the remarks of the Dandekar Committee in connection with a more radical remedy to tackle the problem of backwardness: "We find the proposal to remove backlog step by step beginning at the bottom so that at each step the most bottom districts are all raised to a certain minimum level attainable within the given resources, not practicable and desirable", Report, 17.32, p. 389.

[37]*Ibid.*, Note of Dissent by Dr. V.V. Borkar, pp. 469-473.

[38]"In Gosal village of Sayla Block, for example, an approach road that was sanctioned was not allowed to be constructed because one segment of population that did not like the idea of the weaker section being connected to the market during the rainy season...This body (the taluka panchayat) did not approve the strategy of concentrated intervention...per the State and Central governments' guidelines"-

R.H. Dholakia and Sudarshan Iyengar: Methodological Issues in Micro-level Planning, 8.1, pp. 26-27.

[39]Cf. "The National Committee would recommend that the primary unit for the identification of backward areas should be the development block", Report, NCDBA, 4.11, p. 35. The Dantwala Committee specifically appointed for block-level planning was more flexible on this point, Report, 10.2, p. 6.

[40]V.M. Rao, The Distant Neighbours: A Fuller View of the Clusters and Their Villages in Abdul Aziz (ed.) Studies in Block Level Planning, Concept Publishing Company, New Delhi, 1983.

Rationale and Limitation of Decentralised Planning

M.L. Dantwala

In spite of frequent refinements and revisions, the planning strategy in developing countries has failed to achieve its objective of growth with social justice. We began by asserting that "the heart of the growth problem lies in maximising the creation of surplus—invest and reinvest it" to accelerate production. The accelerated production was identified as growth. The pursuit of this policy did yield somewhat higher rates of growth (GNP) in comparison with historical standards, but it had hardly any impact on the severity of poverty and unemployment. The disillusionment with the growth theory and its GNP indicator came rather suddenly and we were advised to "stand economic theory on its head, since a rising growth rate is no guarantee against worsening poverty." GNP was dethroned and a direct attack on mass poverty was prescribed as the most appropriate strategy of development. For more than a decade this precept for poverty elimination adorned the blueprints of the five year plans of several developing countries. Unfortunately, the results have not been very different from those when GNP symbolised the hallmark of development.

This paper does not deal with the rise and fall of economic theories or their consequences. But it does seem that the repeated disillusionment with strategies of planning has probably turned the search towards the mechanics of planning. After "standing economic theory on its head" failed to produce expected results, it is being suggested that what is needed now is to "stand the planning process on its head". In other words, we should plan from below, or as second best, decentralise the planning process. The failure of planning to meet the challenge of poverty, inequality and unemployment was attributed to the highly centralised nature of planning. Consequently, the emphasis was shifted to decentralisation. Decentralisation also has a record of more than a decade. After the initial enthusiasm, the sobering influence of the technical, administrative and political problems associated with decentralised development rekindled the search for an appropriate methodology of planning. There is now a better appreciation of the relevance of macro as well as micro-planning to meet the challenge of poverty and unemployment. But "the methodology to mesh in planning from top and planning from below through a two-way linkage in the planning process" is still in a formative stage. The process through which such a methodology can be developed should commence by setting down clearly the roles of national level and local level planning in the strategy of development, the imperatives by which these roles are determined, and the rationale as well as the limitations of the two processes. Second, some indication should be given about the nature of obstacles to the 'meshing in' process, whether they are political, technological, administrative or organisational. A tentative attempt is made in this paper to deal with those problems, based almost entirely on the Indian experience. It should however be recognised that several such attempts would be needed before an acceptable blueprint of a two-way planning methodology is developed. At best, our attempt will help to obtain some insights into the problems involved in evolving such a methodology.

We should like to start the discussion at the conceptual level by examining three major issues: (1) the rationale of decentralisation, (2) the limitations of decentralisation, and (3) the contribution of decentralisation to the problem of eradication of poverty. The central theme which emerges from this discussion is the critical importance of integration of sectoral plans and the difficulty of persuading the vertical command line, the ministries and departments at the state headquarters, to accept the discipline of planning which would permit the integration of their projects at the horizontal (district) level.

POVERTY AND THE PLANNING PROCESS

Poverty is a complex phenomenon, a product of a system with interlocked political, economic and social components. As such, poverty cannot be eliminated by merely restructuring the planning process. At best, an appropriate planning system can play a critical supporting role in a comprehensive strategy of eradicating poverty.

It needs to be emphasised that decentralised planning is not a substitute for planning at the national level. The development strategy and the policy frame for poverty eradication have to be evolved at the national level. Laying down a set of priorities, fiscal and monetary policy, transport, communication, energy, science and technology policies, to name a few, all belong to the sphere of macro planning and each of them has a direct or indirect impact on the poverty problem. For example, government expenditure is known to affect income distribution. A study of the distribution of benefits of government expenditure in India reveals that "at the all-India level, the share of the poor in benefits (in 1975-76) works out to only one-third of that of the non-poor."[1] Since the share of the poor in the tax burden at 26 per cent is not much smaller than that in benefits from government expenditure, the author comes to the conclusion that "for a large majority of the poor the fiscal system turns out to be regressive."

The macro plan not only sets a limit to the scope of feasible decentralisation, it also conditions the effectiveness of decentralised development geared to the eradication of poverty. For example, if inflation is not contained poverty would be aggravated. But this in no way detracts from the necessity of decentralised planning, nor does it diminish its crucial role in the task of the removal of poverty and improving income distribution. Assuming that the national plan has formulated appropriate policies for the removal of poverty and inequality, the operative part of the plan has necessarily to be carried out at a fairly decentralised level, a district, a block or a cluster of villages. Decentralisation will not be of much avail if national policies for redistributive justice are inadequate or faulty, nor will appropriate policies bear fruit if a proper mechanism is not evolved to disaggregate the problem at the dispersed levels where it actually manifests itself.

Policies have to be translated into programmes and these programmes have to be devised and their implementation organised in the context of differing local situations. The rather dismal performance of the macro plans in regard to their objectives of eradication of poverty and unemployment and improvement in income distribution, is in no small measure due to the imperfections of the planning process and the weakness of the planning and implementing machinery at the district and lower levels.

A clear perception of the problem of poverty and of the process which generates and sustains it is necessary if planning is to perform a useful role in its eradication. A comprehensive discussion of the theme of poverty is beyond the scope of this paper and the author's competence; yet a few observations which depart from the usual analysis of the problem may be helpful.

There is no dispute that it is the socio-economic system that generates poverty and its inseparable counterpart, affluence. But whichever be the system, it cannot be sustained without the backing of value judgements which implicitly, if not explicitly, endorse the outcome of the system. The roots of these value judgements are deeper than those of the system. Planning, reformist or revolutionary, which proceeds on the assumption that the two are irretrievably interrelated and hence an attack on the prevailing socio-economic system will automatically destroy values and attitudes which sustain it, may achieve some outward results but the results will not be enduring. Of all the plan objectives, eradication of poverty involves not merely a structural change but a more basic change in the value system. Even radically altered structures and institutions can be manipulated if the values which impart esteem to affluence and view poverty as misfortune have not changed.

No less a person than Chairman Mao has conceded that "a mere public ownership of production cannot usher in socialism, because such a change by itself does not rid men's minds of selfishness, personal concept or the desire to have the better of others, nor end workers' alienation arising from division of labour." To this we may add Joan Robinson's observation:

"Soviet experience shows that power, privilege, and access to education can form the basis of class distinctions," notwithstanding the structural change in the system's economic foundation.[2]

Rationale of Decentralisation

The merit of decentralised planning is derived from its ability to discover dormant resources and skills and its endeavour to activise them. Structural, technological, institutional and organisational obstacles to overall growth as well as its equitable spread can also be better identified when viewed in the proximity of the specific area and the people. More importantly, every area, however small, has its inherited social and cultural ethos which the planner has to understand if he is planning for the people and not merely for the area. Better perception of the situation by itself may not be a sufficient condition for the effective removal of obstacles to growth and equity, but their exposure with empirical backing would certainly help to generate pressures which would become increasingly difficult to resist. There are numerous recorded instances, albeit isolated and not necessarily universally replicable, which show that when opportunities are revealed and technological-organisational inputs are provided, commendable results are achieved through community action. Awareness among the disadvantaged can also lead to clashes and conflicts, but this too should be viewed as a positive factor in the struggle against poverty.

To illustrate the point regarding perception, take the case of poverty and unemployment. For the central planner, poverty and unemployment are macro phenomena seen through a highly aggregated array of statistics. Such statistical information is necessary for formulating a national plan but not sufficient for devising programmes for poverty removal. With such technical coefficients as he may have access to, the central planner can estimate employment which would be generated in different sectors by the plan outlay. If the exercise reveals that employment generation through the plan outlay is likely to fall short of publicised targets, he may incorporate in the plan a few special labour-intensive projects to narrow the gap, and deliver homilies on appropriate technology, product-mix, factor pricing and so forth. But this is as far as he can go.

It is one thing to understand poverty, quite another to understand the poor. The central planner sees poverty in the abstract and prescribes global solutions. What is needed, however, is to know the poor, identify them, understand their social, economic and cultural disabilities and, above all, understand the local setting and its institutions under which poverty is generated and sustained, before solutions can be conceived, concretised and set into action. Employment generation and anti-poverty programmes therefore have to be area and community specific, taking into account the differing development potential as well as the constraints of each area and each community. All this can be done with the full cognizance of its attendant implications only at the local level of planning. As the saying goes, you cannot tend a flock of sheep from a camel's back; in the same way you cannot eliminate poverty from the elevation of a central plan, however thorough and earnest.

Take a concrete case illustrated by a field study in Tamil Nadu conducted by the Madras Institute of Development Studies. The researchers "were continually impressed with the fact that most of the tasks sought to be promoted under the DPAP and IRDP could not be accomplished, except on the basis of village level decisions and village level cooperation. Neighbouring farmers had to agree for field channels to be rationally aligned and excavated, and thereafter, in the equitable regulation of water. Contour-bunding and other soil conservation works, which extended across boundaries of private field ownership could not be taken up without the consent and cooperation of all who were involved."[3]

Another aspect of rural development for which decentralisation would be helpful, indeed essential, is the integration of projects launched by different ministries and their departments. There is abundant evidence which establishes that one of the main factors responsible for the less than optimal performance of rural projects was the lack of inter-departmental coordination. Planners now do understand the importance of linkages; nonetheless each ministry is keen to launch its own project, and even a separate agency to implement it with a ritualistic exhortation that the project should be 'dovetailed' with the other ongoing projects. In fact, what the concerned Department really expects is that other agencies or Departments will dovetail their projects with the one it has launched. This competitive zeal to regard one's own project as central to rural development to which other projects should cohere inevitably results in sub-optimal performance. A Planning Commission's paper on planning machinery in the states admits that "the integrity of district planning is seriously threatened by the multiplicity of decision-making agencies such as the panchayati raj institutions, cooperative, and public sector enterprises (there are 22 State Corporations in Maharashtra), SFDA/DPAP/CAD, District Industries Centres, etc."

The point is missed that after departmental projects are finalised and commenced, the scope for effective inter-departmental coordination will be severely limited. Integrated development will have meaning only when project proposals of different departments are submitted to a departmentally unaffiliated technical team working under a specially constituted district planning authority. The team, under the guidance of the local planning authority, will scrutinise the departmental projects and mould them into a single development plan consistent with the local, regional and national priorities, and development potential of the area and the available financial and material resources. The team would carefully assess the past experience of successes and failures and the factors behind them. This exercise may also help persuade the state departments or other district representatives to alter or amend their proposals.

A close scrutiny of forward and backward linkages of the bundle of project proposals may reveal an unsuspected scope for economy in resource use and cost reduction. The attempt would be to get the best return from the total area development plan rather than from each individual project. It is conceivable that the return from the integrated plan may fall short of the sum total of what was unrealistically projected in individual projects. But hopefully, there would be less of the phenomenon of half-finished projects, extended gestation and eventual cost escalation, as has invariably happened in the past.

It hardly needs saying that local level planning does not connote "doing in the state capitals or at district headquarters the same kind of exercises as are done at the national level." The entire process of preparing an area plan has to have a distinctive character. Its perception of problems has a human dimension, its assessment of the achievable reflects historical experience, its design displays linkages, its action plan avoids reliance on vested interests and attempts to build up countervailing forces.

One other aspect of decentralisation which has not received the attention it deserves is what may be termed decentralisation of the talent hierarchy. Talent has a tendency to float to the top, denuding the lower strata of sustenance needed for growth. Whether it is in the realm of politics, administration or profession, talent gets concentrated at the top. We have seen that area planning is not a job for a parvenu. Besides, it is easier to sit down and formulate a plan, be it for growth or for growth with social justice, than to set it in motion in remote areas and among remote people. People in rural areas, particularly the poor have a protective suspicion of any outside intervention and it is not easy to make them understand the intent of the Plan and elicit their cooperation. Within such environment, if area planning is to succeed it will need persons not only with talent but also with tact, patience, perseverance and, above all, empathy. Moreover, at the district level, the processes of plan formulation and its implementation are closer. Hence, the problem of matching performance with promise is more pressing for the district planner.

It is therefore necessary to equip the district planning authority with a multi-disciplinary planning team under the leadership of a person well-versed in the technique and discipline of planning. The main qualification for the membership of the planning team would be professional competence but since the plan it produces has to have a high degree of acceptability by the implementing agencies, they too should be represented on the planning team. Further, since a substantial portion of plan expenditure is now met through institutional finance, credit institutions must also be represented on the team.

Limits to Decentralisation

In a federal state like India, decentralisation of planning authority and financial resources has to take place first from the Union to the state governments and then from the state governments to the district or the block. The legislative and fiscal jurisdictions of the central and the state governments are defined by the Constitution. There is a provision in the Constitution which enables periodical adjustment in the matter of sharing of tax revenues between the Centre and the states through the Finance Commission appointed once in five years. State governments also receive "central assistance" under the Five Year Plans and annual budgets of the central government. While the details of these arrangements are of little interest to our theme, the point is that the states, towards whom the first move in decentralisation is to be made, feel—rightly or otherwise—that their planning endeavour is constrained by the paucity of financial resources.

In the context of the decentralisation debate, one somewhat curious feature of Indian planning may be noted. A large number of special programmes for the weaker sections, such as, Small Farmers' Development Agency (SFDA), Marginal Farmers and Agricultural Labourers (MFAL) Development Agencies, Drought-Prone Area Programme (DPAP), the Accelerated Rural Water Supply Programme (ARWSP), House Site for the Landless and Food for Work, were and many of them still are, "centrally sponsored".

The device of Centrally Sponsored Schemes (CSS) illustrates sharply the sort of contrary pulls which affect the process of decentralisation. While successively a larger share of development outlays has been allotted to the states, the Planning Commission and the Central ministries have expanded the coverage of the CSS. Thus the expenditure on CSS has increased from Rs. 2,860 million during the entire Second Five Year Plan to Rs. 8,740 million in a single year 1978-79. We cite at some length the justification for this arrangement as the same has been provided by a former Deputy Chairman of the Planning Commission: "There are problems of national concern which cannot be left to states because of their inter-state implications like population planning, inter-state power transmission lines, etc."[4] Apart from this argument which has some validity, it is further stated that "There are other plan priorities where the states should be interested but because of *their power structure or because of limited vision* or lack of resources, they have to be specially spurred and induced. Many of the interesting experiments in agricultural planning like SFDA, MFAL and CDA, etc. have come through centrally sponsored schemes"[5] (emphasis added).

The statement raises some important issues. Is the power structure in the states more reactionary than at the Centre? As for the limited vision, is it suggested that the concern for the poor is more pronounced at the Centre than at the states? Though *prima facie* such presumptions may appear unwarranted and may be viewed as an affront to the state leadership, if idealistic perceptions are tempered by stark realities as they prevail in many of the Indian states, the view quoted above may not be all that objectionable. Besides, there are concrete instances which confirm the apprehensions of the Planning Commission. Some of the Centrally Sponsored Schemes are entirely financed by the Centre and for others the expenditure is shared usually on a fifty-fifty basis. When it was explained to the states that assistance under CSS was additional and the unavailed amount would not be available as general plan assistance, there was pressure from several states to augment the scope of CSS and expenditure on them. The relevant state departments exercised pressure on their governments and Central ministries also joined the game with a view to extend their own sectoral empires. On the other hand, "A study of the use of centrally planned schemes would reveal that these have not been used (implemented) by some states and money allotted to them surrendered, even when there was no sharing involved."[6]

The former Deputy Chairman asks a very pertinent question: "Which authorities should move first in an attack on backwardness (and let us add poverty) and how far can one push the other?" He does not give a categorical answer, but from his unquestionably intimate knowledge, he laments, "State plan priorities themselves are different from what their interests require. Higher educational institutions, large prestigious industries, etc., are preferred to new primary schools, adult classes, village industries centres, extension work, etc. . . . On a problem like consolidation of holdings and land reforms which in many ways is the essence of agricultural development, some states have lagged behind others."[7] It is a well-known fact that in one state even the recording of land rights was suspended under pressure from the landlords.

At the other end, there are states which consider themselves more progressive than the Centre and probably are. They not only question the presumption by the Centre of greater concern for the poor, but consider it a stratagem to obstruct the radical orientation of state leadership and to preserve the balance of power in their (central leadership's) favour.

Be that as it may, at what level the power structure reflecting the vested interests is more assertive and pernicious is a question which social scientists have to investigate. On their findings will depend the extent to which decentralisation will be in the interest of the poor. One observation however can be made. The manipulative power of vested interests over the state apparatus concerned with planning (for the poor or the rest) and implementation increases as the area becomes smaller. But this is no reason for withholding decentralisation because the potential for mobilisation of countervailing forces is also greater when issues are more area specific.

The second stage of decentralisation is from the states to the districts. Here, the pattern of devolution of planning functions and financial resources to the districts varies a great deal. In some states like Maharashtra and Gujarat, a prescribed share—30 to 40 per cent—of the state's total plan outlay is allocated for district level schemes though a large part of it (80 per cent in Gujarat) is set aside for "normal schemes to be proposed (at the state level) in the light of priorities and guidelines given by the state."

The composition of the district planning authority also varies considerably from state to state. In Maharashtra, for example, the District Planning and Development Council has as its Chairman a "designated minister" in the state government. Another minister and the divisional commissioner serve as vice-chairmen. In Gujarat, on the other hand, the District Collector acts as the chairman and the District Panchayat President as the vice-chairman. In West Bengal, the Zilla Parishad (the District Panchayat) is put in charge of planning but more so for implementation of the district projects. This brief information may be of some relevance in judging the nature and extent of the decentralisation process prevalent in the states.

Local planning has to operate within the scope defined for it from above. Even so, the local planning authority need not view itself as a passive recipient of projects and programmes handed down to it by the state or central government. If it takes such a view or the planning authorities at higher levels so restrict its operational role, the contribution of local level planning by way of a more perceptive planning and more purposeful implementation would be at best marginal. Precisely how much autonomy should be given to the local planning authority, in which fields, and with how much financial resources, is an issue which would require elaborate discussion. One point may however be stressed. The local planning authority should be given maximum latitude in regard to the development and welfare programmes concerning the target group which would obviously consist of the weaker sections of the population. This is necessary because it should be laid down that the performance of the local planning authority and implementing agencies will be judged primarily by the extent to which they succeed in augmenting and strengthening the skill and the asset base and hence the productivity and income of the weaker sections of the population within its jurisdiction.

Planning from Below

Planning from below as a logical extension of the principle of decentralisation has considerable ideological appeal. It is, however, necessary to view it in a proper perspective and recognise its limitations. Presumably, planning from below would mean that the planning process should begin at the level of the village or a cluster of villages. Such village plans will be assembled and suitably dovetailed at the taluka or block level and would become block plans and, through a similar process during upward journey, would assume the status of the district and ultimately the state plan. Such a plan, it is contended, will reflect peoples' aspirations and felt needs as distinct from the technocrat's and bureaucrat's perception of the content and direction of development.

Though the idea has an idealistic appeal, it has several flaws which cannot be ignored. All problems of an area—a village, a block or a district—even such obvious ones like poverty, and ill-health, do not necessarily originate in the concerned area inasmuch as their causes lie outside the area and therefore their solutions have to be found outside as well. Drought-prone areas, waterlogging, or soil depletion are instances in point. River valley projects or soil conservation schemes have to be planned on a watershed basis which may transcend more than one area. Power generation and the transport system too have to be planned on a larger canvass. No doubt, all such projects have an area content even at the planning stage but more in the process of implementation. As noted earlier, consultation with local authorities and the local people and their informed judgement must find a place in trans-area planning.

The proposition that the plan should reflect people's aspirations and felt needs assumes a harmonious society. In an unequal society, more often than not, a planner will be confronted with conflicting aspirations, the deprivations of one section may be a consequence of the privileges enjoyed by another section. A question will then arise about whose aspirations and felt needs the planner should endeavour to fulfil, unless it is specified that he should consider the removal of poverty as the supreme felt need and aspiration.

In spite of such a dilemma, if a planner is put under pressure to devise a plan tailored mainly for the fulfilment of an assortment of felt needs, he will be driven to finding cosmetic solutions, appeasing instead of planning. This is precisely the process through which populism takes hold of the politician, and from which the planner at least should be saved.

There are, of course, many felt needs which reflect convergence of all interests which no planner can ignore, nor does he have the privilege of replacing people's perception with his own perception of felt needs. But if there is anything like a science of planning which would justify making a distinction between a planner and a politician, the planner should have the freedom to chart out the path for the fulfilment of deprived people's felt needs. This path may not be the shortest or the quickest, but within the limitations of socio-economic parameters and his own professional competence, the surest. The political leadership will of course have the final authority to accept or reject the planner's plan.

All in all, if a wholly or largely centralised planning has its infirmities, a fanatical advocacy of planning from below is not free from them. Planning, especially in a big country like India, had to be a two-way process at more than one level: between the Centre and the state (or a region), between the state and its districts, and between the district and the block or a cluster of villages. Given the commitment to the principle of decentralisation, the modalities of the process should better be evolved through trial and error rather than prescribed as a blueprint. The question of sharing of authority and financial resources will never be free from controversy. Power equations will dominate the controversy, aggravate regional feelings, e.g. on sharing of inter-state river waters, location of a steel plant. But this is part of the game in a democracy.

It has already been stated that it is primarily at the national level that major policy decisions are taken which in one way or the other affect the effectiveness of measures for the eradication of poverty and unemployment. Only if these policies are in consonance with the policy needed for poverty eradication would a discussion on restructuring of planning machinery be useful. The whole plan, and not just a part of it under the caption "special programmes for the weaker sections", must reflect a commitment to poverty eradication. No policy, no project should be inconsistent with the objective of poverty removal. If the commitment of the national leadership to poverty eradication is lukewarm, it will severely hamper effective action at the state or local level. In a federal structure, if some of the constituent states are governed by a party with a more radical orientation, a somewhat more energetic action for poverty removal can be initiated, but in the short run of say five or ten years, the achievements in these states and the rest will not be outstandingly different. Thus, the scope for the (decentralised) local authority to formulate plans for eradication of poverty and implementing them will be determined to a considerable extent by the latitude permitted by the state and central governments to the local planning authority.

The Hope Belied

It is now generally admitted that the expectation that decentraiisation of planning will help to improve performance, particularly in respect of achievement of social justice has not been realised. Many explanations are given for the failure of decentralisation to provide stimulus, as was hoped, to rural development whose primary objective is to eradicate poverty and unemployment. A fuller discussion of this theme is beyond the scope of this paper. Briefly, we shall contend that though poverty cannot be eliminated altogether without a total social reconstruction or structural change involving property relations, considerable ground can be gained in the struggle for poverty eradication through a better planning process and planning mechanism. To put it differently, not all the failures of anti-poverty programmes can be attributed to the opposition of the vested interests. A good many of them fail through sheer inefficiency, bad planning and unintelligent mechanisms of implementation. If this were not so, projects and programmes such as power generation, major irrigation, soil conservation, production of fertilisers, cement and steel, which are demonstrably in the interest of the haves, would not have performed so poorly as they have done.

To cite a typical example: "Acute coal shortage has severely hampered work on the second phase of the Rajasthan Canal.... The main work of lining the canal and water course in the command area has come to a virtual standstill....The problem of coal supply has been persisting for the last two years....Against the requirement of 90,000 tonnes of coal for 1980-81, the supply so far—mid-January 1981—was only about 8,000 tonnes....The nation is in fact losing Rs. 5,000 million annually in terms of food production because of the delay in executing the projects."[8] Much of such mismatch can be traced to the compartmentalised system of decision-making at the Centre and corresponding absence of a competent machinery to formulate an integrated area plan at local levels. If steps are taken to decentralise decision-making in areas appropriate for each level of the decentralised system and if the implementation system is revamped, there is reason to believe that many of the failures of programmes for the benefit of the weaker section can be avoided. We would go further and stress that in the absence of such reorganisation of the planning and implementation system, even with the best of will these programmes will not succeed.

The major shortcoming of the decentralisation experiments (most of them are still in the experimental stage) as they are being conducted in India and in most of the Asian countries, apart from their half-heartedness, is the lack of appreciation of the necessity (or unwillingness) to constitute a planning authority at the local level with a high enough status assisted by a multi-disciplinary planning team. And the major obstacle in establishing such a planning apparatus is the training, tradition and culture of the administrative system which is accustomed to a one-way hierarchical line of command from the state to the district, the taluka and village levels.

Confirmation of the futility of a piecemeal approach to the anti-poverty programme comes from a more prestigious source, a World Bank research publication. Adelman and Robinson[9] have constructed an economy-wide computable general-equilibrium model as a laboratory to test the impact of policy measures aimed at poverty elimination and better income distribution over the short to medium run. The model is rooted in the economy of South Korea. As their findings have received wide publicity and are likely to figure prominently in the animated debate on the problem of poverty, we take the liberty of quoting them at some length.

The Adelman-Robinson model reveals that "policy instruments in current use are largely ineffective when used singly because the effects of even substantial government intervention are quickly dissipated over time, with a few of the trickle-down effects." However, it also shows that "with an integrated well-balanced, mutually reinforcing selection of development strategy and anti-deprivation policy packages, substantial improvement is possible over relevant time periods." The authors contended that such coordinated packages are feasible within the existing economic structure, but warn that "they (will) have a major impact on the relative position of different socio-economic groups and hence on the balance of power within the country."

The model simulated half a dozen programmes for rural economy individually and in combinations: land reform, cooperatives, productivity and marketing, public works and industry, consumption subsidy, education and demographic change. Without going into details, we may highlight two major outcomes from the model. Rural development including land reforms yields the best result in terms of both growth and income distribution. The package dramatically reduces the extent of poverty and is very favourable for overall income distribution. However, the programme which excludes land reform is noticeably less effective. "Total production and income drop off somewhat, the size of poverty population increases substantially and the overall distribution is more unequal...the average incomes of the bottom two deciles are down 7 per cent."[10]

The contribution that redistribution of assets (land ownership, for example) can make is difficult to quantify. But the case for redistribution does not depend on such measurement. Inequality, particularly glaring inequality such as is seen in the coexistence of poverty and affluence, besides being indefensible as an economic phenomenon, is normally repugnant. Yet, if it is contended that redistribution is the sole or major solution to the problem of poverty, the case for decentralisation would lose much of its force, for the simple reason that policy decisions and legislative action for any worthwhile redistribution will have to be taken at a much higher level. Decentralisation can play a positive role in poverty eradication mainly in two ways. A planning authority at the district level equipped with adequate sanctions and resources is in a better position to arrest the process of impoverishment through more specific identification of exploitative instruments, such as rents, interest-rates, trading margins, etc., which generate and sustain poverty. It can initiate countervailing action by more effective enforcement of legislative sanctions and strengthening non-exploitative arrangements, such as institutional credit, cooperative marketing and public distribution. Additionally, it can help to channel a larger than proportionate share of public, private and institutional investment with supportive services—extension, training, technology upgradation, input supply, marketing—to the weaker section of the population. It can also prevent the trickle-up in the special programmes for the weaker sections and improve their performance. The total impact of this course of action may not be dramatic but it will definitely change the course of the income stream in favour of the poor. In any case, if such a reorientation is to be achieved, it can be done only through an authentic decentralised planning and implementation machinery.

PEOPLE'S PARTICIPATION: A SKEPTICAL NOTE

The search for an appropriate planning methodology is quite conspicuous in the ongoing debate on development. The search, it seems, has identified two components of the methodology as critical to the achievement of the development goal of growth with social justice: (1) local level planning, and (2) people's participation. On the face of it, the emphasis placed on these components is unexceptionable. But a new wave, if this becomes one, like "standing economic theory on its head", carries with it a danger of uncritical acceptance.

In Section I we pointed out the limitations of decentralisation. This section attempts to discuss the scope and limitations of people's participation. We all know that people's participation is a basic postulate of democratic polity, and mechanisms like adult suffrage have been devised to ensure such participation. Yet there is considerable skepticism about the representative character of elected legislatures. The experience of experiments in developing a decentralised structure of planning is not dissimilar. In an unequal society, democratic or decentralised political or planning mechanisms do not succeed in ensuring genuine people's participation.

People's participation in decentralised planning is constrained by political as well as technical factors.

The Political Factors

A big fillip was given to the establishment of local level—district, block and village-bodies known as Panchayati Raj Institutions (PRIs)—following the recommendation of a study team (1958) widely known as Balvantray Mehta Study Team. The team had argued that there should be administrative decentralisation for effective implementation of development programmes and that decentralised administration should be under the control of elected bodies. "Community development can be real only when the community understands its problems, realises its responsibilities, exercises the necessary powers through its chosen representatives and maintains a constant vigilance on local administration." The National Development Council, the apex decision-making body in the field of planning, endorsed the study team's recommendations and suggested that each state should work out the structure of PRI which suited its conditions best. Within a few years, in the early sixties, most of the country was covered by Panchayati Raj Institutions. The total number of gram (village) panchayats covered 90 per cent of the rural population; out of 4,974 blocks in the country 4,033 had established samitis, and out of 399 districts, in 262 Zilla (district) Parishads were established.

Two decades later, in 1978, the Asoka Mehta Committee reporting on Panchayati Raj Institutions observed: "The story of Panchayati Raj has been a story of ups and downs. It seems to have passed through three phases: the phase of ascendancy (1959-64); the phase of stagnation (1965-69); and the phase of decline (1969-77)."

One fails to see any 'ups' in this chronology. Be that as it may, the Asoka Mehta Committee blames the bureaucracy and political jealously for the weakening of the panchayati raj system. The system of line hierarchy makes bureaucracy averse to any horizontal cut off. It could not "easily get adjusted to working under the supervision of elected representatives at levels below the State," who incidentally were not always made of the stuff which would command respect and allegiance. At the political level, the state leadership did not relish the rise of a rival centre of power in the districts. "Some of the State Governments would postpone the holding of elections or supersede some of the important tiers (of PRI) for one reason or the other." The crux of the matter was however "the lukewarm attitude of the political elite at higher levels towards strengthening the democratic process at the grassroots. Of particular significance in this connection is the relative cooling off of enthusiasm of Members of Parliament (MPs) and Members of Legislative Assembly (MLAs) in some of the States towards Panchayati Raj *because they would perceive a threat in the emerging Panchayati Raj leadership to their position in their constituencies*" (*emphasis added*).

The Asoka Mehta Committee was not oblivious to the 'inadequacies' of the PRIs. It notes: "PRIs are dominated by economically and socially privileged sections of society and have as such facilitated the emergence of oligarchic forces yielding no benefits to weaker sections. The performance of PRIs has been vitiated by political factionalism. . . . Corruption, inefficiency, scant respect for procedures, political interference in day-to-day administration, parochial loyalties, motivated action, power concentration instead of service consciousness—all these have seriously limited the utility of the Panchayati Raj for the average villager."

It may be true, as the Asoka Mehta Committee says, that the panchayati raj system was not given a fair trial. That the experiment is not a total loss should also be accepted. It commenced "a process of democratic seed-drilling in the Indian soil." From a developmental angle "it helped rural people cultivate a development psyche." In any case, there is no escape from developing sooner or later appropriate political, administrative and planning systems which do not lead to centralisation of all authority, especially if eradication of poverty and unemployment is the main objective of the planning effort.

Technological Constraints

The technological constraint to the two-way planning process or planning from below which would elicit people's participation is more difficult to explain. On the one hand, there is a growing recognition of the fact that planning of even simple programmes like location of rural service centres or implementation of minimum needs programme involves a great deal of expertise, if costs of these programmes are to be kept within acceptable limits. There is therefore a constant emphasis on professionalisation of the planning personnel. On the other hand, there is an equally forceful exhortation to involve the people who are to be the beneficiaries of the programmes in the formulation of the programme. It seems to us that the task of reconciliation of the technical requirements of a programme with popular wishes and expectations can be very frustrating. At the academic level it may not be difficult to suggest a *modus operandi* for bringing about such a reconciliation. But consider an example or two from a real life situation at a much higher level of maturity. The question of equitable sharing of river waters between adjoining states in India has defied solution over decades. The matter has been referred to one expert committee after another. Their reports, based on purely technical considerations, have not been acceptable to one state or the other, sometimes both. Unending efforts are made to resolve the issue through negotiations between the Chief Ministers of concerned states. Only on rare occasions have such negotiations been successful. More often, the matter is referred to a tribunal for arbitration for which there is provision in the Constitution. Even the verdicts of the tribunals have not been found acceptable to the contending states. If such is the case in reconciling *technical* requirement (supposed to be politically neutral) and the *popular* demands at the level of states—often governed by the same political party—the assumption that the district planning team need not face any serious problem in accommodating people's aspirations in its technical plan would be naive.

If one is to take a constructive view of the scope and limits of people's participation in planning, one should spell out the various facets of participation. Mary R. Hollensteiner cites six modes of people's participation[11]: The first mode involves only the educated and monied people in the community without the participation of the 'grassroots' or the beneficiaries. The second mode is one in which the people or the beneficiaries are asked to legitimise or ratify projects identified and formulated by the Government. In the third mode of participation, the people are consulted about the project but they do not actively participate in the planning and management of the project. In the fourth mode, the people are consulted from the very start and they actively participate in the planning and management of projects. In the fifth mode, the people or the beneficiaries are represented in the highest policy-making body of the agency. Finally, in the sixth mode, the representatives of the people control the highest policy-making body of the agency.

The seminar may deliberate on the mode at which it would be realistic to pitch people's participation. The seminar may also consider how to ensure that 'the representatives of the people' are representatives of the poor and even if they are, how far they will be able to assert their rights and obtain for the poor their due share in the benefits of planning, when such assertion is likely to involve curtailment of the benefits currently enjoyed by the 'educated and monied' people. In a community in which the livelihood of the poor depends upon the support—or tolerance—of the rich, assertion of their rights by the poor carries a high risk of reprisals. The upsurge in atrocities against the scheduled castes/tribes bears testimony to such an outcome.

In India there are institutions in which the representation of the rich is deliberately barred or restricted. But such provisions do not succeed in preventing the entry of the rich into such institutions through devious means. If by any chance the rich cannot get into the institutions, they manage to destroy them or more prudently make them non-functional. To cite one example: A scheme of setting up Farmers Service Societies (FSS) was introduced in 1973-74. The FSS was to function as a primary society undertaking all activities conducive to the economic development of its members. The scheme envisaged that the control of FSS would vest in a Board of Directors in which two-thirds of the elected members would represent the weaker sections with a view to creating favourable conditions for the flow of credit, services and technical guidance to the weaker sections. The model bye-laws circulated by the Government of India provided for representation to the weaker sections by five out of seven elected members.

A review of the performance of FSS conducted by the Reserve Bank of India in 1980 however revealed that the above provision of the bye-law had been 'diluted' or not strictly followed in several states. The review further discovered that "in seven out of 13 FSS in (one) State, State Government officials, merchants, traders, lawyers, lecturers, etc. were representing small farmers."

The moral is clear. Whatever institutional devices one may forge to ensure people's participation to serve the interests of the weaker sections, it is difficult to avoid the structural composition of an unequal society being reflected in the composition and control of grassroot institutions. Thus, we are driven into an ironical position under which instead of the people's representative acting as a countervailing force against the higher level planning bodies in the interests of the weaker sections, the latter has to intervene to ensure that the democratic process at the grassroots does not result in the dominance of the 'educated and monied' class over the institutions built to safeguard the interests of the poor.

While people's participation, involvement and control in local level planning must remain the ultimate objective in the evolution of planning methodology, a starry-eyed approach to the problem may do more harm than good to planning for the poor.

The seminar should attempt to demolish this skeptical view on people's participation.

A Postscript

The general precept is that there should be no bifurcation between the planning and the implementing responsibilities. But in regard to people's participation it may not be improper to determine differentially their involvement in plan formulation and plan implementation, the latter being more extensive than the former. True, if there is total non-involvement of the people in planning, it would be idle to expect their responsive cooperation in implementation. This brings us back to the 'mode' or level at which a synthesis can be conceived between the technical abstruseness of a plan (or a project) and people's desire to understand if not influence what is being planned for them. Thinking aloud, it may be suggested that the planner—an expert or an official—should confer with the people about the broad outline of the plan/project, its social and economic objectives, the gains likely to accrue to the community and the financial and physical costs involved, e.g. in realignment of farm boundaries for a network of field channels, compulsory use of pesticides, preferred cropping pattern, rationing of available water, etc. At this stage, the planner should express his eagerness to solicit their advice particularly in regard to the past experience and likely obstacles—primarily social and political—in implementation of the plan. One must not be so naive as to expect a necessarily sober or even a unanimous response. On the contrary, it is not inconceivable that the planner may raise a hornets' nest in broaching the subject. Factions, animosities and conflicts of interest which may be lying dormant may come alive if the accrual of benefits does not conform to the prevailing power equations. And if we are planning for the poor, redistribution of assets and benefits in their favour has to be the essence of the plan. Unequal distribution of the gains of development to correct the inherited unequal distribution of assets and income is the heart of the process of growth *with* social justice. Perhaps with tact and moderation serious cleavages may be avoided. The planner will need political support in the task of enlisting people's participation.

But surely there would be many projects and programmes in

which there need not be any clash of interest: drinking water, link roads, primary education and health. One should neither anticipate—nor exaggerate—the complexities of consultation.

To come back to the mode of participation, the issue may be posed slightly differently. Are we aiming at: (a) the people formulating the plan with the assistance of the expert, or (b) the other way round, i.e., the expert planning with the assistance of the people? It may be submitted that we begin with the latter and graduate towards the former.

In the sphere of implementation, however, both the scope and the possibilities of evoking people's participation are much wider and immediate, i.e. no gradation process is necessary. People in poor countries are used to paternalistic ordering. They want the elders—the government, the *zamindar* or the *mukhia* —not only to think for them but to act for them. There is no suggestion here to perpetuate or even exploit this patron-client relationship for the purpose of development planning. What is implied is that the people may not refuse participation in the implementation simply because they were not fully involved in the formulation of the plan. They would appreciate the fact that they have been kept informed and consulted about the broad features of the plan, its objectives and its benefits. On this basis it should be possible to evoke their participation in the implementation of the plan, preferably through established voluntary agencies, formal and non-formal groups—cooperatives, panchayats, youth and women's associations, educational and cultural bodies. This type of people's participation is crucial to the success of a broad-based development effort. It would be prudent to begin with an exercise which holds promise of success.

Voluntary agencies should be encouraged to assume greater responsibility in implementing particularly the beneficiary-oriented programmes. Government's administrative machinery is neither adequate nor does it have the requisite motivation to undertake the task. The magnitude of the organisational problems of implementing anti-poverty programmes is stupendous. Let us have a look at some of its aspects.

The number of person living below the poverty level in India, as defined in the Five Year Plan documents, was estimated (in 1978) at 290 million.

The number of inhabited villages in India according to the 1971 population census was 575,721 out of which 150,100 had a population of less than 200 each and another 168,512 villages had a population of between 200 and 499. Imagine the organisational problem of catering to such a vast multitude of people spread over lakhs of distant villages with poor accessibility.

Between 1978 and 1988, the number of school-going population (in the age of 6 to 14) is estimated to increase by 72 million. The additional teacher requirement of handling this enrolment would be 1.59 lakhs during 1978-83 and 1.98 lakhs during 1983-88. Similar estimates could be given about the additional requirements of primary health centres, nurses, midwives, etc.

Surely, the official agencies cannot cope with problems of such magnitudes, without the active participation or rather involvement of the people.

CONCLUDING OBSERVATIONS

The Indian experience suggests that the early enthusiasm for encouraging decentralisation through Panchayati Raj Institutions, following the recommendations of the Balwantrai Mehta Committee (1958) and the more recent strong support lent to it by the Asoka Mehta Committee (1978), has cooled off and there is a distinct trend towards entrusting district planning to bodies presided over either by a minister of the state or to the District Collector. The president of the Zilla Parishad had been reduced to a secondary position.[1] There is also some reluctance to constitute interdisciplinary planning teams, though strongly recommended by the National Planning Commission with a promise of financial support for the establishment of such planning teams. The experiment of involving professional institutions and voluntary agencies in the formulation of area plans has also lost momentum.

Is there then some retrogression in the much publicised drive towards decentralisation in planning? If so, what could be the reasons? Any one or a combination of the following explanations is possible. One, the state leadership, whatever may be its rhetoric, is averse to the idea of decentralisation mainly out of political consideration of preventing the emergence of a rival political force at the district level, emanating from the same political party or a party in opposition. Two, the line bureaucracy at the state headquarters is not reconciled to the idea of dilution of its departmental authority implied in the establishment of a horizontal decision-making body entitled to alter or amend departmental plans for the purpose of integration. Three, which would reject the argument of personal jealousies or power equations as the principal obstacle to decentralisation becoming operational, would contend that in the very nature of things there are genuine limitations to decentralised planning and people's participation. Developmental planning has to begin as a national exercise and at each successive step down it becomes increasingly residual. This is the logic of planning, it cannot be otherwise. Both the scope and the content of planning shrink at each successive lower level of planning. This does not mean the inevitability of centralised planning. Decentralisation has considerable merit, but not to recognise its limitation would be doing a disservice to the cause of decentralisation.

The more one thinks about India's planning process as it has evolved over the last three decades, the more aware one becomes of the limits to decentralisation. The limits are of three types: political, administrative and technological. It can be assumed that the political and administrative obstacles can be removed through better understanding and open debate.

A modern state in the modern world unavoidably has to take policy decisions encompassing a wide spectrum of the national economy and geography. Even in the sphere of agriculture, which is rightly perceived as an eminently local affair, policy decisions have to be taken at the national level, for example, in regard to incentives to production of food and commodities in short supply, their prices, imports and exports, fertiliser availability through domestic production and imports, major irrigation projects, etc.

Surprisingly, most of the special projects pertaining to the weaker sections, backward areas and rural welfare—SFDA, DPAP, tribal areas, rural works programmes and its many variants like food for work, drinking water, etc., were also either centrally sponsored and/or centrally financed and quite a few of them by United Nations agencies and under the aid programmes of a number of foreign governments and voluntary organisations like Oxfam or CARE.

It has been observed, for example, that in Maharashtra even the intensity of the DPAP varied according to the sponsorship. In areas (blocks) where the programme was assisted by the World Bank the intensity was the highest. Where the programme was centrally sponsored and in which the outlay was shared equally by the Centre and the state, the intensity was much less, and it was least in areas where the programme was financed entirely by the state government. The status and the strength of the administrative set-up also varied according to the sponsorship. Thus, in the World Bank-assisted areas, the head of the DPAP is a high ranking officer with the status of a collector endowed with authority to control the line departmental officers.

The propriety of the United Nations agencies sponsoring rural development programmes in developing countries has not been questioned. By the same logic, if the central governments deem it to be their responsibility to sponsor such programmes in their own countries and not leave it to local initiative, such propriety would be difficult to challenge.

A view can be taken that this sort of paternalistic approach is wrong and that the central government (in a big country like India) should squarely place the responsibility of rural development and eradication of poverty and unemployment on the state governments and the latter should do likewise in respect of their districts, with an assurance of adequate financial and technical support as may be necessary. If the latter fail in the task, they will be accountable to their respective communities and electorates.

Personally I would support such an approach. At the same time, one must not ignore the fact that in such a denouement the weaker sections will be completely at the mercy of the local vested interests—class and caste. Numerous instances of atrocities on scheduled castes and the tribals have been reported. The point to note is that central assistance—Border Security Force, Central Reserve Police and the army—have had to be invoked for restoring law and order. Can one depend upon those very people who under the slightest pretext commit unspeakable atrocities on the downtrodden to promote their victims' development and welfare?

In spite of such a persuasive justification for central (and foreign?) intervention for IRD and growth with social justice, I have taken the view that decentralisation in planning and implementation of rural development programmes is not only desirable but necessary. In fact, without community action, responsive cooperation, if not initiative, no worthwhile rural development—in agriculture, health, education, housing, etc—can take place. And I would set great store by non-official and voluntary agencies to persevere in this effort irrespective of the Government's attitude towards them. Governments or people in power, by and large, are enlightened only as far as the self-interest of their class or caste is concerned. Change, revolutionary or reformist, has come historically from minority, dissident groups.

Where do all these reflections leave us? Centralisation in decision making both in regard to growth and social justice is unavoidable. At the same time, without genuine decentralisation, local initiative and responsive cooperation and organisation of the poor, projects and programmes of rural development for the benefit of the poor will either remain on paper or will be distorted through a trickle-up process. Call this a dilemma, ambivalence or double-think at worst.

The contribution which the local planning authority can make need not be judged by its rather limited jurisdiction and financial resources made available to it. Though the local authority is not permitted to make any major alterations in the sectoral allocations to what is called—in Gujarat and Maharashtra—normal district level' schemes as proposed by the state government, the local authority, in consultation with the district level departmental officers, will apparently have a good deal of latitude in the choice of schemes. In any case, its recommendations will have the backing of local knowledge and experience in regard to the needs, the potential and the constraints of the area, and will as such be superior to the decisions which would have been taken by the state planning body. Besides, with the knowledge of what has been recommended and approved by the state planning body, it can keep a better watch on the implementation. In the discretionary component (20 per cent) it will evidently have full freedom to plan and take care of the missing links in the 'normal' schemes, if any.

More importantly, if the local leadership is dynamic, is responsive to needs of the people—particularly the disadvantaged groups—and enjoys their trust, a large number of development and welfare programmes can be undertaken for which the major inputs are will and organisation. No plan, however comprehensive, is exhaustive in the sense that what is not covered by it does not exist. There are literally scores of activities—schemes and programmes—which do not enter into the vision of the planner but nonetheless are highly relevant to local needs. A large number of voluntary agencies are currently undertaking such activities with varying degrees of success.[12]

Such a planning body at the local level will not consider itself merely as a channel to communicate the demands—expressed as needs—of the local pressure groups but as a responsible body which in the light of closely observed potential and constraints of the area community would suggest development projects/programmes which would in its best judgement maximise social and economic returns to scarce financial and physical resources made available to it. If that body is competently persuasive it can make a larger demand on the national/state pool of resources backed by a convincing array of data and arguments. The plans of lower level planning authorities will carry weight and command respect with the higher level planning bodies only when they are competently and realistically formulated. This would need training of the local planner not simply in the methodology of project formulation but in the discipline of planning.

The most critical desideratum in the planning apparatus at the local level is the absence of a well-qualified full-time multidisciplinary team to assist the local planning authority. It will be the function of this team to examine the linkages between all projects and programmes proposed for the district, whatever be their source or sponsorship—whether World Bank assisted, centrally sponsored, state departmental, formulated by special agencies (such as SFDA, DPAP) or by state corporations (irrigation, forest, etc.). The scrutiny of linkages may reveal the loose ends and the scope for economising on resource use through mutual reinforcement and compatibility. To the extent possible, the team will estimate the costs and benefits and their distribution between the different classes and income groups to ensure the social justice aspect of planning.

While a few state governments in India—Maharashtra and Gujarat for example—have constituted district planning authorities, the importance of multi-disciplinary teams to assist the decision-making bodies has not yet been appreciated fully. May be the expenditure involved is a deterring factor. The shortage of qualified personnel may be another, though it would be curious in a country which time and again bemoans the prevalence of large unemployment of educated youth.

It would not be an exaggeration to say that the whole idea of decentralised planning has been confounded by the clash of interests of the vertical and the horizontal lines of command. This clash is not confined to the different wings of the bureaucracy. Ministers in charge of their departments also resent meddling with their plan by a different authority at the district level. Thus, what is involved in the successful implementation of the concept of integrated area development is nothing short of a change in attitudes all along the line, or in the political system in which the attitudes are formed.

As 'outsiders' we can at best redefine the respective roles of the vertical and horizontal lines of command to bring about a possible reconciliation between the two. First, the planning team itself will be multi-disciplinary and the departments' points of view would be adequately reflected if not represented in its deliberations. It would not be an 'independent' body in the sense that its doors would be closed to the departmental bureaucracy and the ministerial authority. At no level, not even the national, is planning just a compilation of state/departmental plans. At the national level state plans are pruned, if need be, and integrated to become a national plan with its sectoral allocation, as at the state level departmental plans are pruned and moulded into state plans. Similarly, if at the district level some integration of the district plans of the departments/ministries is needed, it need not be viewed as an unwarranted interference.

As for the district level officers of the departments, their status would be enhanced rather than reduced inasmuch as the integrated district plan in whose formulation they have participated would be more of *their* plan than the one handed down to them from above by their departmental superiors.

No district planning authority can ignore the broad policies and priorities laid down by the concerned state. For example, if the Government of Maharashtra has adopted the policy of employment guarantee, no district planning authority could delete EGS from its plan. It should thus be clear that the district planning team does not override the authority of any minister (or department), much less that of the ministry or the Council of Ministers.

Besides, there can be priorities within priorities. Just as a state can pick and choose its priorities (or alter the emphases) from the broad band of national priorities and even add its own if it does not conflict with the latter, the district could do the same in the light of its assessed potential, deficiencies and constraints. The minister in charge of a particular portfolio should be satisfied so long as all the district plans put together do not whittle down his portfolio's targets and programme.

As for the technocrat at the state headquarters (Chief Executive Engineer, Irrigation, for example) it should be explained to him that the district planning team will not (we presume) question the technical component of his district plan; its main concern is: (a) to examine its forward and backward linkages and bring them in alignment, and (b) if such examination reveals the necessity to subtract from (or add to) the physical or financial component of a departmental plan, it should have authority to do so. (There may not be enough pasture land to support a dairy scheme.) The department will be a gainer and not a loser as a consequence since such an exercise improves the quality of its plan and the prospects of its successful implementation.

The district team would no doubt pick and choose its priorities within state priorities as noted above and as a result the integrated plan may be significantly different from the plan made up of the bundle of district projects as presented by the departments. But this too should not matter, for if each district succeeds in optimising the output from its existing and potential resources and achieves a more equitable distribution of the output, the totality of the integrated district plan would yield better results than the totality of the unintegrated district departmental plans.

It is necessary to distinguish project formulation from plan formulation. Project formulation is primarily a technical exercise, while plan formulation is a broader economic exercise concerned with the allocation of scarce resources to achieve ends incorporated in the policy frame of the plan. The function of the department is to formulate a technically and financially sound project(s), the function of the planner is to integrate projects into a sound plan.

NOTES

1. This paper forms part of the study on "Two-Way Planning: Logic and Limitations—A Critical Review of Indian Experience" prepared for the FAO Regional Office for Asia and the Pacific, Bangkok, Thailand in 1981 and revised subsequently. The study was presented at the Expert Consultation on Two-Way Process in Agriculture and Rural Development Planning, organised by FAO in Bangkok from 1-4 February, 1983.
2. This impression is confirmed by what is stated in a note by the Planning Commission: "For the last several years in many States Panchayati Raj Institutions at the district level such as Zilla Parishads and District Panchayats were given the task of district level planning. The situation has now undergone a change. In some of the States where the district level PRI became effective, the State Governments, for various reasons, found it desirable to entrust the planning function to other new bodies. In Maharashtra, we now have the District Planning and Development Councils, and in Gujarat the District Planning Boards, which have taken over the planning functions of PRIs. In other States, Zilla Parishads and other district level PRIs continue to have the planning function but only in a formal sense. In fact they have been superseded and elections to these bodies have been delayed in a number of States." (Note on "Planning at the District Level", Planning Commission, Government of India (mimeo)).

REFERENCES

[1]Gupta, Anand. *Who Benefits from Government Expenditure in India*, Centre for Monitoring Indian Economy, Bombay, July 1980.

[2]Robinson, Joan. *The Cultural Revolution in China*, A Pellcan Original, Penguin Books Ltd., England, 1969.

[3]Madras Institute of Development Studies. *Structure and Intervention*, Madras, August 1980 (unpublished).

[4]Lakdawala, D.T. *Plan Finances in a Federal Economy*, Dr. V.S. Krishna Endowment Lectures, Andhra University, Waltair, 1979.

[5]*Ibid.*

[6]*Ibid.*

[7]*Ibid.*

[8]*The Times of India.* "Coal Nightmare for Dream Canal", New Delhi, January 21, 1981 (UNI).

[9]Adelman, Irma and Sherman Robinson. *Income Distribution Policy in Developing Countries: A Case Study of Korea*, published for World Bank, Oxford University Press, New York, 1978.

[10]*Ibid.*

[11]Hollensteiner, Mary R. "People Power: Community Participation in the Planning and Implementation of Human Settlement", Philippine Studies, 1978. Quoted by T.K. Jayaraman, "Peoples' Participation in Watershed Management Projects", *Indian Journal of Public Administration*, Vol. XXVI, No. 4.

[12]Many of these are reported in *Voluntary Action*—Monthly Journal of the Association of Voluntary Agencies (AVARD), New Delhi.

PART III

Choice of Implementing Agencies

Proceedings

Rural development, like any other area of public administration in India, has not suffered from a lack of proclaimed policies and good intentions. Where it has been found lacking very greatly, however, has been in the implementation. In his paper, "The Alternative: District Government?", Nirmal Mukarji analyses the problems of implementation and proposes some structural changes in the administrative machinery entrusted with the implementation of rural development programmes.

According to him, the crux of the problem of implementation lies in the dichotomy between the managerial model of rural development administration in which the bureaucracy represented by the district collector and the block development officer play the pivotal role, and the democratic model in which the community through people's representation plays the pivotal role. Development administration in India has been almost entirely designed on the lines of the managerial model and this model has contributed little to the progress of rural development. If any worthwhile headway is to be made, rural development administration has to be restructured in a more democratic fashion and people's participation has to be ensured by the setting up of a third tier of government at the district level which is not only for the people but also *by* and *of* the people. Such a district government should have constitutionally defined powers with functional autonomy, representation through a system of direct elections, and assured finances. The district government should replace the collector pattern and directly control the district bureaucracy. The restructuring of district development administration on such lines presupposes the need for political awareness. This means that rural development must move out of its 'cozy technical field' and reckon with the possibilities and problems of political influence.

Kamla Chowdhry, Nirmala Murthy and Ranjit Gupta, in their papers discuss some specific cases which illustrate the problems of implementation which confront agencies of various kinds in India.* Their case study analyses offer insights into some of the major human, social, organisational and political problems associated with the implementation of rural development programmes.

Chowdhry's paper discusses three cases of projects involved in afforestation and development of uncultivated lands: one by a voluntary agency, the second by a government research agency, and the third by a government department.

The first project carried out by a Gandhian agency called the Dasholi Gram Swarajya Mandal (DGSM) in Western U.P., under the leadership of Chandi Prasad Bhatt, organised Bhoodhan activities and tried to generate an awareness among people of the need to preserve their rapidly deteriorating environment, especially the land and forests. The second case deals with the efforts of the Central Soil and Water Conservation Research and Training Institute (CSWCRTI) to resolve the problem of siltation of a lake and the afforestation of degraded land in the lake's catchment area. The agency was able to win the participation of the community in its efforts by making them realise that soil conservation work would help them obtain supplementary irrigation facilities and redeem them from dependence on the vagaries of the monsoons. Besides achieving success in its desiltation and afforestation efforts, the project led to a number of socio-economic changes in the community which contributed to improvements in the living habits of the people. In the case of the third project, a government department initiated a programme for establishing tree plantations. A number of related tasks such as building canal banks, railway sides, village woodlots, strip plantations and seedling farm forests, and promoting community self-help were under-

*The fifth paper, "Comprehensive Rural Development: The CADC Experiment" by Biplab Dasgupta, was not presented at the seminar due to the author's absence, and hence could not be discussed.

taken. As a result, some improvements were effected in matters concerning the community as a whole, but the main beneficiaries were the rich and the powerful sections of the community.

The evidence from the case studies of the lack of success of the government department in bringing home benefits to the poor seems to suggest that bureaucratic structures may not be effective in substantially improving the conditions of the poor, although such structures are necessary when large-scale programmes demanding mobilisation of considerable resources have to be undertaken. The situation thus presents a dilemma. A voluntary agency of the DGSM type, which is small and built around a charismatic individual, may be highly successful in mobilising the poor, having them participate in various activities, and inculcating self-reliance in them. But its work may be incapable of expansion and replication. On the other hand, a government department which is encumbered by various limitations, which prevent it from reaching the poor directly has the capabilities to undertake large-scale projects from which some benefits may indirectly trickle down to the poor.

Nirmala Murthy discusses two contrasting approaches to rural development. Self Employed Women's Association (SEWA), a well-known and well-established organisation, began with the objective of organising women agricultural labourers for better wages and economic development, later branching out into a number of other welfare-oriented activities such as training women to undertake various income-generating activities, providing training for literacy, and setting up cooperatives. A different approach was adopted by Mahiti, a small, relatively unknown group of young professionals, whose strategy was to evolve information linkages which would create, as a basis for emancipatory action, awareness among underdeveloped communities about the resources to which they could gain access and the kinds of government development programmes from which they could benefit.

The two agencies were driven by common motives of poverty eradication and emancipation from exploitation. But they differed widely in their strategies and methods: one emphasised immediate, tangible benefits; the other sought to generate awareness and self-reliance which are expected to yield longer-term benefits. The first agency has won wide recognition and approval; the second has yet to establish its credibility.

The experiences of the two agencies suggest that if poor people who are socially divided on the lines of caste, class and sex, are to be organised for development and self-reliance, a sense of cohesiveness and mutuality must be created among them by helping them learn to work together on activities that yield direct economic benefits to them. Another implication is that for the gains of development to reach the poor, some sort of middle-level power group is necessary to act as a bridge between the bureaucracy and the people. Also, pressures from both above and below are necessary to goad local development agencies into action, and these pressures can be generated with the assistance of external agencies. The experiences also indicate that sections of the community which benefit from development programmes may develop a vested interest in preventing the diffusion of their newly acquired capabilities to other sections which have not yet enjoyed the fruits of development.

Ranjit Gupta analyses the performance of two prominent voluntary agencies, the Association of Sarva Seva Farms (ASSEFA), and the Mysore Resettlement and Development Agency (MYRADA), evaluating their strengths and weaknesses. Such agencies have made valuable contributions to rural development in the country but these contributions are miniscule when looked at against the background of the unfinished task of development, and the time and resources expended by these agencies. Therefore, he suggests that despite the drawbacks of government agencies which are known for their sluggish performance, the responsibility for carrying out development on as large a scale as is required in the country, has to be borne and discharged by the government. Since the government performs this role mainly through the district administration, it is necessary to pay attention to improving the capability of the district administration by developing ways of matching micro-planning with the structures and capabilities of development agencies and administration.

In the discussion that followed, reaction to Mukarji's paper ranged from qualified approval to strong opposition from among the participants. If we are serious about giving more prominence to politics, Kurien said, we have to be equally serious about defining the character of that politics because politics has both a desirable and an undesirable side to it. Politicisation of local level bodies should mean that such bodies should become much more concerned about local and economic issues rather than with remote political issues of a purely administrative nature. Kurien was in favour of having an elected body with special responsibility for planning and administration at the local level. The scope of this body would be very limited which would enable it to discharge its duties better. Politicisation of local bodies would be a step in the right direction if it helps ordinary people engaged in normal occupations to get better representation in bodies that make crucial decisions.

Dantwala, endorsing the substance of Kurien's contention, expressed the view that conditions are not ripe for a representative form of direct level government or a third force. Such a form of government might remove some of the drawbacks of the present administrative and political structures, but would throw up different types of problems. The idea of a third tier of government at the local level appears to be democratic, but in reality such a government will not be truly representative because of the character of our society. More than 50 per cent of the country's population live in a state of dire poverty and subordination, incapacitated from exercising free choice in an election. Under these circumstances, elections simply cannot ensure genuine people's representation. A representative form of district government therefore will not be an improvement. An organisation which can act as a third force has to be, by and large, outside the arena of party politics and power struggles. This does not mean that it would be politically neutral; whenever necessary it would resort to political action to protect the rights of the poor and end their exploitation. But considering the manner in which elections in India are fought, Dantwala did not believe that elected representatives, who would be affiliated to political parties, could perform this role. Until our society becomes more egalitarian and people become capable of meaningfully exercising their vote in a democratic system, there is no alternative except to continue relying on the bureaucracy. Admittedly, the bureaucracy is not free from corruption, but this is because it has been contaminated by politicians.

Some participants were less optimistic about the role of bureaucrats. Murthy doubted whether the bureaucracy, itself corrupt and notorious for its nexus with corrupt politicians, has the capacity and the commitment to function as the third block of a democratic development system. Experience has shown that the bureaucracy has invariably allowed itself to be used for the personal political ends of the people in power.

Another pitfall in the way of representative district administration, Sanjoy Das Gupta pointed out, is that the poorest groups that should benefit the most from rural development do not have *de facto* representation even in existing institutions. Unless they can be effectively represented, representative democracy cannot succeed. On the contrary, if a district government were to be set up now (under existing conditions), the district collector would always be able to pass on the blame for non-performance to the representatives, and the district government system will therefore only increase the power of the collector without making him accountable. As it is, even today the bureaucrat enjoys far too much protection and so can afford to take his accountability lightly.

Lakdawala raised questions concerning the operational aspects of the proposed system of local government which suggest that giving full representation to the people is no easy task. Given the way local bodies function today, it is probable that local bodies may have to be superseded. If so, how would one define the powers of supersession? As far as finances are concerned, if the local bodies are to have complete financial autonomy, coordination of plans with state and national plans would not be possible. Therefore, there would have to be some system whereby local level plans are approved of at higher levels. These are details which have to be looked into carefully because differences in detail can defeat agreement on the principle of democratic local government.

In his response to the issues raised, Mukarji argued that we cannot continue to repose faith in the bureaucracy and non-party activities until the uncertain day when people have been liberated from their state of dependence. The future, he said, cannot be built around the collector; neither can development wait until people are ready for representative democracy. The collector is after all an instrument of the state and is subordinate to the dictates of those who hold power in the state. He therefore cannot protect the poor against vested interests. A representative local government, on the other hand, would provide the impetus for the emergence of countervailing forces that have to be mobilised if development is not to be sabotaged by vested interests. Mukarji clarified that it was in this context that he had mentioned politicisation. By this he meant an increasing awareness of political rights and mobilising people to participate in the functioning of a democratic system. Today our democratic system exists only at the top of the social hierarchy. Such a democracy has failed to develop nurseries to produce new leaders and so only corrupt leaders emerge. The potential of a representative democratic system involving the third tier needs to be exploited so that a new vibrant leadership emerges.

Some participants felt that greater politicisation is an important prerequisite as well as an objective of the democratisation of development planning and implementation. Dipankar Gupta believed that politicisation is important for the replication of successful development programmes, for without it, we would have to depend upon new entrepreneurs and charismatic persons to generate and sustain new programmes every time.

Ranjit Gupta felt that an increasing sense of political entitlement has helped bringing about significant change in our society and that if this process can be accelerated people can begin to look after their own uplift rather than have to depend upon agencies. Nevertheless, the advent of a district level government is still a long way off, and in the meanwhile we need to encourage and organise many more agenc es like MYRADA and ASSEFA. He suggested the need to induct yonng professionals who should be trained and encouraged to work as development entrepreneurs independently of existing agencies.

The case studies presented by Chowdhry, Murthy and Ranjit Gupta provide some indications of the potential efficacy of encouraging non-governmental agencies to aid in the task of rural development. Gaikwad brought attention to the factors suggested by the studies contributing to the success of the implementing agencies described. First, every successsful programme was spearheaded by a leader, an entrepreneur, who was a product of the immediate environment in which the agency was situated. Second, a programme was successful when it was able to provide direct economic benefits to the people. Third, success occurred when a programme was built around some industry, as in the case of SEWA which began to organise women in establishing a dairy industry. Fourth, successful replication of programmes depended on the nature of the commodity which an agency produced and the type of organisation required. For instance, attempts to replicate the Amul experiment have not met with much success whereas experiments involving sugar cooperatives were quickly replicated. This suggests that replication of rural development experiments may not lead to favourable results because conditions vary from place to place. Programmes and agencies designed to promote rural development, therefore, have to be situation-specific and area-specific. The experiments also suggest that it may not be fruitful to train or educate people to become entrepreneurs in rural development, although it may well be feasible to train people to become managers in the field of rural development. Attempts to replicate entrepreneurship in the past have not been successful as the experiences of the training centres in Marathwada and Baroda have shown. When it comes to issues like poverty and development, many young people who venture into this field are guided more by emotion than by reason. The failure rate among aspiring rural development entrepreneurs is therefore high. So it may be wiser to concentrate on providing support and encouragement to entrepreneurs who are already identified or to those who show potential rather than try to produce entrepreneurs in training institutes.

Haldipur, on the other hand, was more optimistic about the replicability of experiments like the Amul experiment. He pointed out that the Amul pattern of cooperative organisation has now been adopted by 17 states and union territories in the country, including the Andaman and Nicobar Islands, and that training of the kind imparted by the Institute of Rural Management at Anand appears to have been successful. Conceptually, the replication of the Anand pattern is quite simple: social mobilisation, building organisations of farmers, collection and processing of surplus milk, ensuring supply of inputs, and marketing—but everything is owned by the beneficiary farmers, and professionals are only employees of the farmers.

Another counterpoint to Gaikwad's came from Deep Joshi who felt that there was need to demystify the development process in the case of successful rural development projects. Success does not depend upon the personality of the leader or entrepreneur—Mishra, the leader of Sukhomajri programme, is only an ordinary person. The reason for the failure to replicate this project probably lies in the political economy dimension of our society rather than in the personalities of people. If development has to await entrepreneurs, then the whole planning process becomes futile.

The experimental nature of most rural development programmes evoked criticism from Amar Siamwalla. Experimentation with rural development projects, he felt, are tantamount to manipulation of people unless the experimenters are willing to bear the consequences of failure. Almost always, it is the beneficiaries of development programmes who have to bear the consequences of failure. Is it fair to expect people who barely manage to earn their daily bread to bear the brunt of experiments? No wonder the poor rarely show enthusiasm for rural development programmes unless they have proof of their success. In many cases, entrepreneurs have initiated experiments and then withdrawn from the scene when they failed leaving the rural people to bear the consequences.

Mahajan felt that the case studies presented also illustrate the dichotomy that exists between huge governmental agencies involved in rural development which enjoy abundant inputs but are short on results, and the small voluntary experiments of entrepreneurs who work with little input but produce good output. He wondered if the two could be synthesised to create viable social technologies for development tasks. David King voiced a related concern about need for social science research to address itself to questions which may provide answers to the problem of replicating successful experiences—on the logic of collective action, conditions influencing political economy, environmental factors, and the modes of creating entrepreneurial structures. The answers to the questions may help demystify the whole process of rural development.

In his summing up of the discussion, Kurien suggested that the process of development need not be identified with any one type of agency, be it voluntary or governmental. In the social process there are certain things common to all agencies, and agencies will attempt to search for and codify these common aspects. At the same time, the function of a voluntary agency is so closely related to the specificity of the situation that every question regarding what an agency should or should not do can at best have a tentative answer: 'it all depends'. Therefore, voluntary agencies should not be too concerned about replicating experiments. The measure of the success of their mission is not in term of the replicability of the work. If replicability were to be the measuring rod, he warned, success not purpose would be the foremost concern. There is a danger that success would defeat purpose. The real test of a voluntary agency is its willingness and ability to die once its task is done. Therefore, the answer to the question of how to bring about synthesis of different modes of rural development strategies is that one should not look for a synthesis.

The Alternative: District Government?

Nirmal Mukarji

The Problem

A distinguished expert in rural development whose voluntary project in Rajasthan is widely known made the following observations in *Yojana* (August 1984):

> If it was in my hands to change the set up what would I do? I would make sure the planner stayed a major portion of his time in the village. . . .
>
> One does not need a degree from a foreign university to come up with a solution at the village level. The planner has the great gift of making simple solutions look complicated. The district and village level functionaries have the ability to demystify processes and adapt them to be understood by the beneficiaries themselves but such skills are not appreciated. . . .
>
> Those who have broken away from the usual way of doing things are considered eccentric within the bureaucracy. Well, if I have to pin my hopes on anyone for planning to have more meaning I would do so on these handful of bureaucrats who are not willing to be dictated to by the system where mediocrity is a qualification.

This view leans heavily on the few members of the bureaucracy who are able and willing to function in new ways untypical of the system. Such persons are presumed to exist in sufficient numbers to make a difference if properly utilised.

One senses in this view an unstated expectation that if this select group were to be enabled to demonstrate success its numbers might increase. There is thus an implicit reliance on administrative reform, limited in scope but good enough to make the desired impact on rural development.

A contrary view is to be found in a study of rural development delivery systems still in the process of being finalised. According to this, the experience of the past one hundred years shows that 'our administration is reform-proof'. The people continue to be outside development planning and implementation. The central issue, therefore, is not what place to give to the *collector*, but rather what place to give to the *community*. The foremost recommendation of the study is that, on the one hand, democratic decentralisation should be given effect to and all technical and administrative staff (such as for land reforms, bonded labour, children and women, scheduled castes and scheduled tribes, agriculture, cooperatives, education, health, animal husbandry, forest, industry) brought under the direction of three-tier elected panchayat bodies at the village, block and district levels and, on the other, the century old rule of the collector should end.

The two views between them state the essence of the problem about implementing agencies. There is general dissatisfaction about the progress of rural development and especially about the adequacy of the bureaucratic system as an implementing machinery. The way out in one case is seen in terms of identifying promising bureaucrats and giving them as free a hand as possible—a basically managerial solution, of which the there can be other variants. In the other case it is seen in terms of making the machinery accountable to the people's representatives—what one might call a democratic solution, of which too there can be several forms. There are other institutional actors in the field: cooperatives, banks, voluntary agencies and professional groups. But they have largely been supportive of complementary roles. The central debate is about the managerial and the democratic approaches. There is no inherent conflict between good management and democratic functioning, but the two approaches have somehow emerged as mutually exclusive alternatives. Therefore one way of perceiving the problem is as a choice between an essentially managerial model and a substantially democratic one.

* * *

A different way of addressing the problem is to ask what exactly it is that has to be implemented, for only then can the issue of implementing agencies be realistically discussed. This involves spelling out broadly the content of rural development plans.

A perusal of plan documents reveals an element of confusion about rural development planning. The First Plan made no mention of rural development as such. Nor, surprisingly, did the Second Plan, which in a sense was the mother of all succeeding plans. It was not till the Third Plan that the term 'rural development' first appeared. This was in the chapter on community development and only in passing. After a period of eclipse (i.e. no mention whatever in the Fifth Plan), it reappeared in a big way in the Draft Sixth Plan; there was a chapter headed "Agriculture and Rural Development". The Sixth Plan clubbed rural development with cooperation. The Approach to the Seventh Plan found a new partner for it in the shape of poverty alleviation. Thus, firstly, the idea of rural development evolved slowly. Secondly, when it did take shape it did so as an adjunct, first of community development, then of agriculture, then of cooperation and, for the projected Seventh Plan, of poverty alleviation. As far as plan documents go, rural development has still to be recognised as an important concept on its own.

The root of this confusion lies in a dichotomy which has persisted since the time when the community development programme was first introduced. On the one hand there are rural components in nearly all sectoral plans, while on the other there are specially fashioned multi-sector programmes such as the schematic budget of community development fame and the Integrated Rural Development Programme (IRDP) of recent years. There is an ancient and entrenched dispute between the ministries and departments of the Union and the state controlling the former and the Ministry of Rural Development and its conterparts in the states which control the latter. The dispute goes right down to the block level, with officers of the sectoral departments ranged against the block development officer. The Ministry of Rural Development controls, which means operates, the funds for, IRDP, the National Rural Employment Programme (NREP) and the scheme for the Training of Youth for Self-Employment (TRYSEM). It also carries the nodal responsibility for the Minimum Needs Programme (MNP). Consequently the block development officer sees his main responsibility in terms of these core programmes, and so do the people. The dichotomy between the sectoral and the core programmes has thus resulted in the content of rural development plans effectively being narrowed down to IRDP, NREP and other such alphabetical creatures. But this makes nonsense of the idea of rural development. As the Sixth Plan stressed, "the development of the rural areas is the concern of all sectors of the economy and these areas draw benefit of development in varying degrees from various sectors."

In this background, another way of viewing the problem is how to resolve the dichotomy between the sectoral and the core components of rural development plans. Coordination is the catchword. But in all the years since community development was launched, the problem of coordination has defied solution. Repeatedly, reliance has been placed on the collector at the district level and the block development officer at the block level, but the process of differentiation in programmes and agencies keeps outpacing the capacity of such coordinators to bring things together. No state minister or head of department feels happy about allowing sectoral officers at or below district level to come under an outsider's coordinating discipline. Nevertheless, unless the dichotomy is resolved rural development will remain bogged down.

* * *

The subject seems to be beset with dichotomies. The term 'implementing agencies' suggested the need to explore what was to be implemented, and the 'what' came out in terms of rural development plans. Implementation conjures up the notion of new schemes, new programmes, in short, new plans. It ignores the unexciting work of maintaining roads and culverts or operating already established schools and health centres. There is a whole world of ongoing development activities which has to be looked after. Periodically, completed schemes of previous plans, under the concept of committed expenditure, keep getting added to ongoing activities. It is an unfortunate fact that, by and large, all non-plan development activities are grossly neglected. In this author's view there is a crying need for the distinction between plan and non-plan activities being abolished so that maintenance and operation receive due attention. Morarji Desai, when Prime Minister, addressed a minute to the then Deputy Chairman, Planning Commission, in which he desired this very point to be examined. Because of its preoccupation with drawing up the Draft Sixth Plan, the then Planning Commission was unable to go into the matter fully. However, some preliminary exercises are understood to have been made which suggested that the idea could be selectively tried out in a few sectors, education being one of them.

The dichotomy between plan and non-plan development activities seems particulary inept in the sphere of rural development. For one thing, rural development generally involves doing individually small things in large numbers. Every time a primary school is expanded or upgraded, or an electricity supply line extended to a couple of villages in addition to the six or seven already served by it, or an additional drinking water point provided in a village, there is an administrative and accounting nightmare with some of the staff and equipment having to be treated as non-plan and the additional as plan. Rural development, more than any other field, requires simplification of procedures so that more gets done with less resource input. Secondly, emphasis on maintenance and operation is vitally important in this field, otherwise health centres without medicines, electric lines without energy and pumpsets out of order can invite rapid disillusionment. Thirdly, since a large part of rural development involves programmes for the downrodden, there must be an element of continuous nurturing of schemes, of households, even of individuals, until viability is attained, however long that may take. This is not possible under a system of five yearly chops. Fourthly, how can one conceive of a well-knit team of rural development workers if the 'knitting' extends only to the plan part of their work, leaving the non-plan aspect uncoordinated?

Consequently, the problem is not simply one of choosing *implementing* agencies for rural development *plans*, but rather one of evolving suitable arrangements for administering all rural development activities, ongoing as well as new.

* * *

The foregoing poses the problem in terms of evolving an appropriate rural development administration. Concern for rural development springs from the neglect of the rural areas, where the bulk of Indians (75 per cent) live, and also where the bulk of India's poor—landless labourers, small and marginal farmers, village artisans (together numbering around 350 million)—are to be found. The concern is entirely justified, and will remain continuingly so as long as the situation on the ground stays substantially unchanged. The few success stories, some ascribable to voluntary agencies and others to official agencies, are heartening, but they also serve to highlight the massive failures elsewhere. Rural development must therefore remain high on the agenda of national concerns.

Is it time, however, to pause and consider whether a genuine concern has, over time, unwittingly converted rural development into a developmental ghetto. The Asoka Mehta Report on Panchayati Raj Institutions, commenting on what it called 'rural-urban continuum', said that "as a part of the process of increased commercialisation of agriculture, growing dependence on extra-local supplies of inputs and search for market avenues by the farmers and producers in the allied sectors for their diverse products, an urban-rural continuum is growing. Smaller towns with a population of 20 to 50 thousand are becoming a part of the rural scene . . . , these are capable of sharing the economic activities of the rural areas, and an inter-dependence is inevitable both for economic reasons and welfare pre-requisites." The Committee drew attention to the fact that small and medium towns had been stagnating for three decades while the bigger towns were steadily growing bigger. It ascribed the phenomenon to the former not having developed functional linkages with their rural hinterlands. Earlier, the Rural Urban Relationship Committee had observed, in 1963, that urbanisation should be considered a "continuous process of transition from rural to urban, treating the present differences as only a stage in the continuum." This evolution from a rural to urban way of life, the Asoka Mehta Committee went on to say, "is a continuous process with sequences ranging from a tiny hamlet to a sizeable city. The question of urban-rural relationship is to be viewed in the context of the needs of a developing economy and the attendant processes of affording higher level of services and facilities to the rural areas. This could be achieved in linking up the rural areas with urban focal points." The short point is that the dichotomy between rural and urban development is unjustified and damages both.

The underlying idea in most rural development programmes is that people should stay where they are and be enabled to improve their lot *in situ*, whether through the land reforms group of measures or through the loan-cum-subsidies group (IRDP, etc.). This makes sense in that the beneficiaries retain their roots. But if members of the weaker sections, especially scheduled castes, wish to end their misery in the villages by moving away to nearby towns for livelihoods, no alternative scheme to assist them seems to have been considered. Presumably because of the barrier between rural and urban development. Employment generation schemes in growth centres and towns through industrial or service sector development coupled with subsidised housing development plans in these places could be the basis for a well-conceived, and hopefully controlled, migration policy, at least for the most hard-pressed sections in the villages. But such new lines of thinking are not possible so long as rural development remains in its rural confine.

The above raises the desirability of formulating the problem in the still wider sense of evolving suitable arrangements for development administration as a whole, spanning both rural and urban development. This would involve doing away with yet another dichotomy, that between rural and urban. The term 'development administration' is used here to connote the activities associated with the well-known group of departments in the development field. It is not used in the academic sense developed by Weidner and others, namely an action-oriented, goal-oriented administrative system. This clarification is necessary simply to avoid controversy, certainly not to argue against action-orientation or goal-orientation.

* * *

What is left out of the ambit of development administration, as defined above, is the triad of law and order, revenue administration and general administration. The last is a catch-all term for the residuary functions which vest in the collector by virtue of his being the state government's man on the spot. Anyone familiar with the district scene knows that these are the areas where authority resides. Theorists of development administration have tended to underrate the importance of these subjects. Practitioners in the development field know better, because they encounter the impeding or facilitating hand of authority all the time. It is a serious blunder to imagine that the developmental side of district administration can be shaped into something satisfactory in isolation of the 'authority' side.

For long development was treated as the poor relation in district administration, those in authority adopting attitudes ranging from amused tolerance to patronising helpfulness. As the idea of development grew, authority began to be drawn in. The first to be affected was revenue administration, because as the custodian of land records it was called upon to implement every type of land reform, whether it was abolition of zamindari or tenancy reform or consolidation of holdings or enforcement of land ceilings. According to the Seventh Plan Approach paper, "Redistributive land reforms that provide a minimum level of landholding to the landless and a measure of security of tenancy are essential for securing the rural agricultural poor against income fluctuations. Where required, consolidation of holdings of marginal farmers and land assignees, as also their organisation into groups and societies backed by financial assistance and administrative and policy support from government should be attempted so that inputs can be directed towards the target beneficiary groups." It is clear that, if this is meant seriously, revenue administration will have to be detached from the authority triad and treated as an integral part of development administration.

The relationship between the other two components of the triad and the development process is linked with the power configuration within states. Law and order and general administration are firmly controlled by the caste-cum-class group which wields power at the state level. So long as development takes forms which favour this group at the district level, as for instance when it focuses attention on agricultural production to the virtual exclusion of other objectives, it has a cosy relationship with them. But when the focus shifts to poverty alleviation and, more especially, organisation of the poor, the picture begins to change. As soon as the conscientisation of the downtrodden, which is at the heart of such programmes, approaches a critical threshold, the power structure perceives a threat. Its instruments of authority at the district level, namely, the machinery for law and order and general administration then adopt an adversary role and thus become impediments to development. These impediments are sometimes overcome by the intervention of the 'eccentric' bureaucrats the expert quoted at the commencement of this paper had in mind, but such interventions are few and in any case transient. Development has yet to find a systematic and durable answer to the calculated obstructionism of authority on the defensive.

This brief discussion of a major and complex issue indicates that the problem goes beyond merely evolving suitable arrangements for development administration. In the larger perspective, it has to be seen as the restructuring of the entire district administration, developmental as well as non-developmental. Indeed, in this view of the problem what has hitherto been generally regarded as non-developmental can no longer remain outside the bounds of developmental thinking. Even this dichotomy, namely, between developmental and non-developmental, must be reconsidered.

* * *

It is implicit in the above formulation that the wider concept of district administration is more sound than narrower ones like implementing agencies or development administration. It is so only because it affords the maximum possibility of clearing up the accumulated clutter of thirty years of planned development. But all this clutter—plan versus non-plan and so forth—has been artificially created and is internal to the administration. Its removal is not only desirable but essential. But the restructuring of district administration, however well that is done, would be nothing more than a bureaucratic exercise, basically of the nature of administrative reform. Would this meet the requirements of development? Where would the people come in?

On the role of the people in development, the First Five Year Plan had the following to say:

> Democratic planning will not succeed unless the sanction of an awakened public opinion operates powerfully . . . . (The people's) own views about their needs and difficulties and the correct solutions must be elicited and given the fullest weight in making the plans, in the execution of which they will be called upon to assist . . . . Means have . . . to be devised to bring the people into association both at the stage of formulation of the plans and in their implementation. . . .

What was visualised was the *association* of the people in plan formulation and implementation, in the former by eliciting their views and giving them full weight and in the latter by calling upon them to assist. It was a case of a paternalistic government giving yet-to-be-awakened people a minimal role. Since democracy had yet to take root, such a conservative attitude was understandable.

Leaving aside the intervening plan documents, the Approach to the Seventh Five Year Plan contains the following statements:

> The State Governments could set apart plan outlays for the schemes and programmes to be planned and implemented at the district level and encourage planning with public participation at the district level for such schemes and programmes.
>
> (Poverty alleviation activities) have to be implemented with the simultaneous involvement of various disciplines or departments in a decentralised framework and the participation of people at the grassroots level through village panchayats, panchayat samitis, zilla parishads, etc.

The role allotted to the people is still minimal. The vocabulary has advanced, for *participation* conveys something more than association, but the content has regressed. In plan formulation, participation has merely to be encouraged and that too only in the case of district level schemes predetermined as such by the state governments. In implementation, people's participation takes second place to the involvement of departments and, so far as one can make out, only in relation to anti-poverty schemes.

It is remarkable that, although democracy has by now taken firm root and political awareness spread phenomenally, the people's role in development is to this day set down in minimal terms. On the plan formulation side, the main constraint seems to be the reluctance of planners to loosen their hold. Thus, for instance, even a people-oriented exercise like the Dantwala Report on Block Level Planning, while rightly favouring the strengthening of planning capability at the district level, was lukewarm about securing public participation. One of the reasons mentioned by it was that the public would first have to be familiarised with the technical constraints of planning (neo-paternalism?). The Hanumantha Rao report on District Planning contains twenty recommendations under the heading 'People's Participation', but its central theme nonetheless is that there should be a district planning cell composed of experts servicing a district planning body headed by the collector. The Sukhamoy Chakravarty (Economic Advisory Council) report on the Decentralisation of Development Planning and Implementation Systems does not even make a pretence that its concern is in any way *democratic* decentralisation.

On the implementation side, it is the state-level political leadership which does not wish to relax its grip. Genuine people's participation at the district (and below) level might dilute its monopoly over patronage and in the long run even challenge its political power.

How then, in the face of these formidable constraints, are the people to be brought in? The problem advances from simply attaining the bureaucratic ultimate of a restructured district administration to taking the first step in a democratic direction by ensuring people's participation. Administration *for* the people is not enough. It must also be *of* the people, at least to the extent the word 'participation' can be stretched. District government rather than merely district administration needs to be thought of.

* * *

This raises the whole question of the role of political development in the developmental process. Planners have tended to deny any role to it, though plan documents contain the usual rhetorical flourishes. One supposes this is because it does not lend itself to quantitative planning. But no account of India's political economy since Independence can exclude the contribution of political development. Indeed, the political side of the total developmental process has been at least as important as the economic, if not more so. There is nothing to preclude policy being planned in this field, even if the model-building type of planning appropriate to the economic side is not possible.

Policy planning in regard to political development would have to deal with at least two critical issues: the distribution of political power, and political institutions. On the first of these the Hanumantha Rao Group on District Planning made the following pertinent observations:

> People's participation at the local levels is necessary primarily to reduce the unequal distribution of power in the rural areas. Studies on poverty in the developing countries have revealed that the generation of poverty is a function of the concentration of power and the monopolisation of resources by the rural elite. People's participation at the local level would, therefore, help bring about a redistribution of both control of resources and of power in favour of the rural poor. . . . Our experience so far in development at the local level has been that those who have the least power obtain the least benefit from planned development. How are we to change this situation, so that the organised participation of (the) 'excluded' and 'marginalised' categories of people would be possible? Thus the central issue here is one of power structure. We cannot evade this issue in local level planning. . . . The central point in the question of public participation. . . is therefore: how to bring about a change in the power structure in various people's institutions in favour of the majority that is poor?

In short the objective of policy planning for political development at and below the district level has to be the redistribution of power on an egalitarian basis.

As regards political institutions, the same Group observed as follows:

> In a broad sense, the issue of popular participation is basically identical with the issue of democracy. Our experience, however, has revealed that democratic decentralisation experiments have fallen a prey to power monopolisation by the rural elite and have given rise to what may be called certain 'inner limits' to public participation. Thus, the formal channel of participation through the Panchayati Raj Institutions, with a view to adhering to democratic principles, has not guaranteed actual people's participation in the running of affairs at the local level. The crucial question, therefore, is: how to promote active mass participation as a central feature of our policy for local level development?

The Group felt that the answer lay in developing new forums through all kinds of spontaneous action groups. Since spontaneity cannot, by definition, be developed, the answer is not satisfactory. But the question is valid. Given the objective of an egalitarian redistribution of power, what sort of political institutions are required?

These considerations of political development suggest that the idea of people's participation must have the clear objective of power redistribution on an egalitarian basis and must be enabled to express itself through appropriate political institutions. District government must, it seems to follow, not only be *for* the people but fully *of* and *by* the people. The problem in the last analysis is not one of district administration or even district government but of representative district government.

Is Panchayati Raj the Answer?

The burden of what has been said so far is that so long as rural development is viewed in sub-systemic terms, it is bound to suffer from constraints that will not only slow its advance but flaw its quality. This will especially be the case if people's participation is given low value and political development none at all. The problem thus has to be seen as one of evolving representative district administration. Does this point to panchayati raj providing a possible answer?

* * *

The Constitution-makers gave scant attention to panchayats. There is, no doubt, Article 40 in the chapter on Directive Principles of State Policy which reads as below:

> The State shall take steps to organise village panchayats and endow them with such powers and authority as may be necessary to enable them to function as units of self-government.

As is well known, the Directive Principles of State Policy are little more than toothless exhortations. This one on panchayats seems to have been inserted in deference to Gandhian thinking. It finds no reflection in the Seventh Schedule listing the powers of the Union and the states. Item 5 of the state list reads as follows:

> Local government, that is to say, the constitution and powers of municipal corporations, improvement trusts, district boards, mining settlement authorities and other local authorities for the purpose of local self-government or village administration.

It is almost as if the draftsmen of the Directive Principles and the Seventh Schedule functioned in watertight compartments, for whereas the former at least spared an article for panchayats the latter found no use even for the word. One is forced to conclude that there was an element of casualness on the part of the Constitution-makers in regard to panchayats.

It was on this slender foundation that the edifice of panchayati raj had to be built. It is interesting to recall that the study team which pioneered the idea of panchayati raj worked on terms of reference which also omitted any mention of panchayats. Balwantray Mehta and his colleague thus displayed a boldness of vision which the Constitution-makers at best gave only a glimpse of. The philosophy of panchayati raj is encapsulated in the following passage of their path-finding report:

> Development cannot progress without responsibility and power. Community development can be real only when the community understands its problems, realises its responsibilities, exercises the necessary powers through its chosen representatives and maintains a constant and intelligent

vigilance on local administration. With this objective, we recommend an early establishment of statutory elective local bodies and devolution to them of the necessary resources, power and authority.

The structure of panchayati raj was envisioned in three tiers from the bottom upwards: directly elected village panchayats, indirectly elected panchayat samitis at the block level and zilla parishads composed of ex-officio members at the district level. The operative level was to be the middle one to which selected developmental functions were to be devolved.

The scheme was applied in the states in varying patterns and with uneven results. Although most states did introduce it, the only ones worth mentioning are Rajasthan and Andhra Pradesh, which were first off the mark and accepted the primacy of blocks samitis, and Maharashtra and Gujarat, which preferred to give first place to zilla parishads. Except in the latter, panchayati raj institutions were not given much to do, but in these two they did well. The Asoka Mehta Report considered that "panchayati raj should not be viewed as a God that has failed". But this report did little to enlarge the vision of the Mehta report, though important refinements were suggested. One of these was that the first point of decentralisation below the state level should be the district rather than the block, which was the position obtaining in Maharashtra and Gujarat. Its overall analysis was that after an initial phase of ascendancy, panchayati raj went through a phase of stagnation, and since 1969 had been in a phase of decline. Subsequent to the report, West Bengal has activated PRIs and Karnataka has legislated to do so; there are indications of change in Andhra Pradesh also, though the detail are as yet unclear. All three states are ruled by political parties which view democratic decentralisation as politically advantageous. The stirrings in these states show that the phase of decline of panchayati raj may perhaps be over.

This brief review indicates that, despite little encouragement from the Constitution, panchayati raj was boldly conceived. During implementation, largely because of insufficient political will, it went into stagnation and decline. Recent developments, in states where the political climate has undergone a change, furnish grounds for cautious hope about its future. Nevertheless, nagging doubts persist about its adequacy.

* * *

The first of these doubts springs from the fact that in the absence of constitutional protection, panchayati raj is exposed to assaults from political, planning and bureaucratic sources. Political assaults emanate from within the states, but planning-cum-bureaucratic assaults are mounted collusively by the Union and the states.

On the political front, panchayati raj tends to be seen as a rival centre of power, and since politics in India is shot through with an obsessive aversion to share power, panchayati raj institutions (PRIs) have had to live in a state of anaemia. PRI laws have by and large created weak institutions, and their implementation has made them weaker. Thus, Haryana had zilla parishads which were merely supervisory bodies, but presumably because they had the potential of being politically troublesome they were suddenly abolished in 1973 and have remained so ever since. The Madhya Pradesh law of 1962 provided for zilla panchayats with similar supervisory functions only but the state government, having with foresight, taken the power to enforce what is liked when, simply refrained from applying this particular portion. All state governments have been niggardly about giving PRIs wothwhile functions, or the necessary finances and administrative powers to go with them. There has been widespread arbitrariness in superseding PRIs, and elections have in many cases not been held for years.

On the planning side, although panchayati raj enactments in several states provide for the task of district planning being entrusted to PRIs, district planning bodies have come up everywhere outside the panchayati raj structure. In Maharashtra and Gujarat, for instance, initially the planning function was with the zilla parishads, but later, Maharashtra constituted district planning and development councils and Gujarat district planning boards. Both have some representatives of PRIs but they are far outnumbered by others, among whom planning experts also figure. Significantly each such body in both states is headed by a state minister. In this way the planning role of PRIs even in the two states that are regarded as pioneers, has been severely eroded.

As for bureaucratic assaults, the process of creating registered societies dominated by bureaucrats to implement specific programmes such as SFDA and MFAL eventually culminated in the formation of all-embracing district rural development agencies (DRDAs). The Swaminathan Report on Programmes for Alleviation of Poverty proclaimed that such agencies had by 1982 "been set up in nearly all the 400 districts of the country". It went on to recommend that the DRDAs should have general coordinating functions with regard to programmes such as IRDP, NREP, MNP, TRYSEM and also programmes to strengthen rural infrastructure. It is important to note that DRDAs have been created at the instance of the Centre and receive funds for programme implementation directly from the Union government. A parallel process is the setting up of corporations again dominated by bureaucrats, to deal with a wide variety of developmental items such as handlooms, milk, credit, marketing scheduled castes' development and even women's development. With the arrival of DRDAs and corporations, development has been heavily bureaucratised. Consequently there is little left for PRIs to do.

One of the important contributions of the Asoka Mehta Report is its support for a constitutional mandate for panchayati raj. The aim should be to forge a consensus on a few basics, such as treating the district as the first point of decentralisation, direct elections rather than indirect, regular elections under the supervision of the Election Commission, the abolition of supersessions, assured finances through periodic state finance commissions, etc. If these basics could be constitutionally protected, PRIs would be better able to withstand assaults on their functioning. PRI laws would acquire much-needed coherence and the scope of arbitrary action would be severely restricted. In their present state PRIs are hardly the kind of answer one is looking for.

* * *

The second and more fundamental doubt arises from the conceptual limitations of panchayati raj. These stem from three origins: one, the fact that panchayati raj was conceived in a developmental context; two that as a system it is built upwards from the village panchayat as the foundational unit; and three, a degree of confusion about its objectives.

From the word 'go', panchayati raj has been seen in developmental terms only. The Balwantrai Mehta Team was, after all, appointed to study community projects and the National Extension Service. Its central recommendation was that the government should divest itself completely of certain responsibilities and "devolve them to a body which will have the entire charge of all development work". Twenty years later, the Asoka Mehta Committee was required to suggest measures to strengthen PRIs "so as to enable a decentralised system of planning and development to be effective". It visualised that "a separate development administration functioning on a decentralised basis would. . . develop along with a composite zilla parishad secretariat". Thus, all thinking has kept PRIs confined to development.

The village panchayat as an idea wears a halo, mainly because it is believed to have existed since Vedic times and is thus treated as a civilisational heritage. Gandhiji's strong advocacy revived the memory of this heritage and, as already observed, village panchayats now find a mention in the Constitution. It is almost sacrilegious to appear to disparage them. But without intending any disparagement the truth must be stated. From the very beginning, the architects of panchayati raj felt it necessary to establish organic links between village panchayats and popular organisations at higher levels. This meant, first of all, that the latter could not have the cleansing mechanism of direct election, for representation had to be provided to the former. Thus panchayat samitis were constituted by indirect election from the village panchayats and zilla parishads by including, among others, the presidents of these samitis ex-officio. Secondly, the need for linkage led to the block rather than the district being chosen as the level at which the "statutorily powerful instrument of the local people's will" would operate, the argument being that the distance between village panchayats and blocks was shorter. But this lengthened the distance between the operative level and the state, for the intervening zilla parishads had virtually no powers. In these two ways the linkage compulsion tended to limit the effectiveness of PRIs. Apparently recognising the problem, the Asoka Mehta report seeks to restore the importance of the district level and recommends an element of direct election for zilla parishads.

The same Asoka Mehta report commented on the lack of clarity about the concept and objectives of panchayati raj. "Some would treat it just as an administrative agency; others as an extension of democracy at the grass roots level; and still others as a charter of rural self-government". Over the years the 'democracy' and 'self-government' factors have diminished. Correspondingly, the factor of 'administrative agency' has grown but only in relative terms. In absolute terms even the agency aspect has diminished with PRIs being gradually denuded of their functions.

Encumbered by such conceptual limitations, panchayati raj does not inspire confidence that it can serve as a base camp for mounting an ascent towards representative district government.

* * *

The third doubt stems from the fact that a quarter century of experience with panchayati raj has yielded no way of thinking of district administration other than the collector pattern inherited from colonial times. The collector as an institution has certainly seen the country through a critical transitional era. But he is already over-stretched, and it is questionable whether it is wise to think of him as there for all time to come. There were hopes that panchayati raj might throw up an alternative, but they have been belied so far. The doubt is that even with rejuvenation from new initiatives like those in West Bengal and Karnataka, panchayati raj may be unable to furnish an alternative pattern.

The two Mehta reports were somewhat ambivalent about panchayati raj vis-a-vis the collector. At one place, for instance, the first Mehta report said there was "little doubt that after a few years the powers vested in the collector. . . may fall into desuetude and may be statutorily withdrawn". But elsewhere it recommended that the collector should be "the captain of the team of officers of all development departments", and should be vested with powers to suspend resolutions of panchayat samitis in certain situations. The second Mehta report stated at one point that "panchayati raj should emerge as a system of democratic local government, discharging developmental, municipal and ultimately, regulatory functions". But at another point it clarified that until regulatory functions were transferred to zilla parishads, the collector must continue to perform these and other functions, such as revenue and law and order. He must also, on behalf of the state government, "ensure the interests of the weaker sections". Faith in democracy in the form of panchayati raj was not, it seems, sufficiently strong to dispense with the guardianship of the collector.

It is almost as if the spread of the democratic idea has had the effect of giving fresh steam to the guardianship concept. A study appended to the Dantwala report usefully lists five patterns of relationship between the collector and PRIs:

1) The collector kept out of the zilla parishad, as in Maharashtra and Gujarat.

2) The collector entitled to participate, as a non-voting member, in zilla parishad meetings, as in Uttar Pradesh and Bihar.

3) The collector associated, as a non-voting member, in a purely advisory capacity, as in Assam, Orissa, Haryana, Punjab and Rajasthan.

4) The collector as chairman of district development councils, as in Karnataka and Tamil Nadu.

5) The collector as a full-fledged member of the zilla parishad and also chairman of all its standing committees, as in Andhra Pradesh.

The study goes on to suggest that the collector's relationship with the zilla parishad should be modelled on that of Delhi's Lieutenant Governor with his Metropolitan Council, for which he should be endowed with sufficient powers so that he remains the central actor in the institutional structures of local politics and administration. Astonishingly, the Dantwala Group commended the approach on the ground that it would satisfy democratic aspirations and at the same time give an important place to the administrator. In effect, this approach would elevate the collector to the level of a lieutenant governor without his being called so.

The trend in government reports is to cling to guardianship at the cost of local democracy. The latest in the series is the Hanumantha Rao Report on District Planning which unabashedly recommends that the collector should be the sheet anchor of implementation of district plans. He should be invested with greater powers and authority in respect of developmental activities. All district level functionaries should be brought under his control, and to ensure their compliance—here a typically bureaucratic provision—he should write their confidential reports. Guardianship is thus sought to be transmuted into satrapy.

In a way, the bureaucratic backlash that the above trend seems to represent is a tribute to the growing power of the democratic idea. A sleeping giant is beginning to wake up and in the process enormous magnitudes of people's power are being unleashed. There has to be an adequate outlet. Panchayati raj does not seem to be one.

Towards Representative District Government

Starting with implementing agencies for rural development the problem unfolded by stages into one of evolving representative district government. But rural development, vitally important though it is, does not by any means constitute the only or even the main justification. There are other and larger reasons for moving towards representative government at the district level.

First of all, there is the democratic argument. This inheres in the very idea of representative government and is consequently reflected at various places in the earlier sections of this paper. What does need to be stressed at this point is that democracy has become a central issue in the country in a way it was not when the Constitution was written, or even when the first Mehta report was published, for then democratic concern was limited mainly to well-meaning visionaries. The history of electoral politics since 1977 provides telling evidence of the change. The Andhra Pradesh episode of August-September, 1984 offers more significant proof, for there the people intervened even though there was no election to mobilise them. There is not enough realisation amongst the intelligentsia of the extraordinary growth of people's power or *lokshakti*, as Jayaprakash Narain called it. It is something like earthlings being unconscious of their planet's celestial motions. Outsiders seem better able to see. The *Bangladesh Observer*, commenting on the Andhra events, wrote: "Rama Rao's reinstatement, in quite a symbolic way, came to be the restoration of democracy whose impact is not peculiarly Indian. It is Asian—as well as African". Pakistan watchers testify that in that country the democratic idea takes encouragement from every success of Indian democracy. So long as democracy was the clinical concern of the enlightened few, its manifestation at local level was in medicinal doses, as in the case of PRIs. Today democracy has become the people's concern, and it will be far more so in the future. Medicinal doses will no longer do. People must have the staple diet of genuine democratic self-governance at local level, not *under* the district bureaucracy but *over* it.

Next, there is the federal argument. The federal question has so far been mired in the debate about Union-state relations, with the Congress pulling in the unitary direction and anti-Congress forces in the federal. The federalists may well win out. If they do, it will be because federalism is recognised as the only way to organise the polity of a large, diverse and populous country like India, deeply penetrated by the democratic idea. The ground will then have been cleared to consider extending the scope of Indian federalism to encompass representative government at district level. A three-tier federation would give district governments the political and constitutional legitimacy that PRIs have lacked. But more importantly, it would give the upper echelons of the polity much needed relief from the pressures of local problems. Genuine political processes in the districts would, on the one hand, absorb participative upsurges from below and, on the other, furnish opportunities for fresh political talent to be inducted and groomed for higher responsibilities. The addition of a third tier would, in all likelihood, strengthen the Indian federation by providing a legitimate outlet for sub-state pluralities and aspirations.

Lastly, there is the argument of bureaucratic collapse. As tasks have multiplied the bureaucracy has expanded. In the process it has become less effective and more corrupt. This is particularly noticeable at and below district level where, after all, the problem of rural development resides (not that all is well at higher levels). District bureaucracies are not only unable to put development programmes through, they often operate as serious obstacles. Large-scale 'leakages' take place in funds meant for development, especially in funds for anti-poverty programmes. There is thus weight in Prof. Raj Krishna's view that the powers of the 'class' of bureaucrats and politicians must somehow be reduced. On the other hand, as Prof Dantwala has realistically observed, the bureaucracy can neither be wished away nor bypassed. Recent trends in many States indicate that the decline in district bureaucracies has turned steeply downwards. Environmentalists have invented the word 'entropication' for lakes that get polluted beyond redemption. If district bureaucracies have to be stopped from crossing over into administrative entropication, it can only be by some external intervention. The replacement of the collector pattern by representative district government could be just such a revivifying intervention for an otherwise decaying system. District bureaucrats would become accountable to district political executives, who being nearer to the people might (at least in the long run) be more responsive to their concerns than far-away state-level politicians.

* * *

Some of the characteristics which a representative district government should possess have figured, explicitly or implicitly, in the foregoing discussion. To recapitulate, these are as follows:

1) District government should form a third tier in India's federal polity, with proper constitutional backing.

2) Its powers should be constitutionally specified, and in the domain so marked out it should have functional autonomy.

3) Its representative character should be ensured by a system of district elections, to be held at regular intervals, under the overall supervision of the Election Commission.

4) Supersessions should be constitutionally barred.

5) Finances to match powers and functions should be assured, through state finance commissions or other means.

6) District government should replace the collector pattern, the district bureaucracy coming squarely under its control.

It is not the intention, nor is it possible in this paper, to convert the above outline into a blueprint. But some aspects need elaboration.

There is a total pool of powers, functions and finances for which the Constitution provides a scheme of sharing between the Union and the states. One way of fitting in a third tier would be to subdivide the State List of powers into three portions: state, district, and concurrent as between these two. But it is questionable whether the State List has enough meat in it to satisfy political aspirations at both state and district levels through such a limited apportioning exercise. The other way would be to have a look at the total pool and distribute powers, functions and finances over the three-tiers afresh, after taking account of the full implications of a three-tier federation. It is well-accepted, the setting up of the Sarkaria Commission being proof of the fact, that mainly for historical reasons the Union is overburdened with powers and functions and overfavoured with finances. If the Union were to be relieved of its fat, the states would have more to share out with the districts. A wider apportioning exercise spanning all three-tiers would clearly be more rational, but perhaps the Sarkaria Commission cannot undertake it under its terms of reference.

The Karnataka Zilla Parishads, Mandal Panchayats and Nyaya Panchayats Bill, 1983, designates the chief executive officers of the zilla parishad as 'chief secretary'; of course the collector retains his separate identify. In West Bengal, the collector is now also the chief executive officer of the zilla parishad. These two are interesting innovations. Taken together they constitute an organisational stepping stone for conceiving of today's collector as tomorrow's chief secretary of district government. It is one of the less noticed facts of Indian administration that, while collectors find it increasingly difficult to deal with sectoral heads, chief secretaries of states and the cabinet secretary at the Union level seldom encounter any such problem. The reason seems to lie in the latter's proximity to the seat of political power. There was a time when the collector too had no problem because he was seen as the embodiment of imperial power. The present day collector has no such advantage. What he needs to become a more effective coordinator is not enhanced administrative power, as many a government committee has recommended, but the political clout that chief secretaryship of district government would automatically give him. District government would, in this view of the matter, at once provide a worthwhile berth for the collector and open a fresh route for solving the hitherto baffling problem of coordination.

In the Indian context the designation 'chief secretary' is associated with a cabinet form of government. The pattern PRIs have tended to follow is that of the mayor-in-council, with the zilla parishad or panchayat samiti being responsible for policy formulation and the chief executive officer or BDO for implementation. Making a distinction between policy formulation and implementation is all right for academic analysis, but does not reflect reality. In practice, elected representatives cannot be separated from implementation, nor indeed the bureaucracy from policy-making. The idea of reserving implementation for bureaucrats seems to have its origin in a vestigial mistrust of the 'natives', in this case the people's representatives. The cabinet system, on the other hand, makes the elected representatives fully responsible for the totality of governance, with the chief secretary and others being all-purpose aides of the cabinet. Being closer to real life this system may be more appropriate for district government. It would also be in symmetry with what obtains at higher levels. Its familiarity might smoothen its introduction as a replacement for the collector pattern.

The idea of district government does not rule out democratic institutions at lower levels. But their composition and functions would need to be thought out afresh, breaking out of the PRI bind and taking account of the constitutionally backed third tier at the district level.

* * *

A question may justifiably be asked whether district governments would meet the fate of PRIs, namely, capture by the rural elite. In most states the capture of PRIs was facilitated by indirect elections. Direct elections would, by this logic, insure district governments against capture. But in Maharashtra PRIs have been captured despite direct elections. The mode of election is thus not the crucial determinant. It is, in fact, socio-economic reality that determines who will wield political power. So far this has favoured the privileged few and consequently it is they who have ruled at the Centre as well as in most of the states. If they capture district governments, there would be nothing extraordinary about it, for already it is largely their writ that runs in the districts, through the official machinery. Real change in political power will come about only by the mobilisation of the unprivileged many. Movements for such mobilisation may have a better chance of crossing the critical threshold in individual districts than over entire states. Thus district government by direct election offers new hope, however slender, for the mobilised many or the organised poor or whatever.

Districts vary considerably in size and population. And their number keeps rising; it was 360 in 1971, 412 in 1981, and may well be over 420 now. With all this, is it wise to make the district the basic unit of representative government? The Asoka Mehta Committee took note of district level variations and yet recommended that the district should be the first point of decentralisation below the state level. It made two sensible suggestions. One was that where structures already exist under the Fifth or the Sixth Schedules of the Constitution (relating to tribal areas and the northeast), these need not be disturbed. The other was that smaller districts, pitched around a million of population, would be desirable. States have in recent years been trying to reduce districts to more manageable sizes. That is the main reason for the numbers going up. Once district government receives constitutional recognition, district boundaries will acquire an element of fixity as state boundaries have. States would, therefore, be well advised to hasten with the task of district reorganisation.

A more fundamental question is that of distance. The Union and state governments are supposed to be distant enough from their electors to function impersonally. Whether they do so in fact, especially in the smaller states, is a separate matter. It is as important for a government to be *impersonal*, that is, just and fair as between individuals and groups, as to be *involved*, i.e. aware of and responsive to the genuine concerns of the people. If the former needs distance the latter requires proximity. District government may be close enough for involvement, but would it be distant enough for impersonal functioning? It is difficult to be categorical. Objectively, populations of a million or more should provide adequate distance. But socio-cultural factors (which, frankly, is a euphism for dominant caste considerations) may make impersonal functioning difficult. People's power could be expected to operate as a corrective, increasingly so as time passes. But an institutional check in the shape of a district ombudsman or *lokayukta*, with a special mandate to keep an eye on the grievances of the weaker sections, would be necessary.

Finally, is this discourse on district government going to do any good to rural development? It is for the experts to answer that. The non-expert is impressed by the law of inverse proportion which seems to operate in this field of rural development: on the one hand, expanding literature, this paper being a modest addition to it, and, on the other, contracting achievements, at least when viewed against rapidly growing aspirations. The law operates in respect of other deadlocked issues also, such as Indo-Pakistan relations or the generalist-specialist controversy. In all such cases it is useful to inquire whether the wrong questions have been asked in the past. The quest for the right question in this case led to the thought that the nation must give serious consideration to a democratic-cum-federal alternative to collector raj. If it does, rural development will surely benefit, as will so much else.

Institution Building: Role and Constraints of Intermediary Agencies

Kamla Chowdhry

INTRODUCTION

In this paper three projects of rural development have been discussed, all engaged in afforestation and the development of uncultivated lands. The first two are considered exceptional projects not only in terms of growth but social equity. The third project, also considered successful in terms of growth objectives, raises questions of social equity. The implementing agency in the first one is a voluntary agency, in the second a governmental research agency, and in the third case, a government department in a North Indian state. The life cycle of each project is analysed keeping in view the main persons involved, achievements in terms of growth and equality, and finally, the constraints of expansion and replication in each case.

DASHOLI GRAM SWARAJYA MANDAL

The Alaknanda, a tributary of the Ganga, has numerous tributaries of its own—Mandakini, Birhi, Garudganga, Tanganigad, Sulgad, Patalganga, Karmnasha, Dhakgadua, Rigigad, Sumaigad and Rishiganga. In 1970, there were devastating floods in the Alaknanda valley inundating an area of 1000 sq km washing away bridges, motor roads, buses, destroying villages and standing crops of paddy. The Ganga canal nearly

300 km from the flood source was choked, taking six months and over Rs. 1 crore to clear it. Kharif crops in 9.5 lakh acres in western Uttar Pradesh could not be irrigated because eight hydro-electric stations went dead and with the result thousands of tube-wells could not be energised. Deaths, devastation and loss were enormous.

There are several interrelated causes of these floods: the roads that have been built with the blasting of the hillsides in the unstable areas where landslides occur, contractors cutting virgin forests, the Forest Department's commercial policies of replacing broad-leaved trees with quick-growing coniferous trees, overgrazing by increased cattle, increased population, all combining to denude the hillsides leaving the slopes barren and bare. The denudation of the hills has made survival difficult not only because of the landslides and soil erosion, but also in terms of availability of food, fuelwood, fodder and water. The men migrate to the plains to find employment, whereas the women are left to look after subsistence agriculture, to search for fuelwood and fodder far away from their homes, and to carry water from long distances because the springs and rivulets once close-by have dried up.

In the Chamoli district of Garhwal, there are at least 450 villages where homes, fields and forests are disappearing because of the ever-increasing floods and landslides. There is not a single year since 1970 when floods and landslides have not occurred, so the people in this region live in fear and terror of even a minor shower.

The Dasholi Gram Swarajya Mandal (DGSM), a Gandhian voluntary agency is located in this very fragile and unstable area, at Gopeshwar, Chamoli district. Although DGSM was established in 1964, Chandi Prasad Bhatt, its founder, spent many years before that as a sarvodaya worker, walking and working in these villages. He toured the valley with *bhoodan* workers, organised the woman to picket the liquor shops because the men used to drink away their earnings, organised a labour cooperative, a resin factory and other such activities to help the poor. In order to protect the trees from the axe of the contractors, he initiated the famous Chipko movement which resulted in a moratorium on tree-felling in this unstable and sensitive region.

In 1970, when the Alaknanda and its tributaries were in flood and had devastated the region, the DGSM began relief operations and used this opportunity to make the people aware of the causes of these floods and the need for an extensive programme of afforestation. The DGSM has started a major movement in the hills by organising eco-development camps and through them creating awareness in the hill communities of the problems of denudation and its causes. These camps are organised in villages with 250 to 300 participants, 75 per cent of whom are village women, with 20 to 50 outsiders—students, professors, social workers and environmentalists. The programme in the camps is of discussion, planning, organising, and *shramdan*—the voluntary contribution of labour. Pits are dug, trees planted and a protective wall built around the village. The Mahila Mandals, the women's groups, agree to protect the newly planted trees and water them and keep their cattle away, whereas, the men agree to look after the wall. There is intensive participation in these camps, strong relationships are built between members of different villages, and there emerges a shared commitment for the protection of the hills and their way of life.

The DGSM has developed its own nurseries of trees that the women want. They found that the Forest Department nurseries were generally of trees of commercial value which the men wanted. The DGSM has also helped the women in building smokeless and fuel efficient *chulhas* (stoves), pit latrines and biogas plants.

The key to the success of the programme is the mobilisation of women in Mahila Mandals. Firewood, fodder and water are primarily the woman's concern in these villages. Consequently, women take more active interest in improving their fuel and fodder supplies and thus reducing the drudgery in their lives. In the eco-camps these issues are highlighted as also the need for control and distribution of these resources by women.

The Mahila Mandals have shown tremendous capacity to take the management of village forests into their own hands, effectively opposing village panchayats and forest panchayats where discussions are in relation to opening of roads and introduction of commercial activities often threatening the well-being of the women and subsistence level of the community.

There is a quiet revolution going on in the Uttar Pradesh hills.

The women are awakening, not only to deal with their subsistence problems of fuel, fodder and water, but wider issues relating to the well-being of their village and of the hill economy. The women are insisting on equal distribution of fodder, thereby changing the power structure in the village. With some taste of success they are moving to broader issues of village development and hill economy and have begun to question the decisions of the men. They are clamouring for schools for their children and have begun to meet government functionaries for demanding their rights.

SUKHOMAJRI PROJECT

At the foothills of the Himalaya are the Shivaliks, Garhwal and Kumaon hills, environmentally perhaps the most degraded hills in the world. Accounts of this area only a century and half ago speak of dense, luxurious and vast forests. Coupled with mining have been decades of railway building which called for high quality timber much of which came from the lower Himalaya. By the turn of the twentieth century, much of the dense forests had given way to boulders, deep gullies and chasms. After Independence, the building of dams, the widening of roads and other such development projects further deteriorated the situation. Increased pressure of grazing also accelerated deforestation and denudation of the hills. The Shivaliks are now bare and barren, hardly able to provide even the subsistence needs of the people and their cattle.

With the cover of trees and grasses all gone, the monsoon water comes down in torrents destroying villages and whatever else comes in its path. The villagers in these hills live in fear of the cataclysmic deluge that comes with each monsoon often carrying their villages and fields into the ever-widening gorge or 'choes' as the local call them.

Sukhomajri, a small village with about 71 families, mostly *gujars*, is in the lower ranges of the Shivaliks. The village has about 240 acres of land, half owned by individual families, and the other half used as common land. The major portion of the catchment is owned by the Forestry Department which leases it to the villagers for grazing. Before the project, the village had 411 animals consisting of goats, buffaloes and bullocks. Not enough was produced either in agriculture or in the surrounding slopes to feed the people or their cattle.

The *gujars* of Sukhomajri trace their origin to seven families that came to the village eight generations ago. There are two *jat* families also who have been in the village for about two generations. Historically, they are poor cultivators and they became very poor once the fodder from the trees and grasses disappeared. Most people in the village are illiterate and few children attend school.

Before the project, the only water in the village came from a muddy rainfed pond in the middle of the village and piped drinking water supply pumped from a nearby spring.

The village had no irrigation water, no electricity, not even a bullock cart for there were no surpluses of harvested crops to be taken to the market. There were no vegetable plots, or fruit trees or fodder crops since all of these required water, which they did not have. The wealth of the village was in their animals, none of them of superior breeds because the more productive animals could not survive with the fodder and water available. The village produced wheat, maize and legumes but these were rainfed crops and often withered because of drought.

Whereas the men of the village tried to find jobs in the nearby cement factory or machine tool factory or at Chandigarh, the women spent most of their energies searching the surrounding countryside for grass and trees that could be cut for fodder and fuel.

Beginning of the Project

Chandigarh, a city designed by Le Corbousier, has a large artificial lake. The lake water recharges the aquifers which feed Chandigarh with its water supply. The people of Chandigarh use the lake for boating and for other recreational purposes and consider it a major beauty spot of Chandigarh.

The Sukhna lake[1] as it is called, was built 445 acres (180 ha) in spread and 28 ft (8.4 m) deep in 1958. Since the lake was created, more than 60 per cent of it was filled by silt from the Shivaliks. The deepest point of the lake, 14 metres, was little more than four metres deep at the start of the Sukhomajri project. The Chandigarh authorities had been spending lakhs of rupees each year for dredging and desilting the lake but each monsoon brought tonnes of silt back again from the Shivaliks.

The forest catchment area of the lake amounts to 3,214 ha, 78.3 per cent of the total catchment area. The surrounding villages graze their cattle in the forest catchment and have been doing so for centuries. Because of the large number of cattle grazing it has led to severe soil erosion and consequently sedimentation in the lake. In an earlier attempt to conserve the soil, the Forest Department had fenced the area and threatened to punish the villagers for violations. These measures, as was to be expected, did not succeed.

Around 1974, the Central Soil and Water Conservation Research and Training Institute (CSWCRTI) was invited to discuss the problem of siltation in the Sukhna lake and requested to do something about it. The head of the Chandigarh centre of CSWCRTI, Shri Mishra, and some of his colleagues surveyed the catchment area on foot. Their observations indicated that the major source of silt was in the higher catchment area which constituted 25 per cent of the total catchment but contributed 80-90 per cent of the total silt load. Shri Mishra recommended a number of check dams near the Sukhomajri village and the planting of *Acacia catechu* and bhabbar grass on contour trenches in the catchment area, *Dalbergia sissoo* in the gullies and other soil conservation measures. These were completed before the monsoon of 1976.

A second check dam in Sukhomajri was built before the monsoon of 1977. In 1977, however, the monsoon failed and the farmers saw their kharif crop of maize withering before their eyes. There was water in the dam and the farmers realised there was life-saving irrigation in it for their crops. It was during this crisis that the farmers realised that the soil conservation work meant for the Sukhna lake could also mean supplemental irrigation for them. Instead of one uncertain crop the farmers could have two assured crops. The mutuality of interest between the Chandigarh authorities, the CSWCRTI and its soil conservation work, and the villagers became mutually reinforcing.

Today, Sukhomajri has three rainfed reservoirs varying between 200 and 400 ft in diameter. All the rain water that falls on one side of the village is caught and channelled into the reservoirs and is then used for irrigating crops and for drinking water. The village people keep their grazing animals out of the watershed areas. Since grazing animals have been kept out and the goats have largely been sold, the area has sprung back to life and is now full of new grasses, shrubs and trees.

Prior to the availability of rain harvested water, villagers were able to raise only a kharif crop, whose success depended on the duration and strength of the monsoon. With the availability of supplemental irrigation, the number of crop rotations has increased varying from 2 to 4. Production increased from 250 quintals of wheat, 500 quintals of wheat straw and 196 quintals of maize in 1977 to 1,015 quintals of wheat, 2,031 quintals of wheat straw, and 356 quintals of maize in 1981. The milk yield too increased from 2,196 litres in 1977 to 4,405 litres in 1981. The grass production in the catchment area increased from 200 kg in 1977 to 2,500 kg per year in 1981.[2]

People's Participation

For the management and control of the reservoir water, a Water Users' Association (WUA) was proposed and accepted. The Ford Foundation which gave a grant to CSWCRTI for operational projects, hired a young management specialist to assist in putting the WUA on a sound footing. After many months of talking to the villagers, and after much discussion all around, a system was established in which every member would be given equal share regardless of the land owned, and the landless too could be members and claim a right to irrigation water.

Another consultant hired was with the objective of working with the women of Sukhomajri. The woman consultant listened to the problems of Sukhomajri women and urged them to take a more active role in the WUA and in conserving the watershed. The women consultant also helped the village women build smokeless *chulhas* for themselves. The women claim that their wood consumption has reduced by one-third to half and that the inside of their huts has become more hygienic. The women of Harijan Nada, a neighbouring village where soil conservation work has also taken place, have been providing 'technical assistance' in *chulha* making to other villagers as far distant as Himachal Pradesh. Because of the easy availability of grass the women now have more time for growing vegetables, collecting bhabbar grass and making rope and for other income-generating activities.

It is clear from the Sukhomajri experience that exhortations for cooperation do not work, especially if these are aimed at people who live on the margin of subsistence. The poor cannot stop grazing their animals especially when the animals are their mainstay of subsistence. When the Forest Department had fenced off the catchment area, the villagers found their way inside in spite of fines and threats. On one occasion, during the early part of the project, when a villager was told not to graze his cattle in the catchment area, he retorted, "Who are you to tell me not to graze my cattle here—my forefathers did it and so will I." Only with increased productivity and increased milk yields resulting from supplemental irrigation, were the villagers of Sukhomajri anxious to invest in conservation measures to preserve and enhance their new way of life.

Another lesson that emerges from the Sukhomajri experience is that social and management systems appropriate to new technology take time to evolve. All the key people involved in the project spent much time learning from the villagers, earning their confidence and respect before they could experiment and introduce new methods going against traditional ways of doing things. Without establishing mutuality of trust, it would have been difficult to establish the new system of equitable water distribution and the management for its effective functioning and control.

In terms of phases, the first phase of the Sukhomajri project (1974-79) was concerned in diagnosis of the problem, building dams and largely improving the technical system. It was in this phase that PVC pipes were laid so that water seepage and evaporation were minimum, sprinklers were experimented with so that more people could share the limited water. The second phase (1980-83) was in improving and ironing out the procedures and problems of WUA, getting the women involved, and establishing the social and management system of the new resources. In the third phase the Sukhomajri project was expanded to Nada and Harijan Nada so that further experience could be gained and modifications made. The experimental and learning phase, therefore, lasted almost a decade, with both governmental and non-governmental agencies playing key roles. It is in the multiplying of the project to the other areas that no clear organisational solution has been found acceptable so far. The real challenge of Sukhomajri is in finding an appropriate strategy and structure for its replication.

SOCIAL FORESTRY IN A NORTH INDIAN STATE

The social forestry programme in this north Indian state is considered one of the most successful programmes in the country. The physical targets of plantations have far exceeded earlier estimates and the total expenditure has been less than anticipated at appraisal. The total area planted during the project period is about 20 per cent above estimates. In terms of plantation achievements, the SFD certainly needs to be congratulated. However, it is worthwhile to look at the objectives of growth and equity as stated and analyse the extent to which these objectives have been achieved.

The project appraisal report (1979) states the objectives as "establishing multipurpose tree plantations that supply fuel and small timber to meet the basic requirements of rural communities; that provide food, fodder, shade and the environmental stability that is necessary for continued food production; and that generate income and employment, both directly by providing jobs in planting, harvesting and marketing and indirectly, by providing raw materials for cottage industries."

In terms of achievements, the 1983 evaluation report gives the following figures of cumulative achievements of SFD plantations:

	Cumulative/ha (1983)		
	SAR	*Actual*	%
Canal banks	11,335	6,095	54
Road sides	4,960	13,215	266
Railway sides	2,930	4,125	146
Degraded forests	9,635	14,050	146
Community self-help	1,600	127	8
Village woodlots	3,540	5,424	153
Seedlings for farm forestry (millions)	5.6	156.4	2,794

The achievements on canal banks are far below the target and roadsides far above the target. The community self-help scheme did not get off the ground although the Forest Department was able to plant in the village woodlots, with the assistance of the village panchayat (village council). The achievement in relation to farm forestry was spectacular, 2794 per cent above the target!

Farm Forestry

In terms of actual achievements the most spectacularly successful part has been farm forestry. The sapling distribution to farmers far exceeds any estimates. The saplings distributed are largely eucalyptus. It is generally believed that these are lifted in large numbers by the well-to-do farmers (reliable figures are not available). The 1983 evaluation report stated "there is poor progress in the problems of involving small farmers in the farm forestry programme." The Forest Department provides these saplings free or at a subsidised rate.

The market for eucalyptus poles and for paper and pulp industry is so profitable that many farmers are converting part of their agricultural fields to eucalyptus plantations for commercial profits. They mention that profits from eucalyptus are much higher than those from crops and that the need for labour and consequently labour trouble is less. One farmer stated that instead of the 12 labourers that he previously hired, he now hired only three.

In general, farm forestry has benefited the larger farmers. Other beneficiaries have been the paper, pulp and pole industries. The poor in general have not benefited from this component of the programme.

Strip Plantations

After farm forestry, the second largest part of the social forestry programme, is plantations on canal banks, roadsides and railway sides. The canal bank plantations have been disappointing but the roadside and railway side plantations have done relatively well. The roadside plantations have visibility; also the accessibility of staff for technical and supervisory inputs is easier. Here, again, the species planted are largely eucalyptus, with some ornamental and fuelwood/fodder trees.

The strip plantations, because of the overwhelming numbers being eucalyptus, will ultimately find their way to the paper, pulp and pole markets. It is suggested by the Forest Department that when this market is saturated, the plantations would be useful to villagers who live close by, for fuelwood.

Community Self-help and Village Woodlots

Only a small part of the programme was to be community self-help plantings in village common lands to demonstrate to the rural people the benefits of afforestation. Even this small effort has not done well at all. Getting community participation by the Forest Department has been difficult and the project seems more or less abandoned. The women still walk several hours in search of fuelwood, twigs and leaves.

We saw women with lacerated hands who had spent hours collecting thorny bushes for fuelwood. We also saw women sweeping leaves in a village where the woodlot scheme was considered a success to collect them for use as fuel. The smokeless *chulha* programme also for which extension had to be provided by the Forest Department had not taken off the ground. The women had no information, no involvement and no benefits from the programme so far.

In the village woodlot programme, the Forest Department had entered into an agreement with the village panchayat wherein the planting and protection was done by forestry staff and the village panchayat was expected to distribute the benefits giving priority to the *antyodaya* families, i.e., the poorest of the poor.

Here, again, the scheme lacked the cooperation of the village community. The benefits of the village woodlot found their way to the panchayat leader and to a few others. None of the landless and poor appeared to have heard of the scheme or received any benefits.

Cottage Industries

One of the objectives stated in the project proposal was to benefit the craftsmen by providing raw materials for cottage industries. The plight of the craftsmen has increased with the disappearance of wood for their traditional occupation. For instance, in Maharashtra, "nearly 70,000 mat and basket weavers of Bhandara and Chandrapore districts are unable to produce sufficient quantities of goods since bamboos, which were once available to them in plenty, have now been earmarked to big paper mills that have been set up in the vicinity."[3]

Since 80 per cent of the plantings are eucalyptus, whether in farm forestry or strip plantations, it is evident that not much attention has been given to the kind of plantations required by craftsmen.

Employment

According to estimates given by the SFD, direct plantings and nurseries have yielded an employment of 8.4 million man-days. The social forestry project is excellent for generating employment for the poor.

In a project costing approximately Rs. 40 crore it is important to raise the question: who benefits? The rhetoric has been that social forestry programme is meant for the rural poor, to promote fuelwood and fodder, to ease the drudgery of craftsmen and women, but all this is far from reality. The SFP has become primarily a commercial project, 70-80 per cent being farm forestry with farmers primarily growing eucalyptus for profit for the paper, pulp and pole industry. In the plantations on public lands too, the poor and landless do not seem to be benefiting. And in the village woodlots, even where the woodlots have been successful, the benefits have gone only to the panchayat leaders and a few others. The project, however, has generated some employment. The success of the project needs to be judged not only from the number of trees planted, but also in terms of who the major beneficiaries have been. This analysis shows that social forestry, like many other anti-poverty programmes, has so far eluded the poor.

CHOICE OF IMPLEMENTING AGENCIES

It is generally realised that understanding of the institution building process has lagged far behind advances in science and technology. Certainly some of the most perplexing and urgent problems of rural development are not technological, but human, organisational, social and political in nature. In this section, the nature of the implementing agency is examined and its potential for large-scale expansion or replication discussed.

Dasholi Gram Swarajya Mandal

DGSM is a Gandhian voluntary agency located in one of the most sensitive regions of Alaknanda, the Garur Ganga watershed. Because of a difficult terrain, direct involvement for developmental activities is in 21 villages, although its influence on other people and institutions in Garhwal and Kumaon is far-reaching. College students, school children, teachers, journalists, scientists have been attracted to the eco-development camps that DGSM organises and these outsiders along with rural men and women, have contributed significantly in terms of ideas and *shramdan*. Some have been inspired into setting up their own voluntary agencies on similar lines.

Earlier, the DGSM was against any outside money, including government funds, for they believed that dependence on government funds would inhibit their independence and their ability to be outspoken critics of government's forest policy. Since 1982, however, DGSM has accepted funds from the Planning Commission for the development of Garur Ganga, and from the Department of Environment for their eco-development camps but are still reluctant to accept foreign funds.

The DGSM is built around the work and personality of Chandi Prasad Bhatt. It has an underlying philosophy of *sarvodaya* and *shramdan* and is different from the so-called professionally managed organisations. The criterion for the selection of colleagues is their ability to share a way of life and their commitment to the cause of hill development. It has about 25 full-time workers, each paid about Rs. 300-400 per month, largely from its own resources, such as the *khadi* shop, and the resin and turpentine units it runs.

The structure consists of a managing committee of eight—three from DGSM, three women from the Mahila Mandals and two local persons. The chief executive is the secretary of the society. There is no other hierarchy in the organisation and as mentioned earlier everyone is paid about the same.

There are certain factors that need to be highlighted about such an implementation agency. Firstly, institutionalisation came about almost a decade after Bhatt started working in the area and gaining knowledge about the people and their problems. Secondly, the institution-building process of DGSM itself took about a decade before it began to focus systematically on the rehabilitation of the slopes and village lands. Thirdly, the leadership and other members are largely local. As locals with a historical memory there are shared experiences of the vagaries of the Alaknanda river and of the death and denudation it leaves behind, and, therefore, a shared concern and commitment about the watershed.

In terms of expansion and replication of activities, this is achieved by influencing other young people in and outside the area. At least five new voluntary organisations have sprung up during the last decade and many existing organisations' work has been influenced in the direction of DGSM's activities. The Appiko movement in Karnataka has drawn its inspiration from the Chipko movement of DGSM and has sent in trainees for learning activist strategies.

The DGSM mentions that in terms of strengthening its activities it needs two kinds of assistance: firstly, an intermediary agency which could be a buffer between it and the government or donor agencies for funds required for its activities such as raising nurseries, building protective walls around the village, biogas plants, *chulhas*, small tanks, etc. The DGSM itself does not want to negotiate and deal with governmental and donor agencies, for the follow-up work requires time and skills of project preparation which in general they do not have. Secondly, they want information about where to find various specialists for help. They need market information for organising marketing of lime, citrus and walnuts, and dissemination of other relevant information.

Gifted leadership and the ability to attract committed young people is the basis of DGSM's success. Its limitations are: not enough professional people in relevant subjects and lack of organisation and management to replicate such work on a wider basis all over the Himalaya. But the awakening of the people and the self-reliance it has been able to generate amongst local people, especially, women has been truly extraordinary. If activities of DGSM and of similar agencies are to be strengthened and expanded, then intermediary institutions which can act as a buffer between such voluntary agencies and government need to be considered.

Central Soil and Water Conservation Research and Training Institute

The implementing agency in the case of Sukhomajri was the CSWCRTI in Chandigarh, a government research institute, under the direction of the Indian Council of Agricultural Research (ICAR). The Sukhomajri project was undertaken because of the heavy siltation in the Sukhna lake and the heavy costs of desiltation. The Chandigarh authorities had requested CSWCRTI to find out the cause and take preventive action. Although the source of soil erosion was soon located, it was also realised that without the cooperation and involvement of the villagers, the watershed could not be protected. The headquarters of CSWCRTI indicated to the project leader in Chandigarh that as a research organisation their role was only research in soil conservation measures and that the collaborative work with the villagers and establishing the social system was not part of their research agenda. The Ford Foundation saw great potential in this project for rural development with economic benefits being linked with conservation measures. It hired several short- and long-term consultants to work with the project leader and develop the social and management aspects of the system. After about a decade's work, both technical and social, Sukhomajri has become a demonstration project for rural development and community management.

The Haryana Forest Department did try to replicate the Sukhomajri project and built 13 reservoirs to preserve forest watersheds. However, the Forest Department could not provide the pipes for irrigation nor did it have the staff to establish the necessary relationships with the community to establish the WUA for community management. The Sukhomajri project had a multi-disciplinary team with access to flexible funds which the Haryana Forest Department did not have. The project, therefore, has not been replicated in terms of benefit to the rural communities or even in terms of the conservation of the watershed.

The replication of the Sukhomajri project has been a matter

of concern. The Planning Commission's team which visited Sukhomajri and Nada wrote in the visitors' book as follows:

> In the recent period I never spent a day as usefully and richly as I did today at Sukhomajri. It is a model of conservation and development with the fullest participation of the people and with immediate benefits accruing to them as to society as a whole. The key to this successful experiment is the concept of social fencing which has been successfully practised here. Dr. Mishra and his colleagues deserve our congratulations for their interest, passion and dedicated work for the cause of the poor. This model is I think fully tested and should be replicated with the creation of necessary institutions. Such an effort needs to be fully supported and encouraged.
>
> sd/-
>
> C.H. Hanumantha Rao
> Member, Planning Commission
> Dated: 23.10.1982

What kind of an institution can be created for replicating the Sukhomajri model? Should it be a core group within CSWCRTI to deal with the technical and social aspects? Or should such replication be undertaken by an existing voluntary agency such as BAIF? Or, should a new replicating agency be set up by government? Should it be a governmental or a non-governmental agency? All these alternatives have been explored but an appropriate replicating agency has not emerged as yet.

Government Department

The implementing agency for the social forestry programme of approximately Rs. 40 crores, was a government department. The department increased its budget and staff to handle the large-scale plantations required. The SFD was highly successful in terms of seedlings raised and trees planted whether through farm forestry or strip plantations. What it has not been successful in, is in getting people's participation and equitable distribution of fuelwood and fodder.

In general, bureaucratic structures are not very effective in getting people's participation. Further, government's delivery system for the poor whether in terms of credit, inputs, health or education does not seem to reach the intended beneficiaries. The poor are either too weak or do not know how to defend their interests. But, where large-scale plantations have to be organised or a special scheme like using six lakh ha of *usar* lands for tussar silk development is to be established, the government can mobilise the necessary skills and resources for such large-scale programmes.

There is a real dilemma in projects of rural development. A voluntary agency which is built around a gifted and a committed person can earn the trust and confidence of the community in which it works. However, it has serious limitations in expanding its work because then it would need a different kind of an organisation and management and, perhaps, leadership. A government department on the other hand has serious limitations in reaching the poor and getting the involvement of the community, but it can undertake large-scale projects which can benefit the poor in an indirect fashion, e.g., the SFD generated an employment of 8.4 million man-days and if the *usar* lands project was implemented it would generate additional employment of three million man-days. Projects of such magnitude requiring access to such large-scale funds would be difficult for a voluntary agency.

CONCLUSIONS

We have seen that there are projects in which the objectives of growth and equity have been achieved. In fact, growth was only possible with the social system of equal distribution of benefits. Both in DGSM and in Sukhomajri the principle of equal distribution was significant in the preservation of the watershed, and, therefore, in the growth of fuelwood, fodder, and the quality of life. Equity, it seems, cannot be imposed from the top, the local communities must realise that only through equal sharing can they get the cooperation of everyone concerned.

In both Sukhomajri and DGSM, the involvement of women was crucial to the success of the projects. In rural development projects, especially when dealing with the very poor and in terms of subsistence needs, the involvement of women becomes necessary. Subsistence in terms of food, fuel, fodder and water are women's concerns, and their involvement and participation are inescapable for the success of the programme. In panchayats and other local bodies of decision-making, the concerns of women are rarely discussed. The men discuss 'development' projects which would bring in a cash economy often at the expense of subsistence needs. The success of the DGSM is in the vigorous involvement of women and in addressing itself to the basic problems of women.

There is a need for a local agency to deal with the problems of growth, equity and distribution. In both DGSM and Sukhomajri, the local agencies worked very well. How equity would fare in a community with large class/caste differences is difficult to predict. In DGSM although there are caste differences, all the village community is poor. In Sukhomajri, except for two *Jat* families, the rest were all *gujars*.

Rural development projects require access to flexible funding. The DGSM had its own limited funds and used *shramdan* for its activities, whereas, the Sukhomajri project had access to Ford Foundation funds for trying out innovative ideas of problem-solving in the social system. Government funding does not seem to be sufficiently flexible for assisting rural development projects.

In both DGSM and in Sukhomajri there is an upward spiral. From a subsistence economy, they are moving to a cash economy, of selling ropes, milk, vegetables in Sukhomajri and of selling citrus, lime and walnut in the case of DGSM. The next step of development needs marketing information and organisation structures wherein the producers can benefit. There is also a new elan in the community, a new hope and confidence in the ability to improve the quality of life. With women's involvement and with the principle of equity, there is a perceptible shift in the power structure of the community and in the dignity of women.

A period of learning from the village community, of establishing trust and confidence is crucial to experimenting with innovative problem-solving. In DGSM and Sukhomajri it took almost a decade of learning, of establishing mutuality which formed the basis for the later success of these projects.

In each case there was a crisis which brought the agency and the people together. The crisis is a time of testing and making commitments. Who is the 'giver' and who is the 'receiver' who is the 'seed' and who is the 'sower' is difficult to separate in such situations. In institution building, as in the human life cycle, each phase of growth depends on the resolution of a previous crisis.

An intermediary service institution was important in each case to bring together people, to build the necessary linkage with outside agencies and to provide the necessary help. In my opinion, the real challenge in rural development in issues of growth and equity, is establishing intermediary institutions which can work with voluntary agencies on the one hand and with government departments on the other hand.

References

[1]Sedimentation of Sukhna Lake, Chandigarh Status Report, 1982, CSWCRTI, Research Centre, July 1983.

[2]Planning Commission, Tour Notes of Planning Commission Team, unpublished document, December 1980.

[3]*Times of India*, August 16, 1984.

more speed and [illegible] the 'same' is difficult to separate in [illegible] In [illegible] in [illegible] upon the human life [illegible] such [illegible] depend on the [illegible] of a per[illegible]

Two Approaches to Rural Development: Case Study of Sewa and Mahiti

Nirmala Murthy

This is a case study of two approaches to rural development, adopted by two different organisations in two neighbouring blocks—Dholka and Dhandhuka of Ahmedabad district. The two organisations are the Self Employed Women's Association (SEWA), and Mahiti. SEWA is well known, nationally and internationally, for its pioneering work in unionising self-employed women. The Mahiti team is a relatively unknown group of young professionals who got interested in rural development when they were involved in the Block Level Planning (BLP) exercise initiated by the Government of Gujarat in 1979. The group calls itself Mahiti which sees its task as sharing information ('Mahiti' means information).

The rural wing of SEWA initiated its rural development work in 1977 in 15 village of Devdholera region in Dholka block. The Mahiti Team started the BLP exercise in March 1979 in Dhandhuka block and later decided to implement the recommended development strategy in seven villages in the Dholera region of Dhandhuka block. SEWA is an organisation of women, working exclusively for women. Mahiti, on the other hand, does not think of itself as a women's organisation though some of its more active and articulate members are women. Unlike SEWA, the Mahiti Team does not believe in programmes that help any one section of the population; it chooses programmes which benefit the whole area.

There are also differences in the ways both SEWA and Mahiti diagnose problems, their approaches to rural development, their intervention strategies, and their response to failures. It is difficult to compare the impact of their approaches in quantitative terms, partly because they have different objectives, and partly because these projects have been in operation for too short a period (four years) to make any sizeable impact. The paper, therefore, compares only the process factors of the two projects and highlights the lessons learnt.

SEWA'S RURAL PROJECT

The SEWA Rural Wing was started in 1977 with the objective of organising women agricultural labourers to form a pressure group to work for minimum wages and economic development. At that time the Textile Labour Association (TLA) of Ahmedabad, of which SEWA was a part, was trying to organise the Agricultural Labourers Association in the rural areas under the Minimum Agricultural Wages Act. SEWA convinced the TLA members that a majority of agricultural labourers were women and they needed to be organised as well. But there was such strong opposition to the women workers being unionised, both from the farmers and from the male workers, that when the SEWA tried to unionise women, many women labourers lost work. There was a severe drought in 1977 and no agricultural work was available in the villages. Men left villages for contract work outside, but the women could not do so. Some of these women came to the SEWA office in Ahmedabad with an appeal for help. Thus began SEWA's involvement in rural development.

Since the people in the villages of Dholka block were familiar with SEWA because of its work in the Agricultural Labour Association its initial entry posed no problem. SEWA conducted a quick survey of the area to understand women's problems, talked to poor women of various castes, and came to the conclusion that their first need was for work, preferably near their homes. It was necessary to create opportunities for non-agricultural work in which different caste groups could participate. The survey by SEWA showed that about 30 per cent of the households were headed by women.

SEWA was also concerned about women controlling their share of income as well as raising their social status. The organisers had observed, for instance, that though women were involved in pre- and post-weaving activities like cleaning the raw wool, spinning, and dyeing, they were not allowed to weave. Weaving was men's job and all income from weaving went to them because they sat on the loom. Potter women and milk-maids did most of the work but they too did not get paid for it. SEWA, therefore, decided that women, specially girls, needed to be trained in non-traditional skills like pottery-making and weaving. The other needs identified were health services for pregnant mothers, creche facilities, and functional literacy for women.

In 1978, SEWA started with an *ambar charkha* project for 25 women in Devdholera village under the Right to Work Scheme of the Khadi and Village Industries Commission (KVIC). Needy women were identified, were trained to operate *charkhas* and were given *charkhas* to take home. SEWA supplied the raw material, paid wages, and the product was lifted by the KVIC. Within a year, 175 women from nearby eight to ten villages got trained. "When the women were in dire need they worked on *charkhas* enthusiastically," reported one SEWA organiser. In some cases the whole family worked on the *charkha* for about 15 hours a day, producing 40-45 hanks earning Rs. 420-450 per month (at the rate of Rs. 0.35 per hank). But these were exceptions. Most women earned between Rs. 150 and 250 per month by doing six to eight hours of hard work at the *charkhas* in addition to their household work. Though they were earning less than a rupee an hour, it was more than what they earned as agricultural labourers. But it was seen as a stop-gap arrangement, and as soon as they found some other occupation or a source of income, like keeping a buffalo or getting a job as local organiser, they gave up working on the *charkha* entirely.

Other income-generating activities started at Devdholera were weaving of khadi blankets, sarees and floor rugs, tailoring, pottery making, and basket making. A milk cooperative was also started. Most of these, except tailoring, were non-traditional skills for women, and their introduction was not easy. Women hesitated to come forward for weaving classes and the weaving teacher, a man, refused to teach them because of the tradititional belief that weaving is a man's job. After much persuasion from SEWA of both the trainees and the trainer, ten women began their training. Within a year, however, four more weaving centres were started for women under the Training for Rural Youth in Self Employment Scheme (TRYSEM) of the government, and about 50 girls and women are under training in these training-cum-production centres.

A tailoring class was opened in 1979 with a teacher appointed from within the village, an illiterate wife of the village tailor. At present ten women of Devdholera are doing tailoring work. But more women wanted to learn tailoring, and SEWA thought that there would not be enough work for all of them in the village. Therefore, the training classes were converted into production units where women made simple garments which were sold in the villages and in Ahmedabad city.

At the SEWA centre at Devdholera 40-50 women and children learn different crafts. The products they produce are sold either locally or through the Gujarat Marketing Federation and the raw materials and equipment are supplied by SEWA. There is a creche where about 30 babies are being looked after. In the evening, literacy classes are held for women. Through these crafts women earn between Rs. 150 and Rs. 200 per month. Table 1 shows the number of women being trained in different crafts and their average monthly income from these activities.

Another major achievement of SEWA is promotion of dairy cooperatives of women. In September 1978, SEWA organised a five day training for twenty milkmaids in cattle care and development. At the end of the training, all twenty women wanted to buy cows or buffaloes. To get a loan to buy cattle, the banks required that their loan applications be guaranteed by the local milk society. SEWA realised that the existing milk societies which were dominated by men and upper castes would not be willing to support women's applications. This practical constraint gave rise to the idea of having an exclusively women's milk society. The idea also fitted well with SEWA's ideology which is a combination of Gandhiism and feminism. It took over a year to register the cooperative society. First, the dairy officers were not sure that women would be able to manage the cooperative. SEWA then agreed to take the responsibility for its operations, and as a result, the first women's

Table 1: Impact of SEWA—JAAGO Activities: Phase-I

Serial number	Activity	Intervention	No. of women
1	Income generation through *khadi* work	*Charkha* training Linkage with *khadi* board Ownership of *charkhas* and wages rest with women only	50
2	Revolving found for milch cattle	Banking loan for cattle to landless labourers Training in dairy development and cattle care	25
3	Organisers' training programme	Leadership-role and skills training Assignment and support to organisers in the post training stage	120
4	Vocational training	Training	60 from three villages
	Carpentry	Compensation through stipend	
	Weaving	Production	
	Tailoring	Local trainers Literacy Help for self-employment	
	Cattle care training	Training at Ahmedabad	
5	Dairy cooperative	Cattle loans	25
		Training in dairy	500
		Cooperative organisation	60
6	Health education	Health training with government hospital staff	80
		Diagnostic camps with treatment/medicine	135
		Immunisation	50
7	Creches		15 villages
8	Literacy classes	Mothers' group meetings	

Table 1: Impact of SEWA—JAAGO Project: Phase-II

Serial number	Activity	Intervention	No. of women
1	Khadi work	Sewa's own *khadi* trust to run a *khadi* unit Maintenance services Three khadi work supervisors trained at KVIC for one year	30 women heads of families
2	Dairy cooperatives	Organisation through cooperatives Training in cooperatives Developing local leadership Cattle loans	60 women in three villages
3	Agriculture training for small and marginal farmers	Training in improved agricultural inputs and practices Exposure and study tours Support and inputs	200 women from 10 villages
4	Legal education camps	Training in social and labour legislation Legal aid at Devdholera	200 in 2 camps
5	Vocational training Weaving Carpentry Pottery Typing Tailoring	Training Marketing support Help for self-employment Local leadership	85
6	Creches		30 from 15 villages each
7	Literacy classes	Literacy Study tours	300 from 15 villages
8	Survey	Data collection through discussion	300
9	Village women's associations	Village level informal meets Tours	300 villages groups in cooperatives

cooperative in Devdholera was registered in March 1980. Initially, the nationalised banks were reluctant to give loans to women, but finally the State Bank of India agreed to give loans to 20 women under guarantee from SEWA. Anticipating such problems, SEWA created a revolving fund from a loan of Rs. 50,000 from the SEWA Bank and donations from some well wishers to give cattle loans to women. Nearly 150 women took the loan. The amounts ranged from Rs. 1200 to Rs. 1800 depending on the animal; the rate of interest was 4 per cent and the repayment period three years. The men were unhappy because only women were given the loans, and because the cooperative was exclusively for women. To pacify them, SEWA agreed to let the men work as secretaries of the societies. The cattle loans, however, were to be given only to women.

In the year 1980, ten such cooperatives were registered from Dholka block; all of them had appointed men as secretaries. Within two years all the cooperatives ran into financial problems and stopped functioning. Financial troubles occurred because the secretaries, on whom women depended to write accounts and to transport milk, cheated in accounts and diverted some of the milk. Further, many women could not bring milk to these societies but were forced to sell it to private traders because they had taken loans from these traders.

To save these societies from closure, SEWA intervened by taking over their operations. First, one or two SEWA organisers were sent to each village to help the local women take charge of the cooperative. Next, women were trained in testing milk fat, supervising collection operations, and in keeping records. Women commerce graduates were hired as internal auditors.

When these steps were taken, four out of ten cooperatives started functioning profitably. Two more are expected to become operational. SEWA's field organisers put in a lot of effort in arranging for loans, ensuring recovery, managing the finances of the cooperatives, getting the cattle insured, and in getting them the necessary medical care.

In addition to these income-generating activities, SEWA organised in each village creches, maternal security scheme, and literacy classes for women. In 1977, the first creche was opened at Zamp village as an entry point for SEWA in that village. In the next two years 15 such creches were started. About 35 children, including three-month-old babies were enrolled in each of these creches. The only difficulty SEWA faced in running the creches was the caste problem. High-caste mothers did not want their children to eat and play with Harijan children. They wanted separate facilities but SEWA did not accede to this demand. However, SEWA agreed to appoint two women, one Harijan and one caste Hindu in each creche.

The Maternal Security Scheme is a small but very popular scheme. Pregnant women who register by paying Rs. 10 as registration fee, are provided with ante-natal care including the requisite immunisations. The new-born are also immunised. After delivery the women are paid Rs. 100 to make up for the lost wages and given a kilogramme of ghee to improve their diet. This enables them to take rest for some time after delivery. The scheme has been found to have significantly reduced the mother and child death rate in the area.

MAHITI TEAM'S MAHITI PROJECT

In March 1979, the Mahiti Team (then called the Planning Team) was a part of the Ahmedabad Study Action Group (ASAG), a voluntary agency specialising in rural housing and development programmes in Ahmedabad district. As part of an exercise in block level planning, the team visited all the villages in that block, 140 in number, collected village profiles, and talked to village people. Through this intense exercise the team members came to the conclusion that the basic constraints on the development of this block were saline land, shortage of drinking water, and deforestation. The team felt strongly that starting schemes like *amber charkha*, carpet weaving and *papad*-making was of little use unless the more basic constraints to block development were removed.

Talking to the village people, the team acquired a very different perspective on the area's problems than the one held by the officials. Government officials at the block level claimed that the area was backward because it had no resources, people were lazy and non-responsive to the development programmes. The team on the other hand, found that the area had many potential resources which needed to be exploited, and that the village people were knowledgeable about their hidden resources, but there were some missing links in their information which, if bridged, would lead people to work for their own development.

Their research revealed that the missing link in the block development effort was systematic and full information about the government's development programmes. Evolving information linkages thus became their strategy. The team members decided to implement this strategy in seven villages of Bhal region of Dhandhuka block which, in their opinion, were economically the most backward areas. In the beginning the team consisted of five to six members, three of them were Ahmedabad-based and the others were local, educated youth. Since then, some old members have left, some new ones have joined. All the new members are from the villages. The team size has, however, remained about the same. The objective of the Mahiti project was to establish a dialogue with the villagers and to help them organise themselves to derive benefits from the developmental schemes. Towards this end the specific activities to be undertaken were:

1) Generating, processing and disseminating development information to the village people,

2) Providing information on problems and potentials of the area to government agencies,

3) Undertaking demonstration projects and giving training to local people,

4) Bringing people together around certain issues for solving their problems, and

5) Providing a forum for exchange of ideas among people, government officials, scientists and technicians.

The Mahiti team was attempting to work on one hand with the government, and on the other, with the people. It was trying to convince government officials that Dhandhuka block had development potential but its backwardness was due to its people not having access to the existing development opportunities. The villagers were not even aware of the various schemes offered by the government, and the government did not have an effective field level set-up to assist the villagers to benefit from these schemes. On the people's side, the team urged the villagers to apply themselves and use their own ingenuity and resources to solve their problems instead of depending on the government entirely.

In Mahiti's view, scarcity of drinking water was the major cause for the seasonal migration and backwardness of Bhal region so it gave priority to the search for a viable solution to the problem. The villagers agreed that it was their main problem and that the ideal solution was to extend the Ingoli pipeline up to their villages, which politicians and government officials had promised to do from time to time. Though people seemed content with this promise, the team members were eager to find alternative solutions until the Ingoli pipeline was extended. They identified four possible techniques: a solar distillation of saline water, reverse osmosis, roof water collection, and lining the pond with a plastic film.

People were not enthusiastic about these temporary solutions, but Mahiti decided to try them out, hoping that if the solutions worked the villagers would be inspired to act. They installed three solar distillation units in three villages (Zanki, Rajpur, Raisangadh) each unit costing Rs. 1,500. Initially, some families agreed to take care of the units. Each unit produced 2.3 litres of water, a very small quantity compared to the need of a family. Soon the units developed problems and people refused to take care of them. This experience was similar to that of CSMCRI (Central Salt Marine Chemical Research Institute) at Bhavanagar: the technology was not appropriate for village conditions.

In case of reverse osmosis, people could not believe that saline water could be made potable by machine. The machine was purchased by the Gram Vikas Trust (a voluntary organisation in Gujarat specially dealing in water projects). But instead of operating the machine itself the Mahiti team asked the Zilla Panchayat to operate it with the idea that the government would then have first-hand information on the viability of this technique. The department agreed in principle, but in one year after its installation the machine was tried out only for five or six days. The officials decided (without much evidence) that the technology was too new, the water produced would be too expensive, and the solution was too temporary to warrant efforts from the government.

Unlike the first two technologies, the idea of lining the pond with plastic to prevent seepage and salination of water was understood better and appealed to villagers. In the summer of 1983 one of the villages, Rahatalav, came forward to try out the experiment. The villagers got some funds sanctioned from the taluka panchayat for excavation. The Indian Petro-chemicals Corporation Limited agreed to provide the plastic film for lining at half the cost, and people agreed to contribute money for purchase of materials. These negotiations took about six months, and in September 1983 digging began, but it stopped halfway because in November young men from the village left, as usual, for outside contract work. Those who remained in the village also stopped working because their wages were not paid on time, and also because the wage rate for this work was lower than the rate they got for road work.

When drinking water was the people's felt need and when they were involved in the solution from the beginning, why did they not put in extra effort to finish the pond? The team tried to persuade people to contribute their labour. During meetings people would agree to contribute labour but no action would follow. After several such meetings, the village panchayat agreed that in the following year (1985) the work would be scheduled when labourers would be available, and the panchayat itself would ensure that the people got paid on time.

Mahiti took up the problem of saline wasteland for which social afforestation seemed to be the viable solution. The Forestry Department believed that nothing could be grown in the saline land of Bhal region while the local people told the Mahiti team that indigenous varieties like prosopis (*ganda baval*) and salvadora (*piloodi*) can grow in this region, and they had economic value. To ascertain these claims, Mahiti took up a demonstration project in 1982 of growing a nursery of local trees for which land was acquired from a village on lease for two years. The land was situated on the banks of a sweet-water pond.

In the first year the nursery failed twice, but the third time the team succeeded in growing seedlings of both prosopis and salvadora. Next, a demonstration plantation was undertaken on six ha of privately-owned and panchayat land. The cost calcul-ations showed that on a one-hectare plot a family would earn Rs. 6,750 per year per hectare from prosopis after five years, and at least Rs. 7,000 from salvadora after seven years (Table 2). The team wanted to demonstrate that these trees could be propagated in that area and that even a poor man could benefit from them. But in its enthusiasm to grow trees the team was not careful in chosing the land for demonstration. The land on which the trees were planted was not particularly bad and it did not belong to the poorest. Therefore, in spite of reasonable success with the plantation, the poor people remained unimpressed.

Table 2: Prosopis on One Hectare

Total plants	:	1,666
(Survival rate 99 per cent)	:	1,500
After 5 years		
Yield (wood)/tree	:	5 mons
∴ Total yield/hectare	:	7,500 mons (1,500×5)
Bone-dry fire-wood would be 30% less.		
∴ Total bone-dry fire-wood	:	5,250 mons
Cost of wood per mon	:	Rs. 6
∴ Total income	:	Rs. 31,500 (5,250×6)
Less expenses	:	Rs. 6,500
Cutting charges Rs. 4,500		
@ Rs. 3 per 5 mons.		
Initial expenses Rs. 2,000		
After 5 years	:	Rs. 25,000

First cutting is done after five years. Then consecutive cuttings are done every four years from which the income will be=Rs. 27,000
∴ Income from one hectare per year will be Rs. 6,750

Income from Piloodi from one hectare

Total number of plants	:	725
Survival	:	700

Year	*Yield per tree*	*Total yield*	*Income*
5th	2 kg×700	= 72 mons×40	=Rs. 2,880
6th	3 kg×700	=105 mons×40	= 4,200
7th	5 kg×700	=175 mons×40	= 7,000
8th	8 kg×700	=280 mons×40	= 11,200
9th	10 kg×700	=350 mons×40	= 14,000

Assuming that the family members will be looking after the farm and plucking berries.

Realising its mistake, the team went back to the people to understand how they could be convinced. The villagers suggested that if the plantation succeeded on very bad saline land near their villages they would be convinced. Following this suggestion, Mahiti acquired a 20-hectare plot of saline wasteland near the village and established a People's Learning Centre at the end of 1983 where various trees, including fruit trees, were planted for demonstration. In 1984, about five varieties of rice were planted on an experimental basis. Planting was done by involving the local people, taking their advice, and without the help of professional experts.

Among the achievements of Mahiti, one can include planting of a number of salvadora trees by people (in July-August, 1984), and the collective application to the government by 75 poor families for acquiring wasteland for salvadora plantations. The impetus for this activity, however, came largely from Aegis Chemical Company, which had offered to help them in plantation and to buy *piloo* seeds directly from the people. The company came to this area through one of the Mahiti members and wanted Mahiti to start a cooperative for salvadora seed collection. Though Mahiti did not want to get directly involved since it was against its principles, it agreed to play the middleman's role only for a demonstration in the first year (summer of 1984). Most people from the seven villages brought their collection of salvadora seeds to Mahiti Centre instead of selling it through a trader and earned Rs. 15-20 extra per maund (20 kg). Together, 292 families collected 1,400 maunds of seeds and earned on an average Rs. 150 per family for two days' labour. For the same quantity a trader would have paid Rs. 80-90. The people appreciated the importance of having a cooperative of their own. As a result, an informed youth organisation came forward to plant salvadora on a 16-acre land collectively, to form a cooperative to collect seeds from the following year onwards and promote a salvadora plantation.

When the team members were busy dealing with larger issues like water and wasteland forestation, some villagers approached them for help in setting up a fishing business. Fishing is a lucrative but tabooed business in this area. People came to Mahiti thinking that like most other voluntary agencies, Mahiti would have money to start a fishing cooperative in which the local people could join. The team did not want to get directly involved so it tried to motivate a group of young Vaghari men from Rahatalav village to set up the fishing cooperative. Since Vagharis are a lower caste, the taboo against fishing among them is not as strong as among the higher castes. The team members helped them in contacting officials for information and to approach banks for loans. After a long delay of 18 months and many frustrating experiences, the Vagharis finally succeeded in setting a fishing cooperative which turned out to be very profitable. In the process, the villagers learnt enough about the fishing business. They contacted a regular buyer and through him built links with the Bombay market so that they no longer needed Mahiti's help.

Seeing this successful example, many other groups have come forward since then and 26 applications for setting up fishing cooperatives have been made to the government from this region. Mahiti's only disappointment in this case is that the group which is now successful does not want to help other groups in the area as was expected. The desire to protect their market may be the real reason, although they say that they have no time to help other groups except in very small ways.

Mahiti continues to perform its promotional and information disseminating role. After two-and-a-half years of concentrated efforts, excluding the first one-and-a-half year spent in fund raising; mostly in two out of seven villages, the people have taken up tree planting and kitchen gardening. In one village some efforts were made to improve the water supply, This is because in these two villages Mahiti has been able to find dedicated workers to serve as team members. The task of finding similar people from other villages remains to be done.

CONCLUSIONS

A discussion of the salient features of the implementing agencies, their entry problems, their approaches to rural development, their strategies and implementation follows the brief description of the two projects. Finally, an attempt is made to derive some lessons from these two experiences.

Salient Features of the Implementing Agencies

Both SEWA and Mahiti are voluntary agencies. SEWA has a well-established identity as a women's organisation and has an ideology which is a combination of Gandhism and feminism of Indian style which reflects in the programme adopted by its Rural Wing. Though looking at the rural conditions SEWA has set aside its traditional role of unionising women for better wages, it is creating income-generating opportunities only for women, when both men and women are in need of income. This is consistent with SEWA's objectives of making women visible, enabling them to control their earnings, and creating local leadership among them. But are women ready for this role? And what is SEWA doing to prepare them for this role?

SEWA, because of its idealism, tends to treat women as an undifferentiated group which they are not. There are differences among them by caste and by class which become obvious through instances like the caste women objecting to the Harijan children being kept in the same creche with their children and the scheduled caste women not joining in the meeting because of the presence of the higher caste women. In milk cooperatives, women wanted men to hold the position of secretary. Women office-bearers allowed themselves to be controlled by men, ignored the instances of malpractice by the latter, and finally when the men were caught and dismissed by SEWA, women office-bearers resigned instead of forging solidarity with the other women. There is little evidence that SEWA has been able to create a sense of mutuality and cohesiveness among women in the face of the many divisive tendencies that exist.

Mahiti does not have an ideology; it has some ideals. For instance, they want to work with the people. The Mahiti team broke off from ASAG because it did not accept ASAG's ideas. ASAG was concerned with building low-cost housing for rural poor while Mahiti wanted to build up a rapport with the people and learn from them about their problems and solutions. Being free from ideology and open-ended in their approach was their strength according to the Mahiti team, but from the villagers' point of view perhaps it was a weakness. Villagers are used to agencies coming with projects and money while here was a group which had neither.

Both the agencies depend on grassroot workers to bring

about change. SEWA selects two women per village after a careful five-phased selection process. Women are selected for their leadership quality, ability to communicate with village women, and confidence to liaise with SEWA and other outside agencies. These women leaders are paid Rs. 300 per month as honorarium.

Mahiti calls and treats its grass-root workers as team members. Mahiti had thought that local educated unemployed youth would serve well as team members because during the BLP exercise they were found to be of great help, but during the implementation of the Mahiti project the wide gap between the educated youth and the illiterate villagers became apparent. Many of them left as they got other jobs.

Mahiti then decided to recruit members from among the villagers. The important qualities looked for in such members were that they should be interested in people's problems, they must be capable of learning and accepting new ideas, must be able to rise above petty jealousies and local rivalries, and work as equals with the people and not as their bosses. Finding such persons was not easy; in three years only three such members were found while seven more villages need such persons. Mahiti has no set notions about who can make a good member because from experience it has been found that a village loafer has turned out to be as good a team member as a leader type person. Mahiti has some romantic ideas about the team approach and a lot of time is spent in team development efforts. The underlying sentiment was expressed thus by one of its members:

> What we tell the villagers to practice we must practice first. If we believe in people's participation we must allow all our team members to participate in our discussions as equals. Some of us cannot be bosses and others workers. If we preach the villagers to be self-sufficient, our team members should not be dependent on Mahiti and Mahiti on the outside support for very long.

Entry Problems

For SEWA the entry was almost by invitation. Women from Dholka went to SEWA because they wanted work and they knew that SEWA could give them work. With SEWA's reputation it was hardly surprising that they got the support of the local administration. Village leaders supported them by renting out rooms to SEWA, allowing use of a public building for their activities, and in one village even donated panchayat land for building a SEWA Centre.

In the beginning, however, when SEWA tried to unionise women agricultural workers there was a lot of resistance from their labourer husbands and farmers. From one or two villages SEWA had to withdraw, and till today, leaders of those villages have refused to let SEWA enter under any guise. After this initial experience SEWA changed its approach to developmental activities and entry into the village was easy.

In each village, SEWA entered by starting a creche because that was seen as a centre around which poor women could be brought together for other activities concerning functional literacy, maternal and child health-care and non-formal education. SEWA thus adopted the path of least resistance as far as the government was concerned.

SEWA had picked up the various government schemes like Training Rural Youth for Self Employment (TRYSEM), Non-Formal Education, Health Education, *Balawadi* (creche) and ran them under their own banner but exclusively for women. The Director of the Rural Wing gave the following explanation;

> We had to have a separate organisation for women at the field level because the existing development structure at the block or the village level would not serve women's interest given their mental conditioning. At the higher level, however, we work through the existing structures. We make use of every government scheme for the benefit of women.

The government welcomes this mode of working: a reputed voluntary agency playing the middleman's role between the governmental development programmes and the intended beneficiaries. But, as one senior executive of SEWA pointed out, instead of coordinating with the government SEWA sometimes ended up taking over the schemes which were often poorly conceived and inadequately supported.

By comparison, Mahiti's entry was somewhat unorthodox

from the point of view of both, the government and the people. When the team was asked to develop a block level plan, it was expected that it would recommend some income generating projects, work out their costs, and the number of beneficiaries. Instead, the team suggested that BLP should be concerned with removing the basic constraints of the area like the saline land and drinking water shortages.

The BLP report argued that in the past many developmental schemes had failed in this block because they were inappropriate for this area and/or the government officials took little interest in making them work. For example, land has been deteriorating every year because of floods from the rivers. The government tried many times to build embankments under scarcity programmes but they were left unfinished and were usually washed away in the following monsoon. Therefore, instead of investing money in new projects the government should try to improve the earlier investments, the report argued. The government did not accept any of the BLP suggestions on the ground that they would not increase the employment potential of the block which was the objective of BLP. The team was asked to come up with employment-generating schemes. There was too wide a gap between the government's thinking and Mahiti's approach for them to appreciate each other's point of view. The officials looked upon the Mahiti team as comprising well-intentioned but inexperienced (perhaps even misguided) youth and virtually ignored it and its report.

The team members criticised the Forestry Department because a nursery scheme which was meant to generate employment among small farmers was actually helping rich farmers since the targets had to be met. This kind of criticism, though valid, evoked hostile responses from the officials; for instance, they would say, 'Show us what you can do!'

Mahiti had problems with villagers as well. The villagers expected that anyone coming from outside would have money and a project. One of the Mahiti members recalled their early experiences in this respect:

> Till late in the evening we would discuss their problems—water and saline land. They would agree that those problems can be solved, perhaps expecting that next we will

offer money. But whenever we said that we expected them to use their resources, ingenuity, and problem solving ability, we could see the change. People would simply nod politely and wait for us to leave.

For the team members, those were frustrating experiences because both the people and the government expected them to do something tangible. The nursery of local species and reverse osmosis machines were seen as 'research projects' for the benefit of the team and, therefore, did not count as help to the poor people. Villagers began to hint that Mahiti should start a fishing cooperative, almost challenging them by saying that the government would not allow this to happen. Some of the team members became eager to take up the challenge and show to the villagers that they were capable of doing something. But after much heated discussion among themselves, the team decided not to get involved directly but to help a group in the village to form a cooperative.

When this fishing cooperative could not get loans for seven months and everybody involved in it was frustrated, the team members were again tempted to advance loans from their own funds. After much discussion they decided against it because that would have created a dependency relationship with the people and the team did not want to be cast in the role of a saviour. Fortunately, the bank loan came through eventually, and the cooperative managed to survive and even flourish. But if this had not happened, how would it have affected Mahiti's image?

The role that Mahiti played both in the fishing cooperative and in the construction of the pond created the impression that at least some of the members were well-connected and had influence in Ahmedabad and Gandhinagar; if they wished, they could make things happen in the village. This image had, to some extent, eased their initial entry but may also have raised people's expectations.

Two Approaches to Rural Development

Both the SEWA and the Mahiti approaches to rural development are similar in a fundamental way: both are attempting to mitigate social and economic exploitation of a certain class of people; SEWA is doing it for women, and Mahiti, for the rural poor. SEWA attempts to raise women's status and confidence through their ability to earn and control their earnings as well as by giving them control over their sources of income. For example, in the milk cooperative, women could not remain just token members while the men controlled the operations. In two cooperatives they were trained in milk testing and in other operations of a milk cooperative. The ultimate goal is to prepare women to gradually take over the buying and selling functions as well as the management of finances. SEWA would like to accomplish this goal quickly, even though the women who are expected to take over are not yet ready for the task.

The experience with the women's milk cooperative is very instructive from that point. The women who attended the initial training in cattle-care during 1978 wanted merely to own a buffalo; membership of the cooperative was thrust upon them. SEWA took the initiative. It encouraged the idea of women's cooperatives, got the cooperatives registered, created rotating funds, and gave loans to women. In the first village, SEWA organisers went to the cattle market with the women to purchase good quality buffaloes. Women who wanted to buy were just observers in this process. As a result, they were not concerned if the animal became ill nor were they bothered about its insurance. They conveniently shifted all the responsibility to SEWA.

The organisers began to feel that the women were not getting involved in the cooperative. Nor had they developed a sense of ownership of the animals. After this experience, in the villages where SEWA was yet to enter, it tried to reduce its involvement by giving women the money to purchase cattle on their own, but later they learnt that almost all of them had purchased poor quality animals. The organisers were not sure whether the women were cheated or they had deliberately purchased poor quality animals to save money. As a result, in those villages milk production was low, and women were unable to repay the loans. This could be interpreted to mean that the women were not yet ready for the role they were given. They were finding the cooperative a burden. They would have preferred to be employed by SEWA.

Mahiti's approach to rural development is to organise the

poor, disadvantaged people around certain issues. The principal assumption is that if people find out about their entitlements and are organised as a force, they can make demands on the system to get them. The assumption raises two questions: How far is Mahiti justified in assuming that the poor will acquire sufficient courage to get organised and make demands on the system just by finding out what they are entitled to? Is the system ready to respond to such demands?

Initially, the team members had believed that the local officials could become development oriented if they knew people's problems and the correct ways of solving them. It did not take them long to realise that a development culture was lacking among the local officials. They were busy trying to get transfers from that block. The only way to get them to act was to put pressure on them from above and create a force of demands from below.

Under what conditions can the poor and disadvantaged generate sufficient pressure to force an action? And, can Mahiti's approach produce these conditions? The issues that Mahiti chose to work on, namely wasteland and drinking water, do not seem to have the force necessary to bring the people together. Mahiti identified having a supply of drinking water as a basic need which when not met would bring people together to generate pressure. But in the view of the people, not having a supply of drinking water was a hardship to be put up with. The basic need according to them was more income. This should have become obvious from the way people behaved rather than what they said. They gave a higher priority to the contract work outside the village which paid higher wages than to the pond digging work in the village which would have given them drinking water.

To generate an effective demand there must be some power behind the people; the power could take the form of money or of political or elite support. In this case, the poor in the villages did not get support from their village leaders. In Rahatalav, the leader effectively stopped people from working on the village pond by offering them slightly higher wages on his private construction work. The only form of power they could have had was the support of an outside group like Mahiti, who have links with the high-ups. But Mahiti deliberately withheld this support, undermining its importance, unlike SEWA which was using it as and when required.

Identification of Problems and Intervention Strategies

In case of SEWA the problem was clearly identified by the women themselves. They wanted some work near their homes. The work package that SEWA could put together was based on its experience in the urban set-up.

SEWA did not try to find out what rural women could do or would like to do. *Charkha* was easy to organise though women were not too keen about it. They accepted it when their need was dire and gave it up as soon as the need ceased to exist. Most women were reluctant to be weavers and potters because it was man's work, though SEWA tried to train them to do men's jobs with the idea of improving women's status. Usually, young girls came forward to learn these skills rather than women, and many of them may have come only because a stipend was being given.

Women showed interest in tailoring and in cane work which seemed to have a limited scope in the villages. This raises the issue of the choice of product. At present, the products are made mostly for the urban market. The centre at Devdholera weaves sarees, carpets, and makes fashionable cane products which are sold in the Ahmedabad market. One reason for choosing these products could be that SEWA did not want to compete with the local weavers who were making *dhotis* for the village market. But this means that women will have to depend on an outside market and on SEWA for a long time. Also, so far no thought has been given to women who have neither the skill nor the capacity to learn. Income-generating opportunities which can be exploited by unskilled women need to be identified.

Mahiti's problem identification was influenced by their BLP findings. While working for BLP they identified saline land and shortage of drinking water as constraints to development. But these were the problems of the area for which most families had worked out individual coping mechanisms. For instance, at least one member from each family works outside the block, in the city of Ahmedabad and Surat. City income has reduced their dependence on land. Thus, according to Mahiti, there is a one-to-one relationship between the area's constraints and poverty, but people in the area do not seem to perceive it that way.

Equating the area's problems with people's problems is perhaps the weakest link in Mahiti's approach. It then expects that people will be committed to solving those problems. If Mahiti wants to demonstrate how people can work together for their own benefit, it will have to select activities in which there is a personal stake for people. Fishing cooperatives is an instance of such activity. On the other hand, if it wants to tackle the larger problems then it must have commensurate resources.

Shifting Strategy in Response to Failures

Finally, it would be interesting to see how these two organisations have responded to their failures and how their strategies have changed over time.

In the case of SEWA there is a consistent pattern: whenever a certain approach failed or ran into difficulties, SEWA accepted responsibility for it and took over the operation before deciding an alternative course of action.

Milk cooperatives are an example of such an approach. When men secretaries put the milk societies into financial crises, SEWA took charge, dismissed the office bearers, put SEWA's own workers, who faced the risk of being assaulted, in charge. Some of the women resented SEWA's control but the organisers had no doubt that as long as SEWA stood guarantee to the banks for the cattle loans it must control the cooperative. Initially, SEWA used to seek the cooperation of the village leaders for starting its activities in the village. When it realised that the leaders were trying to get benefits for their family members and friends in return, it stopped the practice. Now all activities are started independently under SEWA's name. There is not much community participation or joint effort at problem solving. Meetings are called when there are problems, but decisions are made largely by the organisers.

Mahiti's approach, on the other hand, is to get ideas from the people and act upon only those ideas which are accepted by the people. In fact, in the beginning Mahiti did not have a separate identity as an organisation symbolised by an office or a centre. Then came the idea of the People's Centre because people wanted a demonstration of tree plantation on saline land.

There was a change in the strategy. Some of the members resisted the idea of a Centre in the beginning because they thought that the Centre would take too much of their time and it would be at the cost of their village activities.

The Centre has influenced their style of functioning. For example, one year many villagers expressed a desire to plant fruit trees after learning from Mahiti that certain fruit trees would grow on their land. So the team bought seedlings from Ahmedabad and offered them to the villagers at cost, charges such as transportation not included. People wanted the seedlings free. They decided not to buy the seedlings, and hoped that eventually Mahiti would distribute the seedlings, free. Mahiti remained firm and, instead, planted the trees on the Centre's land. In the following year many families arranged to buy seedlings on their own. If Mahiti did not have a Centre it would have, perhaps, yielded to people's pressure, and the following year others would have expected them to do the same.

Mahiti has also realised that by insisting that people get involved in learning about a new technology when they were not fully aware of its benefits, would not be beneficial to anybody. When the reverse osmosis machine was installed for experimentation, neither the people nor the officials showed curiosity. The machine remained unused and the team repeatedly tried to approach the officials and people and motivate them to try out this solution. Mahiti itself did not try out the machine and demonstrate its usefulness because it believed that if the people were not involved from the beginning they would not accept the solution. Thus a perfectly useful experiment was sacrificed for the sake of a principle. Over time, the team has modified its stand. Mahiti has started activities only for demonstration purpose in which people's participation is considered desirable but not necessary.

Team members now spend more time at the Centre, creating a distance between the villagers and themselves, though they wish that people would use the Centre and the land around it as their laboratory. In July-August 1984, the idea of a centre was extended to the villages by renting a house in each village to be used as a demonstration centre. Mahiti members have already realised the usefulness of having such centres. Perhaps they should have started with the village centres.

Evaluation and Recommendations

It would be unreasonable to evaluate the impact of these projects since both are still evolving, and much can be expected from them in the future. But whether the strategies followed by them are consistent with rural development objectives or not can be assessed, and some lessons can be learnt from their experiences.

Both the agencies are aiming at reducing poverty and social and economic exploitation. SEWA's approach emphasises immediate and direct results. In each village where SEWA is working there are about a dozen women directly benefiting from their intervention. Some of them are grass-roots workers, some work in the creche, others, are getting income in the form of stipends from the training centres. To that extent, these schemes are meeting one of the felt needs of some women, majority of whom are poor but not always the poorest.

The more important objective of rural development is to develop self-reliance among the rural poor where SEWA has achieved very little so far. If anything, there has developed a dependency, i.e., employer-employee relationship between SEWA and the rural women. This type of relationship certainly cannot be sustained over a very long time and cannot be extended to a large number of women.

Both SEWA and Mahiti may find that the goal of self-reliance, that is, being able to sustain activities without external support, is difficult to achieve. The people that they are trying to help are living at a subsistence level at which it is difficult for them to come together to work for self-sufficiency in the face of many divisive forces like caste, class, sex, and in the midst of poverty. To organise these people, which is what both the agencies are attempting to do, it may be necessary to create a sense of mutuality and cohesiveness among them. Experience from other projects has shown that this mutuality can be achieved only under two conditions: one, if the intervenors are prepared to spend their time with the group so that it can learn to work together; and two, if the people are brought together to work on activities which will yield benefits directly to themselves. That is, people can learn to work together cohesively on an income-generating activity on which they have an exclusive claim and only if they can control the entry of others into their group. The fisheries cooperative which Mahiti helped to develop has these characteristics, and it is working very effectively perhaps because of it.

The Mahiti team is ready to give a lot of time to the people but the issues that they have chosen to work on do not have immediate personal appeal. People got together to start a fisheries cooperative but could not come together to dig a village pond which would have benefited all. SEWA organisers spend very little time with the village women but in their scheme the grass-roots level leaders are expected to bring women together. This idea has many practical limitations. Only two or three leaders out of thirty, would be effective. And that is to be expected because SEWA is looking for women with inherent leadership qualities. Such women are difficult to find in the villages and not many of them belong to the poorest class. Thus, to achieve self-reliance both the agencies will have to modify their approaches somewhat, in terms of what activities to select, how many to choose, and how much time to spend in building village level groups.

Another important conclusion that emerges from these case studies is that it is necessary to develop a middle-level power group between the local bureaucracy and the people in order to ensure that the gains of development flow to the people.

Both these organisations have found that local development agencies can be forced into action only if there are pressures from both above and below. SEWA hopes to generate these pressures at the village level through the grass-roots workers. But these leaders by themselves would be helpless individually unless they are supported by an outside organisation like SEWA. Mahiti is attempting to develop a regional team in which a group of villages would come together and support each other in solving their problems. The concept behind this approach is that usually all villages in a region share common problems like water scarcity and saline land. If they got together and approached the local officials as a group, they would be more effective than they would be if they approached them as individuals. In this design, the need for an outside support group is not perceived. In practice, however, the local teams have taken too long to form. And if and when they do form, they would face the twin problems of evolving a power base necessary to put pressure on the local officials and at the same time guarding themselves against being corrupted by that power.

Present experience shows that when local groups have formed especially for income-generating schemes, these groups have attempted to become exclusive by closing entry to other village members. This tendency can be observed among the members of the fishing cooperatives. Since the cooperatives became profitable, the original members have refused to expand the group. In none of SEWA's activities has this happened because SEWA is controlling the entry and the exit. This indicates that the concept of a regional or local level power group may have some problems though clearly they are needed for people to derive the benefits of development. Both SEWA and Mahiti, therefore, will have to concentrate on evolving alternative structures which can function effectively.

Similar Concern but Varying Approaches: A Case Study of ASSEFA and MYRADA

Ranjit Gupta

The original intent was to conduct a case study of two voluntary agencies (non-governmental organisations) sharing similar concern or involved in similar activities such as development of the landless rural poor, but following different approaches and differing in their ways of working. The idea was also to select agencies operating in several rural clusters in quite a few districts for a reasonably long stretch of time with varying degrees of 'success'.

Two Voluntary Agencies

After some initial probing the choice fell on the Association of Sarva Seva Farms, primarily based in Tamil Nadu, and the Mysore Resettlement and Development Agency, primarily based in Karnataka (popularly, the first is referred to as 'Assefa' and, the second, as 'Myrada'.)

In terms of area of operation and scale of activities, both are several times larger than most voluntary agencies in the country. Both originated around the same time, Myrada in 1968 and Assefa in 1969. Both started with more or less similar ends in view: Myrada to resettle Tibetan refugees and local landless families on government or public land, usually wasteland, and Assefa to resettle the landless rural poor on the lands —usually waste or degraded land—acquired through Bhoodan and Gramdan movements launched by Vinoba and further broadened by Jayaprakash Narayan.

ASSEFA

From 1951 when Vinoba launched the Bhoodan (land-gift) movement till about 1963, when the land gifts virtually came to an end, the movement collected from landowners in various parts of the country over four million acres for redistribution to the landless. Though about one-third of this land was distributed to the landless, most of the Bhoodan allottees could not cultivate the land because they did not have the resources or means to do so. For all practical purposes they remained landless wage earners.

The idea of starting Sarva Seva farms was conceived in 1969 to bridge this gap. Assefa emerged from the work initiated towards this end by the Tamil Nadu Sarvodaya Mandal and the Tamil Nadu Bhoodan Board. Three individuals who played key roles in translating the idea into action and establishing Assefa are Giovanni Ermiglia, a retired Italian professor representing the Movimento Sviluppo E Pace (Torino, Italy), S. Jagannathan, a Sarvodaya leader, and S. Loganathan, a young activist.

The first farm of 70 acres with 35 Bhoodan allottees owning and managing it, was started in 1969 in Ramnad district of Tamil Nadu. It was a success. The allottees, who live in nearby villages, worked with Loganathan to reclaim and develop the 70-acre farm. The land was levelled and cleared of rocks and scrub. Seven wells were dug. Water flowed to irrigate the entire farm and made it alive.

The 'success' generated enthusiasm. It also brought support and strengthened the team's confidence in itself to carry the work further by adding more farms. By 1976, the number of farms rose to 10. Funds for starting and running these farms came from the Movimento Sviluppo E Pace (MSP). Support from more donor agencies, including the European Economic Community (EEC), followed.

By 1978, there were 16 farms in five districts of Tamil Nadu covering about 800 acres of land and 364 Bhoodan families. It was at this stage that Assefa was formally founded as a registered body with headquarters at Madurai, Tamil Nadu. In terms of number of farms established and landless families resettled, the progress thereafter has been rapid (Table 1).

Table 1: State-wise Distribution of Sarva Seva Farms (January 1983)

State	No. of Farms	Area (acres)	No. of Families
Tamil Nadu*	36	2033	898
Bihar	15	1142	601
Maharashtra	15	1222	254
Rajasthan	1	85	22
Karnataka	1	342	66
Total	68	4824	1841

*Excludes one project on Gramdan land and another on forest fallow land, both in Madurai district, covering 3,200 acres and 1,452 families.
Source: *ASSEFA Profile*, Madurai.

Although development and multiplication of Sarva Seva farms to settle the Bhoodan allottees—mostly Harijans and tribals—remains the dominant concern of Assefa, it has started enlarging its interest and range of activities. Since 1980 the package of activities has been both expanded and diversified to include programmes like development of animal husbandry, forestry, rural industries, health, nutrition, education and housing.

Organisationally, Assefa is a four-tier structure. At the all-India level there is the working committee of the Association, which works under the guidance of the General Body. The committee is composed of nine members (Sarvodaya leaders) drawn from different parts of the country. The General Body decides the overall policy and operates through the working committee. For day-to-day decisions there is a three member executive committee elected from amongst the members of the working committee.

At the second tier there are state committees to coordinate and oversee the working of the Sarva Seva farms in the state.

The state committees consist of eminent Sarvodaya leaders of the state, social workers and professionals.

At the third tier there are project committees which are responsible for planning and implementation of the projects. A typical project may cover more than one Sarva Seva farm in a district or a block. The project committee comprises local Sarvodaya leaders and senior members of the project staff. The committee has direct access to the central organ of Assefa from which it receives financial, human and technical support.

The individual Sarva Seva farm constitutes the fourth tier. The decision-making body here is the Gram Sabha (village assembly) of the allottees. Assefa is represented at this level by a *sevak* (community worker). Financial and technical support is made available to the farm through the project committee. The ultimate test is to make the the farm viable and develop the allottees' capability to manage it on their own. At this point the farm is handed over to the allottees' Gram Sabha and the project committee withdraws. So far only a few farms have been handed over to the Gram Sabhas [1].

MYRADA

Myrada, with headquarters at Bangalore was founded in 1968 as a registered society with the objective of resettling Tibetan refugees in Karnataka. In the mid-1950s, when Tibetan refugees first came to India, they were settled in the Himalayan belt of North India where they found employment mainly in road construction works. After these works were completed, most of them had no stable source of income. Resettlement programmes for them had to be taken up afresh. As the results of the efforts made in this direction by governmental bodies were not encouraging, Myrada was established as a private or voluntary body to implement and coordinate the resettlement programme in Karnataka in collaboration with the State Government and other agencies. Its first board was composed of senior state officials, political leaders, specialists, and representatives of international non-government organisations.

Myrada completed the Tibetan resettlement programme comprising five projects in 1978. Twenty thousand Tibetans were resettled on 15,000 acres of government land in Cauvery valley,

Mungod, Lakshmipura, Chowkur and Kollegal villages of Karnataka. The projects were executed on 'turnkey' basis. Work in all projects started with clearing and reclamation of forests followed by land development, tubewell irrigation, construction of roads and bridges, hospitals and schools, housing, electricity, and similar facilities and services to settle the Tibetan families as agriculturists. Cooperative societies for distribution of inputs, and marketing of outputs, banks, and handicraft centres were also established. Training in farming, animal husbandry, and dairying was imparted to enable the Tibetans, herdsmen by tradition, to settle down in a totally new environment.

Successful completion of these projects and the experience gained in resettlement and land development encouraged Myrada to take up a similar project, this time with a view to resettle 38 bonded labour families who were freed in 1964 by the government of Tamil Nadu. Though each of these families received from the Government a plot of 3 acres in Kongahalli village of Periyar district, none of them could put it to any use for lack of resources and follow-up support. For 16 years the land they received remained barren, uncultivated. Myrada took up the project in 1980. The first thing it did was to construct houses for the allottees. Soon it dug a bore well, developed the land, and helped and encouraged the allottees to settle down as land owning cultivators. All this took time, demanded patience to deal with people and enthusiasm and skills to cope with a continuous stream of problems.

Similar projects, including what Myrada calls, 'integrated rural development projects', were added in subsequent years. Presently, it is involved in four resettlement projects and six integrated rural development projects. Why these are called 'integrated rural development projects' or what they stand for, is not clear. But they are not very different from the 'non-integrated' pieces schemes in bureaucratic terminology—which most development agencies tend to pick up either because the donor agencies (national or international) supporting them expect them to do so or because they themselves want to do what others in the field are doing, or both. While the outcome is generally more of the same, some agencies do manage to handle the same tasks more innovatively. Myrada's tubewell irrigation for small farmers is a case in point.

The location and coverage of Myrada's four resettlement projects and six IRD projects, which are in progress, are given in Table 2.

Organisationally, Myrada is composed of two parts: (i) the central office at Bangalore, and (ii) the projects situated 60 to 2,000 km away from the central office. The latter with an annual budget of Rs. 650,000 is headed by a full-time director. He is assisted by several subject matter specialists and supporting administrative and technical staff. The central office is responsible for raising and managing resources, staff recruitment and training, coordination and monitoring of project activities, and providing expertise in specialised fields to the project staff.

Each project, with a project officer heading it, is sub-divided into two or three geographical territories called 'sectors'. The sector staff, with sector officer as incharge, include one or more extension officers and a small group of field workers. The subject matter specialists based at the central office also report to the project officer.

Most members of the 350-strong Myrada staff are young. Superannuated civil and defence personnel constitute a significant part of the rest. Quite a few project officers had a full career in the defence services before they joined Myrada. The first director of Myrada was himself a senior defence official.

Strengths and Limitations

The success of the two agencies is perhaps best reflected by their growth and ability to attract young workers to work for the landless poor. One with radical views may differ with their approach and ways of working. One looking for possibilities of mounting massive efforts matching the massive size of the problem may view their work and contributions as inconsequential. Both may be right. But viewed from their perspective, their size and resources, they have surely done better than most others working in similar fields.

This does not mean that they have done well in all the fields in which they are active. Where they seem to have done well, in some cases remarkably well, is in their efforts to resettle the landless—on Bhoodan land in the case of Assefa and on government land in the case of Myrada. Despite certain similarities,

Table 2: Resettlement and Integrated RD Projects of Myrada (December 1983)

Project	District/State	Coverage	Funding Agency
Resettlement Project			
1. Kadri I (landless labour)	Ananthapur/Andhra	200 families/2000 acres	Canadian Hunger Foundation
2. Kadri II (landless labour)	Ananthapur/Andhra	200 families/2000 acres	Swiss Development Corporation
3. Sri Lankan repatriates	Madurai/Tamil Nadu	180 families/360 acres	Netherlands Committee for Refugees
4. Kongahalli (bonded labour)	Periyar/Tamil Nadu	38 families/200 acres	OXFAM, CRS, FORRAD, etc
IRD Projects			
1. HD Kote Taluk	Mysore/Karnataka	229 villages	FPP International, USA
2. Holalkere Taluk	Chitradurga/Karnataka	30 villages	Agro-Action, West Germany
3. Kollegal Taluk	Mysore/Karnataka	33 villages	TRAS, Canada
4. Bangarpet Taluk	Kolar/Karnataka	49 villages	MAF, Canada
5. Talvadi Taluk	Periyar/Tamil Nadu	113 villages	Agro-Action, West Germany
6. Nongkhlow Project	Khasi Hills/Meghalaya	140 villages	Agro-Action, West Germany

Source: *Myrada Newsletter*, December 1984, Bangalore.

there are basic differences in their orientation, approach, and style of functioning.

Assefa is a Gandhian body sharing the values and culture of what has come to be known as Gandhism. The hold of ritualised practices and attachment to a work culture which Vinoba symbolised are still very strong. Like most Gandhian bodies the organisation is a good deal personalised around the leader. Myrada, on t e other hand, is essentially professional in orientation and bureaucratic in organisational structure.

MYRADA

It neither subscribes to any "ism', nor has one of its own. While this makes the organisation more open to new ideas, such bodies involved in rural development seem to suffer from a general weakness—the temptation to pick up whatever comes their way and in the process end up doing something of everything.

Added to this, when a voluntary agency seeks to professionalise itself without a clear vision of the people it wishes to serve and develop, the approach changes, wittingly or otherwise, from 'developing the people' to 'managing them'. This shift is clearly indicated in a Myrada document, titled 'Capitalization Study'. In a chapter describing some aspects of the Myrada organisation, it poses and attempts to answer four questions:[1]

1) How does Myrada *manage* its people?
2) How does Myrada *manage* its finances?
3) How does Myrada *manage* its operations?
4) How does Myrada *manage* its environment?

Each statement is loaded. Emphatic. *Myrada manages*. In contrast, an Assefa document spells out the Assefa vision or "philosophy" as follows:[2]

> In the Development Philosophy of Assefa, community organization stands first. Assefa uses socio-economic programmes as a medium for organization, education and animation of communities, ensuring people's participation, development of local leadership and decision-making processes.

The two passages quoted from the documents of the two agencies sum up the difference in their approach and attitude towards development. Other differences—in intervention strategy, planning methods, and ways of working—follow from this basic difference.

The Myrada strategy shares several elements of the strategy evolved and adopted by Amul Dairy and subsequently used elsewhere in the country by the National Dairy Development Board (NDDB). However, whereas the Amul strategy—popularly called the 'Anand pattern'—is confined to only dairy development with emphasis on vertical integration of activities, the Myrada strategy seems to be based on those elements of the strategy which it could put across the board covering diverse fields of development, with or without vertical integration. This could be due to its involvement in projects like resettlement of the resourceless and area development, both pushing it to look for and work in more than one field simultaneously.

According to Myrada, the intervention strategy it follows consists of four parts or stages:[3]

1) *Preparatory Stage*: A spearhead team surveys the area, forms village societies, identifies leaders, provides them with training facilities, motivates small community actions, and prepares a project using the data collected through survey and discussions with villagers, banks, cooperatives, and government agencies.

2) *Formative Stage*: This includes the building of basic infrastructure—land development, irrigation, establishment of services and facilities including—in the case of resettlement projects—construction of roads and bridges, housing, schools and hospitals, etc.

3) *Consolidation Stages*: It is not clear what this stage really is. The impression one gets from Myrada documents and discussions with its staff is that the endeavour at this stage is to revitalise institutions like cooperatives and secure aids and sanctions from a number of organisations, including government departments and banks, to implement the projects.

4) *Withdrawal*: The ultimate stage when the activities and institutions like cooperatives are handed over to the target groups enabling Myrada to withdraw for good. This is the most critical stage. The aim is laudable. However, except in the case

of the Tibetan Refugee Resettlement projects, this stage does not seem to have been achieved [2].

Conceptually, however, all the four stages are well conceived and are relevant to realising the aims of rural development. Being more professional than most voluntary agencies in the country, Myrada is also quite systematic in its approach to grass-roots planning. Besides village survey and project formulation undertaken at the entry stage, a more elaborate planning exercise is attempted at the post-entry stage. The exercise involves:

1) *Family-oriented planning:* The attempt here is to identify the socio-economic status of each family in the 'target group', and evolve a plan in physical and financial terms for increasing the family's income. These are aggregated villagewise to assess the level of resources, infrastructure and credit facilities needed for each village. Sources to raise the required resources are then identified. These include both donor agencies supporting Myrada and government schemes, including institutional credit from banks and cooperatives.

2) *Activity-oriented planning*: The aggregated family plans are used as a basis to identify and select activities such as irrigation works for small farmers, stockman centre for animal husbandry support, and rural industry for local artisans. "The focus here is on such issues as the number and type of beneficiaries, equipment and facilities needed, manpower and training required, level of investment and credit requirements, financial viability etc.[4]

3) *Institution-oriented planning*: By and large this is confined to examining the feasibility of revitalising village cooperatives. The exercise usually involves preparation of diagnostic studies, the underlying intention (or hope) being to facilitate Myrada's eventual withdrawal from the area.

ASSEFA

If rigorous and systematic planning, professional competence and technical expertise are the main strengths of Myrada, the ability to work with—as against managing—the resourceless landless with a sense of humility appears to be the foremost strength of Assefa. Partly because of this reason and partly because it is less professionally managed but interested in acquiring more professional competence, Assefa is more open to researchers interested in a gaining closer, even critical, understanding of its work than Myrada. It has also published a few reports providing data from its internal records about the economics or viability of the Sarva Seva farms [3].

Depending on the legal status of the land on which the Assefa farms are organised, the farms are classified into three categories, each governed by a separate set of rules:

1) *Bhoodan holding*, where the land is allotted to individuals who are governed by the rules prescribed by the Bhoodan Board.

2) *Gramdan land*, where a "community" constituting the Gram Sabha is governed by a set of regulations imposed by the Gram Sabha itself under the guidance or direction of the Bhoodan Board.

3) *Government/forest fallow land*, occupied by individuals and ratified by the state government. The landholders here are governed by the rules prescribed by the state government through the revenue department.

The approach to organise the farms is partly conditioned by their legal status and the rules and constraints associated with the status. For example, in 'Bhoodan holding', where individuals are the owners of the land allotted to them, it is difficult to organise the farm and relate it with general village development activities. This is more so when the allottees are few and therefore in a minority vis-a-vis the village population. The farm, or more correctly the allottees owning it, tend to get isolated from the mainstream of village life. Assefa considers this a 'danger' that need to be avoided [4].

In the case of 'Gramdan land', where the entire village—the Gram Sabha—is involved, Assefa has to undertake a range of activities to reach various sections of the village population. However, in this category, it has only one project covering two villages (2,000 acres, 780 families) in Natham block, Madurai district. Besides land development, the activities started in these villages are health, education, and rural industries.

The emphasis in the third category of farms, 'government/forest fallow land', is on maintaining links with government departments at one end and with landholders at the other. In this category also there is only one farm covering 1,200 acres and 672 families in two villages of Nilakottai block, Madurai.

Neither of the two can really be called a 'farm'. They are essentially programmes or projects with land development as one of the important activities. As against these two, Assefa has 68 farms of Bhoodan land. Clearly this is the most important achievement of Assefa.

The first two farms were started in 1969 with assistance from MSP, Italy. In the next eight years, another eight were added, most of them with assistance from MSP. Till this period (1969-77), the attempts were confined to only five districts in Tamil Nadu: Madurai (5 farms), Ramnad (5), Coimbatore (4), and Pudukottai and Tirunelveli (one each). Expansion to other states began in 1978 when eight more farms were started—six in Gaya district of Bihar, one in Kota district, Rajasthan, and one in Madurai district, Tamil Nadu.

From 24 farms established till 1978, the number jumped to 50 in 1979, when, beside MSP and other donor agencies, the European Economic Community (EEC) stepped in to promote Assefa's growth. Sixteen of the 26 new farms thus started with assistance from EEC; the remaining 10 with assistance from MSP. Assistance from these and other donor agencies helped adding 13 farms in 1982 and 5 in 1983.

The average size of the 68 farms is 71 acres. The number of families settled works out to 28 per farm. However, the size of the farms varies widely—from 9 acres with 9 families (a farm in Madurai district) to 342 acres with 66 families (a farm in Tumkur, Karnataka). In terms of the number of families settled, the largest happens to be a farm in Coimbatore, Tamil Nadu, with 100 families owning 3 acres each. Some idea of the variations in farm size and the number of families per farm can be obtained from Table 3.

What does Assefa do to establish and develop the farms? The planning process, efforts, and achievements vary, understandably, from farm to farm or from one situation to another. But a pattern does seem to have emerged over time. It involves a series of steps or actions, some undertaken sequentially, some simultaneously. A somewhat loose classification of these, showing the stages of growth, is given as follows:

1) *Rapport Building*; From the Bhoodan Board and know-

Table 3: Size-wise Distribution of Assefa Farms

Size of holding (acres)	Farm		No. of families per farm
	No.	Avg Size (Acres)	
Below 10	1	9.0	9
10—30	12	22.6	12
30—50	15	34.9	15
50—75	13	62.0	27
75—100	16	89.0	36
Over 100	11	163.2	53
Total	68	71.0	28

Source: Assefa records.

ledgeable Sarvodaya workers, the areas/locations where work needs to be or could be started are ascertained. Concerns such as desirability and logistics influence the eventual choice. The choice may fall on one or more of the suggested locations. Efforts to build rapport with the Bhoodan allottees in particular and other villagers in the selected locations follow. Many visits are made by Assefa workers and several rounds of discussions with the Bhoodan allottees are held to persuade them to start the farm. *This takes time* [5].

2) *Building Infrastructure:* Activities undertaken at this stage are similar to those Myrada does in the 'formative stage'. The activities include land reclamation, levelling and bunding of lands for irrigation, digging of open wells, deepening and widening of existing wells, installation of pumpsets, formation of channels and underground pipelines, provision of basic services and production aids like farm implements and draft animals [6].

3) *Group Farming and Capability Building*: Depending on the size of the farm and the number of wells dug/deepened, the allottees are divided into two or more groups—usually one group per well. The groups, along with Assefa workers, then prepare the crop plan for the farm and work out ways of implementing it, which involve assignment of roles and tasks to each

group and to each member of a group. The tasks include procurement of inputs, cultivation, marketing, and management of group farming functions and activities. The process continues with many ups and downs.

4) *Self-management and Assefa Withdrawal*: Depending on the level and quality of self-management capabilities acquired by the allottees as a collective body, the handing over of the farm to them takes place, enabling Assefa to withdraw from the scene. The time it takes to reach this stage is uncertain dependent as it is on a variety of factors, particularly the results achieved in relation to making the farm viable and the dynamics of group working.

A group formed around a specific or a set of economic activities by outside intervenors tends to acquire one of the following attributes depending on the nature and quality of interventions [7].

1) The group, particularly if members of the group happen to belong to the disadvantaged sections of the rural society, becomes so dependent on the intervenors that the intervenors see virtually no way of withdrawing except at the cost of letting the group and the activity disintegrate.

2) The group and its capability to self-manage progress through several stages of 'group cohesion—confidence in group working—control by some over others—conflict within group leading to factionalism—collusion and crisis'. The crisis may lead to total breakdown or ironically to a new level of cohesion. The cycle may repeat but the chances of total breakdown keep declining as new levels of cohesion are reached through successive stages of group building (See Chart on page 325).

The intervenors can withdraw with a fair degree of confidence that the group and the activity will continue and generally do so after the group has gone through two or more stages of progression described above. Assefa has been able to do this only in respect of four or five of the 68 farms. This handful of farms, which were started 12-15 years ago and have been handed over to the allottees, are reportedly doing well. 'Uchapatti' in Madurai district is one of them. It surely is a success story, and it may be worth noting some of its achievements.

The farm with an area of about 33.5 acres allotted to 13 landless Harijan families (at 2.5 acres each) was founded by

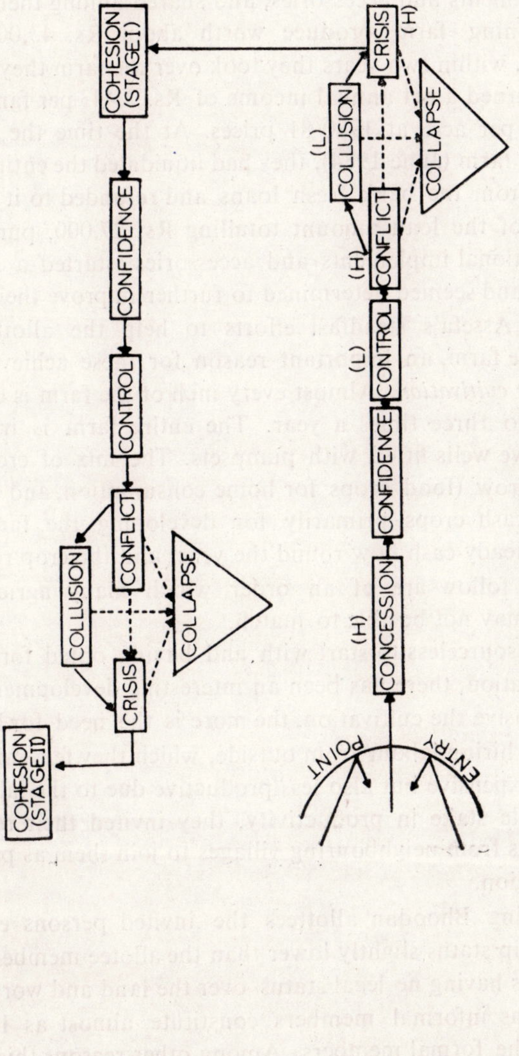

Chart: Successive stages of group building

Assefa in 1970. Assefa handed over the farm to the allottees in 1978 after developing it fully at a total cost (investment) of about Rs. 97,000 or Rs. 2,900 per acre and recovering Rs. 74,600 through income from sale of farm produce and an old oil engine. The allottees, who agreed to repay the unrecovered balance to a local bank from which the amount was obtained as loan, did it within two years. In addition, they invested Rs. 9,400 in farm implements and accessories, and shared among themselves the remaining farm produce worth about Rs. 43,000. Put differently, within two years they took over the farm they managed and earned a net annual income of Rs. 3,443 per family or Rs. 1,085 per acre at 1980-81 prices. At the time the author visited the farm (June 1984), they had liquidated the entire loan, obtained from the bank fresh loans and refunded to it all but Rs. 6,500 of the loan amount totalling Rs. 27,000, purchased some additional implements and accessories, started a sericulture unit, and seemed determined to further improve their lot.

Besides Assefa's steadfast efforts to help the allottees to develop the farm, an important reason for these achievements is *intensive cultivation.* Almost every inch of the farm is cultivated two to three times a year. The entire farm is irrigated through five wells fitted with pumpsets. The mix of crops the allottees grow (food crops for home consumption, and vegetables and cash crops primarily for developing the farm and ensuring steady cash flow round the year) and the crop rotation plan they follow are of an order which many agricultural scientists may not be able to match.

Being resourceless to start with and having opted for intensive cultivation, there has been an interesting development. The more intensive the cultivation, the more is the need for labour. Instead of hiring labour from outside, which they felt might be not only expensive but also less productive due to the labourers having little stake in productivity, they invited their relatives and friends from neighbouring villages to join them as partners in production.

Not being Bhoodan allottees the invited persons enjoy a membership status slightly lower than the allotee members. The newcomers having no legal status over the land and working in the farm as informal members constitute almost as large a group as the formal members. Among other reasons this is due to the fact that each formal member has inducted one relative or friend to preserve the balance of power. The motivation is more income from the farm for themselves, the process is political and democratic.

The informal members participate in all activities of the farm, even in decision-making, but they have no right to vote. It is likely that they also receive a little less than the formal members.

Another feature worth noting is that while intensive cultivation has substantially increased the net income per acre, the income per member (formal+informal) or family, has remained, in real terms, more or less constant in the past three to four years. No generalisation is intended. But the case, even though it may be atypical, suggests that the poor, as they succeed in achieving a better status, are socially as well as economically attracted to share the gains with their less fortunate kith and kin. They may cross the poverty threshold and yet remain poor.

More than income, the achievement of Uchapatti is reflected by the confidence the allottees have gained in their ability to manage their farm and to deal with the external agencies, government as well as non-government. When asked what they thought they had gained most by working together and developing the farm, the allottees, who are all Harijans and were either landless or bonded labourers earlier, said:

> We have gained recognition in the village. Other castes, who were our masters earlier, now not only listen but also pay attention to what we say. Members of the forward castes also visit our farm. Some of them even work as wage labourers in the peak season.

One of the allottees with whom the author had a prolonged discussion said that before he joined the farm he was an agricultural labourer. He married the daughter of a bonded labourer in Uchapatti and started living with her. It was his father-in-law who received in 1956 a piece of land on which the farm is built. He inherited the plot from his father-in-law after he died. In the initial years when he joined the farm he, like others, was extremely poor. "While the cash income even now is far too inadequate", he said, "my food habits have changed radically for the better. As the farm now grows pulses and vegetables, besides cereals, all the allottee families now eat well. It is no longer rice and salt once or twice a day, but also pulses, vegetables, oil and tea."

He has recently built a new house. All his children of school-going age go to school. According to him, all of them including himself and other members of the family are better dressed and better fed. One of his worries, he said, was that he was not sure whether any of his sons would like to work in the farm, and even if they did, whether they would work as painstakingly as himself to keep it going.

Projects like Uchapatti and some of the resettlement projects of Myrada represent, no doubt, the strengths and achievements of the two agencies. The contributions they have made in this field are surely valuable.

But viewed from another perspective, the scale of the contributions made vis-a-vis the size of the problem and the time and resources spent to achieve these, one sees how little they have been able to achieve. Take for example Assefa, which is larger in size and, in terms of scale, has contributed several times more than Myrada in resettling the landless. It has taken nearly 15 years to establish the 68 farms covering 4,800 acres of the 1.29 million acres of land distributed to the Bhoodan allottees two to three decades ago. No doubt the work is very difficult and hazardous. But 15 years and only 0.4% of the distributed land reclaimed suggest that even if Assefa were to raise the coverage from 0.4% to 10%, it will take over 350 years to reach the level. One can, of course, assume that the rate of progress will increase with passage of time. But how much? Twice? Thrice? Surely not more. At three times the present rate, it will still take more than 125 years. Add to this the time it takes to make the farms viable and hand them over to the allottees, the road seems to stretch to eternity [8].

This does not mean that the fault lies with Assefa or with its approach. Nor is it intended to belittle the contributions it has made. Both Assefa and Myrada should continue with the work they are committed to, and we wish them well. The point being stressed is how much more needs to be done and who can or will do it.

It is questions like these that prompted the author to expand the scope of the study and take a look at governmental programmes, like the Integrated Rural Development Programme (IRDP), which also aim at improving the incomes and status of the rural poor.

* * *

There is a growing view that the performance of government agencies involved in rural development being dismally poor, and as bureaucracy will always be bureaucracy, rural development cannot be achieved by them. We do not wish to support or reject the view. But we do think that the issue is academic in as much as it ignores the fact that government or government agencies will continue to be involved in rural development in a country like ours for a long time to come. What is more, rural development across the country on a scale commensurate with the size of the problem, cannot be undertaken by any agency *except* the government. And as the government performs this role—at the level where action for rural development is needed—essentially through the district administration, it is important that we pay serious attention to the problems and possibilities of improving the capability of district administration to plan and implement the programmes effectively.

It was with this notion that the author spent some time in a district—Uttara Kannada or Karwar as it is commonly called—in Karnataka to gain a better understanding of IRDP and the scope for improving the capability of the implementing agency, District Rural Development Society (DRDS). The district was chosen for no reason other than the opportunity and facilities that the DRDS Director extended to the author to indulge in this exercise and the attempts that he himself was making to grapple with the problem.

IRDP IN KARWAR

As stated earlier, the basic aim of the IRDP is to increase the incomes of the rural poor such as agricultural labourers, small and marginal farmers, and village artisans. The programme seeks to achieve this by providing assistance—both technical and financial—directly to individual members of the target group, usually one per household.

Households are identified on the basis of annual incomes not exceeding a prescribed limit (currently about Rs. 3,600). All rural households in a district within this limit are eligible to receive financial assistance—credit and subsidy—to purchase some productive or income-generating assets like livestock, pumpsets agricultural implements, and to dig wells, etc. Provision for institutional credit and subsidy ranging from 25 per cent to 50 per cent of the total value of the assets is an important feature of the programme.

Implementation Agency

Planning and administration of IRDP and other programmes of development in a district vest with the District Rural Development Society, a registered body established under the Societies Registration Act. For all practical purposes, however, it is an official organ of the district administration. Being a registered body, a legal entity, however, it enjoys greater financial autonomy and relatively more freedom and flexibility than the traditional district set-up. Administratively however, the difference is marginal. Like the collectorate or the district administration at large, which is headed by a District Collector, DRDS is headed by a senior district official—usually an IAS officer—next only to the District Collector. In Karnataka he holds a dual position, one as Director, DRDS, and another as Special Deputy Commissioner.

The tasks and responsibilities of DRDS are:

1) Identification of eligible beneficiaries involving periodic household/village surveys.

2) Formulation of income generation schemes and their implementation with a view to increase the income of each beneficiary. Though not publicly stated, the long-term objective remains eradication of rural poverty.

3) Mobilisation of resources, mainly subsidy and institutional credit, and timely disbursement of various inputs and assistance to the identified members of the target groups.

4) Verification of assets to assess what the beneficiaries received or acquired, whether any leakages occurred, and if so where and how.

5) Integration of various elements of the programme including coordination of activities within DRDS and with other participating agencies like banks and development departments/functionaries at various levels.

6) Continuous monitoring and periodic evaluation of the progress and impact of the programme.

7) On the basis of these, to make changes wherever required, formulate future plans of action, establish and strengthen links, improve the quality and performance of the programme—all with a view to expedite the realisation of the long-term aim: eradication of poverty.

By any standard these are very complex and challenging tasks. The sheer size and complexity of the programme demand not only close monitoring but, more importantly, careful planning and effective management.

Approach

A village-wise household survey in every district is carried out to identify persons who are eligible to participate in the programme as well as to facilitate the formulation of income generation schemes or activities for them. The survey involves collection of data indicating the social and economic conditions of the households, their incomes and assets, etc. The survey team, which in Karnataka is headed by a Block Development Officer (BDO), includes the functionaries of other development departments like agriculture, irrigation, horticulture, fisheries, and industries.

The cluster approach involving identification of suitable clusters of villages as the focal points of development is used to facilitate the formulation and implementation of schemes as also to make the tasks of the participating agencies easier. The village clusters are determined keeping in view the nature and level of infrastructure available, the size and composition of population, location of scheduled castes and scheduled tribes settlements, presence of credit and other institutions, etc.

Identification of eligible households/beneficiaries started several years ago with the launching of programmes like Small Farmers Development Agency (SFDA) and *Antyodaya.* IRDP aims at covering all eligible households in a phased manner starting with about 600 beneficiaries per block in the initial

Table 4: Schemewise Distribution of Beneficiaries, Credit and Subsidy (IRDP in Karwar: 1980-84)

Particulars	Scheme/Sector						
	Agriculture	Irrigation	Animal Husbandry	Fisheries	Rural Crafts	Others	Total
No. of Beneficiaries							
1980-81 (April-March)	1873	206	637	592	232	74	3614
1981-82	2822	324	1933	1567	593	338	7577
1982-83	3366	319	4173	1042	1457	418	10775
1983-84	2527	295	3521	903	2658	11	9915
Subsidy (Rs. lakh)							
1980-81	4.28	2.71	6.75	14.10	1.01	0.26	29.11
1981-82	10.45	4.04	13.85	33.06	1.90	0.63	62.93
1982-83	24.56	3.19	28.31	18.99	6.50	1.03	82.58
1983-84	16.12	3.28	27.37	16.28	13.87	0.26	77.18
Credit/Loans (Rs. lakh)							
1980-81	9.56	6.99	14.41	33.51	2.03	0.82	67.32
1981-82	23.86	7.78	31.61	67.07	3.80	1.67	135.79
1982-83	65.56	8.54	60.34	68.65	13.00	2.50	218.59
1983-84	41.37	6.85	69.99	27.36	27.73	0.79	174.09

Subsidy per Beneficiary (*Rs.*)							
1980-81	229	1316	1060	2382	435	351	805
1981-82	370	938	717	2111	320	186	831
1982-83	730	1000	678	1822	446	246	766
1983-84	638	1112	777	1803	522	2364	778
Loans per Beneficiary (*Rs.*)							
1980-81	510	3393	2262	5660	875	1108	1863
1981-82	846	2401	1635	4280	641	494	1792
1982-83	1948	2677	1446	6588	892	598	2029
1983-84	1637	2322	1988	3030	1043	7182	1756

Source: 1984-85 Annual Plan for IRDP in Uttara Kannada District, Government of Karnataka, Bangalore, 1984.

years to 800 or more in subsequent years. As there are several blocks in a district, the number of villagers receiving IRDP loans and subsidies every year can be as high as 10,000. In Karwar district, for example, in 1982-83 10,775 villagers received IRDP loans and subsidies to the tune of about Rs. 30 million. In the following year, another 9,915 received similar assistance totalling over Rs. 25 million. Subsidy in the two years constituted 30-40% of the total assistance (See Table 4).

Gaps to Fill

How much additional income the programme beneficiaries have derived from this assistance we do not know. In fact, we have no reliable information about the contribution IRDPs in different parts of the country may have made towards raising the income of the rural poor. Yet this is the most critical information one needs in order to appreciate or assess the impact and usefulness of IRDP. This is a major gap.

While this gap needs to be filled, the more critical task that needs to be completed first is to evolve and suggest a simple but well-designed and workable method which implementing agencies like DRDS could adopt and follow to ensure that the programme activities do generate the desired additional income. So far, our response to the challenge has been generally to stress the importance of planning, execution and monitoring; to suggest guidelines for micro or area planning for administrative units like the district or block; to reiterate the need for better implementation and management *inter alia* through training in various fields including project formulation and appraisal; and so on.

All these are, no doubt, important and necessary. Several attempts have also been made to incorporate these elements or practices at appropriate levels. Yet no significant headway has been made. *Why*? There could be several reasons including those elaborated by Prof. Dantwala in his paper, "Rationale and Limitation of Decentralised Planning", and Dr. Lakdawala in his paper, "Consistency between Macro and Micro Planning". We do not wish to repeat these. What we would like to do, instead, is to add a few more points keeping in view the needs and capability of implementing agencies like the district administration.

Officials or functionaries at this level understand two things most clearly: 'scheme' (or schemes) and 'target' (or targets). They understand equally well the position they occupy in the 'hierarchy' and what it means in administrative—bureaucratic-terms. Their work culture, orientation, practices and folklore are woven around these three key phrases. Suggest or prescribe anything new which does not fit into this scheme and they will transform it to bring it in line with the scheme. More often than not the transformation takes place through distortions of various sorts.

There are at least two ways of looking at this process. One is to prescribe the required changes or innovations with or without further prescriptions and hope for the best. Most planners, reformers, and scholars seem to have followed this route. Another, which very few seem to have taken note of and virtually none seems to have found the time or the interest to explore, is to accept the system—its work culture, structure, practices and orientation—as given, and detail the prescriptions which will fit in with the scheme-target-hierarchy framework.

We need not reject the first. Indeed, whatever more we need to do to make it effective, we should. At the same time, however, we need to explore with equal vigour, if not more, the second alternative too. This would involve:

1) breaking down the micro or area plan into schemes or a protfolio of schemes,

2) realistically assessing their income generating potential and evolving the feasible organisation, work plan, and investment which are necessary to realise the potential, and

3) sequencing the schemes and activities in accordance with the notion of integration as well as with the priorities of the departments/agencies likely to be involved in the implementation of the scheme/activity.

Planners tend to give a great deal more attention to the *what* of the plan than to the *how*. Even if this helps formulating a plan appropriate to the needs of the area, it remains untuned to existing political structures and to the capacities of the government agencies which would have to implement it.

To sum up, it is our contention that to make local level planning (including programmes like IRDP) more effective, we will have to explore and develop ways of matching the micro-planning methodology with the structures and capacities of the district development administration/agencies. To be meaningful and effective such a methodology will have to find answers to several questions such as:

1) How to develop and locate a simple but efficient information system at the district level for planning and monitoring?

2) How to effectively overcome existing bureaucratic obstacles to local level action for rurai development?

3) How to bring about more effective mobilisation of already committed or available resources for promoting the development of the people in the district, particularly the disadvantaged groups?

4) What processes and mechanisms are needed to mobilise/organise the disadvantaged as effective demand groups?

5) How to relate and use the planning process to meet the growing aspirations of the disadvantaged groups who have none or very little resources to grow?

Notes

* I am grateful to ASSEFA and MYRADA for extending the support and information I needed to conduct the study and enriching my understanding of their approaches to development, their aims, activities and accomplishments. I received valuable assistance from Shri M.P. Vasimalai and Shri Vijay Mahajan of PRADAN in conducting this part of the study, and from Shri Sanjay Das Gupta, Director of DRDS, Uttara Kannada, in gaining better understanding of the Integrated Rural Development Programme, some aspects of which are presented in Part II of the paper. I am indebted to them.

1. Uchapatti is one such farm. Some aspects of this farm, which the author visited, are discussed elsewhere in the paper.
2. Myrada mentions a few more resettlement projects as having been handed over to local cooperatives. One of the IRD projects is also reported to have been handed over to a local voluntary agency. But one does not know whether the handed over projects are continuing or closed; and if continuing, how well or badly.
3. Whether Myrada's numerous exercises include collection of such data to study the economics of its projects, or their contributions to improving the income of the target group, is not known. In all likelihood no such exercise has yet been attempted. At least the author could not obtain any such information from Myrada.
4. Why Assefa considers this a 'danger' or what sort of danger it envisages is not clear. It could be that it views such a development inconsistent with its goal, sarvodaya, meaning 'development of all'

as a community. Or it could be that it sees that if a handful of the oppressed try to move away from village life and yet remain in the village, the village majority may not like it, and may even retaliate and suppress them further.

5. The risk of change, however small or beneficial it may be, is very high for villagers surviving at the subsistence level. The poorer they are the higher is the risk and the lower is the risk-taking capability. It is one thing to listen to the well-meant suggestions of well-meaning people, essentially outsiders. It is quite another to accept and act upon them. The risk could be as high and foolish as switching over from subsistence to starvation or worse. The upshot: the intervenors have to provide convincing assurances and back them up by deed to raise the villagers' risk-taking capability to a level required to bring about the change.
6. Unlike Myrada, construction activities like housing, schools and hospitals are normally not undertaken by Assefa. This could be due to Assefa's concern not to isolate the Bhoodan allottees from other sections of the village population. or because the allottees have houses or huts of their own in the village where the Bhoodan land is donated, or both. Another reason could be Assefa's wanting to spend on building infrastructure only so much as is necessary to make the land productive, and not any more.
7. The observations on group formation process and the chart depicting the process are based largely on author's own involvement in rural development, both as intervenor and researcher, particularly in the Jawaja Experiment.
8. One can add more constraints, such as the financial, technical and human resources needed to carry out the work. But there is no need to add them.

REFERENCES

[1]Myrada, *Capitalization Study* (mimeo), p. 58.
[2]Assefa, *ASSEFA Objectives and Their Achievements*, (mimeo), p. 7.
[3]Myrada, *op. cit.*, p. 13.
[4]*Ibid.*, p. 73.

Comprehensive Rural Development: The CADC Experience

Biplab Dasgupta

The Original Concept

The setting up of the West Bengal Comprehensive Area Development Corporation (WBCADC) in 1975 was, in a sense, an admission of the failure of the existing rural development administration of West Bengal centred around the Block Development Office. The idea was to replace the blocks by the CADC projects within a given time period of five to ten years, but it was thought that the new set up would not become a replica of the block network. To start with, CADC would not be a government department but a statutory autonomous corporation established under an Act passed in 1974. While the Chief Minister would be its chairman, the State Agricultural Minister its vice-chairman, and a number of senior ministers and civil servants including the Chief Secretary its Board Members, the Corporation itself would be autonomous in its functioning and somewhat free from the bureaucratic norms and regulations which impede the working of government departments. The Executive Vice-Chairman, its chief executive officer, would be a social scientist or a social worker, in order to provide the organisation with a non-bureaucratic approach.

Another major aspect of this new organisation was its emphasis on institutional finance for rural development. It was thought that CADC would not become a drain on the state's budgetary resources. The commitment of the state would be limited to salaries and establishment expenses, while development expenditure would be financed by way of bank loans, refinanced by Agricultural Refinance and Development Corporation (ARDC, now NABARD), and recovered from the beneficiaries themselves in the form of prices charged for various inputs and services. This, in fact, was one of the main attractions of this organisation from the point of view of the state government of the time. The idea of rural development without large scale subsidy could not fail to impress a government short of money.

A third aspect was the emphasis on a 'comprehensive' approach. In a sense, this was no different from the original concept of development blocks in the early fifties, excepting for the fact that the focus was on tubewell irrigation—deep and shallow varieties. It was expected that once the tubewells were installed and water flowed, the agriculturists would rush to utilise this for double cropping, and it would be possible to extend the acreage considerably in addition to increasing productivity per unit of land. This was to be the main activity, supplemented by 'service centres' which would supply fertiliser, pesticides and high yielding seed varieties as well as spray machines and diesel pump sets on hire. Some relief activities in the form of *dharmagolas* were also launched, where the idea was that the agricultural labourers would make regular contributions to a fund which would entitle them to obtain from the *dharmagolas* during off-season, paddy (as loan) equivalent in value to twice their contribution. Another, called 'special schemes' was to provide loans ranging from Rs. 50 to Rs. 200 to small time traders, shopkeepers and village artisans.

A fourth aspect was the form of organisation. At the project level the employees were of two types. Those selected by the headquarter, mainly officers, were called CADC employees, while those recruited locally and paid between Rs. 180 and Rs. 235 as a lump sum wage, to work mainly as village organisers, nightguards, and weighmen to service centres, were known as CADP (Comprehensive Area Development Project) employees. The latter were supposed to be volunteers working part-time, while in effect they were working full time.

Fifthly, a number of large-scale cooperatives were formed,

called Farmers Service Cooperative Societies (FSCS), one for each project area, which were in the main responsible for the disbursement of loans through banks. Both the Chairman and the Managing Director were CADC employees (except for three projects where the MD was a bank employee). It was presumed that all the primary cooperative societies in the area would be dissolved or merged with FSCS, so that this would become the sole lending agency in the area operating on behalf of the banks for agricultural purposes.

This was CADC in its original conception. The concept was identified in the public mind with Pannalal Dasgupta, a one-time Marxist revolutionary who was the guiding spirit behind the organisation as a member of the State Planning Board. His main associate was the first Executive Vice-Chairman (EVC) of the organisation, Dr Ajit Narayan Bose, a government planner but also a social scientist with a publication on Calcutta's input-output model to his credit. However, the concept was far from original, and its parenthood legitimately belongs to the World Bank. The Comilla model in neighbouring Bangladesh is not dissimilar in its orientation, with its emphasis on bank financed development spearheaded by the small scale irrigation projects drawing sub-surface water.

Three Phases

In its nine years of life so far, CADC has passed through three distinct phases. The first phase, the formative period, continued from 1975 up to June 1977, for slightly more than two years. It was during this period that twenty projects were launched, each covering a cultivated area of between 10,000 and 18,000 acres, around 40-50 villages, and between 30,000 and 100,000 people. In each project a number of deep/shallow tubewells were installed, service centres and dharmagolas were set up, and in 16 projects loans were offered through FSCS. Most of these activities had only begun when, following the state assembly election in June 1977, the state government was changed, and a new, Left Front government took over the state administration. Since the left wing parties had always been critical of CADC as a 'gimmick' and as having no chance of success, it was rumoured that the organisation would now be dissolved. The new government took some time to make up its mind, and eventually decided to keep it, but changed the Executive Vice-Chairman in November 1978 in order to give it a new orientation which would be in keeping with the rural development strategy of the Left Front government. The third phase therefore began after November 1978.

At the beginning of this last period, the organisation was beset with many problems, some of which grew out of the uncertainty regarding the future of the organisation, and some resulting from the new aspirations of the rural population following the victory of the Left Front. A major problem was with the price charged for water which, based on full-cost principle, was fixed at Rs. 10 per acre of *boro* paddy cultivation, compared to Rs. 2 per acre charged by government-owned tubewells. This caused resentment among the farmers who failed to distinguish between the govenment and the CADC, and demanded equal price for water irrespective of the source. A second problem was with the CADP temporary staff on fixed pay at the project level, who demanded parity with state government employees working at the village level, and opposed the distinction between CADC and CADP employees. But the main problem was the lack of communication between CADC and the rural population it was supposed to serve. This was partly because no conscious effort was made by CADC to involve the beneficiaries in decision-making, and partly because of its association with a discredited government and the timing of its birth during the period of Emergency Rule. In the public eye it was often labelled as a tool of the World Bank, and of a foreign-based conspiracy against the people of India. Furthermore, during the intervening period, between June 1977 and November 1978, the morale of employees suffered, discipline eroded, and various forms of corruption associated with loan advance and fertiliser sale erupted.

NEW OBJECTIVES

The new regime of CADC had to redefine its objectives, besides correcting the organisational maladies. An important consideration in this was the rural development strategy of the new state government, which made the local level panchayats the foci of its development programme. After the 1978 panchayat elections at three levels—district (zilla parishad), block (panchayat samiti) and clusters of about 10 villages (gram panchayat)—these new bodies were given a great deal of responsibility, power and money. In this changed social and political context, CADC could not play the role originally envisaged by its founders. There could be no question of covering the entire rural Bengal with a network of CADC projects supplanting the blocks, nor could there be any question of bypassing the panchayats.

The number of projects was therefore frozen, and the declared objective became to work with the panchayat. In order to translate this objective into practice, project level advisory boards (PAB) were formed with the chairman of the local panchayat samiti as its chairman, and with representatives of the panchayats and also various government departments and banks as its members. The PABs now meet once a month, review the work of the project, make decisions on location of various facilities and selection of beneficiaries, help in settling disputes particularly with regard to the distribution of irrigation water, fix priorities for work, and otherwise help with the running of the project. CADC is no longer an isolated bureaucratic enclave, but an integral part of the village society where it exists. PAB chairmen are also permanent invitees to the state level meetings with project directors, where most of the major decisions are taken, to be subsequently approved by the Board. At the district level a council has been set up, with the Chairman of Zilla Parishad as its chairman, and with both panchayat and government representatives as members, in order to integrate the work of CADC project in an area with district level planning.

But the question remained: what can CADC do which is not already being done by either the panchayats or the blocks? The answer CADC came up with was: experimentation with new crops, seed varieties, practices, technologies and institutions. In this CADC had a number of advantages. The twenty-one CADC projects (one in Ajodhya Hills in 1982), whose selection was influenced less by agro-climatic than by political considerations, were found, despite the haphazard method of their selection, to represent all the major features of life in rural Bengal. Every district contains at least one CADC project, and some of them (e.g. Darjeeling, West Dinajpore, Nadia, 24 Parganas,

Purulia and Midnapore) two such projects. These cover all the main agro-climatic zones, from the Himalayan foothills, Gangetic and coastal plains to the semi-arid extension of Chota Nagpur plateau, and practically all types of soil conditions, water sources and cropping patterns. Besides, these contain both highly developed (e.g. Boinchi, Hooghly) and very backward (Goalpokhur, West Dinajpore) areas, and those with tribal, Muslim and low-caste majority in the population. Therefore, any experiment which works in CADC ought to work in the rest of West Bengal. Another advantage is the youth of its employees and of the organisation itself, which contains a large proportion of highly motivated workers who work because they love work and enjoy working with the people. Furthermore, being small in geographical coverage, the damage done by failed experiments cannot be considerable. In fact, such failures would be no less important than successes. On the other hand, a technology, institution or crop, once successful in an area, can be widely adapted in the district where it is located. This in fact is one of the reasons behind the creation of district level councils for coordination with the district authorities. CADC would not any longer work for the area under its jurisdiction; its objective would be to serve the entire rural population of the state even when it is functioning only in some pockets.

Three other objectives, in addition to the involvement of the panchayat and the emphasis on experimentation were as follows: comprehensive approach, bias in favour of the weaker sections, and emphasis on self-reliance. The full-cost principle in fixing the prices of services and inputs was dropped. Rather than taking each activity in isolation and attempting to balance its costs and prices, a broader social cost-benefit approach was adopted. It was found that the application of the full-cost principle would, in fact, make the price of irrigation water for *boro* paddy cultivation around Rs. 1,400 per acre, which would price out all but a few of the beneficiaries. One of the main reasons for this was the underutilisation of existing irrigation facilities because earlier the computed cost figures were based on the assumption of full utilisation which cannot be realised without a more guaranteed power supply, generous credit provision and more elaborate extension activities. On the other hand, a subsidised water supply would make a high contribution to social benefit in terms of higher food production, employment and income generation. Following the recommendation of a high-power committee (of which the author was the convenor), the water rate of CADC tubewells was brought in line with that of the government-tubewells, at a level of Rs 5 per acre-inch. Organisationally, the distinction between CADC and CADP was abolished, and the project employees were offered salaries which were on par with those of government employees with similar responsibilities. And, through a concerted drive against corruption—leading to the dismissal of 25 employees of practically all ranks—corruption and indiscipline were brought under control.

These provides the framework within which CADC has been operating over the past six years. CADC can boast of quite a number of successes during the period, and there is now a better appreciation of the problems, pitfalls and limitations in carrying out a programme of rural development.

Comprehensive Approach—The Organisational Form

One of the strong points of CADC is its comprehensive approach, compared to the blinkered departmentalist approach of most of government functionaries. In a typical project, there are between 60 and 80 employees, about 10 of whom are specialist officers. The specialists are told that while as agriculturists, veterinary surgeons or engineers, they are expected to serve the entire project, they are also required to act as 'adopters' or team leaders for a cluster of four to five villages, where they would be responsible for everything from adult education to fish farming. All the CADC personnel working in the cluster would come under their responsibility, as also those like health workers, and artisans under various schemes who are associated with CADC in that cluster. While as a specialist he should know everything about something which is his line of specialisation, he should at the same time know something about everything in order to be able to meaningfully apply his expertise in the rural environment. This principle of organisation applies also to all the senior personnel in the headquarters—including the Accounts Officer and the Administrative Secretary—who too, are put in charge of projects as 'adopters' in order to help with the project-headquarter coordination. It is not rare to find an engineer enthusiastically participating in agricultural extension in CADC projects, or an accountant lecturing in adult education centres on broiler chicken production.

One of the key functionaries at the project level is the village organiser, who is in charge of multiple functions, and is expected to discharge any type of responsibility which is assigned to him. Some of them have been given specialist training in animal husbandry, fishery, plant protection, health work, or similar activities, and almost all of them are trained in agriculture in general, but they can be called upon to perform a variety of functions such as cashiers, work assistants, operators of consumers' stores or service centres, as well as field level workers. From carrying loads if necessary, to writing campaign posters and lecturing to non-formal students, the flexible nature of their jobs is an important aspect of the working of CADC. This is not easy, since the tendency is for the employees to prefer work in one particular line, particularly if it is considered to be a high-status activity, and for the specialist officers at the project or headquarters levels to insist that the village organisers specialising in their fields should not be given other jobs. But so far such pressure for introducing a 'caste system' in the division of labour among the village organisers has been successfully resisted. The important task facing CADC is to stimulate the interest of the employees in all aspects of rural development, while at the same time taking care to see that in the process the specialists do not become transformed into generalists.

NEW ACTIVITIES

In order to make CADC activities comprehensive the organisation has moved into many new areas over the past six years, as compared to the original focus on tubewell irrigation. Such development has followed a certain logical order. For example, the question has been asked, what are the main needs of an agriculturist, and how best can these needs be satisfied? Tubewells—some canals and bunding of spring water—to provide irrigation; service centres to provide inputs other than water; FSCS to provide loans; and village organisers to make provision for extension. The next question is, having reaped the harvest, what problems would an agriculturist face for which CADC support might be necessary. He would need storage facility—so in every project godowns of varying capacity from 100 to 500 metric tonnes have been erected. Since a good part of the grain is stored within the farm, and the storage loss from pest attack, disease and damp conditions can be considerable, over the past few years a major effort of CADC has been towards the improvement of such storage structures. In addition, there are community *dharmagolas*, which have already been mentioned.

He would also need help with marketing, particularly in case of jute—so bailing presses have been added to the godowns, and arrangements have been made to purchase jute at the officially fixed rate on behalf of the Jute Corporation of India. Three cold storages are going to be built—again with the objective of stabilising the prices of potato and vegetables. Ninety units of power *ghani* have been recently installed, with the objective of providing a ready market for mustard produced in the area, and arrangements have been made for the setting up of a ginger processing plant and a fruit processing plant (*gaighata*). All these are to ensure that the agriculturist does not find himself at the wrong end of the market after having produced a bumper crop.

Another way the agriculturist might lose is in terms of the price he has to pay for procuring non-agricultural goods. As for agricultural inputs such as fertiliser, pesticides, seeds, diesel pumps, spraying machines, power tillers, etc., this 'terms of trade' problem is obviated by their supply through the service centres, each project having three to four such centres. As for the others, a network of consumers' stores, again three to four per project, ensures supply of cheap clothing, cooking oil, rationed rice, and other provisions for the agriculturist at a subsidised price. The consumers stores have proved to be highly popular with the rural poor, particularly for the janata clothing.

Non-agricultural Activities

There are obvious limits to a strategy of rural development which is solely concerned with agricultural activities. The main constraint is land, and the land-man ratio is steadily declining with population increase. Whereas extension of irrigation facility and the consequent increase in double cropping has a 'land-augmenting' effect, there are limits to the rate at which such an increase is possible. For this reason, CADC has been forced to stray out of an exclusive concern with agriculture, and to look for non-agricultural income-generating and employment-creating activities which would also add to production. Three major areas have been identified for this purpose: animal husbandry, fishery and rural industries.

Of these, the work on fisheries so far has been somewhat tentative, mainly in the shape of demonstration of composite fish farms. However, its future is immense. There is no shortage of large and small water bodies all over West Bengal where some fishing activity goes on. What is needed is a scientific approach, training of villagers, and the provision of some inputs. For the larger water bodies, some infrastructural investments are necessary in bunding and setting up sluice gates. One major difficulty lies with alternative uses of water for irrigation and fishery. The tendency among the agriculturists is to use the water for irrigation purposes, to the extent where the survival of the fish population would be at stake. In areas where waterlogging is a serious problem during the rainy months, the demand from the agriculturists is for drainage and not for its use for fish production. Joint ownership of ponds by extended families is another problem when the individual family units are in conflict with one another as regards the use of water. On the other hand, where the demonstration farm with different types of fish, each operating in different layers of the water body, has been successful, the idea of composite pisciculture has caught the imagination of the people. One of our most successful experiments has been in Naxalbari where, usually, the sandy soil does not hold water and the tanks become dry after the rainy season. Our success in improving the soil with dolomite and other inputs and making the tank usuable all round the year, has encouraged other villagers to initiate fish farming in the neighbouring villages.

With the animal husbandry programme we were immediately faced with two serious constraints. First, the failure of the cattle purchase loan schemes of the banks in the past. Many such purchases had been fictitious, and loans had been advanced without examining the repayment possibilities. Where the purchases were genuine, the high-breed animals were not given the needed food or care and, as a consequence, many of them died soon, or produced much less milk than expected even when they remained alive. A large proportion among the defaulting loanees all over the state are those who made such purchases of cattle.

A second difficulty lies with the supply of fodder. Before the 1793 permanent settlement, it was a common practice to allocate a part of the village land under communal possession for grazing purposes. Since then a good part of such land has been privatised. In recent years, cultivation has been extended to marginal land which had hitherto remained fallow, and hence is now available for grazing. With the extension of double cropping, the opportunity for grazing over a larger area during at least half the year has been reduced. With the introduction of high yielding varieties, the amount of hay available as a by-product has been reduced. Furthermore, as the land-man ratio is becoming increasingly unfavourable, there is growing pressure on the government to distribute vested land, a large part of which is of poor quality and was so far available for grazing and for field crop cultivation. With the extension of irrigation facilities, the land which was unsuitable for cultivation before has been brought under cultivation. In other words, an animal husbandry programme based on the assumption that the animals would graze on fallow land is no longer tenable. The growing conflict between graziers and agriculturists in many villages is a socio-economic problem which can only be satisfactorily solved by way of commercial fodder production, but so far the government agencies have given little thought to this. Nor has there been much integration between the departments of agriculture and animal husbandry, despite the fact that the inclusion of fodder crop in the cropping pattern generally helps nitrogen fixation, and thereby adds to soil productivity.

There are other problems too, such as the difficulties faced in preserving the quality of semen, the problem of maintenance of bulls in natural service, and so on. While the veterinary surgeons working in CADC projects have to give a certain amount of time for curing the cattle, the main emphasis in CADC programmes has been on fodder production and on smaller animals. Our programme with pig breeding in Naxalbari has become quite popular with the local tribals, and arrangements have been made for setting up similar units in Debra and Falakata. Poultry farming is another programme with a favourable future. It is intended to make CADC projects among the major centres of broiler chicken production, supplying the urban centres nearby as also distant cities such as Calcutta. The support obtained under the special component plan for the scheduled castes, and under the tribal sub-plan (certain areas with tribal majority) have been mostly used in these directions. In some of the projects artificial insemination centres have been introduced, but the animals under the natural service programme have generally not survived long, largely because of our wrong selection of beneficiaries who are too poor to afford food for such big animals, and who even when such help is given by way of a loan or grant, tend to divert its uses.

Neither of these two programmes of fishery and animal husbandry is expected to provide full support to beneficiary families. The same is the case with the rural industries programme, which too aims at supplementing the income of the family from other sources. Initially such programmes took the traditional form of tailoring, *chira*-making, paddy husking, tile making, and so on. We soon came to realise that such activities would not succeed in generating much income, and cannot be introduced on a large scale in a particular area. Two types of programmes which have been taken up in recent years have been for *charkhas* and power *ghanis*, both financially supported by the State Khadi Board. So far nine *charkha* units have been installed which have provided employment to 300 women, and have included polyester and muslin units; and ninety power *ghanis* have been installed, producing 450 tons of oil every year. But the most successful rural industries programme under CADC has been the one on wool-knitting in Kalimpong, with an annual turnover of around Rs. 10 lakhs, and providing support to about 300 women.

In all these cases the problems faced can be listed in the following order of importance: market, supply of raw materials, spare parts and maintenance, training, motivation on the part of the individual beneficiary, and finance. It is to be noted that finance has been put as a problem of minor importance compared to others.

Many of these activities has been made parts of a composite

programme on women and children. Women, rather than men, have been given preference in several such activities. This is partly because of our commitment to undertake economic activities for women, supplementary to other programmes for them including those relating to education and health. But this is also because many of the activities selected by us can be more efficiently handled by women, e.g. the programme on poultry, wool-knitting, muslin-*charkha*, or pig-rearing. In addition, such activities, more often than not, cut across disciplinewise boundaries. The programme on power *ghani* is linked with several other programmes: bee-keeping (because bees have a symbiotic relationship with mustard), mustard production, oil processing, and the production of oil cakes as a by-product which can be consumed by cattle or fish.

Many such activities are also included under our special programmes for scheduled castes, tribals and sharecroppers, in addition to women. This is another aspect of CADC work which is new, and makes it relevant to the poor majority. But, perhaps, the most radical departure from the original CADC concept can be witnessed in cases of programmes on education and health. Both of these faced serious opposition from the agricultural purists from within and outside the government, who thought that this was not what CADC was supposed to do. A similar objection was raised when CADC undertook *operation barga* in areas under its jurisdiction, on the ground that the organisation was moving away from its primary concern for agricultural production. The justification given for launching these programmes was that agricultural production cannot be increased, or at any rate cannot be increased on the fields of the poor majority, without structural changes which can be brought about through such programmes on land reform, education and health.

Over the past five years, CADC has been running 600 adult education centres which have become the leading component of the state government programme in this field. Every year seminars and workshops have been sponsored to bring together those working on non-formal and adult education, both government and non-government agencies, to exchange experiences and reorient the programmes in the light of the lessons learnt collectively. This programme has made the greatest impact in the backward tribal areas and among women. In addition to regular teaching, popular lectures, film shows, cultural and sports activities, processions and meetings have been part of the ten-month course. Each centre has been given a transistor so that teaching can be supplemented by radio discussions. Despite all these efforts, many problems have remained, including the high drop out rate of the agricultural labourers and sharecroppers during the rainy season.

The health programme supported by UNICEF contains two components—infrastructural and educational. Each village is being served by a drinking water tubewell, and a number of demonstration toilets have been constructed. Large scale immunisation of children with triple antigen and other injections, has been supported by the health department. These three steps are likely to go a long way in reducing the incidence of diseases. But a greater emphasis has been given on health education through health workers, who played a major role during the recent outbreak of gastro-enteritis and kept both the incidence and the casualty rate at a comparatively low level in CADC areas. Special programmes for crippled children and on nutrition have also been launched.

Both of these programmes on education and health, which also include components such as 70 centres for non-formal education for children aged 9-15 and creche-cum-balwari for the younger children of working mothers, help to increase the general level of awareness of the village population, and thereby also indirectly help to stimulate agricultural production. The adult education centres in particular are used as bases for agricultural extension work in project areas. The success with these programmes has been far from uniform. Immunisation and drinking water programmes have been more successful than the one on toilets. Non-formal education programmes have generally failed, while the performance with creches has been better.

Much depends on the persons responsible for such programmes—instructors or health workers at the village level. If they are motivated and enjoy working among the villagers for its own sake, the programme succeeds; but if they see it as a step towards regular jobs in CADC, they tend to give more effort to ingratiate themselves with the CADC personnel rather than serving the villagers. Without a voluntary spirit, this kind of work, with little supervision from the top, has little chance of success. It is fortunate in the case of CADC that the proportion of dedicated volunteers working on Rs. 50 per month as honorarium is quite high.

All these would indicate the range of activities CADC is engaged in. These would also underline its inter-disciplinary as well as comprehensive approach. However, despite all these, agriculture remains the basic activity of CADC, and the lion's share of time and resources is spent in augmenting agricultural production.

NEW EXPERIMENTS

Over the past six years, a number of experiments have been conducted in different projects of CADC with varying degrees of success. Here I will outline only some of these, to indicate both our areas of interest and also the social and economic hurdles such experiments have to contend with.

Seed Multiplication

Here the objective is to make West Bengal self-sufficient in seed production in the case of a number of major crops within the coming five to six years. A beginning was made with wheat seed multiplication in Saharjore, Purulia, four years ago. In 1983-84 about 350 acres were covered, and this year more than 1,000 acres are expected to be covered. Similarly, successful experimentation with jute seed production in Ajodhya Hills, Purulia, shows that it is possible for the state to avoid jute seed import from far away Maharashtra. Potato seed production is undertaken in Boinchee and Kalna. Other projects, including Sonamukhi, Bankura, Kalimpong, and Darjeeling, have taken an initiative in the multiplication of seeds.

New Crops

One of the objectives has been to introduce and try out new crops in different agro-climatic environments. The usual procedure is to begin with some demonstration farms, and to go for large-scale extension after success has been achieved. In addition to potato, jute, mustard, fodder crops, some trees and food crops are introduced in new environments through this process. Processing activities, whether for jute, ginger, mustard, tomato, or some such crop, aim at providing the producer with a fair and remunerative price.

New Technologies

There is a fairly long list of technologies adapted to specific agro-climatic environments, most of which rely on local resources, economise on energy use, and are maintainable by local skilled manpower. In the three north Bengal districts where the water level is high and within 25-30 feet, bamboo tubewells have been installed, and various technical problems which have arisen in their use have been solved. In Kalimpong, high-drums have been introduced which help to lift spring water up to 150 feet without the need for electricity or diesel. In Nalhati, infiltration galleries have been constructed to draw water from the dry river bed, and serve 150-200 acres of command area. In Saharjore, infiltration galleries take advantage of gravity flow, and do not require power for its operation. Improvised submersible pumps, called *mini-deep*, have helped to keep the water flowing under heavy draw-down conditions during the dry months. Experiments with different designs, materials, and varying mix of such materials have been made for building houses, toilets and community centres.

One lesson learnt from the CADC experience is that the agriculturists, despite their educational backwardness, have been quick to adopt new technologies and practices when the superiority of these have been conclusively demonstrated to them. Only ten years ago there were few irrigation tubewells in the countryside, and very few of the agriculturists used fertiliser, pesticides or new seed varieties. It was believed that those who use irrigation water manufactured by men would forfeit their claim on the rainwater distributed by God. It was also widely believed that fertilisers and pesticides are bad for the soil and would destroy productivity. Today, not only have such superstitions been largely overcome, but the demand for those inputs far outstrips their supply. While at the beginning it appeared to be a highly sophisticated technology, now diesel pump sets and shallow or deep tubewells can be operated by ordinary uneducated villagers without much trouble. In many places the villagers themselves, albeit illegally, often repair the faults on the electricity lines rather than wait for days for the personnel of the State Electricity Board to come. But one seldom hears of casualties from electric shock resulting from such activities. All these prove that the technological problems are not as insurmountable as are often made out to be by those who would prefer the villagers to continue with their traditional technology.

New Institutions

Experiments have not been confined to crops, seed varieties or technologies. Among the new institutions sponsored, the foremost has been the FSCS, which will be discussed below in detail. One of the major experiments which failed has been with joint farming in Balarampore, Cooch Bihar. After having worked with this scheme for four years it was dropped because the collective self-interest was far outweighed by the interest of the members in obtaining CADC financial support. But even this failed experiment was not without any value. Another joint farming cooperative recently launched among the tribal agriculturists of Singhivita of Naxalbari has tried to avoid the mistakes committed in the first experiment.

Through these experiments the productivity in CADC areas has been considerably increased. In each case, many technical, administrative, as well as socio-economic hurdles had to be crossed. There were vested interests who opposed the modernisation of agriculture, and there were others who could be easily misled because of their backwardness. When wheat seed production was initiated in Saharjore, the simple tribal cultivator in the area, used to cultivating one crop in the year and producing for self-consumption, was reluctant to produce another crop, and that too for sale and not for his own consumption. His reluctance grew when he was told that even his previous kharif production would have to be altered, and new quick-maturing rice varieties would have to be sown in order to complete harvesting by early November, in time for the planting of the wheat seed. But greater resistance came from those who used whatever little water was available in the area for *boro* paddy cultivation, and were reluctant to shift to wheat production, despite the fact that the water requirement of the wheat crop was one-fourth of that needed for *boro* paddy cultivation. Their own self-interest came in the way of the programme which was meant to cover an area four times larger but using the same amount of water. Then there were others who were afraid that success with this programme would make the subservient tribals independent of their influence, and so opposed the programme tooth and nail, going to the extent of circulating the rumour that the lands cultivating wheat seed would be taken over by CADC, and intimidating the CADC staff.

SELF-RELIANCE

A major objective of CADC is to promote self-reliance. This is easier said than done. Over the years the villagers have been taught to become dependent on the government, even for those activities which they themselves are capable of undertaking without much trouble. The traditional institutions of self-help, including exchange labour, common teams for harvesting over the entire village land, and communal labour mobilisation for building village roads or bamboo bridges across canals and small streams, have been eroded and replaced by new attitudes which are highly individualistic on the one hand, and heavily dependent on the government on the other. It is against this background that CADC's declared policy of handing over all its activities and assets in a particular project within five to six years would have to be examined. The common reaction—from both villagers and civil servants in Calcutta—is that this would not be feasible and certainly not within the time schedule prescribed by CADC. But already a beginning has been made.

In the new programmes sponsored by CADC, the usual practice is to ask the local panchayat to be formally responsible for it. For example, the local panchayat issues appointment letters to adult education instructors and health workers, and the payment of their honoraria is made through them. This also helps to neutralise any expectation they may have regarding their being eventually absorbed as regular CADC staff. Although the programme is presently administered by CADC, and also financed by it, the panchayats are expected to take over the *de facto* responsibilities too within the given time period.

Another recent decision has been to replace CADC staff by

'commission operators' in cases of a number of activities. For example, a service centre usually requires a salesman, a weighman and a nightguard, and their aggregate salary far outweighs the commission obtained on turnover from such activities. Over the past three years, the practice has been to give the responsibility to a local young man, who works on a commission, and it is up to him to arrange weighmen, nightguard etc. should he feel any need for such support. Similarly, shallow (and some deep) tubewells, consumers' stores, marketing outlets etc. have been handed over to the commission operators.

Another important step, operational over the past one year, has been to incorporate the consumers' stores, service centres, godowns, and marketing activities, as also activities like seed multiplication, into the FSCS. The membership of these societies has increased up to 5,000 to 6,000 in most cases, and the turnover to between 20 lakhs and 50 lakhs. The addition of these activities has increased the viability of these large cooperatives. Whereas initially these were managed entirely by CADC, over the past three years the responsibility for the management has been handed over to the elected Board of Directors. Although the Chairman and the Managing Director of FSCS continue to be the nominees of CADC, it is expected that the officials would be withdrawn over the coming two-three year period. Vigorous training of FSCS directors has been launched so that the financial viability of these large-scale cooperatives is not threatened by the complete take-over by the villagers themselves.

The most serious problem facing these cooperatives is the low rate of loan repayment. Until recently, villagers looked upon the cooperatives as government departments, and upon the loans as government grants or subsidies. The repayment habit was not developed. During the early years of CADC a great number of loans were distributed without taking into account the financial viability of the scheme or the repayment ability of the loanee. As a consequence, the number of defaulters is exceedingly high in many villagers, and many of them are unable to repay now. Nor do the banks seem to be determined to recover their loans—the number of cases filed is usually very low, reminder notices are seldom sent, and the ARCS is usually too busy with other activities to attend to these cases. Vested interests also do not wish the banking system to develop roots in rural soils; it is often they who whisper to the villagers not to repay the loan. When a few years back the state government offered full interest subsidy to those who repaid their loan within a stipulated period, these vested interests circulated a rumour that this was just the first step—that eventually even the principal would be waived.

In case of CADC the repayment position in the north Bengal projects is very low, but the situation is considerably better in the southern Bengal projects. Cases, notices, propaganda against the defaulters with capacity to repay, all these help to improve the recovery rate. Over the past six years, a great deal of improvement has been registered in terms of loan repayment, but CADC has still a long way to go before the repayment level becomes satisfactory.

FSCS is not the only cooperative form which is being tried by CADC. We have already mentioned the experience with joint farming. Moreover, in addition to FSCS, separate cooperatives for pisciculture, dairy and poultry are being introduced; and for women, Mahila Samitis registered with the Registrar of Societies are instrumental in giving their economic activities the necessary organisational shape.

Another experiment has been with the beneficiary committees of shallow tubewells. In May, last year, it was decided to hand over the 126 shallow tubewells in Deganga, 24 Parganas, to the beneficiary committee as an experiment. The committee members were not paid any kind of remuneration or honorarium; the only payment received by them was the bus fare and tea and biscuits when they visited the project headquarter once a month. They were given training in operating tubewells, and were taught how to maintain logbooks for recording the use of tubewells, how to collect water rate and deposit it to the bank, and so on. At the end of the one year period, the agreement with the beneficiary committee has been renewed for another year—and this time they themselves have eagerly sought renewal. Over this year not a single motor has been stolen, only one motor was burnt, and the water rate collection has been the highest ever recorded. Having benefited from this experiment, CADC has extended this type of management to all the CADC projects excepting two. This is an important step forward, and unique in the state. It is hoped that the experience with beneficiary committees in tubewell operation and management in CADC areas would be replicated elsewhere. The only support they require from CADC is when there is a serious breakdown of the power system.

A NEW TYPE OF ORGANISATION

CADC is also experimenting with its own organisation. Close links with the panchayat is itself an important experience for a public sector organisation. We have seen therole the panchayat plays in project advisory boards, in location decisions and beneficiary selection, in settling disputes, and in the selection of personnel for CADC and CADC sponsored activities. The panchayat also helps with the extension work. New seeds are often introduced in the fields of prominent panchayat members, to whom a large number of villagers come for advice, and with whom they can communicate more easily than with the village organisers. Various kinds of training is given to the panchayat members, with the expectation that they would transmit their knowledge to others. Before every agricultural season it is routine for the CADC staff to meet each gram panchayat separately, to review the previous season, and to plan for the coming one. In these discussions, the panchayat members raise questions about new pests and diseases, availability of pesticides and fertilisers, cropping patterns and so on. The field level village organisers are expected to attend the gram panchayat office once a week, to take messages from the office to them, and to communicate messages on their behalf to the project headquarters. In the performance reports of the project employees, space has been allocated for the comments of the panchayat *pradhan* and the *sabhapati* of the panchayat samiti. All these have brought the two organisations working in the same area closer to each other.

In the early phase, a section of the CADC staff expressed unhappiness with the role given to the panchayat. Having worked together for six years, such misgivings have disappeared. However, there are still one or two among the officers who privately resent this role, but publicly hobnob with the top panchayat leaders and cold shoulder the lower level panchayat members. There are some CADC employees who unscrupulously use their contact with the panchayats to lobby for promotion, against transfer, or against some of their own colleagues. But this is more the exception than the rule. Most CADC employees appreciate the plus points of the presence of the panchayat in their functioning e.g. in settling disputes on selecting beneficiaries. One of the things which is continuously emphasised in CADC meetings is that the panchayat is a collective entity, and CADC's close relationship with the panchayat is not equivalent to catering to the wishes and needs of individual panchayat members.

Another major organisational aspect is the issue of balance between discipline and democracy. So far, discipline has been maintained and rigorous punishments including dismissal have been given to many offending employees. Dismissal of 25 employees out of a total 1,500 employees is indeed a high proportion. It is now known that those indulging in corrupt practices or indulging in serious breach of discipline would be severely punished. On the other hand, a certain tradition of democracy has been established too. Weekly staff meetings are a regular feature of CADC project work. Both the unions—of the officers and other employees—are highly active, and regularly meet the CADC management at the project and headquarters levels. The union representatives are regularly invited to Project Advisory Board and District Council meetings, and also to the state level meeting of the project directors and panchayat leaders. They are given special leave to attend union meetings or for union work, and CADC vehicles and officials facilities are extended to them during conference and other major activities. All these have fostered a common understanding between the management and the union.

A third aspect is the relationship between employees holding different ranks. In order to forestall the growth of a caste system, recreation clubs and cultural activities have been sponsored where employees of all ranks jointly take part—from the Executive Vice-Chairman to the office peon. A proof of the success of this approach has been seen in the fact that over the past six years there has been no serious conflict between the management and the unions. On the other hand, whenever the CADC staff have been harassed or intimidated by powerful men in the village, both the unions and the management together have fought against it and have extracted apologies from the offenders.

A major problem facing the work of CADC is that the more it works, the more varied the work becomes, the greater becomes the expectations which cannot be fulfilled. The basic funding for CADC comes from the Department of Agriculture, which covers its establishment expenses, but for development activities CADC has to rely on the grants obtained from various government departments, central agencies such as NCDC or ICAR or Save Grain Campaign, or from external bodies such as UNICEF, in addition to the funding received from the district authorities. The fund available is too small in relation to the need. Another major problem is the tendency towards bureaucratisation in its mode of functioning. Flexible decisions based on the merit of each case give way to rigid rules and procedures regulating personnel as well as developmental activities. Every decision sets a precedence, even when it is clearly stated that it should not, and keeping this in mind one has to be very careful in making new decisions which might be right in one particular case, but which might set a wrong precedence for others.

PART IV

Reconciling Growth and Social Justice

Proceedings

From the early seventies, the strategy of rural development in India has been claimed to be one of a direct attack on poverty. While the Fifth Plan relied on a macro strategy to accelerate growth and redistribute income from the rich to the poor, the Sixth Plan's strategy, in contrast, was a micro-strategy targetted specifically at the poorest sections of society to whom the benefits of growth had failed to trickle down.

In "Reconciling Growth and Social Justice: Strategies versus Structure?", Kurien argues that administrative interventions in India are based on the prevailing structural characteristics of the economy. It is these structural characteristics which give shape and form to growth processes and which determine what will be produced, how much, for whom, and so on. Therefore, given the inequitable structure of our economy, if growth is to be reconciled with social justice, the crucial issues to be addressed are not only these related to the fundamental development strategy to be adopted, but also those related to the basic features of the structure of the economy.

The basic structural characteristics of the Indian economy, according to Kurien, are private ownership of resources with a substantial proportion of the population not having any non-labour resources, and the highly skewed distribution of these resources among those who own them. Within this structure, the strategy of stimulating and supporting the utilisation of resources to increase the output of goods and services to the poor has only succeeded in the benefits being cornered by those already well-to-do sections who control resources and power. The interventionist strategy that has been used to eradicate poverty, therefore, is an attempt to correct the *consequences* of an inequitous structure without altering the structural characteristics themselves.

Kurien suggests two necessary conditions for the success of an interventionist strategy favouring the weaker sections. These conditions are: that the initial distribution of resource-power is not too inequitable, and that the strategies are accompanied by some redistribution of basic resources and assets. He raises the question of whether the strategy can be used as a means of transforming political processes so that changes in the structural characteristics of the economy can be initiated and growth thereby become socially responsive.

Dantwala, in "Reconciling Growth and Social Justice: Agrarian Structure and Poverty", questions the predominance given by Kurien to structural change as a precondition for the success of anti-poverty programmes. His argument is that structural change is at best a necessary condition for eradication of poverty but not a sufficient condition. Furthermore, too much emphasis is placed on land redistribution as a means of bringing about structural change. Land is no longer a critical resource. There are a number of other resources whose control and distribution are feasible and useful for ensuring greater growth with justice, such as water resources, ecologically degraded lands, and modern varieties of seeds and fertilisers. Merely bringing about an equitable distribution of land is unlikely to help in achieving the goal of growth with justice because even a radical redistribution of land will not materially alter the economic and political power structure. The preoccupation with land and its redistribution, Dantwala stresses, has resulted in the neglect of other means of augmenting income flows to the poor such as evolving an egalitarian basis for the development of ancillary industries, animal husbandry, forestry, and fisheries. These are areas in which vested interests are not yet firmly established and are more amenable to efforts at building a more egalitarian structure. Dantwala also disagrees with Kurien's basic thesis that an interventionist strategy aimed at correcting consequences of structure will not alter the characteristics of the structure. By using appropriate policy interventions that systematically modify structural consequences, changes in the crystallised structure can be induced. The establishment and strengthening of countervailing non-exploitative institutions may be more effective in enhancing the bargaining power of the poor than attempts at changing the structure.

The discussion after the presentations centred around two main issues: whether the structural changes which Kurien talked about are in fact a precondition for equitable growth, and the sort of structural changes that may be appropriate for India. Several participants from other Asian countries contributed to the discussion by recounting the experiences of their countries in the quest for growth with justice.

Hirashima felt that when one talks about structural change through land redistribution, there is need to distinguish between landless labourers and other poor in the rural areas who possess some land. This being the case, there can be no uniform solution to the removal of rural poverty. There are two important implications of land redistribution that policy makers must keep in view. First, if an egalitarian redistribution is carried out, the country will end up having a large number of non-viable units. Second, if the ceiling on landholdings is lowered to reduce concentration of landholdings in the hands of well-to-do farmers, land would have to be taken away from the already efficient farmer. This is not only economically undesirable but also politically impractical.

Another reason why structural reform through land redistribution may not be feasible, according to him, is the relationship that exists between productivity and land value. If the rent-land price ratio is taken as the measure of the rate of return on investment in land, one would find that historically the ratio has been much higher than the interest rate imposed by institutional banking systems, cooperatives, and even moneylenders. According to his estimates, the rent-land price ratio in India in 1850 was as high as about 56 per cent. That is why the moneylender, whose interest rate was about 36 per cent, came into the land market. However, by the time the Land Alienation Act was executed in 1900, the ratio had dropped to 12 per cent and the participation of the moneylender was reduced. At present, the ratio is about 2 per cent. The implication of this analysis is that since rent is a proxy for productivity, and according to rent theory there is a proportional relationship between land price and rent, if productivity increases, rent also increases. Therefore, we should expect that land price should also increase proportionately. But this has never been the case even in undivided Punjab. When the rent-land price ratio is as low as 2 per cent one cannot participate in the land market unless substantial capital is available without opportunity cost. While productivity can be increased by improvement in the institutional set-up and technology, the impact on land price would be substantial. Given this historical situation, it is very difficult to imagine how structural change can be brought about by changes in the ownership of landed property. A related issue is that the use of high-yielding varieties of grain can push up the rent-land price ratio to a very high level. But in order to utilise high-yielding varieties, the government would have to invest a lot of money in infrastructure, especially irrigation. As long as this situation exists, we cannot expect that the incremental upgrading of the poor is possible through improvements in technology, prices, and so on.

Economic considerations apart, there are many political, social and administrative factors that make the task of land redistribution a very difficult one. In the late 1950's, the Bhoodan and Gramdan movements in India made concerted attempts at land reform through acquisition, redistribution and collectivisation of lands for the poor and landless farmers. The movements enjoyed initial success, but eventually fell into disarray and were, as Mahajan put it, subverted and replaced by the Panchayati Raj system, Dantwala ascribed the failure of these attempts to the excessive concern of the movement leaders with the collection of land and to the neglect of cultivation and redistribution which were felt to be the responsibility of the government. Even Vinoba Bhave was completely seized by the goal of meeting targets in the collection of land; he became too elated by the success of his attempts to think beyond the accumulation of land.

Social norms and customs, Gaikwad points out, have been another critical factor in the failure of structural reforms pertaining to land distribution. In India, the distribution of property is determined by social customs which have found legal sanction in Hindu Law. Due to the prevalence of the joint family system in the rural areas, most people who are ostensibly landlords do not really own the land exclusively. They are often only *kartas* on behalf of the joint family that owns the land. If the joint family breaks up, it results in fragmentation of land. Unless social norms and the laws of inheritance are modified, structural change does not seem feasible. At the same time, these issues are too delicate and politically explosive for policy makers to interfere with.

The experiences of other Asian countries as recounted by the foreign participants in the seminar suggested that the problems of reconciling growth with justice are not peculiar to India.

In Bangladesh land reforms were initiated after the partition to alleviate the plight of the farmers. The zamindars who functioned as intermediary revenue collectors were replaced by government agents. Land ceilings and mechanisms for acquiring surplus land were instituted. But the implementation of land reform policies was always poor due to problems such as the sorry state of land records, the Muslim laws of inheritance which allowed boys as well as girls a share in the land, and apathetic administration. One of the major problems in a country with 8 million farm households and only 22 million acres of cultivable lands is that most farms are by and large very small in size. Despite some improvements in productivity through technological innovations, the possibilities of equitable land redistribution in a land-poor country, compounded by the weaknesses in the administrative structure, have severe limitations.

The Philippines' experience has also been marked by a number of ups and down. After independence in 1963, the Congress initiated a number of structural agrarian reforms without having to be goaded by pressures from below. Little was done to pursue these reforms thereafter. However, the introduction of new rice technology in the 1960s and the MASAGANA-99 programme led to increases in rice productivity. It was only in 1971, after pressure from now organised peasant groups, that further reforms in the form of revisions in agrarian reform codes were introduced. The peasant movements came to be suppressed after the imposition of martial law in 1972, but the new government continued to introduce a number of agrarian reform measures, such as the agrarian reform programme, village association programme, and compulsory membership of beneficiaries in cooperatives. Gradually, however, what started as measures intended to benefit the poor tilted in favour of rich agri-business corporations. When the government found in the 1980s that the country had a very large foreign debt that was impossible to repay, the focus shifted to big agri-business multinational corporations which were relied upon to bring about a quick improvement in economic conditions. With this reversal in agrarian reforms the small farmers were once again at a disadvantage. Quite a few studies showed that those who had benefited from earlier reforms now became landlords themselves and hired landless labourers to work for them. In effect, a second generation of landlords and landless labourers came into being. The Philippines' experience corroborates the point Hirashima made earlier, that rural development is not a homogeneous process and that it affects different groups in different ways—often in ways unintended and undesired by the initiators of the reforms.

Discussion on Gaikwad's suggestion that structural reforms could be best introduced by reversing the privatisation and degradation of common lands through proper administration indicated that it suffered from a number of possible drawbacks. David King illustrated the point by narrating the Philippines' experience in 1975. To curb the rapid degradation of forest lands the Philippines Government passed a presidential decree placing all land above 18° slope in the hands of the public sector. Nine years later the tide of degradation has not been stemmed; instead, a number of problems have cropped up. A number of groups which were displaced by the implementation of the decree are in conflict with the government. The original occupants of the uplands became illegal squatters overnight and were forced to flee further into more remote areas or to break the law for want of any other alternative course of action. The power given to maintain control over these newly acquired lands is being used to further private interests by influential individuals and groups. Recognising these problems and in an effort to deal with them, the Bureau of Forest Development of the Philippines introduced a programme of integrated social forestry. The programme consists of a series of measures such as granting 1 to 25-year occupancy leases and the establishment of communal tree farms to provide equitable access to forest resources. King suggested that in seeking means to improve growth and equity we need to develop technologies of using land that do not degrade the environment further and yet provide livelihood to a large number of people. The work on wasteland development in India described by Chowdhry has been a big step in this direction, but has been slow to make any major inroads.

The discussion on the importance of structural changes for achieving the goals of growth and justice once again highlighted the varying points of view among the participants on the aims of rural development in India. Visaria felt that if rural development is to achieve anything by way of improving the conditions of the poor, it would have to aim at changing the level of agricultural production and productivity. Improvements in agricultural production would in turn have a cumulative effect on other dimensions of rural life. The decline in death rate during 1971-81 and the improvement in the literacy rate he cited as examples supporting his view. He further pointed out that the difference between the literacy rates of the small and large farmers is much smaller than what one would have expected.

Conceding that rural development programmes have had some success in poverty eradication when measured in terms of use of fertilisers and spread of livestock, V.M Rao argued that, if measured against the criteria that really matter namely the spread of education and access to institutional finance, the success has been very marginal. Rural development, he said, may have succeeded in raising the level of expectations of the poor, but it has not succeeded in fulfilling all of them. This is likely to have an important—and perhaps unpleasant—consequence in social-political terms: as people achieve a certain standard of living and become aware of their unfulfilled expectations, political mobilisation and agitation are likely to increase sharply. The peasant movements that have emerged in the country in recent times may be just a forecast of the things to come. There may well come a time when the poor are mobilised to the extent that they acquire control of micro-level institutions.

Ranjit Gupta suggested that even the poor who do not possess any assets can acquire resources if they get organised around a bundle of roles, and not merely one or two roles which the state or the resourceful can easily control or suppress. If they succeed in doing so, they may find it easier to transfer and use the advantages of non-political roles to strengthen their economic and political interests.

In concluding the session, Lakdawala expressed agreement with the contention that structural change is a precondition for growth with justice. He, however, questioned the validity of the proposition that development strategies in India have failed to reconcile growth with justice because they ignored or glossed over inequities in the economic structure. Changes in the marketing system and public finance and the setting up of cooperative institutions are some of the measures taken during the last few years which have brought about some changes in the structural characteristics of the economy. Public finance has helped reduce or control concentration of resources in the hands of a few. Public investments has accounted for almost 40 per cent, and public expenditure for about 35-40 per cent of the respective budgets. Other indicators also suggest that some improvements in the lot of the poor have been achieved: death rates have declined even among the very poor and per capita consumption of goods which are not consumed by the rich has increased considerably. To attribute increase in per capita consumption to increase in indebtedness among the poor, Lakdawala felt, was implausible, and one cannot dismiss the increase in consumption as being a deceptive indicator. Development inevitably affects some groups adversely. But on the whole it has improved the conditions of the poor in India.

Reconciling Growth and Social Justice: Strategies versus Structure?

C.T. Kurien

The need to reconcile growth and social justice has been an explicit objective of our economic policy from the very early stages of planned development. According to the First Year Plan document: "The urge to economic and social change under present conditions comes from the fact of poverty and of inequalities in income, wealth and opportunity. The elimination of poverty cannot obviously be achieved merely be redistributing existing wealth. Nor can a programme aiming only at raising production remove existing inequalities. Only a simultaneous advance along both these lines can create conditions in which the community can put forth its best efforts for promoting development."

After three and a half decades of planned development we do not seem to have made much progress towards the achievement of the cherished objective. After a careful evaluation of the first three decades of planned economic development in which the progress achieved on many fronts was fully acknowledged, the *Draft Five Year Plan 1978-83* document stated: "We must face the fact that the most important objectives of planning have not been achieved, the most cherished goals seem to be almost as distant today as when we set out on the road to planned development." If the stubborn persistence of mass poverty is any indication at all, the situation even today is much the same.

Over these years the strategies of our development policies and their outcomes have been critically evaluated. In this paper, therefore, I shall concentrate on the present strategy that we have adopted for reconciling the twin objectives of growth and social justice and also look at some recent studies relating to performance and the analysis of performance.

As for strategy, from the early seventies we have been attempting what is officially claimed to be a 'direct attack' on poverty. In one of the preparatory documents leading to the formulation of the Fifth Five Year Plan it was stated: "In elaborating our strategy of development in earlier Plan documents we seem to have assumed that a fast rate of growth of national income will create more and fuller employment and also produce higher living standards for the poor. We also seem to have assumed that for reduction of disparities in income and wealth, the scope of redistributive policies is severely limited. However, the economy has now reached a stage where larger availability of resources makes it possible to launch a direct attack on unemployment, underemployment and poverty, and also assume adequate growth."[1] A new strategy of combining redistribution with growth was implied by the statement, partly because of a new understanding of the problem and partly because of the feeling that the economy has reached a stage where some redistribution has become possible. The Fifth Plan's strategy of 'direct attack' on poverty was a *macro* strategy to accelerate growth and to redistribute income from the top three deciles of the population to the bottom three deciles in the attempt to lift the poorest of the poor above the poverty line.

The Sixth Plan's strategy is also one of growth with redistribution. After identifying accelerated progress towards the removal of poverty, generation of gainful employment and technological and economic self-reliance as the objectives of planned development, the plan document says: "Experience shows that a substantial acceleration in the overall rate of growth of our economy, as measured by the growth of gross domestic product in real terms, is an essential condition for the realisation of these objectives. However, there is also convincing evidence which points to the limited effectiveness of trickle down effect. Therefore, consistent with our overall social and economic objectives, public policies will have to acquire a sharper redistribution focus in raising the share of the poorer sections in national income, consumption and in the utilisation of public services."[2] But in contrast to the Fifth Plan's macro strategy, what has been proposed in the Sixth Plan is a detailed *micro* strategy to tackle the problem of poverty. "The poorest sections belong to the families of landless labour, small and marginal farmers, rural artisans, scheduled castes, scheduled tribes and socially and economically backward classes. The household will remain the basic unit of poverty eradication in target group oriented programmes. Families differ in such vital respects as dependency ratios, asset holding, skills and even the ability to perform manual labour on public works. Hence each household below the poverty line will have to be assisted through an appropriate package of technologies, services and asset transfer programmes."[3]

* * *

The present strategy is, therefore, one of combining growth with 'target group' programmes to eradicate poverty and to underline the component of social justice in planned economic development. The target programme is essentially an interventionist strategy. In order to appraise its contribution to the reconciliation of growth with social justice it is, therefore, necessary to evaluate the impact of growth on different groups in the economy and to see how far the target group approach succeeds in directing the benefits of growth to the weaker sections.

The discussion of the relationship between growth and equity has a long history. I shall skip the earlier stages of this discussion which concentrated on the theoretical aspects of the pattern of income distribution over time, as also the earlier empirical studies.[4] Within our country what gave a new turn to the discussion was the introduction of the new agricultural strategy —the 'green revolution'—in the mid sixties. A couple of early studies of the phenomenon which attracted considerable attention had indicated that the benefits of growth via the new strategy were accruing primarily, if not exclusively, to the larger and richer farmers.[5] There were also suggestions that the new strategy was impoverishing the smaller farmers and agricultural labourers.[6] Since then several field studies have been conducted and a recent review of some of these studies and their findings leads a scholar to conclude that over time there has been a wide diffusion of the new technology among farmers irrespective of farm size and tenurial status.[7] He also notes that "in areas where the relative access to product and factor markets has been unequal among the farmers, due to various economic, social and political factors . . . the gains from the new technology have been disproportionately shared by the large farmers." Another recent study of the relationship between the green revolution and income distribution in Punjab also arrives at a similar conclusion.[8] The authors note a fairly uniform spread of the new technology among the smallest of the farmers (with operational holdings 0.10 to 2.49 acres) to the largest farmers (with over 25.00 acres) out of a total of 1,663 households from 180 villages in the state that constituted their sample. Their view is that this is mainly because the irrigation base of the large and small farmers is about the same. At the same time they note also that about a third of the marginal farmers (tilling less than 2.5 acres of land) and about a fourth of small farmers (tilling between 2.5 and 5.0 acres of land) are living below the poverty line and show substantial deficits in terms of their total earnings (the difference between farm business income plus non-farm income and consumption expenditure). About these farmers the authors observe: "Their production efficiency notwithstanding, these farmers are unable to earn adequate per capita income from crop production because of their small land base. They are, therefore, obliged to engage themselves in a wide range of non-farm activities and are able to obtain higher per capita earnings from such activities. Consequently, the distribution of total household income (of which income from non-farm activities is an important constituent for marginal and small farmers) is much less iniquitous than land or farm income distribution. Unfortunately, however, in spite of putting in very hard labour both in farm and non-farm activities quite a few among them are not able to save themselves from the clutches of poverty. It is indeed a disquieting feature of the Indian agrarian situation that even in the heartland of the green revolution about one-third of the marginal farmers and about one-fourth of the small farmers are living below the poverty line."

Since the study was about farming households they did not have anything to say about the impact of the green revolution on agricultural labourers about which some controversy was generated on the basis of earlier studies. At the all India level a main source of evidence regarding earnings of rural labourers is the *Rural Labour Enquiry 1974-75*: *Final Report on Wages and Earnings of Rural Labour Households* which made a comparison of average daily real earnings of men belonging to agricultural labour households between 1964-65 and 1974-75 and showed that at the all-India level in real terms the 1974-75 wage earnings was only 88 per cent of what it was in 1964-65 and that wage earnings had gone up only in Uttar Pradesh, Punjab-Haryana and Jammu and Kashmir.[9]

Village studies making intertemporal comparisons of growth processes and their impact on different sections in the village community may throw light on this phenomenon noticed at the all India level. Two village resurveys recently conducted by the Madras Institute of Development Studies deserve special attention.[10] These two villages were studied originally in 1916-18 by Gilbert Slater, then Professor of Economics, Madras University, and his students and have been resurveyed in 1937 and 1967 prior to the latest resurvey conducted in 1981 and 1982. Iruvelpattu in South Arcot district and close to a major town, Villupuram, is an agricultural village which experienced modernisation and the green revolution in recent years. Since Independence, particularly, it has come to have more roads, electricity, a primary health centre and many other amenities. With 147 cultivators and 256 agricultural labourers according to the 1981 Census, the village also had 78 wells fitted with pumpsets used for irrigation. There were three tractors in the village, a rice mill, a truck and a couple of cars. Many farmers have adopted the high yielding varieties of paddy and in the case of some of them yield per acre was as high as 2,300 kg although such high yields were by no means widespread. Yield per acre depended very much on the extent to which fertilisers were used. In spite of all these striking changes the wage rate of agricultural labourers in terms of paddy units in 1981 was at best the same as it was at the time of the 1937 resurvey, and for female workers it was indeed much less. There was some increase in employment because of technological changes, but "even with more days of employment, the wage levels of agricultural households remain such that their real earnings are below minimal subsistence norms" and "altogether, some 200 agricultural labourer and marginal cultivator households or 62 per cent of the total number of 323 households in Iruvelpattu can be considered to be absolutely poor."

The story is about the same in Palakurichi, the second Slater Village resurveyed. Located in Thanjavur district, Palakurichi is also a primarily paddy producing village. The distinguishing feature of the village is that it is one where the agricultural labourers have been organised by the Communist Party of India since 1939 and by the Community Party of India (Marxist) after the split in the party. As a result of collective bargaining and agitations wage rates have been formally revised upwards on many occasions. But because of the rising wage rates there has been a tendency on the part of farmers to mechanise agricultural operations. In a village of less than 120 cultivators and over 450 agricultural labourers, there are now nine tractors and "there is a substantial mechanisation of ploughing, rethreshing and farm transport". A comparison of the real earnings of agricultural labourers between 1937 and 1982 leads to the conclusion that "the hard-won wage improvements have only served to maintain year-round real earnings at most at about the same level as they were about four decades ago. Annual earnings of agricultural labourers come to no more than 75 per cent of what can be considered a minimal poverty line."

These studies have been referred to not to substantiate any hypotheses regarding the relationship between growth and poverty eradication and certainly not to imply that growth has an inevitable adverse consequence on all weaker sections. That certainly cannot be the case and any number of instances can be produced of agricultural labourers, small farmers, rural artisans and other sections of the rural community who have become better off over time as a result of the growth process. And yet if, as the evidence available shows, the overall impact of growth has not been favourable to a particular section such as agricultural labourers, or the poverty situation has not substantially improved as a result of growth, it is important to gain better understanding of the actual processes of growth which are more clearly captured at the ground micro level than at the aggregate macro level.[11] It is regrettable that there are very few ground level case studies that document the complexities of the growth process. After all, the growth process is never a smooth flow. It is more like a churning up process with differential impacts on different sections in society and even on different sub-groups such as households within fairly homogeneously defined sections like agricultural labourers. In the churning up process some go up and some go down and yet others may be largely unaffected. If so a case can be made—and must be made—that the most important task in the study of growth is not to convert it into a simple numerical index, but to identify, as meticulously as possible, the complexity which is its very essence and then to see whether its main characteristics can be adequately explained.[12] It must be evident also that assumptions such as that increase in real income over any specified period is uniform across all expenditure or social classes are patently absurd although they may be extremely convenient to generate desired numerical values as has been done in the Mid-Term Appraisal of the Sixth Plan.[13]

* * *

Some more of these issues are taken up later, but against the background of the discussion of the impact of growth on the poorer sections we can now turn to an examination of the target group approach to the eradication of poverty. The specific instances given above have illustrated the failure of growth to trickle down, and it would appear that even a long period of time may not by itself make much of a difference. Hence the principle underlying the target group approach—that special efforts to reach the poorer sections are necessary—is certainly valid. And, as the Sixth Five Year Plan *framework* document eloquently indicated, the poorer sections are not all alike. Hence designing programmes for each of the identifiable sub-groups, going down to the household level, if possible, is also eminently reasonable. For these reasons it is also evident that such programmes become essentially administered projects.

Consequently, in evaluating the target group approach the administrative aspect has to be given careful consideration.[14] A recent review of the performance of a wide variety of target group programmes has suggested that the administrative aspect itself consists of two components, implementation and strategy.[15] A host of problems relating to the implementation of these programmes have been identified such as frequent transfers of key officials, inadequate assessment of the ability of beneficiaries to utilise programme service, carelessness in identifying the beneficiaries etc., not to speak of instances of corruption. But problems of implementation are not all of this kind. There is, as one study indicates, the problem of the attitude of *nishkamiya karma* transferred to the field of public administration: officials were dedicated and hardworking, but indifferent to the ultimate results![16] The authors of the view referred to above suggest that the problems of implementation may not all be at the operational level or because of lack of commitment of the officials and lack of political will on the part of the policy makers. They note instances where the programmes performed poorly even when there was an honest intention to implement and the leadership was committed, and hence surmise that it is possible that weaker sections failed to benefit from such programmes, not because implementation was the hurdle, but rather because their design or strategies were at fault. According to them strategy implies "the dynamic process by which the programme strategy, organisational structure and processes are appropriately aligned with the demands of the environment". The six propositions that they put forward on the basis of their review of the successes and failures of the programmes they have examined will bring out more clearly what they mean by strategy. The six propositions are:

1) The weaker sections of the population are likely to benefit from a programme when its service is designed to meet varying needs of beneficiary groups through a process of adaptation over time where necessary.

2) The stronger the vertical and horizontal linkages in a programme service, the greater the chances that the programme will benefit the weaker sections.

3) The weaker sections are likely to benefit from a programme when its service is so designed that its appropriation by others is rendered difficult or unprofitable.

4) The more participative the process of identification of the intended beneficiaries, the greater the chance that programme benefits will reach them.

5) The lower the technological and institutional barriers to

entry in the design of a programme, the higher the likelihood that the weaker sections will benefit from its service.

6) The stronger the participation of poor beneficiaries or their organisations in the planning and implementation of the programme, the higher the probability that benefits will flow to weaker sections.

Those who are familiar with the special beneficiary programmes will appreciate the validity and strength of these propositions and will have no difficulty in agreeing with the final conclusion of the authors that "careful attention to programme strategy might make a difference to the accrual of benefits to the weaker sections". But there is a major question that arises from the approach. Can a strategy of this kind be worked out and implemented entirely through administrative procedures and decisions (given the best of political will and a most committed bureaucracy) or is it likely to run into structural problems? This question is crucial because many people take the view that strategic and structural aspects can be neatly sorted out and kept in separate compartments.

Such dichotomies arise from a lack of understanding of the underlying links between the structure and working of a system and in particular the constraints that structure imposes on possible options of operation. 'Structure' gets identified with property relationships[17] and it is assumed that the choice of property relationships is simply a matter of personal preferences or ideological predilictions which need not be and should not be brought into discussions of growth and growth strategies which are considered to be in the sphere of technical and administrative decisions. But structure—defined as the manner in which resources are owned and controlled and the considerations that govern their use—cannot but have a bearing on production decisions and consequently on growth processes. Where resources are privately owned, unequally distributed and used principally to add to the command over resources, decisions regarding what will be produced, how they will be produced and how the produce will be shared among different sections in society will be made primarily on the basis of the given distribution of resource power in the system. In other words, the growth processes and the distributive processes are embedded in the basic economic structure of the system. This does not mean that administrative interventions based on broader social and political considerations cannot regulate and modify the economic processes. They can. But they do not operate in a vacuum, but must negotiate through the innate economic processes of the system. It is the relative strength of the two forces that will determine the outcome in each specific instance.

In some instances the structural elements can be so pervasive that even the most carefully designed strategies may not only fail, but can turn out to be counter-productive as well. An illustration of this kind is provided by R. Sinha et al. in their work *Income Distribution, Growth and Basic Needs in India.*[18] Basing themselves largely on Indian data that describe the structural characteristics of the system, they simulate alternative intervention strategies to trace their consequences on different sections in society. Consider a (fairly realistic) case where the lowest income groups in the rural areas derive around 63 per cent of their income from agriculture, but whose share in the value added of that sector is as low as 11 per cent. Consider further that over 75 per cent of their expenditure is on food and that their marginal propensity to consume agricultural output is over 85 per cent. Under these conditions examine the impact of a net income injection of an additional income to this class. Because they spend the bulk of this increment on food, and because income generated in the agricultural sector is heavily skewed in favour of the top income group in the rural areas, the accrual of income to the bottom class creates a major spill over income to the top rural group. Tracing the spill overs thus generated among different rural and urban classes interrelated through income generation and expenditure patterns, the simulation model shows that the spill over effect of a net injection of one rupee to the rural bottom class would result in an overall increase in incomes of Rs. 1,916 in the rural areas distributed as Re. 0.213 to the bottom class, Re. 0.520 to the middle class and Rs. 1.183 to the top class (apart from an income generation of Re. 0.640 in the urban areas). What is important to note there are not the numbers, but the spill over pattern resulting from the structural aspects.

A dynamic simulation model of the impact of intervention within given structural parameters was tried out by Irma Adelman and Sherman Robinson for South Korea.[19] Taking into account wage and price adjustments over time, possibilities of substitutions in the production processes as well as in consumption, investment patterns based on profitability considerations and expections, they consider a variety of anti-poverty programmes and work out their longer-term implications.[20] On the basis of their exercises they arrive at two major conclusions. "First, and perhaps surprisingly, we find that most anti-poverty policies eventually help the rich and middle income groups more then they help the poor. This is so even when, as in our experiments, the rich are taxed quite progressively to finance the programmes, the programmes are designed so that their initial impact is quite specific in favouring the lower income groups, and there is no graft, corruption, diversion or stupidity in their execution. This trickle-up effect was evident in a great many different policy experiments and is difficult to avoid. Second, our experience with a wide range of policies indicates that it is much easier to make the income distribution worse than to improve it."

The Korean study has been more of an experimental exercise than the Indian study mentioned above even though it was based on actual basic data. Here again what is significant is not the (pessimistic) conclusion but the pervasive impact of the structure of the economy on a variety of policy interventions. As Adelman and Robinson indicate, the main point of their study is that it underlines "the view that the distribution of income is firmly rooted in the structure of the economy, and that its path over time depends on the fundamental development strategy chosen by society. Once the basic development strategy is chosen, single-pronged programmes that do not include large direct transfers of assets or income can constitute, at best, moderately effective programmes."

* * *

In examining the possibilities of reconciling growth and social justice, therefore, the crucial issues are the basic features of the structure of the economy and the fundamental development strategy we have been following. As for the structure of the economy, no major change has been effected or even attempted since Independence except zamindari abolition. Consequently, the basic structure of the economy continues to be private ownership of resources with a substantial proportion of the population not having any non-labour resources at all and the distribution of these resources being highly skewed among those who own them. The fundamental development strategy we have adopted is to stimulate and support the utilisation of resources within the basic structure to bring about an increase in the output of goods and services subject to some overall supervision by the state to ensure that the processes so generated do not go contrary to some accepted social objectives. The problem of the reconciliation of growth and social justice is the extent to which the innate propensities of the economic structure are compatible with the social objectives which are, for that structure, extraneous considerations.

The logic that underlines the structure and propels it is to use resources to come to have more resources. Its major instrument is the market mechanism which informs resource owners through price signals the kinds of goods and services they should produce so as to maximise their own resource accumulation which, consequently, also ensures that production decisions respond to resource power with the implication that access to what becomes available is also based on resource power. It is on to such a structure that we have been trying to graft or superimpose the goals of social justice—eradication of poverty and unemployment, let us say—via administrative strategies and interventions.

In recent years these strategies have been of two kinds, the macro strategy of the Fifth Five Year Plan and the micro strategy of the Sixth Plan. The former is a thing of the past, and yet some observations about it may be useful for the continuing discussion regarding the reconciliation of growth and social justice. The Fifth Plan's strategy was to attempt to influence production actively and directly by reducing the resource power of the top income earners and by diverting it to the bottom group. While the strategy itself was greatly celebrated at least among academic circles, very little has been heard about it after it was launched into action, and so it must be presumed that it did not work. Even if it were to work initially, it is doubtful if it would have been sustained for long because what was attempted was only to reduce the *consumption* of the top income groups without much interference with the income generating measures. Hence, if the strategy were to be successful, it would have led to an increase in asset accumulation at the top over time which would have only added resource power at that level thereby futher reinforcing the natural propensities of the system.

With that comment we can turn to the latest strategy of trying to modify the normal processes of the system by micro interventions in favour of the resourceless sections. As has already been noted, the claim that is being made now (in the *Mid-term Appraisal*, for instance) is that poverty is being reduced by the combined effects of the growth process and of the special programmes. One of the crucial assumptions underlying the argument is that the benefits of growth accrue uniformly to all income groups, or more generally to all sections of society. The tenability of that assumption must now be examined more carefully. What is required for such a scrutiny is not statistical information about aggregate growth and income distributions, but a clear examination of specific growth processes. We shall refer to two types of problems. The first consists of instances where intended production processes are nullified and reversed through the natural operations of the system. As our first example we may take up a problem dealt with in the *Mid-term Appraisal*. In making a review of the past performance of the agricultural sector, the *Appraisal* notes that both wheat and paddy had registered impressive growth performance in the past but the other cereals like bajra, maize and ragi have been laggards. The reasons identified are also simple and straightforward: these cereals are cultivated in the rain-shadow belt of the country which generally receives inadequate rainfall marked by a wide degree of variability and uncertainty. The recommendation for the better performance of the laggards also follows—make more irrigation water available in the areas where these cereals are grown.

This is a good example of treating growth as a purely technical phenomenon devoid of all the structural elements. But studies that have examined the problem have documented the structural aspects which seem to offer a more adequate explanation of the poor growth performance of the "inferior" cereals[21]: they are produced by the poorer farmers because they have low paid-out costs, lower risk and higher component of fodder. The demand for these crops is largely confined to rural areas and to poor consumers in urban areas. These crops are neither widely traded nor receive official patronage and support comparable to superior cereals like wheat and rice. Consequently, when an opportunity presents itself, as for instance when irrigation water is made available, the normal tendency, particularly among larger farmers who are increasingly commercially motivated, is to move over from the inferior cereals to the market oriented wheat and paddy. Such changes in cropping pattern determined by structural aspects, are taking place in many parts of the country.[22]

The point to note here is that changes in cropping pattern of this kind are usually into high value crops (particularly if the movement happens to be into a crop like tobacco or sugar cane, and such shifts are not uncommon) and hence they make a better contribution to 'growth' even when they may impoverish the poorer sections further. When 'growth' is evaluated in value terms and the values are determined by market forces backed by resource power, changes of this kind are but natural. One of the most glaring instances of this class of phenomena was the sharp increase in the price of prawns as a result of the development of the export market, the entry of big commercial concerns into fishing and the problems it presented to the poorer traditional fisherfolk.[23] The net result of these changes was an increase in fish production in *value* terms without any significant increase in the *volume* of production and a substantial erosion of the real earnings and disruption of livelihood patterns of the coastal fishing community.

That takes us to the second problem of technological progress associated with growth adversely affecting the traditional workers in different walks of life. The introduction of motor trawlers in coastal fishing has made big inroads into working and living conditions of fisherfolk who can have no economic access to such technology. The same problem has descended upon those who have been depending on hand-printing of textiles.[24] The displacement of handloom workers (and of output) by the phenomenal growth of the powerloom sector is a manifestation of the same problem on a much larger scale.[25]

In the case of the latter two, and to a limited extent even of the first, it can be argued that since legislation exists to curb indiscriminate mechanisation the problem is basically an administrative one of improper or inadequate administration, and that consequently there is no structural issue involved. To be sure, the question of implementation (or more accurately the lack of implementation) is a major issue here. But one must probe also how implementable these regulations are *against* the normal working of the system propelled by resource power. After all, instances of this kind are indicative of the attempts made by resource power to frustrate social decisions and to the extent they succeed—and several other instances can be cited—they show the ability of resource power to resort to subtle and not so subtle measures to achieve its objectives in opposition to social policies and often *even through* social policies.[26]

Hence the question of the possibilities of designing strategies that are foolproof against the all pervasive aspects of the structure is very crucial in attempting to reconcile growth and social justice. We may take a second look at the six propositions cited earlier and consider how many of them are feasible in the context of the structural characteristics. For instance, where those who have resources look out for any and every opportunity to make more resources, to what extent is it possible to design programmes which cannot be appropriated by those who are not members of the target group, and hence, by definition, have greater resource power than the intended beneficiaries? How much participation of the poorer sections can effectively be ensured in the planning and implementation of the special programmes when they have to struggle hard even to get minimum wage legislations implemented? And to what extent can the poorer sections organise themselves when the stronger ones perceive such organisations as a threat to their interests? The Palakurichi study mentioned above showed how long the struggles of the weaker sections had to be to get 'concessions' from the powers that be, and how soon these concessions get eroded by the normal operations of the system. The Iruvelpattu study records the attempts of the agricultural labourers to organise themselves for a wage bargain at the time of the 1982 harvest and how easily it was frustrated by the landlords who brought in labourers from outside the village, got the harvest done and thus nipped in the bud the attempt of those who have no resources to achieve some power through organisational strength.

Another correlate of the growth process within our structure which has been having an adverse effect on the poorer sections, particularly in the rural areas, deserves to be touched upon mainly because it has not received much attention. According to official pronouncements in the early years of policy formulation for planned economic development, our economy was to become increasingly socialised over time. The Second Five Year Plan document, for instance, had very eloquent sections on the socialistic orientation built into our plan strategies with a growing public sector becoming the vanguard of the progress towards a socialistic pattern of society. These sentiments were repeated by the Third Plan document also. Of course the insistence that we do not want to become dogmatic about socialism prevented the need to spell out in any specific manner the features of the socialism of our imagination. But one thing we can be sure of. If socialism connotes in any sense greater socialisation of ownership of resources and of the manner of their utilisation, there has been no move in that direction during the past couple of decades. Indeed, the trend has been in the opposite direction, towards greater privatisation of the ownership and use of resources. This is somewhat difficult to document in a quantitative sense, but its features can easily be assessed. In the rural areas, of course, privatisation is related largely to the ownership and use of land. Several factors have contributed to this. Many post-independence reform measures such as land ceiling legislations, distribution of land to the landless and tenancy protection measures have increased the awareness of exclusive ownership rights. The increase in the productivity of land as a result of technological improvements has further contributed to the desire to establish and jealously guard the right of ownership. The growth of the banking system in the rural areas and the increased supply of credit has also led to the emphasis on exclusive ownership of land, as title deeds that affirm exclusive ownership are frequently required and used as collateral for loans. The possibilities of having other forms of assets have strengthened the tendency further. Agricultural implements of various kinds and a wide array of consumer durables have become symbols of private ownership.

One impact of this emphasis on private ownership has been to undermine the position of those who traditionally could not have any claims to ownership of land, particularly the landless agricultural labourers and more specially the scheduled castes among them. In the changing ethos of ownership they have also been losing some of the traditional claims and concessions that they were entitled to in the rural social relationships of the past. Traditional rural society was hierarchical and iniquitous, but it was also one of mutual obligations even when these were largely to the advantage of the stronger sections. But growing privatisation of resources and the commercialisation of economic activity have almost completely marginalised the weaker sections who find increasingly that they have to buy many things which they formerly used to receive in the form of traditional claims, and have nothing other than their labour power to sell and frequently there is not much market demand for it either. Special mention must be made of the manner in which common property resources—grazing lands, wasteland, forests, water resources—are coming to be eroded through the interrelated processes of privatisation and marketisation. A recent study has estimated that in some parts of the country income accruing from such resources constituted over 40 per cent of the gross household income of labourers and small farmers.[27] This may reflect certain regional pecularities and the share may not be so high in other parts of the country. But it is common knowledge that fodder for cattle, fuel and roofing materials were obtained from 'the commons' in most village settlements, but that these are increasingly getting commercialised through the efforts of those who preceive opportunities for private resource accumulation through the effective privatisation of erstwhile common property resources. If free access can be prevented, effective access will naturally come to be related to resource power, and those who have command over resources will be able to *sell* to others goods which were freely available to all at one time. There are bits of evidence to show that the commercialisation of the commons is a close correlate of growth, modernisation and development.[28]

Finally, it must be noted that these various factors make it difficult for the resourceless to acquire resources through the normal operations of the system. One reason for this is that those who have more resource power will use it to compete away resources from those who have less, and in this process the market, naturally, will be the ally of those who have more. Secondly, the working of the market in this context will be such that those who rely primarily on labour for earnings will find the prices of the assets moving up much more and much faster than their labour incomes. The growing disparity in the asset price-labour income ratio is a common feature of growth that takes place within structures like ours and is mediated through the inflationary process. It is, therefore, not surprising that although the ownership of land has changed hands in recent years (from members of the highest caste to those below them, for instance) there has been little tendency for land to come within reach of the poorer sections.

* * *

This is the structural milieu within which the reconciliation of growth and social justice must be considered. It may be recapitulated a follows: The structure of the economy is characterised by the private ownership of non-labour resources and these are very unequally distributed with a sizeable proportion of the population being totally deprived of them. In this system production and distribution are determined primarily by the unequal resource power and are geared to the accumulation of resources through resources. Those without adequate resource power are, therefore, virtually excluded from the benefits of the operations of the system. What strategies such as target group programmes attempt to do is to achieve through administrative interventions some *redistributions* in favour of those who do not have resource power. The interventionist strategy, therefore, is an attempt to correct the structural consequences without altering the structural characteristics. The attempt is to use political and administrative power to moderate the functioning of resource power. But the situation is not one where two opposing powers confront each other for a determination of relative strengh. For, while political and administrative power try to moderate resource power, resource power can influence and pervade over political power also, and political power is derived from resource power to a large extent, although not entirely. Hence the situation is one of constantly shifting power configurations resulting from the interplay of a variety of considerations. The outcome, therefore, is not *a priori* determinate. However, it is possible to indicate some conditions that will contribute to the success of the strategy (and conversely the absence of which will thwart the strategy).

We can say, for instance, that even in the context of production and growth based on resource power, an interventionist strategy favouring the weaker sections will be more successful where the distribution of resource power initially is not too glaring. Under such circumstances, the 'weaker sections' may have at least enough resource power to take advantage of interventions in their favour, and the redistributive function that political power has to perform may be only marginal. The redistributive strategies in high income capitalist countries belong to this category and are known to have a large measure of success, especially when the redistribution is attempted through publicly subsidised services than the actual transfer of resources. Within countries too, regions that may have had more favourable 'initial' conditions may have a better chance of reconciling growth and social justice through interventionist measures than others.

Secondly, interventionist strategies may become more effective when they are accompanied by some redistribution of the basic resources and assets as well. In principle, this reflected in the Sixth Plan's strategy for the eradication of poverty. It shows awareness of some of the structural impediments that have to be removed if the strategy is to have a fair chance of success. It recognises the need to take possession of and distribute ceiling surplus lands, to accelerate the process of consolidation of land, to confer ownership rights on tenants, to straighten land records and to provide house-sites to the landless. However, the *Mid-term Appraisal* has shown that little has been done along these lines and the indications are that instead of dealing with at least some of these structural issues, the decision has been to convert the strategy into one of administrative implementation of financial allocations alone.

Thirdly, since the interventions are into an on-going structural process, their longer term impact, through spill-overs and spin-offs can be to reverse a favourable initial impact. For instance, interventions that raise the absolute level of income of some target groups initially, but which also add to the resource power of the better off sections simultaneously and thus increase the inequalities in resource power, may turn out to be self-defeating in the long run. Thus an interventionist strategy in favour of small farmers that enables them to cross the poverty line in one year is no guarantee that they may not be pushed down subsequently through loss of assets through the normal operations of the system which confer more resources power to the larger farmers in the meanwhile. In other words, the developmental processes within our structure strengthen the resource position of some, but undermine that of others [29] The structural processes generate both growth and poverty, and very seldom are interventionist strategies sufficiently aware of these longer term implications or able to combat them effectively.

It is also important to take note of a specific political dimension of interventionism as a strategy. Within a democratic set up with adult franchise as one of its major tenets and where the majority of voters expect improvement in the living conditions through political processes, social justice becomes not only a goal to be aimed at, but also a criterion by which political processes and parties will be evaluated. Because many of the voters are potential beneficiaries of special programmes, the designing and advertising of these programmes become a major component of political activity. The visibility of the target group strategy—something being done for every section of society, however selective the programme may turn out to be within that section—gives it special political advantage that no government and no political party is likely to give up. It can be used to canvass and sustain support for party programmes and to build up the image of leaders as benefactors. It thus becomes an integral part of the political processes as long as rulers and ruled consider politics as a benefit-sharing process rather than a change-inducing process.

A question to consider, therefore, is whether the strategy can be used as an instrument to transform the political processes and to initiate changes in the structural characteristics of the economy. Indeed the strategy has that latent potential. It communieates the principle that even the least in society have rights. It announces that the administration must be responsive to the needs and rights of the people. It introduces an element of accountability into the administrative system. It opens up the possibility of participation in the development process. If these latent potentials can be energised, they can be used to mount pressure from below to loosen some of the rigidities of the system and to ensure that growth becomes more socially responsive. But the task is not an easy one.

REFERENCES

[1]*Approach to the Fifth Plan 1974-79.*

[2]*Sixth Five Year Plan 1980-85*, para 3-61.

[3]*Sixth Five Year Plan 1980-85: A Framework.*

It may be pointed out that the *Framework* shows some ambiguity about the relative roles of growth and special programmes in the eradication of poverty. "An increase in the productive potential of the economy is an essential condition for finding effective solutions to the problems of poverty. At the same time, *recognising the constraints which limit the scope for higher growth rate medium-term*, more direct means of reducing the incidence of *poverty in the stage of transition* would have to be employed" (Para 30, emphasis added). It would then appear that special programmes are assigned only a transitional role till the constraints that exist on growth are removed.

[4]See Irma Adelman and Cynthis Taft Morris, *Economic Growth and Social Equity in Developing Countries* (Stanford, Stanford University Press, 1973) especially Chapter 4 for reference to earlier studies, particularly of a theoretical nature. Hollis Chenery *et al., Redistribution with Growth* (Oxford, Oxford University Press, 1974) has a bibliography of studies relating to the theme. For the Indian discussion on the subject see T.N. Srinivasan and P.K. Bardhan (eds) *Poverty and Income Distribution in India* (Calcutta, Statistical Publishing Society, 1974) and C.T. Kurien, *Poverty, Planning and Social Transformation* (New Delhi, Allied Publishers, 1978).

[5]Francine Frankel, *India's Green Revolution* (Princeton, Princeton University Press, 1971) C.H. Hanumantha Rao, *Technological Change and Distribution of Gains in Indian Agriculture* (New Delhi, Macmillan, 1975).

[6]P.K. Bardhan, "Green Revolution and Agricultural Labourers", *Economic and Political Weekly*, Special Number, July 1970.

[7]M. Prahladachar, "Income Distribution Effects of the Green Revolution in India: A Review of Empirical Evidence", *World Development*, Vol. 11, No. 11, November 1983.

[8]G.S. Bhalla and C.K. Chadha, "Green Revolution and the Small Peasant: A Study of Income Distribution in Punjab Agriculture," *Economic and Political Weekly*, May 15 & 22, 1982.

[9]In a recent paper A. Vaidyanathan supplements this with information relating to the levels and patterns of consumption and states: "There is compelling evidence, from diverse sources, of a decline in rural wages of rural labour." A. Vaidyanathan, "Impact of Development on Rural Wage Labour in India" (cyclo-styled). That the process of growth can leave behind sections of the population, particularly those who depend solely on wage incomes because they have no assets, is documented also by Gilbert Etienne's field studies reported in his *India's Changing Rural Scene 1963-1979* (Delhi, Oxford University Press, 1982). This is particularly relevant because the thrust of Etienne's work is to show through informal intertemporal comparisons of villages in many parts of the country how growth and modernisation improve the living conditions of people.

[10]S. Guhan and Joan P. Mencher, *Iruvelpattu Revisited*, Working Paper No. 28, Madras Institute of Development Studies, September 1982 published in *Economic and Political Weekly*, June 4 & 11 1983, and S. Guhan, *Palakurich: A Resurvey*, Working Paper No. 42 Madras Institute of Development Studies, November, 1983.

[11]For an analysis of the micro level processes that prevent weaker sections from sharing the benefits of growth see C.T. Kurien, "Development and the Livelihood of People," text of a lecture delivered at Institute of Development Studies, Jaipur, April, 1984.

[12]See C.T. Kurien, "What is Growth?" *Economic and Political Weekly*, December 23, 1972 for discussion of this issue in context of the impact of growth on poverty.

[13]According to para 2.35 of the *Appraisal*, "The Sixth Plan Document assumed a reduction in the percentage of people below the poverty line from 47 per cent to 30 per cent. . . Over 1980-81 and 1981-82, a large number of families below the poverty line are expected to have crossed it because of the rise in their real income partly through the adoption of specific poverty alleviation programmes like IRDP and NREP. The exact distribution pattern of expenditure below and above the poverty line will not be available until the results of the National Sample Survey for the year 1983 become available. Until that time, the number and percentage of people below the poverty line may be estimated on the basis of *the assumption that increase in real income is uniform in all the expenditure classes* and the number of families brought above the povertyline is relatable directly to the corresponding expenditure in IRDP and NREP. Adopting this method, the percentage of poverty, it is estimated, came down to 41.5 and the total number of persons below poverty to 242 million in 1981-82. Thus, over the two years 1980-82, 34 per cent of the total Plan target of people to be taken above the poverty line were so taken" (emphasis added).

The claims themselves and the methods used in arriving at the figures have been challenged. In particular see K. Sundaram and Suresh D. Tendulkar, "Poverty in the Mid-term Appraisal"

Economic and Political Weekly, November 5-12, 1983 and Raj Krishna, "Growth, Investment and Poverty in Mid-term Appraisal of Sixth Plan" *Economic and Political Weekly*, Nov. 19, 1983. From the point of view of the present paper the major issue is the clause emphasised above. The validity of the assumption will be scrutinised in the subsequent sections of the paper.

[14]See David C. Korten and Felipe B. Alfonso (eds) *Bureaucracy and the Poor* (Singapore, McGraw-Hill International, 1981).

[15]Samuel Paul and Ashok Subramanian, "Development Programmes for the Poor: Do Strategies Make a Difference? *Economic and Political Weekly*, March 5, 1983.

[16]Madras Institute of Development Studies, *Structure and Intervention.* An Evaluation of DPAP, IRDP and related programmes in Ramanathapuram and Dharmapuri districts of Tamil Nadu, (August, 1980).

[17]"In the literature on development, there are two rather parallel views on the reasons why development programmes fail to benefit the weaker sections. One traces the problem to the absence of structural changes in society. According to this view, unless society is radically restructured and productive assets are more equitably distributed, the poorer sections of the population cannot benefit from the gains of development." Samuel Paul and Ashok Subramanian, *loc. cit.*

[18]R. Sinha et al., *Income Distribution Growth Need Basic Needs in India* (London, Croom Helm, 1979). The models in the book are based on Indian empirical data.

[19]Irma Adelman and Sherman Robinson, *Income Distribution Policies in Developing Countries—A Case Study of Korea* (Oxford University Press, 1978).

[20]The programmes tried out included changes in tax policies, consumption subsidies, price support measures, limited land redistribution, public works programmes, technological adaptation etc. and different combinations of these.

[21]N.S. Jodha and R.P. Singh, "Factors Constraining Growth of Coarse Grain Crops in Semi-arid Tropical India" *Indian Journal of Agricultural Economics*, Vol. XXXVII, No. 3 July-Sep. 1982.

[22]For a Study of shifts in cropping pattern from millets to paddy in Tamil Nadu when water becomes available see C.T. Kurien, *Dynamics of Rural Transformation—A Study of Tamil Nadu: 1950-75* (Madras, Orient Longman, 1981).

[23]John Kurien, "Entry of Big Business into Fishing: Its impact on the Fish Economy" *Economic and Political Weekly*, Sep. 9, 1978.

[24]For a more recent study of the same phenomenon see Jean-Philippe Plateau, "The Drive Towards Mechanisation of Small-scale Fisheries in Kerala: A Study of the Transformation Process of Traditional Village Societies", *Development and Change*, Vol. 15, No. 1, January 1984.

[24]L.C. Jain and Rita Kapadia, "Hand-Printing is Dying: Impact of Indiscriminate Mechanisation", *Economic and Political Weekly*, March 17, 1984.

[25]L.C. Jain, "Handlooms Face Liquidation: Powerlooms Mock at Yojana Bhawan", *Economic and Political Weekly*, Aug. 27, 1983.

[26]M.L. Dantwala cites several instances of this kind in "Rural Development—Investment without Organisation" *Economic and Political Weekly*, April 30, 1983.

[27]N.S. Jodha, "Market Forces and Erosion of Common Property Resources" paper presented at the International Workshop on Agricultural Markets in the Semi-Arid Tropics, ICRISAT Centre, October 1983.

[28]G. Parthasarathy and V. Pothana, "Structural Constraints to Growth with Equity Strategy in Agriculture: Some Lessons from Village Studies in Andhra Pradesh" paper presented at the Silver Jubilee National Seminar, Institute of Economic Growth, Delhi, April, 1984.

[29]A problem that is surfacing in many parts of the country is related to the privatisation and commercialisation of water by those who are enabled to do so through technological possibilities and administrative policies. Large farmers who are subsidised to go in for tube wells on their own land are now in a position to *sell* water to their neighbours who may get high yielding variety of seeds and credit at concessional rate through the appropriate target group programmes. But 'water rents' can be as high as one third of the total produce to be given in kind to the kindly neighbour who makes available a scarce input! For documentation see Guhan and Menchar, *op. cit*.

Reconciling Growth and Social Justice: Agrarian Structure and Poverty

M.L. Dantwala

Many explanations are offered for the failure of special programmes for the weaker sections—IRDP, NREP, 20-Point Programme, etc.—to make any significant impact on the magnitude of poverty and unemployment. The failure is attributed to the technocratic approach, administrative inefficiency, lack of motivation and urban bias of political leadership and bureaucracy, organisational weakness, non-application of refined management techniques and faulty delivery system. Hesitant approach to decentralisation of planning and decision-making and the consequent absence of people's participation, *ad hoc* and piecemeal approach, inadequate attention to forward and backward linkages and lack of coordination amongst implementing agencies at the local (district) level are also emphasised as being responsible for poor results. Several case studies have established the validity of one or all of the above explanations.

But a more substantive explanation which has gained wide academic acceptability and prestige is the one which attributes the failure to the economic and political power structure which has vested interests in maintaining the status quo. The vested interests may not exhibit open hostility to the programmes, but resort to dubious ways to defeat the purpose, and divert the benefits to themselves. More fundamentally, it is contended that even without resort to such manipulation, the iniquitous economic structure itself ensures that any development programme, even if it is targeted towards the weaker section, would automatically bring more benefit to those who have resources than to those who have none:

> . . . since the interventions are into an on-going structural process, their longer term impact, through spill overs and spin offs can be to reverse a favourable initial impact. For instance, interventions that raise the absolute level of income of some target groups initially, but which also add to the resource power of the better off sections simultaneously and thus increase the inequalities in resource power, may turn out to be self-defeating in the long run. Thus an interventionist strategy in favour of small farmers that enables them to cross the poverty line in one year is no guarantee that they may not be pushed down subsequently through loss of assets through the normal operations of the system which confer more resource power to the larger farmers in the meanwhile. In other words, the developmental processes within our structure strengthen the resource position of some, but undermine that of others. The structural processes generate both growth and poverty, and very seldom are interventionist strategies sufficiently aware of these longer term implications or able to combat them effectively.[1]

If the iniquitous structural milieu is to be accepted as the principal reason behind the failure of the anti-poverty programmes, all other explanations such as faulty planning, and bureaucratic ineptitude, would become irrelevant, or at best marginal. Assuming that structural change is a prior condition for the success of each and every programme for eradication of poverty, a few further questions will have to be answered.

I think it would be fair to say that what the structuralists are contending is that structural change is a necessary *pre-condition* for the solution of the poverty problem and not that it is *a sufficient* condition. In other words, it is not contended that once the structural change—primarily more equal distribution of resources/entitlements—takes place, poverty, unemployment and exploitation would disappear. There is ample historical experience to show that a just ownership (cooperative or collective) of resources does not necessarily create a just society or generate just attitudes, just behaviour and respect for human dignity—goals which the abolition of poverty seeks to achieve.

The first question is: if an equitable resource structure is a necessary but not a sufficient condition. what are the other supplementary or supportive conditions? Without waiting for an answer from others, let us hazard an answer.

Poverty removal is not purely an economic or a social issue. We desire and struggle to eradicate poverty because we cherish certain values. We believe that it is 'wrong' to tolerate a situation which subjects a vast (or even a small) section of the society to 'sub-human' conditions of living. Words like 'wrong' and 'sub-human' connote a moral principle. This, it would be said, is obvious. Our contention is that it is not so obvious in the structuralist view. The word moral is rarely used in the structuralist argument. It may not be deliberate, but perhaps it is, for words like morality—call it ethics, if you like—are believed to be an escapist strategem to sidetrack the basic issue of inequitous ownership of property and all the evils it generates. To come to the point, if structural change is to achieve some basic goals like the elimination of exploitation of man by man, it should be specifically linked to a value system from which it derives its urge. Devoid of its moral content, structural change may end up in a worse form of tyranny than we are witnessing today. Is it the fear of being dubbed un-Marxist or a sanctimonious reformist which inhibits us from introducing a moral dimension in the case for structural change?

The point does not end here. If a moral dimension is relevant to structural change, it is equally relevant to other components of the economic system, bureaucracy, management, institutions. All these need 'technical' or 'operational' improvements (I don't find more appropriate words), but the outcome of all these improvements will not be what we desire it to be, unless they too imbibe the moral purpose of change. We have superb scientists, technocrats and managers, but the world is not any the better for it.

Let us come down to a more mundane level. Here the first question is: what precise structural change have we in mind? Mainly, if not solely, a more equal distribution of ownership of land. To put it bluntly, though necessary and highly desirable, realisation of equity through redistribution of land is no longer a viable option for more than one reason. The main reason is not the political unfeasibility of the proposition. Though the prevailing political configuration is the major obstacle for redistribution of land ownership, we do not put it up as the main reason for not considering it a live issue. In fact, if the main obstacle were political it would make it very much a live issue. Our reason for giving land redistribution secondary place is that even a radical redistribution of land will not materially alter the economic and more so political power structure, if the degree of radicalism is determined by a common urban and rural norm. Even if the *exemption* limit—inclusive of the permitted deductions—currently applicable to non-agricultural income and wealth is considered as the *maximum* (ceiling) permitted income and wealth for the landowner, the amount of 'surplus' land which may become available, will be too meagre for its distribution to significantly reduce the inequality in the ownership of land. If the permitted post-tax non-agricultural income and wealth are accepted as norms for agricultural income and wealth, hardly any surplus will materialise. This line of argument will be questioned on two grounds. First, there is considerable concealed or *benami* land ownership. So is the case with non-agricultural income and wealth, perhaps with a much bigger dimension. Second, land is a very special asset from which a vast portion of labour force derives its livelihood. As such, norms pertaining to it cannot be the same as those applied to non-agricultural assets. If land is such a special asset, why not advocate its nationalisation as has been done for banking and life insurance. We honestly believe that even a semblance of equality in access to land ownership cannot be achieved without its collectivisation. But if private ownership is to be permitted, we cannot have a double standard: one for agricultural income/asset and another vastly generous for non-agricultural income.

More important, land ownership is no longer the major source of economic and political power which it was in good old days. Count those who wield money power and political power. How many of them are big landlords. The sociology of power is still not clear. On the face of it, it seems like you need a lot of unscrupulousness rather than land to acquire political power and to a slightly less extent, money power. So, if we are concerned with the incubus of the economic and political power structure as a major obstacle to the success of anti-poverty programmes, we should look at least occasionally elsewhere instead of hammering only at iniquitous landownership. The changes over time in the pattern of landownership indicate de-concentration at the top and concentration at the bottom. The swelling (almost doubling in three decades) in the number of marginal farmers and in the ranks of landless labour is thus not related to increasing concentration of landownership at the top. Both the number of large landowner households and the area in their possession have in fact declined sharply. How do we relate the two phenomena—reduction in the magnitude of large land ownership and increasing poverty—in the analysis of the poverty problem?

The facts and the line of argument advanced do not imply a plea for the abandonment of the policy of imposition of a ceiling on individual/family holding. Legislation for imposition of a ceiling has been enacted, made more stringent by stages, and the concept has been socially and politically accepted. As admitted by the Planning Commission in plan documents and appraisals, the enforcement of the legislation has been lax and by and large ineffective. It would be wholly appropriate to expose the loopholes in the legislation, administrative lapses, the evasions, and extract the maximum possible surplus. The point we are making, is that the redistribution of such surplus will have an insignificant contribution, needs amendment. Even if the meagre surplus land can be utilised to provide house-sites with a small farm yard to the landless, it will reduce their helpless dependence on the landowner and strengthen their resistance capacity.

A more important point which we wish to emphasise is that land redistribution does not exhaust the range and scope of resource redistribution. There are other resources as important as land, whose 'privatisation' has not been as total as in the case of land. One such resource is underground water. This resource is being privatised on an increasing scale, but even now considerable potential is lying untapped. This author had pleaded for social control, if not socialisation, of this resource some 20 years ago. The Government of India was moving in this direction (regulation of ground water use) and a

Model Bill was drafted for the purpose as early as in 1970. But the move has been stalled. Why are our academicians not taking up this cause instead of flogging what for all practical purpose seems to be a lifeless issue—land redistribution?

Another resource is the ecologically degraded 175 million hectares of land. Prem Shankar Jha has suggested that even if 50 million hectares of such land is brought under fuelwood trees, it will not only provide an ecologically safe source of energy generation at a lower per unit cost than that of oil, but also generate "50 million additional full time jobs, or provide 100 extra mandays of work per year to 125 million underemployed people in the rural areas." (*Times of India*, July 24, 1984).

Ways will have to be found to stop privatisation of this resource (ecologically degraded land) and put it to community use for generating income and employment for the poor. Resources and their productivity are not static. Redistribution need not be thought of only in terms of the existing privatised resources. There are plenty of untapped dormant or low yield resources. It would be easier to stop and, if need be, reverse (socialise) their privatisation. The attachment of the owners to such resources is much less than to the land under cultivation, because the yield from them is low and the cost of developing them for higher profitability is beyond their means.

Apart from the scope for redistribution of untapped or dormant resources, there is scope for 'reverse discrimination' in the deployment of development investment and incremental income in favour of the disadvantaged groups. The aim of anti-poverty programmes is the same. But many social scientists are convinced that these programmes are intrinsically incapable of eradicating poverty, not simply because they are being poorly conceived, badly managed, and if not sabotaged or manipulated by vested interests to appropriate the accruing gains, but for a more fundamental reason. It is argued that "what strategies such as target group programmes attempt to do is to act through administrative interventions (to enable) some *redistributions* in favour of those who do not have resource power (emphasis in original). The interventionist strategy, therefore, is an attempt to *correct* the structural *consequences without altering the structural characteristics*."[1] (emphasis added).

It is difficult to accept the argument. If the 'structural consequences' are *systematically corrected*, and distribution of incremental income is steadily deployed to build up the resource base of the poor, it is reasonable to expect that over a period of time, the 'structural characteristics' will not remain unaffected. It is something like quantity transforming itself into quality. Apart from this, the target group approach does not rule out the attempt to alter structural characteristics. On the contrary, we have suggested elsewhere (*Report of the Working Group on Block Level Planning*) that the ultimate aim of rural development should be to progressively change the asset structure and make it more egalitarian. Our difference with the structuralist view—if we understand it correctly—is that we do not accept the proposition that structural change *through* land distribution must precede all other measures for poverty removal, and that if this is not done the latter are doomed to failure.

Their and our goals are identical: an egalitarian and non-exploitative society which, we agree, cannot be achieved without a fully egalitarian ownership of productive assets and skills. We include skills, because the biggest privilege today, besides political power, is education and specialised knowledge. Those who possess this resource are not excessively shy to privatise it for personal gain and status. But such an egalitarian structure cannot be brought about instantly. We therefore suggest initiating a process of progressive erosion of the prevailing power structure through policy interventions which would start changing the 'consequences' of the structure, and simultaneously chip off the protruding edges of the structure itself, for example, by putting a ceiling on large landholdings.

We also believe that we should not leave the task to the political process. The ultimate objective is to change the social ethos. Capture of power may be a necessary instrument and therefore an intermediate goal. The trouble is that the intermediate often becomes the end. Having captured power, we lose interest in the ultimate goal. New vested interests replace old interests. The colour changes, the content remains the same.

It should also be emphasised that land ownership is not today a major source of exploitation of the poor, nor the most lucrative source of gain from the development process. The prime source for amassing wealth is trade and corruption in collusion with those in authority—political or administrative.

Many artisans have exceptional skills and yet are perpetually poor. Their legitimate earnings are laundered by middlemen who supply them raw material and credit and pre-empt the purchase of their products. Why is this phenomenon underplayed and land redistribution excessively emphasised? Is it contended that once you take care of the inequity in land ownership, all such ugly features of the system will disappear? Or the ugly features cannot simply be eliminated without first removing the inequality in land ownership?

I think the analysis of the processes which generate poverty on the one hand and affluence on the other has got stuck in intellectual ruts. It is necessary to pull it out and refine it with a more open-minded debate.

To avoid ambiguity about my stand on 'structural' change I should like to sum up by recording a few specific statements:

1) Elimination of poverty on a durable basis can be achieved only by ensuring that all rural households, especially those currently below the poverty line, have an entitlement to productive assets and skills which provide them gainful employment and adequate earnings to enable them to live above subsistence level.

2) The objective of providing such entitlements to the (poor) rural households can be achieved through (a) redistribution of existing productive assets, *and* by (b) adopting a deliberate policy augmenting the flow of income stream towards poor households and facilitating acquisition of assets generated by public investments, *and* (c) plugging the sources of exploitation of the poor households by establishing non-exploitative institutions for providing tenure security, credit, supply of inputs and marketing of output, etc. In our view all the three are *equally* important and we should not underrate the contribution which (b) and (c) can make to removal of poverty. We do not accept the view that (b) and (c) are mere corollaries of (a), and that unless (a) is achieved gains from (b) and (c) will be illusory.

3) The most valuable asset in the rural economy is land. Its equitable distribution would thus involve transfer of land ownership from the large owners to the small and marginal owners and the landless. The land ceiling legislation should therefore be strictly enforced. But a critical assessment of the composition of land ownership and the quantum of surplus

likely to be derived through enforcement of ceiling legislation suggest that the surplus will be quite inadequate for the purpose of providing productive assets to all those who need them and insufficient to provide above-subsistence level of living. This does not mean that the idea of land redistribution should be given up. The policy of imposition of land ceiling has gained a wide measure of acceptability. Its pursuit will serve two equity objectives. It will reduce inequality—in our view marginally—and even the inadequate surplus can be utilised at least to provide house-sites and work places to a large number of the dependent poor. We, however, do not believe that such redistribution will break the existing power structure. At best, it will weaken it and/or strengthen the resistance of the poor to exploitation. Hence, other avenues which would facilitate removal of poverty or arrest the process of poverty removal need to be explored.

4) The importance of land as an input for agricultural production has diminished and that of other inputs such as irrigation, modern varieties of seed, fertilisers, etc. has correspondingly increased. It would be easier to redirect and augment their availability—through susidies and physical controls—to the poor landowners.

5) There is an equally large scope for augmenting the income flows towards the poor from a strongly egalitarian—even socialistic—approach to the development of ancillary industries like animal husbandry, forestry, fisheries, etc. The vested interests are yet not firmly established in these fields, though the process has begun. There is an imperative need to reach an academic consensus on the policy in these fields which will benefit the poor and alter the income stream in their favour. Pre-occupation with land distribution has resulted in the neglect of these potentially powerful instruments for building a more egalitarian economic structure.

6) Much of the poverty can be traced to an exploitative institutional network—land tenure (sharecropping tenancy), credit, marketing, input supply. It may be admitted that the structure and the institutions are offsprings closely inter-related. But this does not mean that the institutions cannot be reformed without a *prior* change in the structure. Besides, our experience shows that while the direct attempt to change the structure has

been almost ineffective, establishment and strengthening of countervailing non-exploitative institutions—credit in particular—is having some impact on the bargaining power of the poor, though even in this field a corrective action is halting and half-hearted.

7) Finally, I have been arguing that structural change without a change in social-ethical values will be superficial and short-lived. The form may change but the purpose (equity) for which it was changed may not be achieved, unless the change is supported by—has the foundation of—internalisation of values which the change represents. My plea is to see 'poverty' not simply as an economic issue, but essentially a moral issue.

Note

1. Kurien, C.T., "Reconciling Growth and Social Justice: Strategies versus Structure?", (1984) (mimeo), pp. 24-25.

PART V

Other Asian Experiences

Presentations*

BANGLADESH

One of Asia's youngest nations, Bangladesh with a population of about 90 million, has a land area of about 35 million acres, of which about 23 million acres are cultivable. Since about 90 per cent of the population live in rural areas and are dependent on agriculture for their livelihood, the conditions prevailing in the rural areas are generally indicative of the state of development of the country as a whole.

The beginnings of rural development can be traced back to the cooperative movement which reached the Bangladesh region as early as 1904. In the twenties work on rural development was spearheaded by volunteers of the national movement, and pursued with zeal by some distinguished civil servants. The Government of Bengal adopted a Rural Reconstruction Programme. This was an important step towards promotion of rural development. Legislation on primary education and debt settlement was enacted in the thirties. The early forties witnessed the expansion of credit cooperatives.

After Independence in 1947, rural development was given greater impetus in Bangladesh (then East Pakistan). Multipurpose cooperatives were promoted. The *zamindari* system which had been established by the British in 1793 was abolished. A Village Agricultural Industrial Development (VAID) programme was started in the 1950s. The main thrust of the programme was towards making villagers self-reliant and help-

*The experiences of Bangladesh, Japan, Nepal and Thailand narrated in this part are based on the presentations orally made by the participants from the respective countries.

ing them build linkages with relevant government departments to obtain support for their development. Like the Community Development Programme in India, the VAID Programme was funded by foreign donors under schemes like the PL 480.

Technology and organisation suited to tackle problems of villagers such as water for winter crops and irrigation projects, received greater attention. To promote the diffusion of new and relevant technology and managerial and organisational skills, a training and research institute was established at Comilla. The institute evolved an interesting approach in its training programmes, keyed to the needs of the rural areas. It adopted one *thana* (a sub-district with an area of about 100 square miles/ 250 villages) as its laboratory. The institute surveyed the villages, collected information, and used it in the classroom. In turn, ideas generated in the classroom were tested directly in the rural areas. Villagers were organised around specific technical inputs such as irrigation equipment for training, group action and group discipline. A Rural Works Programme was formulated for expansion of rural physical infrastructure (all-weather roads, drains, culverts), supply of agricultural inputs, agricultural extension, and credit services. The Comilla experiment met with considerable success and was replicated in other parts of the country.

Village based cooperatives (Krishak Samabaya Samitis—KSS) supported by *thana*-based institutions called Thana Central Cooperative Associations (TCCA) were organised. Unlike the earlier cooperatives which were largely credit-oriented, the new cooperatives were production-oriented and worked to develop and diffuse appropriate technology for improving agricultural production.

After liberation in 1971, Bangladesh adopted more comprehensive rural development plans. Such plans regarded the *thana* as the focal point for development in the rural areas and farmers were looked upon as key change agents. Bureaucrats and technocrats were oriented to operate more as development agents than as just administrators. The Government encouraged the formation of cooperative federations at the national level. A Ministry of Local Government, Rural Development and Cooperatives, and a Rural Development Board were set up.

A large number of non-government organisations (NGOs) emerged after 1971. In collaboration with the UNO and other international agencies, the NGOs launched a variety of development programmes at local levels. Bangladesh does not, however, have a single umbrella—NGO; ties between the NGOs and the government have been weak.

Many useful changes are now taking place in rural Bangladesh. A variety of target-oriented projects for the disadvantaged groups such as the landless, the near-landless and women in agriculture, health and home-based occupations (e.g., weaving and poultry keeping) have been promoted.

The rapidity with which villagers have adopted innovations such as high-yielding varieties of seeds and new methods of cultivation, and the use of fertilisers and pesticides, indicate that the climate for rural development in Bangladesh is favourable. But on the whole, the impact of rural development has been feeble and there remains much room for improvement. Better coordination of the activities of different organisations would lower costs and facilitate greater efficiency. This is important for a country which has limited resources to invest. Another aspect is the need to harness such resources as water. Most of all, there is need to pay attention to the intangible but crucial aspects of the development process, namely, the values and ideals of the people, their motivation to change, and a clear vision of a better way of life.

JAPAN

Of all the countries in Asia, Japan has enjoyed the most spectacular growth and development during the last few decades. About one-sixth of the total land area in Japan is under cultivation. With rural households totalling about 5 million, this works out to be about one hectare of cultivated land per agricultural household. Only about 11 per cent of the Japanese population are engaged in agriculture, and they contribute 5 per cent to the country's GNP.

The key to Japan's progress may be found in the Japanese policy of giving predominance to industrial development, since land is a scarce commodity and not much reliance can be placed on agriculture. About 70 per cent of the population engaged in agriculture contribute less than 1 per cent to the GNP. As against this, nearly 70 per cent of the farm households in Japan earn more income from non-agricultural sources than they do from the agricultural ones. Unlike in most other countries, the process of industrialisation has been integrated with traditional social structures and community relations, thus offsetting the social costs of modernisation which most other developed and developing nations have had to bear.

Given the unique features of Japanese society, it is perhaps not strange that there has been no formal concept of rural development in Japan. On the other hand, although the country is centrally governed, the management of development has been firmly rooted in grassroots community relationships. The household is the basic unit of consumption and production, and the community shares all major assets. One such asset is irrigation. The main source of irrigation is surface water. The plots of land used in farming do not have separate inlets for water and the farmers depend upon water flowing from neighbouring plots. The individual farmer consequently has little freedom, and unity among the community members is essential for the economic survival of the farmers. Other factors strengthening community ties are the existence of common pasture-lands and community-based technology. All these features explain why there is only negligible difference between the labour inputs and land productivities of owners and tenant-farmers.

The Japanese government has played a pivotal role in the development of agriculture and farming. As early as 1868, 70 per cent of the country's irrigation infrastructure had been completed. However, the benefits of irrigation were highly skewed in favour of the productive agricultural areas. After the Meiji restoration, attempts were made to modify the differential productive capacities of farm households. As a result, differences between the productivities of high and low yielding areas were drastically reduced. Even so, until 1946 pockets of poverty continued to exist, primarily due to the skewed distribution of land ownership and the high tenancy ratio. Forty per cent of the land was under tenant cultivation, and the ratio of disposable income of owner-farmers to that of tenant-farmers was 100 : 70. These conditions were drastically changed by a series of land reforms initiated by the Western occupation forces after the Second World War. Through the reforms land titles were transferred from owners to tenants. Since there were no conspicuous differences between the technology employed by owner-farmers and that employed by tenants, these changes did not affect productivity. Also, because large numbers from among the agricultural workforce moved out into the rapidly growing small and medium-scale industrial settlements, land reforms did not seriously affect the size of operational holdings.

The transfer of labour resources from the agricultural to industrial sector was facilitated by the primogeniture system of inheritance in existence since 1883. As the eldest son of a household alone is entitled to inherit the land and other assets of the family, the other children are compelled to seek non-agricultural employment.

The strong emphasis on education has been another critical factor in the transformation of Japanese society. Technical education forms part of general education, imparting skills in the fields of agriculture, commerce, modern technology, etc. By spending a good part of their disposable incomes on the education of their children, particularly on technical and vocational education, the Japanese have managed to avoid the poverty trap.

One of the lessons which the Japanese experience suggests is that eradication of poverty is virtually impossible without structural changes in the ownership and distribution of land and other assets. Poverty cannot be eradicated through piecemeal efforts confined to one or a few sectors of the economy. The effects of linkage between sectors and within sectors have to be studied and the plan of action formulated using an approach which deals with the entire macro-system (for instance, the linkages between agriculture and industry, between farmers and farmers' organisations, between farmers' organisations and local bodies, and so on). This is necessary because development is an integrated process requiring simultaneous action on a variety of fronts.

The development process in Japan also suggests that popular participation cannot be relied on as a magic formula for progress. The poor in the third world cannot be expected to 'participate' in activities which, in their perception based on past experiences, have done little to improve their lives substantially. Neither can one attribute past failures to lethargy on the part of the poor. The failure has been due to the lethargy on the part of government and political leaders. What is required, therefore, is more energetic and meaningful participation from these quarters. The leaders have to be drawn from within the local communities because only such leaders are likely to identify with the poor and commit themselves to their well-being and growth.

NEPAL

The initial efforts at rural development in Nepal started after 1950 when it began to open its doors to the outside world. In the early phase of rural development, a number of Village Development Programmes (VDPs) were started at the local level with a focus on training farmers to use new methods of cultivation using improved seeds and modern fertilizers.

In the late 1950s, Nepal adopted the panchayat system of government at the local level. The responsibility for rural development was vested in the panchayat organisations. Subsequently the small area development programmes were introduced to promote development in the remote areas of the country. The panchayat system led to the growth of a number of organisations such as farmers', women's and youth organisations. However, none of these organisations has yet been involved in the implementation of programmes. Besides these, there emerged a number of non-governmental organisations (NGOs) working in such fields as health care and welfare of women.

The Small Farmers' Development Programme (SFDP) was initiated in 1975. The programme began with a pilot study to identify the small farmer and to devise a development programme catering to his needs. The small farmer was any person who depended for his livelihood on agriculture, fishing, cottage industries, or small landholdings, or who was a tenant sharecropper, a landless labourer, or a skilled labourer whose annual family income did not exceed Rs. 950. A number of such small farmer families were identified and assisted to organise themselves into groups consisting of 10-15 farmers. These groups were to carry out group-based activities using institutional credit. A special feature of SFDP was the introduction of a group savings scheme which was intended to develop self-reliance and independence of small farmers from moneylenders and landlords.

This experiment continued for about four years during which it was found that the beneficiary farmers achieved significant improvement in their living conditions compared to the farmers not covered by SFDP. In 1982, the success of SFDP prompted the International Fund for Agricultural Development to finance the expansion of the programme. Currently, the programme runs in 48 districts and covers about 24,000 households. In addition to credit and agricultural activities, these programmes include a number of social activities such as adult education and family planning.

Political commitment from the government and policy making bodies like the National Agricultural Board have significantly bolstered the progress of rural development in Nepal. However, the Nepalese experience suggests that while people's participation is both possible and desirable, it is not a panacea for all problems of rural development. There is a danger that as implementing agencies become bureaucratised and governmental involvement increases, popular participation may decline.

THAILAND

The background against which rural development acquired prominence in Thailand is different from that of other Asian countries because unlike the latter, Thailand was never directly colonised.

Land being not as scarce as in other Asian countries, Thailand was able to achieve substantial increases in agricultural production after the Second World War, mainly through area expansion. As a result, its dependence on imports of agricultural produce is low. Thailand's economy is greatly dependent on trade in agricultural produce; its main problem is to find markets for its produce.

Measures that led to rural change in Thailand have to be understood in the context of its political milieu. Traditionally, Thailand has had weak central political power. Rural development programmes were often executed with the covert motive of consolidating political influence at the centre and maintaining political control over the country, particularly over the rural areas of Thailand which were dominated by various provincial power groups. Public investment in development was made on the consideration of expansion of political control regardless of economic returns. For instance, public investment in the expansion of the railway system was preferred over investment in irrigation because a good railway system facilitated greater territorial control. Political control was also acquired through a process of 'internal colonisation' by which the government won domination over provinces, and provincial elites were either eliminated or co-opted.

After the Second World War, the bureaucratic class which wrested political control out of the hands of the monarchy, dominated the central government. One positive aspect of this change was the increasing use of the public sector to speed up development. In 1958, with aid from the World Bank and other foreign agencies and with the liberalisation of the Thai economy, a beginning in building an infrastructure for agricultural development was made. The period between 1958 and 1973 witnessed rapid economic growth.

In 1973, the coalition at the centre collapsed. In order to build political bases among the rural masses, the 'elite' moved into the rural areas with a plethora of development schemes. The military government continued to take interest in rural development and introduced a number of measures to strengthen marketing support, rural credit, technology and other facilities. By 1982, a formal rural development programme was promulgated with the objective of redressing imbalances in the social infrastructure, providing better education and health facilities, setting up rice and cattle banks, etc.

While these measures have brought about rapid changes in Thailand's rural areas, they cannot really be said to constitute development because they have not brought about the changes needed in socio-economic structures. Large pockets of poverty in the developed areas of the country remain, and the number of landless labourers has actually increased.

A major role in the development of rural Thailand was played by the private sector through large agri-business corporations which, due to the liberalisation of the economy, emerged as powerful engines of growth. Frustrated with the inefficiencies of the political system, bureaucrats too turned towards the private sector to initiate changes in the rural areas. Business corporations introduced a variety of new economic practices in the rural areas.

The role of Non-Government Organisations (NGOs) in Thailand's rural development has been much less conspicuous than in other countries. Because of the state's strong control over the rural areas, NGOs were hard put to enter the stage and had to be content with playing a somewhat furtive role, financed by foreign agencies, and viewed with suspicion by the government as being possible front organisations of subversive elements.

China: Development of Small Towns in the Delta of Yangtze River

Yuan Bao-min

The delta of the Yangtze river is a rich area of China. The physical environment and economic conditions are very good for agricultural production. This area has a temperate climate and abundant water resources which makes it ideal for the development of agriculture, fishery, animal husbandry and sideline production. Industry and commerce also flourish here. Today, the density of population in this region is 200 persons per square kilometre.

Before the founding of new China, the main residents of the small town were merchants, handicraft workers, and other employed people. With the establishment of the People's Republic of China in 1949, reforms were carried out in agriculture, privately owned industrial and commercial enterprises, purchase and supply of farm produce and sideline products. The structure of the economy of the town underwent a change. Where there were wholesale grain stores, oil mills, workshops and old-style Chinese private banks, now stand grain distribution stations, food product factories, provision shops, and departments owned by the state or the collective.

In 1978, the Third Plenary Session of the Twelfth Central Committee of the Communist Party of China issued a declaration on reform of the economic structure. The document declared clearly that a socialist planned economy is based on public ownership in which the law of value must be consciously followed and applied. The full development of a commodity economy is an indispensable stage in the economic growth of society and a prerequisite for economic modernisation.

In order to develop a socialist commodity economy, small towns were to be regarded and run as commercial as well as science and education centres. In the past few years, a great number of old towns were recovered and new ones set up. In these towns, the population increased rapidly. According to some estimates, from 1982 to 1983 the population of the towns increased by more than 30 per cent.

The system of contracted responsibility for production with remuneration linked to output was introduced across the countryside. This step got rid of absolute egalitarianism in distribution and brought into play the enormous initiative of the peasants for building socialism. As a result, productivity increased sharply and the output of grain doubled. The grain output in excess of production quotas and other non-planned products were allowed to be sold in the market by the farmers in the small towns. In this way the value of trade was raised. For example, in a small town called Qing Feng, near Nantong, one of the 14 coastal cities in Jiangau province, the value of trade had grown by more than 100 per cent between 1978 and 1983.

Numerous township enterprises have been set up in recent years. The scale of these enterprises is not large, but there is a great deal of variety and quantity. They include a food product factory, a feed processing plant, a repair and spare parts workshop, a clothing factory, a tailoring workshop, a general store, and a book store.

Another result of the reforms was that the standard of living of the peasants and workers has improved. A survey around Wuxi, South Jiangsu province, brought this out. Last year, per capita income in the countryside was more than 400 yuan ($ 220), with the highest reaching 500 yuan. Only three years ago, it was 100 yuan. Part of the income had been invested in the township enterprises and agricultural production; day-to-day expenses and savings accounted for the rest.

Postal and telecommunications facilities promote the development of small towns. An efficient transport network using waterways, railways, and highways covers this area and connect it with major cities. As a rule, the transport service is run by the government, but several cars and ships came to be owned and managed by private enterprise recently.

Finally, support from the government is another important factor in the development of small towns. The state banks, both the People's Bank of China and the Agricultural Bank of China, provided large loans to the township enterprises and farmers.

As a supplement to the state economy, the collective and individual economics are allowed to grow. To facilitate commodity circulation, cold storages and warehouses are also being built with both state funds and money raised both collectively and from individuals.

The development of small towns is an event of historic significance. It provides surplus labour with the opportunity to take up an occupation and thus prevents the migration of the rural population into urban areas. It gradually works to reduce the distinction between the town and the country.

In conclusion, from experience of developing small towns in the delta of the Yangtze river we may glean the following lessons:

The development of small towns was caused chiefly by the policy of the Chinese government. China is socialist society with a planned economy based on public ownership of means of production. Historical experience shows that the socialist planning system should combine uniformity with flexibility. Diversified economic forms and various methods of management must also be developed.

The main tasks in China's rural areas and small towns are to raise productivity, open channels of circulation, and develop commodity production with a view to stabilising and improving the production responsibility system. With the efforts of the people, the small towns will make progress; they can expect to quadruple the gross agro-industrial output value by the end of this century.

Rural Development Strategies in the Philippines: Some Perspectives

Antonio J. Ledesma, SJ

Since independence in 1946, several strategies in rural development have been tried out in the Philippines. Non-government organisations, including church-related groups, have initiated and implemented a number of these strategies. Other programmes have been legislated and implemented by government agencies. These strategies are looked into under three headings corresponding to the post-war decades of the 50s, '60s and '70s.

Community Development in the '50s

In the aftermath of the Second World War, one major social force left in the rural areas was the *Hukbalahap*, a guerrilla army initially organised against the Japanese but later turned into a peasant-based rebel army against the landlords and the newly constituted government of the Philippines Republic.

The latter half of the '40s and the early years of the '50s was a period of continuing agrarian unrest over the key issue of land reform, particularly in the densely populated rice-growing areas of Central Luzon.

The charismatic leadership of Ramon Magsaysay turned the tide against the communist insurgency by the mid-'50s. Laws on share tenancy and land reform were passed, although they could not be fully implemented.

On the whole, the government strategy in countering rural unrest was to resettle peasant families and former *Huks* in frontier areas in Mindanao. In Central Luzon itself, the

Philippine Rural Reconstruction Movement (PRRM) was among the first privately funded organisations to introduce the concept of community development (or the CD approach). PRRM was an extension of Dr. Yen's rural reconstruction movement in mainland China and the Sino-American Joint Commission on Rural Reconstruction in Taiwan. The model entailed the fielding of CD workers in one or several neighbouring villages to initiate community projects under the four dimensions of livelihood, health, education and self-reliance.

Following the CD approach, the Magsaysay administration created a special office called the Presidential Assistant on Community Development (PACD) to field government personnel in the rural areas. Much was accomplished in terms of concrete services like the installation of artesian wells in many villages. However, the CD approach was premised on a model of a homogeneous rural community which ignored inherently conflictful issues such as concentration of land ownership, insecurity of land tenure for tenant farmers, and lack of peasant organisations.

Peasant Organising in the '60s

Radicalised peasant groups had been forced to go underground, but legally sanctioned peasant organisations began to rise in the late '50s and throughout the '60s. Notable among these was the Federation of Free Farmers (FFF) which organised tenant-farmers by offering them legal aid and moral support in fighting for their tenancy rights. At its peak in the late '60s, the FFF had its members in practically all the rice-growing areas of the archipelago, and its membership was 300,000. Its founder had a hand in drafting the Land Reform Code of 1963 under President Diosdado Macapagal. In 1971, FFF members and sympathisers led the protracted live-in demonstration in front of the Congress building to pressurise legislators to revise the code of agrarian reforms.

Parallel to the rise of farmers' organisation was the increasing role of church groups in social action. Banking on a membership of four-fifths of the population, the bishops of the Catholic Church set up Social Action Centres in most of their dioceses. These were federated under the National Secretariat for Social Actions (NASSA). Church involvement was heightened by a nationwide Rural Congress in 1968 which stressed the social teachings of the Second Vatican Council and papal social encyclicals such as *Pacim in Terris* and *Populorum Progressio.*

Initially, social action meant social welfare services for distressed groups like undernourished children, flood victims, and displaced farmers, and for other groups the formation of credit unions and cooperatives, particularly in town centres servicing the rural areas. Notable among these efforts was the promotion of credit unions in the prelatures of Antique and Infants. In the Misamis Oriental-Bukidnon areas, the extension service of Xavier University's College of Agriculture spearheaded a similar movement.

In the sugar province of Negros Occidental, the Diocesan Social Action Center helped unionise sugar workers, culminating in a protracted strike against a major sugar mill by the end of the decade. It was also during this period that student activism on national issues became pronounced. A number of student activists joined left-of-centre groups to push for needed reforms, particularly on the eve of the Constitutional Convention in 1970. Other students preferred more radical paths. All were clamouring for social change.

Community Organising in the '70s

It was in this context of heightened social activism by students, church groups, and farmers' organisations that martial law was declared by President Ferdinand Marcos in 1972, bringing in its wake a whole new strategy of rural development.

If the '60s was the decade of activism among the NGOs, the '70s was the period for government planners to design and implement their programmes. First among these was the extension of agrarian reform to all rice and corn tenanted lands. Coupled with this was the *Samahang Nayon* (Barrio Association) programme which made it compulsory for the agrarian reform beneficiaries to join this nationwide cooperative structure. A uniform presidential decree for cooperatives was also promulgated which led to the suppression of many privately initiated cooperatives.

With the introduction of new rice varieties, the *Masagana-99* (Bountiful Harvest-99 Cavans) programme was launched to provide free credit without collateral security to small farmers and increase rice productivity. By the early '80s, another nationwide credit programme was announced to promote livelihood activities in the rural areas. Meanwhile, massive infrastructure projects for building dams, irrigation networks, highways and bridges were also introduced. However, the largest share of the national budget still went to the military during this period.

Partly because the government had co-opted a majority of the economic activities in the rural areas, and partly owing to the dangers inherent in militarisation, the NGOs turned to community organising (CO), first in urban neighbourhoods and later in the rural setting.

CO work is issue-oriented at the local level. It can also be instrumental in the defence of human rights for an individual or for an entire community. It requires a specially trained CO worker to help local villagers identify key issues; map out the strategies to deal with the local, district, and even national officers; and finally mobilise local participants including women and children to press their demands. In the course of time, many of these NGOs have evolved their own style of CO work, graduating from the initial Freire and Alinsky models to a more *Filipino* version.

Some government agencies like the National Irrigation Administration and the Land Bank of the Philippines have begun to contract the NGOs to field CO workers in their areas of operation to ensure fulfilment of expectations of both villagers and line agencies.

Going beyond specific issues, Basic Christian Communities (BCCs) have also been formed in a number of church dioceses. Through the BCC structure, villagers are organised from the grassroots level of a neighbourhood cell to the village chapel community, and upwards to the zone, parish and diocese levels. In this setting, conscientisation takes place, adult education becomes a weekly activity, and people's participation becomes institutionalised. It is because of these features that BCCs have sometimes been viewed either as "subversive" or as a democratic exercise of people's power.

Four Dimensions in Philippine Rural Development

With the current political uncertainties in the country, it is difficult to foretell the direction which rural development is likely to follow in the years ahead. It is easier to point out some current parameters and the four key dimensions of rural development strategies.

From 20 million in 1946, the Philippine population has now grown to 53 million, and is projected to reach 80 million by the year 2000. The country is currently undergoing the most serious economic crisis since the war, with a $ 25 billion foreign debt and a 60 per cent inflation rate. Lately, policy makers have given up hopes of speedy industrialisation and focussed their efforts on agri-business in the rural areas instead. It is in this light that the four key dimensions in Philippine rural development need to be considered.

Firstly, the nation has had a tradition of rural unrest which, far from diminishing, has reached revolutionary proportions.

Secondly, despite government attempts at structural reforms, 'free enterprise' market forces continue to dominate the rural areas resulting in the entry of multinational agri-business corporations, particularly in Mindanao, and continued economic hardships for small farmers as a result of rising fertilizer prices, lack of price supports, etc.

Thirdly, NGOs have been in the forefront in evolving various strategies for rural development, but they have limited resources, and hence the scope of their activities is restricted.

Fourthly, the government itself has either tended to co-opt, to contain, or to confront these rural development strategies from other sectors The Government has also brought about a staggering economic—as well as political—crisis, the solution to which is not yet in sight.

In many ways, a viable strategy for rural development is intimately linked to the life of the nation itself. But how this can be brought about remains a challenge to all the protagonists on the Philippine stage today.

INDEX